SOCIAL PROBLEMS
AND
SOCIAL POLICY:
The American Experience

This is a volume in the Arno Press Series

SOCIAL PROBLEMS AND SOCIAL POLICY:
The American Experience

Advisory Editor
Gerald N. Grob

Editorial Board
Clarke A. Chambers
Blanche D. Coll
Walter I. Trattner

*See last pages of this volume
for a complete list of titles.*

HISTORY

OF THE

PHILADELPHIA ALMSHOUSES

AND

HOSPITALS

CHARLES LAWRENCE

ARNO PRESS

A New York Times Company

New York — 1976

Editorial Supervision: SHEILA MEHLMAN

———◆———

Reprint Edition 1976 by Arno Press Inc.

Reprinted from a copy in The Friend's Historical
  Library of Swarthmore College

SOCIAL PROBLEMS AND SOCIAL POLICY: The American Experience
ISBN for complete set: 0-405-07474-3
See last pages of this volume for titles.

Manufactured in the United States of America

———◆———

Library of Congress Cataloging in Publication Data

Lawrence, Charles, b. 1837-   comp.
    History of the Philadelphia almshouses and hospitals.

    (Social problems and social policy--the American
experience)
    Reprint of the ed. published by C. Lawrence, Phila-
delphia.
    1. Philadelphia. Almshouse--History. 2. Phila-
delphia--Hospitals--History. 3. Philadelphia.
Guardians for the Relief and Employment of the Poor.
4. Philadelphia. Dept. of Charities and correction.
I. Title. II. Series.
HV99.P5L4 1975   361.6'3'0974811   75-17231
ISBN 0-405-07500-6

HISTORY

OF THE

PHILADELPHIA ALMSHOUSES

AND

HOSPITALS

FRONT ENTRANCE, ADMINISTRATION BUILDING.

HISTORY

OF THE

PHILADELPHIA ALMSHOUSES

AND

HOSPITALS

FROM THE BEGINNING OF THE EIGHTEENTH TO THE ENDING OF
THE NINETEENTH CENTURIES,

COVERING A PERIOD OF

NEARLY TWO HUNDRED YEARS

SHOWING THE MODE OF

DISTRIBUTING PUBLIC RELIEF THROUGH THE MANAGEMENT OF
THE BOARDS OF OVERSEERS OF THE POOR, GUARDIANS
OF THE POOR AND THE DIRECTORS OF THE
DEPARTMENT OF CHARITIES AND
CORRECTION

WITH AN APPENDIX

CONTAINING A LIST OF FORMER VISITING AND RESIDENT PHYSICIANS

ILLUSTRATED FROM PHOTOGRAPHS

COMPILED AND PUBLISHED BY

CHARLES LAWRENCE

SUPERINTENDENT FROM 1891 TO 1900

1905

TO

MAJOR WILLIAM H. LAMBERT,

WHOSE EXCELLENT SERVICES

AS

PRESIDENT OF THE BOARD OF DIRECTORS

OF

THE DEPARTMENT OF CHARITIES AND CORRECTION

SHOULD EVER BE

HELD IN GRATEFUL REMEMBRANCE

THIS

VOLUME IS DEDICATED

AS

A SLIGHT TOKEN OF RESPECT AND ESTEEM.

PREFACE.

IN THE preparation of the following " History of the Philadelphia Almshouses and Hospitals" the fact was borne in mind that history must be a truthful account of happenings and anything inserted that is not true destroys its value and it ceases to be reliable.

In collecting the data all kinds of official records, minute books, laws, ordinances, reports, addresses, histories and newspapers were consulted to obtain the desired information ; in fact, consideration was given to everything available that was trustworthy. This was arranged to make a continued and connected statement of the government of the institutions and the distribution of the public charities from the beginning of the Eighteenth to the close of the Nineteenth Centuries, covering a period of nearly two hundred years.

The great difficulties under which some of the Guardians of the Poor labored are referred to, and enough stated to show the character of the men engaged in the work.

The principal events that created scandal and reflected on the management are shown from official records and they tend to make the good work performed appear brighter and better by comparison.

The great improvement made in the treatment of the inmates, especially in the Insane and Hospital Departments, are noted, and it is very gratifying to know that with the exception of the limited capacity of the wards it will compare favorably with that of any in this country.

As the transferring of the ground purchased for the present Almshouse, to other Trustees for other purposes, prevents the proper enlargement of buildings for the accommodation of the constantly growing population, thereby necessitating removal, the ordinances providing for the transfers are quoted fully, together with the provisos and agreements forming part of them. A careful reading will show how much they have been complied with.

Nine years experience as Superintendent of the institution, in addition to a knowledge of the details of previous administrations, were of considerable value in preparing the manuscript, and although much labor was involved it was cheerfully given in an endeavor to make it as near complete as possible.

A carefully prepared list of the former Visiting and Resident Physicians will be found in the Appendix.

C. L.

CONTENTS.

7

and from the House to Darby Road Provided for—Notice Given of the Sale of the Spruce Street Property—Terms of Sale Reported—Price of Ground Limited to $125,000—Richard Smethurst's Bid—Failed to Pay—Again Offered but Not Sold—Sold at Last—Commissioners Surrender House of Employment and Women's Almshouse—Notice Regarding Out-door Relief—Auctioneer Wolbert Paid—Childrens' Asylum on Fifth Street Sold—Description of New Almshouse —Ferry Established—River Banks Constructed—Graveyard—Stone Barn and Farm House Built—School-Room Furnished for Children—First Steward of Blockley—Cost to Date.

CHAPTER XII.

How Blockley Got Its Name—Efforts to Utilize the Labor of Inmates—Report on Dependent Foreigners—List of Guardians—Pleasant Ending of the Work of the Commissioners—How Other Almshouses in the County were Authorized—Auditing Committee's Report of the Cost—Head Money—Case of John Enhart and Eliza Worl—Panic of 1837—Commissioners of Moyamensing Desire to have the Benefits of Blockley—Cost of Maintaining the Steward's Table—Changes Made—Report on Distribution of Meat—Tie Vote on the Election of Steward.

CHAPTER XIII.

Another Change in Management—Charges Against the Secretary of the Board —Solicitor Requested to Enter Suit—Treasurer also a Defaulter—Report on the Cause of Pauperism—Mismanagement Shown—Moyamensing Admitted—Lack of Management in the Medical Department—Resident Physicians Leave Without Giving Notice—Revolting Conditions Shown by Report of Committee —Change in Management—Chief Resident Physician Elected.

CHAPTER XIV.

Protest Regarding Graveyard—Nurse Welsh and Guardian Abbott—Vote of Censure—Mr. Abbott Again—Newspaper Comment—Poor Heating and Ventilation—Dr. Benedict Reports on the Temperature of the Insane Department —Contract made for Apparatus to Remedy it—Trouble with Mr. Stewart, a Member of the Board—Reply to the Grand Jury.

CHAPTER XV.

Cholera Again in 1849—Precautionary Measures Taken—Hospital Opened—Alarming Death Rate in Almshouse—Committee's Report—Resignation of Dr. Benedict—Election of Dr. Haines—First Female Physician Employed—Heating Apparatus not Satisfactory—Board Refuses to Pay Bill—Suit Entered—Settled by Compromise—Resolution of Board—Building Purchased for Office on North Seventh Street—Charges Against Certain Members of the Board Investigated—Two Reports Made—Bad State of Affairs Shown by Subsequent Report—Mr. Abbott Mixed Up in the Disreputable Business—Resolution to Expel Two Members Laid on the Table.

14 Contents.

ILLUSTRATIONS.

FRIENDS ALMSHOUSE ON WALNUT STREET.

HISTORY

OF THE

PHILADELPHIA ALMSHOUSES

AND

HOSPITALS.

CHAPTER I.

DESCRIPTION OF FIRST ALMSHOUSE—SPRUCE STREET ALMSHOUSE OPENED.

WHEN William Penn sailed for America, on the ship Welcome, of three hundred tons burden, knowing that his voyage and residence there would keep him separated from his family during a considerable time, he left a letter addressed to his wife and children, in which he said: "Pity the distressed and hold out a hand of help to them; it may be your case; and as you mete to others God will mete to you again."

The Founder of Pennsylvania was honorably descended, his paternal ancestors, for several generations, having been persons of high respectability and considerable note in the world.

His grandfather, Giles Penn, was a captain in the English Navy. His father, Sir William Penn, at an early age, became a distinguished naval officer, and passed through the successive grades of promotion, so that at the early age of thirty-one he was created Vice-Admiral.

The father was much annoyed by the persistency with which his son William clung to the teachings of Thomas Loe, a preacher of the Society of Friends. He remonstrated with him, beat him, and turned him out of his home, but all in vain. The younger William was expelled from college and suffered confinement in prisons on several occasions, and for long terms, for preaching heresy, as it was termed; but he adhered to what he considered was the true faith, and no sect had a better advocate than he proved to be.

The " Friends " who came with him to this country, which was to be " the haven of rest for the oppressed of all nations," were, no doubt, men of sterling qualities; they believed in the sentiment expressed in the letter referred to, and it is not surprising to see that the first almshouse established in the Colonies was that of the Friends, located on the grounds belonging to John Martin, between Third and Fourth Streets, on the south side of Walnut Street, in the city of Philadelphia.

Even in the selection of the name for their new home, Philadelphia, City of Brotherly Love, the spirit of Christian charity is manifested.

In early writings it appears that " no one need ever starve or be in want in this fruitful country," and as the founders were industrious, prudent people, the assertion was probably true at that period.

In time, idle persons came drifting in among them and sickness or misfortune overtook some of those early settlers, so that they required assistance from the more fortunate. This was rendered privately, as friend to neighbor, until it became so burdensome, to a few, that it was deemed essential to have some public way of relieving the necessities of the poor, and to levy an equal tax on all to provide the means for that purpose.

As early as the year 1700, an " Act for the better provision of the Poor " was passed, but the Queen repealed it.

In 1705 the Assembly passed a law that provided that Justices of the Peace should annually elect two " Overseers of the Poor." for each Township, and authorized them to levy a tax of one penny per pound on real and personal property of citizens, and four shillings per head on all citizens not otherwise rated, " to be employed for the relief of poor, indigent and impotent persons, inhabiting within the said Township." The money so collected appears to have been distributed to the families in need, as the names of some who received it were entered in the " Poor Book."

Tramps were not encouraged, and idleness was not considered as good form in those days. Councils passed a resolution, in 1712, which declared : " The poor of this city, Dayly Increasing, it is ye opinion of this Council that a workhouse be immediately hired to Imploy poor P'sons and sufficients P'sons appointed to keep them at work."

The Overseers were directed to attend to this matter, and they were subsequently authorized to " find a convenient building for a workhouse."

The Friends Almshouse was established in 1713. John Martin, a tailor, who died in 1702, devised the property on Walnut Street to Thomas Chalkley, Ralph Jackson and John Michener. The will did not provide that they should hold it for any trust, or object ; yet, " it was understood from conversations with Martin, in his life time, that he intended that his estate should be disposed of for the use of the poor Friends, according to the directions of the Society."

Small houses were erected for the purpose, but the front building was not built until 1729.

These buildings were described as being very quaint in appearance and character. The main one on Walnut Street occupied the whole front of the lot, and " the central portion of it rose above a simply ornamented doorway to an open-arched entrance which led from the street by steps to the garden and buildings in the rear." There were six small houses in a row with entrances from the yard.

This almshouse was strictly sectarian, and none but members of the Society, having charge of it, could be received within its walls. It had but few inmates, as the Quakers were generally thrifty and economical and did not have to be supported in an almshouse. A few old women were there, and it was frequently called the "Quaker Nunnery." As it was not a place for the support of the poor of all denominations, it could not be considered a public almshouse, and its usefulness was very much restricted.

An order was issued, in 1717, that compelled all persons who received relief from the Overseers of the Poor, to wear upon the right sleeve of the outer garment a Roman P, together with the initials of the county, city or place of which the pauper was an inhabitant. The letters were to be of red or blue cloth, as the Overseers should designate. Every one who refused to wear such letters was liable to have their relief suspended or withdrawn, and also to be whipped and kept at hard labor for twenty-one days.

In that year an Act was passed to authorize the erection of Workhouses in Philadelphia, Bristol and Chester. It was directed that a Workhouse should be built in Philadelphia within three years, but that was not complied with. The out-door system of relief was still maintained.

The dependent class increased in number to such an extent that the Overseers of the Poor presented a memorial to the Assembly, in 1729, which explained the difficulty of providing for the great number of poor persons from foreign ports and neighboring provinces, as well as for the insolvent debtors, their wives and children. The city recommended the application for relief, and the Legislature resolved to "loan the Mayor and Commonality £1000, to be applied to the purchase of ground and erection of an Almshouse for the use of the poor of the city."

The money was received in 1730, and the Mayor, Alderman Plumstead and James Steel were appointed a committee to select a place, prepare plans and make estimates.

A square of ground, a green meadow, bounded by Third and Fourth, Spruce and Pine Streets, was bought from Aldren Allen for £200, and a brick building was erected in 1731 or 1732. The main front faced Third Street; there was a piazza all around the building, and the house somewhat resembled the Friends' Almshouse. The large gate was on Spruce Street, and there was an entrance, by a stile, from Third Street.

A hospital for the accommodation of the sick and insane was established in connection with the Almshouse, and that was the inauguration of a system which has been continued up to the present time.

The Philadelphia Hospital is, no doubt, the oldest hospital in continuous service in this country.

The Assembly passed a statute on March 29, 1735, which regulated the manner in which persons who came into the city of Philadelphia, or any township or borough, except those who came from Europe, might obtain a legal settlement. This was a very serious question, and the Act was to prevent the dependent class from drifting from place to place, and to provide for their support where they belonged. Housekeepers and others who received persons not having legal settlements into their dwellings, were bound to give notice to the " Overseers of the Poor " under penalty. The Act stated: " The Almshouse built for the city of Philadelphia may, if well regulated, be of service and help to ease the inhabitants of the taxes yearly assessed on them for the maintenance of the poor."

Authority was given to the Mayor, Recorder and Aldermen to appoint a Superintendent of the Almshouse. The preamble stated: " Complaints have been made against Overseers of the Poor who have supplied the poor with necessities out of their own stores and shops at exorbitant prices, and also against Overseers who have paid unreasonable accounts to their friends and dependents for services done the poor."

It appears that there were people in those early days, like some of later date, who would stoop to anything to gain profit for themselves. Removing the appointment of the Superintendent from the Overseers, was intended as a check upon the Board.

The number of applicants for admission became so large that in a few years the Almshouse was too small to receive them all, and in 1764 the Overseers again called upon the Assembly to assist them. In their petition they called attention to the crowded condition, and stated " that into rooms but ten or eleven feet square we have been obliged to put four or six men. The church was turned into a lodging room with fifteen beds."

No action appears to have been taken at the time. The Overseers renewed their application to the Assembly in 1766, and again called attention to their crowded condition.

The number of paupers requiring care and assistance at that time was two hundred and twenty. In addition to the people in the House there were one hundred and fifty out-pensioners. The cost for the support of the poor in 1765 had been three thousand and two hundred dollars.

The attention of persons of means had been attracted to the urgent duty of relieving the necessities of the poor, and it was proposed that if the Assembly would charter a Corporation with power to establish and maintain an Almshouse and House of Employ-- ment, such a company should be formed.

An Act was passed on February 8, 1766, entitled, " An Act for the better employment, relief and support of the poor within the city of Philadelphia, District of Southwark, the Townships of Moyamensing and Passyunk and the Northern Liberties." It provided that every person who contributed ten pounds towards the purposes of the Almshouse became a member of the Corporation with power to elect twelve Managers, a Treasurer, etc. They were incorporated as " Contributors to the Relief and Employment of the Poor within the City of Philadelphia."

They were authorized to borrow on mortgage of the Almshouse property on Third Street £2000, and to pay that over to the Managers of the Almshouse Corporation for the purchase of ground, the erection of buildings, etc., as soon as they raised a stock of £1,500. They were to erect a commodious building, one part of which was to be used for the reception and maintenance of persons who were poor and helpless, and the other as a House of Employment, or Workhouse, for the lodging and employment of poor persons who were able to work.

The Contributors held their first meeting in the Courthouse, on the corner of Second and Market Streets, on the twelfth day of May, 1766.

In addition to the regular officers, a board of Managers was elected. The gentlemen selected were Joseph Fox, Philip Lyng, Abel James, William Masters, Luke Morris, Joseph Redman, John Palmer, Hugh Roberts, Jacob Lewis, Enoch Story, Samuel Rhodes and Joseph Wharton. They were all well known, respectable and influential citizens.

After a number of conferences, it was finally concluded to buy the lot of ground bounded by Spruce, Pine, Tenth and Eleventh Streets, belonging to the Widow Callender, at the price of £800. Governor John Penn assisted in securing the site.

A subscription of £1,500 having been raised, a mortgage on the building and ground for the sum of £2,000 was executed. The Managers adopted as the motto for the seal of the Corporation, "Charity, Justice and Industry."

In the meantime, Overseers of the Poor were elected in the city, districts and townships, and they took charge of the administration of outdoor relief and the general expenditure of public charities. The Overseers were Joseph Potts, John Elton, Samuel Davis, Joseph Moulder, Joseph Watkins, David Evans, James Irvine, Nicholas Garrison, Benjamin Paschal, Bryan Wilkinson, Christopher Ludovick and James Whitehall. The tax-levy for their purposes was threepence in the pound. In addition to the amount raised by this assessment, the Board had the income of ground rents amounting to £45 16s. 8d. per annum and frequent donations from wealthy persons.

The plans for the new institution were agreed upon and the erection of the buildings immediately followed. In Scharff and Westcott's "History of Philadelphia," they were described as follows: "The buildings were opened in October, 1767. The Almshouse was laid out in the form of an L, one hundred and eighty feet by forty, two stories in height, joined by a turret thirty feet square and four stories high. The House of Employment was on the west side of the lot, running south from Spruce Street, fronting Eleventh Street, also in shape of an L, so that the entire range of buildings inclosed on three sides a quadrangular space. A large central building was erected on Spruce Street, which stood between the L's.

"The first story of the Almshouse and House of Employment on the interior was a cloister of open arches. The buildings on Tenth and Eleventh Streets occupied two stories and a garret. The main central building when finished was three stories in height, with a hip roof surmounted by a small cupola.

"A habit soon grew up among the people of calling this establishment the 'Bettering House,' a title which in time became somewhat an epithet of contempt. Two hundred and eighty-four persons were admitted into the Almshouse in October, 1767, and in three months the number had increased to three hundred and sixty-eight. The inmates of the House of Employment were soon put to work, and in it were made various kinds of goods, principally of wool, hemp and flax. When in years after cotton began to be grown in the United States, the manufacture of that fibre became an important industry in the establishment."

The Overseers of the Poor and the Managers of the House of Employment soon had their disagreements and difficulties. The Managers had been in the habit of extending relief to needy persons outside of the institution, but finding this imposed a heavy tax upon their resources, had resolved to cut off the "pensioners," as the outside poor were termed. The Overseers denounced this action and claimed that they were greatly annoyed by applicants for relief which they could not furnish. Much suffering was caused by the action of the Managers of the House of Employment, and the Overseers determined that they would not appoint any more committees to visit the Home and confer with the Managers, as they had previously done.

John Dickinson, Esq., a wealthy and influential young man, married an estimable young lady in 1770, and he celebrated the event by sending to the Overseers of the Poor £200, to be distributed under their direction among deserving applicants for relief. He endeavored to share some of his happiness with those who were not accustomed to much pleasure and joy. The Overseers passed resolutions congratulating him upon his fortunate choice of a partner, and wishing him prosperity and happiness. They also thanked him for his generous gift.

Mr. Dickinson was a talented young lawyer of a generous nature, with a mind of his own and with the courage of his convictions. He dared to oppose the Declaration of Independence; but, after the Continental Congress decided to adopt that wonderful document, there were few abler or more devoted friends to support the cause than John Dickinson of Pennsylvania. History associates his name with that of Franklin and says, " They had as much to do as any other two men who can be named in uniting the colonies and preparing them for resistance." He relieved the sorrows of many households and set a worthy example for others to follow ; he deemed the course he pursued to be wiser than spending thousands on a wedding tour.

In September, 1770, the Overseers of the Poor were compelled to take action in regard to the Nova Scotia exiles, known as " Neutrals," who had settled in Philadelphia, and who had become a serious burden on the taxpayers. When the British captured Nova Scotia, they deemed it a matter of State policy to transport the French residents and distribute them among the Colonies. In 1756 a number of the families that had been driven from their homes and ruined financially arrived in Philadelphia. Anthony Benezet took a great interest in them ; they were provided with shelter in a long range of one-story wooden houses on the north side of Pine Street, between Fifth and Sixth Streets. They were indolent, refused to mingle with the other colonists and had no ambition to do anything to help themselves. They became burdensome ; so the authorities, to compel them to do something, resolved to have their children bound out to other people, giving as a reason that their parents had lived long enough at the public expense. The Overseers sent a remonstrance to the Assembly, representing that the neutrals, through age, sickness and infirmities, were incapable of providing for themselves, and had been ordered to remove from the houses provided for them. They appealed to the Assembly to take some action for their relief.

Thomas Fisher, one of the Overseers, in 1774 agreed to take the Neutrals, or Arcadians, under his special charge and distribute among them the appropriations made to supply their wants ; and in that and the succeeding year the Assembly granted £200 for the purpose. It has been stated that from 1756 until the Revolutionary War began, these people were a continual burden to the community and a heavy tax upon its charity. Some authorities say that they disappeared in a body at the sign of war, and settled near New Orleans. George W. Cable, in his story of Bonaventure, speaks of the Arcadians in that section, and probably they were descendants of that race. The winter of 1775 was a very severe one in Philadelphia. The Overseers were kept very busy, and the Almshouse and House of Employment were crowded. The Overseers appointed a committee of two to visit the institution every week and to confer with the Managers.

John Petty and William Carter died, and in their wills it was provided that certain sums should be used for the purchase and distribution of bread among the poor. One portion of it was distributed in February, and the other in March, 1776. A bellman and public crier were employed to notify those in want of it, as to where and when it could be procured. Our forefathers did not have as many newspapers as we have at the present time.

At that period the Overseers were Capt. Samuel Smith, Samuel Murdoch, James Reynolds, Michael Schubert, William Garrigues, Lewis Karcher, William Wills, Leonard Kessler, Joseph Mifflin and Samuel Garrigues. The peculiar manner in which the Overseers were selected prevented even the best members from serving more than one year. As the term was about to expire the names of sixty citizens were sent to Court, and the judges selected twelve Overseers from the list, to serve for the ensuing year. As the Overseers would not send their own names, their services were lost to the community.

The minutes of the Board of Managers for September 2, 1776, says: "The number of troops that are passing through the city and making use of the Court House renders it extremely inconvenient to meet there;" and it was resolved that "the Board should hold its sessions at the sign of the Golden Fleece." A number of poor and disabled soldiers were admitted into the House of Employment, and the Overseers were active in relieving the wants of the families of those who were fighting the battles of their country.

Those were trying times for the poor; the Overseers found great difficulty in collecting money and were not able to do much. Every one was expected to help the country, and could not give much to relieve the poor.

CHAPTER II.

A T about this time, Col. Francis Gurney was ordered by the Committee of Safety to quarter a number of Continental militia, who were very sick with dysentery, in the Almshouse. The managers and physicians strongly objected to the order, as it was calculated to endanger the health of the House. Notwithstanding the objection, Col. Gurney took possession ; the poor inmates were transferred to the west building, and the troops were put into the southeast wing of the House of Employment.

No meetings were held between November 25, 1776, and January, 1777, owing to " the alarming situation of the times," as mentioned in the minutes of the Board. On the latter date, five members—Messrs. George Meade, Benjamin Gibbs, David Schaffer, Samuel Read and Mordecai Lewis—met to consider what could be done to relieve some of the worst cases of suffering.

Mr. Thomas Willing placed one hundred cords of wood at the disposal of the Overseers, and other donations were received from various charitable individuals.

Soon after this a new and full Board was appointed by the Court; but the British army under Gen. Howe took possession of Philadelphia, and the Overseers were unable to perform their functions. In October the sick belonging to Gen. Howe's army filled the entire east wing.

The Board of Managers was ordered to clear the House for the King's troops; they refused to do so. The British officials turned the inmates, about two hundred in number—poor, miserable creatures—out in the streets. To save them from perishing, the managers had them placed, some in the Freemason's Lodge, some in the Friends' Meetinghouse and others in Carpenters' Hall, where they were provided for until the British left the city, in June, 1778.

Only eighty-two of the two hundred survived the exposure and were taken back to the Almshouse.

No one could realize the terrible trials through which the patriotic colonists passed in those days "that tried men's souls." Want and distress accompanied by acts of cruelty were familiar sights; but, believing in the righteousness of their cause, they never faltered.

The Overseers of the Poor did not resume their sessions until July 22, 1778. The minutes of the meeting of that date states: "The British army having at length evacuated this city after having possession of it about nine months—during which time there has been no legal care taken of the poor—at a Court of Aldermen, the following citizens were appointed Overseers for the ensuing twelve months: William Pritchard, John Stille, Philip Moxen, William Woodhouse, Robert Aitken, Jonathan Meredith, Andrew Guyer, Nicholas Weaver, Jacob Kimsley, Peter Cooper, John Linnington and Samuel Wetherill, Jr." These were prominent, able and humane gentlemen.

A conference was held with the Magistrates and it was determined to borrow the sum of £2000, to be repaid out of the proceeds of the tax levy as soon as possible.

A subscription was opened and the amount required was soon obtained.

The southeast wing of the House of Employment, which had been used as an Almshouse, was at this time occupied by wounded soldiers of the Continental army. The Overseers were not anxious to deprive them of such shelter, but they thought that as the poor of the city were thus excluded from the building erected for their use, rent should be paid, so that it could be added to the relief fund of the Board.

The rent asked for was eventually paid by Isaac Melchor, the Barrack Master.

The Assembly passed an act authorizing the Overseers to borrow £5000, to be appropriated to the relief of the poor, and preparatory steps were taken for reorganizing the poor department. But the Board found it impossible to borrow any money, in 1779, in consequence of the depreciated state of the Continental currency, which produced universal distrust. The Overseers generously resolved to advance the sum of $300 each, and take the risk of being repaid when better days should come.

At the meeting of the Board held on the 23d of December, 1779, the following communication was read: "Gentlemen—I am not, and have not been, for several years, an inhabitant of this State; yet, from a sincere affection for the people, I am persuaded I shall heartily wish their happiness in every respect. These sentiments have led me to think of the distress to which many worthy families in this city, not properly the objects of the laws of relief, may be reduced in the course of the winter that is setting in early and probably will prove severe. I therefore beg leave to put £1000 in your hands, to be distributed in such manner as your prudence and humanity shall dictate.

"I flatter myself that you will pardon the liberty I take on this occasion, as I presume the nature of your office and a general acquaintance will render a compliance with this request not very troublesome, and I am convinced if it should be so, your benevolence would receive pleasure by dispensing even the little assistance this mite will afford to those to whom it may be necessary. If the weather should moderate, so as to open the river, you shall be freely welcome to order two hundred cords of wood to be cut on my estate in Kent, and, perhaps, I can spare a larger quantity. The land is close to navigable water, and wood has been brought from the neighborhood to Philadelphia this Fall, allowing one-half the profit to the owner, which shows the conveyance to be easy. If it should not be convenient to accept the offer this season, you, gentlemen, or your successors may have the wood against next season. It appears to me that an undertaking of the kind may be of considerable service to many of your valuable fellow-citizens, though the grant, on my part, is very small, as I intend to clear the ground. I am, with great regard,

"Your humble servant,

"JOHN DICKINSON."

The Board expressed its thanks to that worthy gentleman for his timely and much appreciated donation.

Mr. Dickinson abandoned the practice of his profession at the commencement of the War, and devoted his time and talents to the public service. No man of his time was more generous to the worthy poor; he was much beloved in Philadelphia. Many persons had been suddenly reduced to want by the progress of the struggle for independence, and the depreciation of the currency. It was to relieve those people that the donation mentioned in the letter was intended. They would have suffered rather than to have asked for relief from the legal authorities, and the Overseers endeavored to reach them through the generosity of Mr. Dickinson, who had been a benefactor on numerous occasions besides those mentioned in the minutes of the Overseers.

The Board labored under many difficulties in the performance of its duties. While the taxes and donations were, in most cases, paid in depreciated currency, specie was demanded for almost everything needed. Every expedient was tried for raising money, but winter arrived and the Board frequently found the treasury empty. When there was any money it soon went, as the number of urgent needs called for its immediate use.

In 1781, the Board consented to rent a portion of the eastern wing of the House of Employment to the "General Government" for the accommodation of the British prisoners who were sick or wounded. This kept many of the poor citizens out of the House; yet, after the treaty of peace was proclaimed, 1784, and the soldiers were removed, the managers were unable to grant all the applications for relief.

Many of the contributors had become impoverished by the events of the Revolution, and the membership and the income of the institution had been so much reduced that, in 1781, the Legislature passed an act which provided that if the corporation could not be kept up, or should cease to act, the Overseers of the Poor should be vested with all the powers of the corporation, and be themselves a corporation under the title of the "Guardians of the Poor of the City of Philadelphia."

On the 3d of March, 1784, the Board of Managers sent a "remonstrance" to the Legislature. The following extract will convey a faint idea of the conditions in Philadelphia at that time : " In the course of the winter, your petitioners have had many and afflicting instances of the utmost human sufferings and accumulated distress in and around the city. They represent that from the rigors of a very severe and tedious winter, the want of employment, with the exorbitant prices of fuel and provisions, the poor have greatly increased, and notwithstanding heavy taxes and liberal donations have been collected and expended for their relief, many remain in great distress. That by the resort of people, both by sea and land, to this metropolis, many become burdensome to the inhabitants, through sickness and misfortunes. That in addition to those, the city and environs are greatly oppressed by numbers of beggars and vagrants, not only from various parts of this State, but from many others of the United States, who, being found in distress in the streets, and daily, of necessity, added to the poor, under our immediate care, already too numerous, amounting to 117 out-pensioners and 230 poor in the Almshouse, about 60 of whom have no legal settlement or right of support in this corporation. But what we would now particularly represent to your honorable House is the distressed situation of several hundred persons, consisting of disbanded soldiers, late of the Pennsylvania Line, their wives and children, with other non-residents, who have this winter taken shelter in the barracks, where they have hitherto been assisted, not only by the liberal donations raised in this city, but also frequently out of the funds under our direction. Notwithstanding which, they are now, at this inclement season, in great distress for almost every necessary of life."

Although the Board earnestly pleaded for the Assembly to take some action for the relief of the sufferers, many of whom had fought gallantly for our independence, no mention is made of any attention having been paid to their petition, and, inasmuch as there were subsequent appeals made, it is to be inferred that no measures were taken to render assistance.

In the minutes of the Overseers can be found such records as :

" 5 shillings given to a wounded soldier," " a half-cord of wood sent to the family of John Davis, the said family being in great distress," and others of the same character. This may help the imagination to form some idea of the misery that prevailed among certain classes in Philadelphia at that period.

In 1784, reports were circulated that "shocking abuses prevailed in the Almshouse." The Overseers appointed a committee to investigate the charges. It was ascertained that all kinds of unwholesome food, including " maggotty butter," had been served to the inmates; that there was a lack of proper clothing, and that women suffering from loathsome diseases were placed among the other females, who, although paupers, were honest, decent and cleanly. The person responsible for this shocking state of affairs appears to have been Mrs. Cummings, the wife of the Steward, who acted as Matron of the House.

The committee thoroughly reformed the course of management, but the Steward's wife was not displaced. She was much frightened by the exposure, and became a better official, serving until she died at her post of duty during the yellow fever epidemic in 1793.

The Overseers of the Poor and the Managers of the House of Employment again " locked horns " in December, 1784, as appears in the minutes of the Overseers by the following report: " According to the rules of the preceding meeting, Mr. Connelly, Mr. Sharswood, Mr. McIlhenny, and Mr. Dorsey waited on the full Board of Managers, and represented to them that this Board considered themselves insulted in a very particular manner, by the Steward of the House, in his telling two of the gentlemen of this Board (who visited them last week) that it was a pimping disposition to come regularly and inspect the internal management of the House; that the reason of two persons being appointed every week from this Board was not to interfere with such—their management—but in order to observe whether the poor persons sent in by them were well and duly provided for; that they considered they had an indisputable right, both in such cases, and as citizens, to visit the House at any time; that during the visits which were weekly made to the House, they observed very great inattention in the management, or stewardship of the House; that those observations were not founded on slight or trivial information, but on such as was at any time to be affirmed to. The whole of which representations was treated very lightly, and in no wise to satisfaction."

The squabble between the two Boards continued for some time, and in February, 1787, the Overseers sent a petition to the Legislature, praying for a change in the law relating to the relief of the poor of Philadelphia, and for the passage of an act to make a revised system, and the consolidation of the Overseers and the Managers of the House of Employment.

Experience had shown the wisdom of complying with this request, as the conflict existing led to much confusion.

The Managers of the House charged the Overseers with being remiss in the collection of taxes and paying the money over to the treasury of the House. The Overseers retorted that "if they, the Managers, could give a more satisfactory expenditure of such monies, it might be the means of their being more speedily collected."

This shows the feeling existing between the two Boards, but the Assembly did not take any action upon the subject at that time.

Troubles seem to have started in other channels and the Board discovered that there were thrifty financiers in those days who were ready to earn an "*honest dollar*" in any way that presented itself, no matter how questionable it might appear to be. The "Potter's Field," or "poor man's burying ground," was located on the ground now known as Washington Square. The following report appears in the minutes of May 17th, 1787:

"The committee appointed from the Board of Overseers of the Poor to inquire into a complaint made to them of John Reynolds, Jailor, who is represented to have extorted money, unwarrantably, for the permission of entering paupers and other poor persons in the Potter's Field, report that their first inquiry was to find under whose care this ground properly was, and finding that the Board of Wardens, as guardians of the property belonging to the city was legally invested with this trust, and, of course, the proper body to make application to, your committee wrote a letter to them, calling

3

their attention to the evil complained of, and desiring an opportunity to prove before them the accusations alleged against the said John Reynolds. This the Board of Wardens granted, and appointed a time for bringing forward the necessary proofs, which your committee was able to do, and did, in a few instances, prove to the satisfaction of said Board that the said John Reynolds had, in some instances, taken a half-dollar and in others a quarter of a dollar, for the privilege of opening the gate of said Potter's Field, for ' fence money,' as he termed it."

The Wardens promised to stop the extortion, but they could not compel Reynolds to return the money he had obtained in that *honorable* manner.

While the gains of that worthy gentleman might not be considered abundant, yet the disposition and ability shown might have lifted him into a position of affluence, if the Overseers had not made themselves so " *officious.*"

Another committee report shows that the average population of the House had increased to 328, and it often reached 400, during the winter months. They were of both sexes and of all ages, "from infancy to dotage." Those who were able to work were generally employed in spinning, knitting, sewing, picking oakum, and the manufacture of linen. About forty paupers were engaged in spinning alone. In consequence of the institution being encumbered with debt, the Managers tried to reduce the expenses by compelling all who were not sick to work at some productive labor.

There were many disreputable characters in the city at this time, and they carried on a lively trade after night, exchanging rum for clothing and bedding belonging to the House. This could be accomplished without difficulty, as the grounds surrounding the institution were not inclosed.

It was a very serious matter, as it not only resulted in loss, but led to drunken disorder and insubordination as well. The Board endeavored to stop this as soon as it was discovered, but much anxiety was caused before some of those engaged in the nefarious business were detected and punished.

SPRUCE STREET ALMSHOUSE, 1767 TO 1834.

There were now more than 300 outside pensioners receiving assistance from the Board.

A complete change in the administration of the public charity was made in the early part of 1788, when the Assembly passed an act which incorporated the Overseers of the Poor of the city and the adjacent districts under the title of " Guardians of the Poor of the City of Philadelphia." The House of Employment, Almshouse, as well as the care of outside poor, were given into charge of Managers appointed by this Board, and the old Board of Managers, which had existed for many years, was abolished.

The new Managers agreed to hold monthly meetings at the House of Employment, and appointed a sub-committee of two, called the " weekly Board of Managers," to visit the House twice every week and supervise and direct all the arrangements. The rules and regulations were amended and made clear in regard to every official's duties.

A notable proposition was made at a meeting held in November, 1788, to allow medical students to practice in the House. It was strongly opposed, and the discussion was spirited and protracted. Finally, the Managers consented to admit the students on trial, and a committee was appointed to frame suitable regulations for their government.

The monthly report of the Managers, presented December 1st, 1788, will give some idea of the financial difficulties of the administration of charity at that period. It said: " At and since the revolution, which placed the management and direction of this institution under our care, the idea of abuses, negligence and want of capacity under the late management hath been pretty generally disseminated. To these causes the embarrassed and encumbered condition of its affairs hath, in a great measure, been ascribed, and from the active and zealous part the Overseers took in the revolution, the public eye has been turned toward them with a fixed expectation of seeing considerable reforms effected. We think it highly necessary therefore, at this time, to state for your serious consideration, a brief review of what progress we have made, and an examination of what lies before us. On our first commencing the management of this institution, it was found, on examination and inquiry, to be encumbered with a load of debt, to an unexpected and alarming amount. A regard for the welfare of the institution and justice to its creditors required that some measures should be pursued to pay off or reduce that debt. The last assessment granted to the late Managers for £8600, although sufficient for the support and employment of the poor, was judged inadequate, if collected in paper money, for the purpose of such payment or reduction. An application was therefore made to the Magistrates for the assessment of that sum in specie, which they were induced to issue their warrants for, on the representation made to them of the embarrassed state of the institution, and that a considerable part of this sum was wanted for and intended to be appropriated to the discharge of its debts. On attempting to collect this tax great murmurs and discontent were expressed at the poor rate being as high in specie, as it had been before in paper money, and considerable opposition was made by some in paying it in specie. We surmounted the difficulties thrown in our way by this opposition, and, in a measure, calmed the discontents of our fellow citizens by alleging that the object of so great a tax was to relieve the institution and its creditors by a considerable diminution of its debts, and to effect this purpose an extraordinary sum was necessary. These circumstances have placed us in a very marked and conspicuous point of view. The creditors of the institution are looking to payment with anxiety, and our fellow-citizens behold us with a steady expectation that we will remove the cause of such extraordinary contributions. And as we have received every sanction and aid that the magistrates could afford us, it now solely rests on us to perform that on which we stated our object to be, and on the event is our reputation at stake."

Those gentlemen recognized their responsibilities, and were determined to faithfully perform their duties. They felt that their "reputation was at stake," and, as they valued the kind they bore, its preservation was deemed of importance, so they resolved to carry out and fulfil all the pledges made before their selection and to not forget what was due to their fellow-citizens and tax payers.

Some officials of later date have not been so particular, as they
looked upon ante-election promises as being buried in the dead
past, and not worthy of a thought.

The details of the management of the House were carefully
scanned by the members of the Board, and while they were ever
ready to give credit when it was due, they did not hesitate to censure
or punish when they felt it was deserved.   The minutes of December 15th, 1788 record that " The Steward and Matron of the House
of Employment were reprimanded on account of some unexplained
deficiencies in the returns of the spinning department. The Board
adopted the following rule : " That in future all deficiencies not
regularly and satisfactorily accounted for, shall be charged to the
Steward or Matron, where such circumstance occurs under his or
her department, and the value of the same shall be stopped out of
his or her wages."

CHAPTER III.

THE physicians on duty at the Almshouse, at this period, were the most distinguished and skillful to be found. Among them were Drs. Samuel Powell Griffiths, John Morris, Samuel Duffield, William Clarkson, William Shippen, Caspar Wistar, Michael Lieb, and Nathan B. Waters, men who have been looked upon as the early lights of science, and whose names are still honored by the members of the profession.

At a meeting of the Board held on March 3d, 1790, the following memorial was adopted and sent to the municipal authorities : "That being informed of your having under consideration the subject of renting out the lot now in use for the interment of deceased strangers, commonly called Potter's Field, we deem it a duty incumbent upon us to address you on the occasion, as affecting, in some degree, the interest committed to our trust, and therefore use the liberty of laying before your view some circumstances which, perhaps, are not generally known, and may be of use in enabling you to judge whether it would not be for public benefit, should you adopt the measure of leasing out said lot, to reserve to the Guardians of the Poor the privilege of having graves dug for the interment of such paupers as may die under their care. We have reason to believe that on due inquiry it would appear that more than 120 persons are annually interred whose coffins are made and graves dug by paupers in this institution, whose labor in any other way, would, from their unskillfulness and incapacity, be very little productive for the public interest, and should the Guardians of the Poor be deprived of their present economical means of making use of their labor in the interment of those for whose funeral expenses the public must pay, this deprivation will impose an additional burthen on our fellow citizens who pay poor taxes, by an increase of expense to which the whole income of the ground proposed to be leased may not bear a due proportion." In

38

answer to this document it was stated that the corporation designed to reserve to the Guardians of the Poor the right of interment in the Potter's Field.

The steward of the House entered complaint against the " invalid pensioners," several of whom had been a burden to the House since the close of the Revolutionary War. It was charged that these disabled soldiers were in the habit of selling their pensions before they became due, thus defrauding the institution of any compensation for their maintenance. A bill in regard to pensions being before the Legislature at the time, steps were taken to have a clause inserted to prevent the pensioners selling their claims. This was accomplished, and afterwards the old soldiers had to pay their way at the Almshouse.

John Cummings was steward of the Almshouse at that time. He had held the position more than twenty years, and had been active and influential in organizing the system upon which this great charity was administered. At a meeting of the Board, held in February, 1792, it was ordered to be entered on the minutes as a recommendation for Mr. Cummings to the succeeding Board, that for more than twenty years " his attention to the various duties of his station has been unremitted, his integrity unimpeached, and his humanity conspicuous." It had the desired effect, as the new Board not only retained him, but increased his salary as well. Mr. Cummings lived in times when faithful services were appreciated.

A memorial was addressed to the Legislature asking for a modification of the poor laws. It appeared that by the 10th section of an Act passed in 1767, the Justices of the Peace were authorized to commit " rogues, vagabonds and other idle and dis solute persons to the House of Employment." This class of inmates became a great nuisance in the institution. The Guardians stated that " children, on whose minds first impressions are the most lasting, were exposed to improper examples, while the more advanced in years, to whom nothing worse than poverty or disease could be imputed, and to alleviate whose distresses the first contributions to the House of Employment were made, were confounded,

with the rogues, the vagabonds and the culprits. Thus this public charity, intended to be a decent and respectable abode for the
poor and infirm, was converted into a place of tumult, disorder and
punishment." At the same time the Board abolished the practice
of distributing a daily allowance of rum to paupers employed by
the institution, having found that such a course only tended to
promote disorder and keep alive a thirst for intoxicating liquor.

In 1793 the city was visited by that terrible plague—yellow
fever. It made its appearance in July, in a lodging house on
Water Street, but it was not until the middle of August that its
progress attracted attention. The Guardians of the Poor refused
to receive any more persons in the Almshouse. This was intended
as a protection to the inmates, but the disease broke out among
them, and many were attacked. Some were sent to the Hospital
at Bush Hill. No one could conceive the conditions at that time.
A panic seized the people, and we are informed by writers that the
streets were filled with fleeing families, who, in their terror, had
not only left their homes, but the stricken of their household.

On every hand one could see carts with rough boxes containing the dead hurrying to the graveyards. Men locked themselves
in their homes; all social intercourse ceased, and one half of the
houses were deserted. The Federal Government removed to Germantown, and all kinds of industry ceased. Coffins were piled
along the streets, and the cry, " bring out your dead ! " could be
heard at intervals. Bodies lay rotting on the highways for want
of burial; whole families were swept away.

It was impossible to procure suitable nurses; only the most
depraved creatures could be hired.

Mayor Clarkson, on September 10th, 1793, called for volunteers to relieve the Guardians of the Poor. Of those remaining in
the city only ten responded, and among them was Stephen Girard,
the French " merchant and mariner." He became the master
spirit of the Committee of Safety. Matthew Carey, in his "account
of the malignant Fever lately Prevalent in Philadelphia," describes
Bush Hill Hospital, as it was in the early part of the epidemic, as
follows : " A profligate, abandoned set of nurses and attendants—

hardly any of good character could be procured—rioted on the provisions and comforts prepared for the sick, who, unless at the hours when the doctors attended, were left entirely destitute of every assistance. The sick, the dying and the dead were indiscriminately mingled together. The ordure and other evacuations of the sick were allowed to remain in the most offensive state imaginable. Not the smallest appearance of order or regularity existed. It was, in fact, a great human slaughter house, where numerous victims were immolated at the altar of riot and intemperance. No wonder, then, that a general dread of the place prevailed, and that a removal to it was considered as the seal of death." Who would volunteer to take charge of such a pest-house?

No one could consider it as being less than suicidal. Stephen Girard, millionaire, with everything to live for, immediately came to the front and offered his services for that benevolent work. He was joined by Peter Helm, a noble Moravian, and, without stopping to attend to any private affairs, they went forth together, divided the work, and for two months both of these heroes spent from six to eight hours every day at the hospital. When they saw the condition of that place they started to reform it. It was a terrible task, but their courage, charity and labor were wonderful. An eye witness of the scenes, in speaking of Girard, said: "He had to encourage and comfort the sick, to hand them necessaries and medicines, to wipe the sweat off their brows, to perform many offices of kindness for them which nothing could render tolerable but the exalted motives that impelled him to this heroic conduct."

It was stated that at least 17,000 people fled from the city, and at one time not more than 23,000 remained. It was estimated that there were nearly 5,000 deaths during the few months the epidemic raged.

When the disease was at its height the visits of the Guardians to the Almshouse were not frequent, but the steward and the medical attendants never deserted their posts. They stuck to their duty, attending to their flock of poor old friendless wrecks.

In December, 1793, the house was again opened to receive persons entitled to aid. At a meeting of the Guardians, after all vestige of the fever had disappeared from the city, the following preamble and resolution were adopted: "The Board, taking into consideration the dangerous and difficult situation in which the steward of this institution was placed, by reason of the prevalence of the late yellow fever, together with the intrepid firmness and resolution with which he, undismayed, adhered to the duties of his place, *Resolved, unanimously*, That the sincerest thanks of the Board be presented to John Cummings, steward of this institution, for his firm, intrepid and vigilant attention to the various and important duties of his office, and that a committee of three be appointed to report this resolution to Mr. Cummings."

The services of the steward were further recognized by an extra appropriation of two hundred dollars for his family. At the same time the matron, Martha Marshall, was also complimented upon the steady heroism she had displayed during the gloomiest period of the pestilence. Martha Marshall, a noble woman, took the place of Mrs. Cummings, wife of the steward, who had died at her post.

The brave and faithful Cummings continued in the service of the institution for more than thirty years, at the end of which age and infirmities compelled him to resign. No officer could have had a greater claim on the gratitude of the public. Honest, industrious, intelligent and resolute, he was always at his post, ready to make any sacrifice for the benefit of those under his care. It is a pleasure to write of such a man, and is doubly so when it is seen that his services were recognized and appreciated. That has a tendency to make good officials and improves the service. When Mr. Cummings resigned Aaron Musgrave was elected to succeed him.

The Board adopted a resolution increasing the steward's salary, but directing him to pay the late steward, during the remainder of his life, the sum of two hundred dollars per annum. The Board endeavored to make the last days of a faithful servant comfortable. It was subsequently discovered that they had no authority to make such an appropriation, and it was revoked. Peter Browne, Esq., paid the amount out of his own purse.

Mr. Musgrave only acted as steward two years. Some officious person made trivial charges against him. He demanded an investigation, and after it was shown that the allegations were false he resigned. Jacob Philips was elected to fill vacancy.

In August, 1798, the yellow fever again made its appearance. The steward was directed to allow no persons to be admitted without a certificate from the attending physicians. Frequent conferences took place between the Guardians, the Board of Health and the managers of the Marine City Hospital for the purpose of securing accommodations for the poor of the city and districts, and to aid persons who desired to remove outside of the city limits. In September it was concluded to solicit a loan on subscription, the money to be used for their purposes. During the month of November between two and three hundred children, utterly destitute, were sent to the Guardians of the Poor, their parents having fallen victims to the fever.

It was stated that during the prevalence of the epidemic, in this year, at least 50,000 persons fled from the city, leaving only about 3,000 remaining in Philadelphia.

In the same year the whooping cough prevailed to an alarming extent; almost every house was visited by it. This was a year of trouble and distress.

In 1803 the institution was crowded. The average population had become so large, being about five hundred and forty, that it was necessary to make additions to the buildings. Mr. Isaac T. Hopper, a well known philanthropist, made a number of suggestions; some additions were made to the premises, and, what was considered, in those days, suitable accommodations for the insane, were arranged. At this time clinical lectures were introduced at the Almshouse, at the request of Dr. Charles Caldwell. The doctor was allowed to introduce and instruct a class of twenty— afterwards forty—students, during his visits to the medical wards, on condition of his becoming responsible for their good deportment. When this was inaugurated many persons considered it as a rather dangerous innovation, as medical students were surrounded by an atmosphere of mystery and suspicion at that period.

In this year an Act was passed by the Legislature which provided that "the Guardians of the Poor, who shall be substantial
housekeepers," shall be elected annually, sixteen by the corporation
of the city, six by Southwark corporation, and eight by the Justices
of the Peace of the township of Northern Liberties." Outside of
the city, Northern Liberties and Southwark the poor were attended
to by the Overseers of their respective districts.

In September, 1803, there was another fever panic in Philadelphia. The Guardians adopted precautions to prevent the disease from getting among the inmates of the Almshouse. They
secured the building known as the Pennsylvania Arsenal for a
temporary hospital. Another building, belonging to Dr. Curry,
situated on the banks of the Schuylkill, near Race street, was
tendered to the Board, fitted up with twenty-five bedsteads and
bedding, and used for the reception of the paupers during the
prevalence of the fever. The pestilence proved very destructive,
and the demands upon the labor and money of those having the
distribution of charity in charge was unceasing. Mr. Philips, the
Steward of the Almshouse, proved worthy of his charge, and
earned the gratitude of the public by his energy and attention to
the sufferings of those around him. He fell a victim to his devo-
tion to duty, and died at his post, in December, 1803. He deserved
a monument, at least, from the people he served.

A serious difficulty, or quarrel, occurred between Doctors
Thomas C. James and Charles Caldwell, both of whom were en-
gaged at the Almshouse. It appeared that Dr. James charged Dr.
Caldwell with altering a figure on one receipt and a date on another
after they had been received from the Treasurer of the College of
Physicians.

The accused demanded an investigation by a committee of the
Guardians. The Managers declined to take such action, in a case
which seemed to them to be nothing but a personal quarrel, and
referred the parties to the legal tribunals.

Dr. Caldwell sent the following communication, November
17th, 1803, to the Board:

"I have reason to believe that Dr. Thomas C. James continues to urge a decision by the Managers of the Almshouse on the subject of the misunderstanding between him and myself. I make no comment on the spirit of determined hostility and inexorable rancor with which he has pursued this business since its commencement.

" If the charges he has alleged against me be well founded, they amount to high offences against the laws of my country. They are also of such nature as to be cognizable by those laws. On my country, therefore, I throw myself, for a fair, legal and impartial trial. From the justice of the government under which I live, I have every assurance that such a trial will be readily obtained. On the issue of that I am willing to rest my reputation and fate, both as an officer of the Almshouse and as a private citizen. And as Dr. James has not brought it to this issue by commencing a prosecution against me, I will certainly do it, by bringing an action against him for his slanders and malice. As I am determined to bring the matter as soon as possible before the proper tribunal, I cannot for a moment suspect that the Board of Managers will come to any decision on it, which might tend to prejudice the public mind, and prevent the current of justice from flowing in its native purity.

" It is impossible for the Board to institute such an investigation as will put them in possession of all the requisite testimony on the subject. Should they undertake to decide on partial testimony, and the decision prove unfavorable to me, they will therefore oblige me to meet a suit under all the adverse impressions which such a decision would necessarily produce on the minds of my fellow-citizens, from among whom a jury must be chosen at no very distant day to decide on the matter in a court of justice. I understand the affair has been laid by Dr. James before his Excellency the Governor, with a request that he would remove me from the Board of Health. The talents, information and uprightness of that gentleman will not be doubted. But his love of justice constitutes a pre-eminent trait in his character. He, therefore, very properly declined taking, at present, any concern in the business, conscious that a removal from the Board of Health would be a prejudice of the question, and tend to a violation of that justice which has been the business of his life to cherish and protect."

The Doctor desired the Board to follow the Governor's example, and the Managers did so.

Dr. James sustained his charges by producing letters from officials connected with the College of Physicians, and seemed unrelenting in his enmity.

At the ensuing election of physicians Dr. Caldwell was dropped, but he was permitted to bring his pupils to the institution. Dr. James was re-elected, and was the cause of considerable comment. The Board showed a weakness. If Dr. Caldwell was not fit to be retained on the staff he certainly should not have been allowed the privilege of taking his class to the House.

Dr. James soon got into difficulty, and a number of distinguished physicians, including Dr. Philip Syng Physic, were requested by the Board to investigate. Their report said: "A complaint of a very serious nature having, at your last meeting, been charged before you against one of the present attending physicians, and by you referred to our judgment, we have, without delay, carefully inquired into the circumstances. They were succinctly these: Dr. James, the physician complained of, prescribed camphor in small doses of ten or fifteen grains for Savage, a maniac, leaving a choice of either quantity to the discretion of the senior pupil, Dr. Scott. The medicine was made up in the form of a mixture, but the portion given at each dose amounted to about thirty grains. This error is not attributable to Dr. James, whose conduct was cautious and correct. The matter, too, was in itself harmless, this patient, while in the Pennsylvania Hospital, having been in the habit of taking quantities of much more considerable amount.

" It is our duty to state our apprehensions that much worse mistakes occur, and these frequently, under the present manner of prescribing. In order that they may, in the future be obviated, we beg to propose that the senior pupil should enter into a book an accurate account of the symptoms with which each patient is affected, and a regular register of the medical treatment.

"The attending physicians may, for their own sakes, and the benefit of their pupils, preserve similar case books, and these will serve as a check upon each other. The measure here urged is not new or unprecedented; it is practiced in all the principal hospitals in Europe; it would not be attended with much trouble, and in a long time would form a collection of medical facts of high value.

"The occurrence which has induced the present communication, solemnly presses upon us as an additional observation, if medicines are not duly administered, if any nurse or other domestic declines administering a medicine, because it does not suit their own conception of what is proper, the patient may, in acute cases, be suddenly destroyed and murder perpetrated by ignorance under the roof of charity. The well being of the patient and the character of the physician demand the removal of any person whatever guilty of conduct subversive of both."

Mr. John Trout, a member of the Board of Managers, was appointed Steward of the Almshouse in April, 1804. It appears that no suitable person could be found to fill the position, and the institution had been left without an efficient superintendent since the death of Mr. Philips. Under these circumstances, Mr. Trout was persuaded to accept the situation. Previous to doing so, he resigned his office as a Guardian.

The report of a committee made on the 3d day of September, 1804, seemed to have some connection with the "additional observation" contained in that of the medical gentlemen who investigated the charges made against Dr. James, although some time elapsed between the dates of the two reports. The committee's investigation appears to have discovered the foundation of the thoughts expressed in the previous report, and the facts were stated to the Board as follows: "The charges made against James Malanafy are: That he has drawn liquor for the patients after they have been discharged from his ward; that he has been frequently intoxicated in such manner as not to be able to administer the medicines prescribed for patients under his immediate care; that, after he has drawn liquor for the patients in his ward, he has taken the same for his own use; that he hath, after the death of a patient, selected the best of the clothing and sent the remainder to the Steward; that a patient named Thomas Loudin drew liquor for eight or ten weeks, but did not get a half-pint from the whole that was drawn; that there were several charges similar to this; that John Moore, a barber, who died three or four weeks ago, was visited by Dr. Petre, who ordered a certain quantity of laudanum to be given him; but instead of the laudanum as ordered, James Malanafy gave him a pill; that in about ten minutes after he gave him the pill, the patient began to feel very uneasy and 'drew breath like a horse,' and he died the next day; that for a considerable time before the Managers ordered the gates to be closed, the tea and coffee received by the patients was such that nobody could tell which was tea and which was coffee."

" The charges against Elizabeth Donnelly are: That she gets intoxicated; that she has declared to one of the patients, now in the ward, that she had sold as much coffee as produced her six dollars, which was a sum sufficient to purchase her a new gown, and at the same time expressed her regret that the other nurses had not had the same opportunities as she enjoyed; and further, that as Malanafy was nurse, she could act as she pleased; that she had destroyed the medicines she should have administered to the patients."

These facts, showing how patients in the hospital had actually been murdered through neglect, or worse, were known to but few persons, and instead of this pair of ungrateful, dishonest murderers being sent to prison and punished as they so richly deserved, they were simply discharged from the institution. One can scarcely believe that such depraved creatures could exist, and it is a sad reflection upon the management of the institution to find that such a condition of affairs had been allowed to continue for any length of time.

CHAPTER IV.

THE Managers saw that it was absolutely necessary to enlarge the accommodations for the constantly increasing numbers that applied to them. The committee reported that the Almshouse was continually crowded, and the constantly increasing population of the city would soon develop an amount of pauperism for which no provision had been made. It was expected that there would be one thousand in the institution during the coming winter. It was resolved to build another addition on Spruce street, between the two buildings then standing, and to erect outhouses and make alterations for the purpose of securing accommodations for several hundred more paupers.

When the Board concluded that the additional buildings would be required, the question of funds was a serious one. There was no money available, and the Legislature was again applied to. The petition sent was as follows:

"That although the beneficial effects of republican government have prevented the claimants of eleemosynary bounty from being in any wise proportionate to the increase of population, yet this, rapidly progressing, has at last attained such a height as to render the present buildings utterly incompetent to the purposes for which they were destined. That your memorialists, involved by their predecessors in a debt of $20,000, one-third of which was unnecessarily incurred from the retention of maniacs in the Pennsylvania Hospital, are unable to erect buildings of the extent which has become at present necessary.

"That the institution comprises a poorhouse, a house for the reception of the aged and infirm, whose condition incapacitates them from earning a subsistence; an orphan and foundling hospital; a ward for lying-in indigent women; apartments adapted to the treatment of the insane; workshops for those who are capable of exercising every species of industry; an extensive hospital for

4 49

poor male and female patients requiring medical and surgical treatment.

" That though each of these departments has, in most cities been separated into distinct establishments, severally endowed with donations, benefactions, legacies and permanent public provisions, yet this complex institution has heretofore occasioned little or no expense to the State.

" That though your memorialists, resting solely on the merits of their cause, would wish to evade any invidious reflection, yet in justice to the distressed, they cannot forbear remarking that the Pennsylvania Hospital, which, rich in estates and property, has received large and repeated assistance from the munificence of former Legislatures, is shut against the poor, and exacts a sum from all those admitted more than equivalent to the expense of their board and lodging, giving only medical treatment gratis. That your memorialists submit another consideration : the merits of the profession in this medical school of Philadelphia have attracted students from all parts of the United States, and some from other countries, thereby saving the exportation of very considerable sums heretofore expended in Europe, and exalting the American character. That the Pennsylvania Hospital, which from the difficulty of admission, on an . average contains no more than from sixty to eighty patients, is not a very important adjunct of the medical school, affording few examples of disease and but limited lessons in practice to the students, while the Almshouse contains, on an average, between six and seven hundred persons, and at present nearly one thousand within its apartments ; and, of course, might be, in this respect, rendered more eminently useful and instructive.

" Finally, your memorialists, conceiving that one-fifth of the admitted paupers being from various and remote parts of the State, gives them a claim on general assistance, but they rest with the more assurance on the respect for science, morals and humanity entertained by their enlightened representatives, and, therefore, pray that, taking the premises into consideration, the Legislature may be pleased to assist them in effecting the necessary alterations and additions to the Almshouse by a grant of $50,000."

This memorial caused considerable discussion and comment, but the amount applied for was not appropriated.

The "malignant fever," which had been the cause of so much distress on its previous visits, again made trouble in August, 1805. A large number of the paupers was attacked, and to prevent the spread of the contagion in the institution, the old sugar house of James Ash was rented for the accommodation of the sick. Patrick McFell was steward at that time. A report was circulated that a sick woman had died in consequence of the neglect of the physicians, and the Guardians of the Poor asked for an investigation. The managers of the House paid no attention to the request.

In November a man named Thomas Barry, who had been an inmate, was promoted to the position of cell keeper, on account of good conduct, then demoted to his former condition as a pauper by reason of unsatisfactory performance of duty, and finally discharged from the House for insubordination, caused considerable anxiety for the Board, and much food for gossip to the community.

It was stated that Barry had publicly declared that " he would consume the factory," which was construed to mean that he would set fire to it. A communication, signed by Barry, appeared in the *Freeman's Journal*, in which he charged gross mismanagement and abuse in the manufacturing department of the Almshouse.

The charges were investigated, and it was found that there was no truth in them. No attempt was made to "consume" the House, but there is nothing to show that Barry was ever prosecuted for the threats he made.

In February, 1806, a communication, signed "Detector," appeared in the *Freeman's Journal*, alleging that certain abuses existed in the Almshouse. The Board demanded the name of the writer, and it was William Ross, the President of the Board. The charges made by Ross were : " That the matron's brother and his wife were in the habit of residing in the House for several months at a time at the public expense ; that the matron had a number of the paupers employed for her individual benefit, for about eighteen months ; that the matron was in the habit of drawing barrels of flour and sugar for her own use, and without the authority of the managers, and finally that members of the Board were in the habit of passing some evenings in the matron's apartments, whereby an undue influence was gained in her favor."

The charges were investigated in a manner. The matron was questioned and denied the allegations, and she was considered innocent. The President was censured and compelled to resign.

Whether the charges were true or not, it was a mean and undignified way to get them before the Board. It would have been much more honorable on the part of Mr. Ross if he had called the attention of his colleagues to what he knew or believed, instead of sending it out to the public through the newspapers. He must have known that it was a contemptible way to act, as he was either ashamed or afraid to sign his name to the papers. Whatever may have been the motive that prompted him, it reflected no credit upon him, either as an official or as a man.

During the month of August, 1807, an epidemic of influenza broke out in the House, attacking both officers and inmates, and prevailing in so violent a form and so general, as to interrupt the ordinary routine of business.

More charges were investigated, and on the 23d of May, 1808, the committee submitted the following report :

" The various subjects submitted for consideration are of a nature sufficiently important to command the serious consideration of the committee. The instances of immorality and depravity that our inquiry and examination made manifest are productive of infinite regret, and incline us to believe that some further provision is necessary for the well government of the House. The daily violation of the ordinary laws of society and of the rules and regulations established by this Board, ought not to be tolerated for a single moment. The pilfering of clothing, provisions, etc., and the introduction of spirituous liquors, with the consequences of drunkenness, elopement and fornication, and the perfectly systematized and good understanding which exists between the persons concerned, have become so flagrant and notorious as loudly to demand the immediate interposition of this Board, and the utmost vigilance and activity of the steward and the officers of the House,

PHILADELPHIA ALMSHOUSE, 1840.

and that offenders may be speedily and exemplarily punished. We are aware that to apply an adequate remedy for diseases so complicated is an undertaking of no common labor ; it is a work that requires time and experience, assisted by all the resolution, skill and industry of the Board to accomplish.

" Permit us to add that it is more surely traced to a sensibility too early excited, an ill-timed relaxation of official severity, or a deficiency of that scrupulous adherence so indispensible in our determination, to which may be added the extreme difficulty of substantiating offenses by legal evidence.

" Suits were commenced by the committee against certain tippling houses in the neighborhood of the institution whose unlawful practices, it is presumed, contributed to increase the irregularities in the House.

" But a prevention, not a punishment, was the object of the Board ; and from the solicitations, several of which the Board heard, and the most solemn assurances of amendment, the committee was prevailed upon to stay the proceedings for the present, the Attorney General having entered a *nol pros.*, at the same time informing them that on the smallest deviation from their present engagements they should be proceeded against with the utmost severity of the law."

The report was accompanied by resolutions providing for the government of the institution, etc., and was adopted.

That report revealed a terrible condition of affairs. There did not appear to be any semblance of management. It was an arraignment of the incompetency of the steward and all connected with the management of the institution ; and no doubt the best course to pursue, under such circumstances, would be to dispense with the services (?) of officials who could allow such demoralization and rascality to exist in any kind of an establishment, and especially in one of that character, without immediately adopting measures to correct the abuses and reform the management of it.

One of the cases that attracted attention was that of Mary Lawyer, an inmate in 1808. She had been in the House several months and was likely to remain there. Her father, Christian

Lawyer, had been a man of means, and when he died he left a will, in which after providing for the payment of his debts, etc., he left "the annual income and the income of all the residue and remainder of his property" to his beloved wife for and during her natural life, if she so long remained his widow, unmarried, and *not otherwise*.

He provided that after the death or marriage of his wife, "whichever shall first happen," all of his estate, real and personal, should go to his five beloved children—Mary, etc.,—to be equally divided between them, except that his daughter Mary and his son John were to receive twenty-seven dollars more than the others.

The wife and John Sheble were appointed executors. The "beloved wife" did not long remain unmarried, but she refused to relinquish the property. The children, most of whom were under age, were left destitute, and Mary, who was of age, was compelled to go to the Almshouse.

John Sheble brought the case to the attention of the Guardians of the Poor, and suit was entered; the unnatural mother fought to the end, but was compelled to surrender, and Mary Lawyer left the Almshouse to live on her share of her father's estate.

It was very fortunate for those poor children that their father had prudently inserted the clause in his will which cut the hard-hearted mother off when she remarried.

The goods manufactured in the Almshouse amounted to considerable, and met with a ready sale. Stephen Girard sent fifty-two hundred pounds of cotton there at one time, for which he was to receive a certain number of counterpanes and covers when they were made. The cash received amounted to a respectable sum, which reduced the cost of maintenance somewhat. The managers received the following notice in December, 1808: "The minutes of the Board of Managers of the Philadelphia Premium Society require of me the agreeable duty of announcing that the sum of $25 has been awarded to the institution over which you so excellently preside as "to the individual or company who first sets up a throwing or thread machine and lodges, as a specimen, at the Philadelphia Society's warehouse, at least sixty pounds weight of the grey and colored kinds (the Scotch slender thread, such as is used by the tailors, upholsterers, bookbinders, etc., being the thread recommended for imitation) and also that the premium of $20, which, for obtainment, requires the best piece of sheeting, thirty-three yards long and nine-eighths wide, made of linen chain and cotton filling, bleached and fit for sale, has been awarded to your institution. Of your second exhibit the circumstance of its being part of thirty thousand yards of cloth completed within the past year does you the greater honor, as you have no motive save the good of the country."

The Philadelphia Premium Society was an association established to promote domestic manufactures and the useful arts; the managers of the Almshouse were justly proud of the honor achieved and greatly encouraged in their work.

The first move for an institution on a large scale, and located on a farm, was made as far back as 1808. The committee suggested that with a farm, a few miles from the city, and containing from three to five hundred acres, the poor, or a greater part of them, could earn their subsistence, and thus diminish the poor tax. Although it was considered advisable to purchase a farm at that time it took about twenty years to accomplish it.

In the minutes of July, 1810, appears the report of a committee regarding the case of a patient, a colored man, named Robert Easton, who jumped from one of the windows of the sick men's wards.

One of the patients lying near Easton's bed saw him get up at about half-past one o'clock and go to the convenience. As that was a usual thing, it caused no alarm. A woman was on a porch near to where he fell, but she did not hear the fall. She heard his groans, and saw him on the ground. She gave the alarm, and James, the assistant to the nurse in the ward, dressed himself and went down to the man. When James asked him how he came there, Easton replied that he had jumped out of the window, because he wanted to die. They carried him up to his bed, when James, thinking the man was insane, and perceiving no injury from the fall, put a chain upon his feet for security. The physicians were notified of the accident immediately. James first informed Dr. Gordon. He desired him to notify Dr. Stewart, and he did so. The doctor inquired if the man was hurt, but did not go to him to see. James said that he did not seem to be, as far as he knew. Dr. Stewart told him to let it go until morning. The unfortunate man was then left in that condition until four o'clock, when James, hearing him groan, and fearing that he might want assistance, went to him and found him evidently dying. No further notice was given to the doctors and the man died in a few minutes after.

The report showed gross negligence on the part of the physicians. They should have examined the man immediately to see whether he was injured, and not take the judgment of an ignorant assistant to the nurse.

The affair caused considerable gossip, and it was asserted that Easton had been put in chains and so badly treated that he had jumped out of the window to escape the cruelty. It was also said that he died for want of medical attention. There was probably some truth in the latter assertion.

The only action taken by the Board was to order the Steward to have iron bars put on the windows. That did not help the reputation of the House in the estimation of the community, and the Almshouse became an object of suspicion. The records show that the physicians gave the Managers a great deal of trouble. There were repeated complaints of violating the rules, neglecting the sick, and interfering with the discipline of the House.

Committees of investigation were appointed, new and more stringent rules framed, and attempts made to enforce them; but the complaints still poured in to the Board. The trouble was, there was no competent head in charge of the institution.

The sale of liquor to the paupers by the proprietors of tippling houses on Spruce street was another source of annoyance to the Managers. Inmates purchased the rum and took it in the House, and drunkenness and disorder was the result. The friends of inmates smuggled it in to them, and the officials did not seem to know what to do about it. The keepers of the taverns were prosecuted, the drunken paupers were punished, but still it continued.

Patrick McFell, who had been Steward several years, was dismissed for not enforcing the rules of the House; not visiting the various departments, and showing a lack of judgment on several occasions. It would have been better for the institution if the action had been taken much sooner. His incompetency had been clearly shown by the condition of the House, as shown by the committee's report in May, 1808.

There was a number of changes made in the manufacturing department; some labor-saving machinery, which had been introduced for the spinning of cotton and wool, was abandoned; all hired labor was dispensed with, and the Superintendent's services were discontinued. For a long time the factory of the Almshouse had been the largest and most productive of any in the city, but the Managers concluded that too much attention had been paid to that department, to the detriment of more important branches. The changes made destroyed its importance in the eyes of the community.

Considerable speculation was indulged in at this time as to the proper course to be taken in regard to the insane patients in the Almshouse. They were placed in dark, close and damp cells in the eastern wing, and the medical gentlemen did not seem to trouble themselves very much about them. They appeared to think that insanity was incurable, and even the mildest cases were in cages like wild beasts, and exposed to the gaze and jeers of heartless visitors, who laughed at them and treated them as though they were monkeys or other animals on exhibition in a zoological garden. The west end was finally selected for the confinement of these poor creatures, but their condition was not much improved. It took a number of years to learn how to treat those unfortunates, but the knowledge has been gained and applied at last.

At a meeting of the Managers on September 20th, 1811, a resolution was adopted which caused considerable comment. The Board had been informed that certain persons had been in the habit of preaching in the sick wards "on the first day of the week," frequently to the injury of the patients. The Managers regarded this as "neither a moral or religious way

of hastening the afflicted into the grave," and probibited its
repetition.

Arrangements were made, however, for preaching the gospel
on Sundays in a part of the House, remote from the hearing of
the sick.

The surgeons reported that they were compelled to perform
severe surgical operations in the room crowded with the sick, and
they spoke of the effects of the spectacle upon the suffering audience, as being terrible and cruel. The Board adopted a resolution to secure an apartment to be devoted exclusively to surgical
operations.

It might well be said that the lot of the poor paupers, in those
days, was not a happy one, and they did not rest on a bed of roses.

CHAPTER V.

THE deplorable condition of the insane patients was again brought to the attention of the Board by the report of the committee appointed, in the early part of 1812, " to investigate and report what measures would be necessary for the improvement of the system of confinement adopted in taking care of these unfortunate creatures." In their report occurs the following horrible statement: " Your committee must confess to the Board their conviction that the comforts of the afflicted maniacs cannot be materially improved, nor their disorder successfully contended with, while they are exposed to the chilling damps of the present lower cells; the confined situation of which, must, in many cases, render useless the best directed efforts of medical skill. The only apertures which are depended upon for the circulation of air being near the ceiling of the apartment, must be, in a great meaure, ineffectual for the purpose; and when your committee reflect upon the consequences that may be apprehended from the damp and stagnant atmosphere acting on a system debilitated, perhaps by disease, under the effects of derangement and the operations of medical treatment, they are induced to feel the subject a very serious one. Among the incurable defects of the present cells, both upper and lower, are noted their proximity to the sick and surgical wards, by which the last moments of the sick are liable to disquietude; and the windows of one half open into a part of the yard the most frequented by the paupers, perhaps of any in the institution; and your committee have no doubt of the ill effects of an opportunity for disturbing, by conversation or interruption, the repose of the wretched tenants of the cells."

That report shows a terrible condition of affairs, and a sad want of intelligence and ability on the part of the officials to change for the better conditions that never should have existed.

The outbreak of the war between the United States and Great Britain caused a large increase of the population of the Almshouse; and, as the demand for goods stimulated the operations of the factory, an opportunity to employ the surplus inmates was afforded, and the manufacturing department again became of service.

A large cotton spinning machine was introduced, and the carding machine, invented by Mr Baxter, set up and operated for a short time, but it was a failure.

Francis Higgins, Steward of the Pennsylvania Hospital, died in February, 1813, when Mr. Samuel Mason, Steward of the Almshouse, was chosen to fill the vacancy. Mr. Mason was complimented by the Board, upon his retirement, for " his indefatigable attention to duty." Mr. J. A. Inslee took his place at the Almshouse.

Much comment was caused by a report presented in March. It read:

" The committee to whom was referred the application of the ' Evangelical Society,' of this State, requesting the grant of the flax ward on Sunday afternoons, for the sole use of the preachers of their society, respectfully report that it appears to have been the practice of this House for a long period of time, and probably from the origin of this institution, to admit the regular preachers of every Christian society on Sunday morning and Sunday afternoon ; that the flax ward being the largest and most convenient room for that purpose, has been appropriated accordingly ; and that, in order to prevent confusion, the Steward has been authorized to receive the applications of the different ministers, and to give them the privilege of holding forth to the people, according to the priority of their applications. Your committee observe that, under this regulation, there appears to have been a constant attendance of preachers, and that the instances of the Sabbath passing away without have been rare; so that expediency cannot be urged in favor of the proposed measure. Another consideration will, no doubt, have weight with the Board. The paupers of this House consists of Baptists, Lutherans, Presbyterians, Catholics, Methodists, Episcopalians and other sectarians. The exclusive grant of one-half of the Sabbath to the disciples of one sect might be deemed a measure savoring of partiality; and, however desirable it might be to secure the attendance of Presbyterian preachers for the afternoon, it might create a dissatisfaction in the disciples of different doctrines, which would counterbalance the good effects arising from it. There is no doubt in the minds of this committee· that if it were generally known that the Board was disposed to grant applications similar to the present, every sect in this city would request the same favor, and justly contend for an equality of claim."

Although the Evangelists were respectfully informed that their requests could not be granted, they did not give it up, and they subsequently succeeded in getting control of the religious instruction. They framed a prayer for the use of the school children, which is entered on the minutes of the Board as follows:

"PRAYER FOR THE ALMSHOUSE SCHOOL.

"Thou Most High and Holy God: we adore Thee as the greatest and best of beings, who art always present with us, to notice our conduct and mark our way. As Thou art an infinitely pure and perfect Being, and we simple creatures who have deserved nothing but eternal punishment, we beseech Thee, most gracious Lord, to look upon us in mercy, and, for the sake of our Lord and Saviour Jesus Christ, pardon all our transgressions and love us freely. We do entreat Thee, O Thou compassionate God, that Thou wilt be pleased to look, in Thy great kindness and compassion, upon these children in their pitiable condition. While we thank Thee that, in the midst of their helplessness and wretchedness, they have here an asylum where their food and raiment are provided for them, and where they are protected from the storm, we pray that their souls may be precious in Thy sight. Blessed Saviour, pity them in their ignorance and miseries. Do unto them as thou didst to the little ones in the days of Thy sojourning in our world. Take them in Thy arms of love and mercy and bless them. Oh, suffer them not to grow up under the negative enmity of their hearts against God, but turn them from sin to holiness, from the way of ungodliness to the path of righteousness. To this end bless the means which are used to train them up in the fear of the Lord, and to teach them the way in which they should go. Let this place, O Lord, become a school of piety and a blessed fountain from which many streams shall flow, to make glad the Church of Christ. Let these children know, in their own happy experience, the gracious fulfilment of that promise of the Lord, 'They that seek me early shall find me.' Oh, may they find the precious Saviour in the midst of their worldly distress and poverty, that blessed treasure which is more valuable than worlds, even the salvation of their souls. Bless, O Lord, this whole institution. May all the sons and daughters of poverty in this place, both old and young, be visited with thy saving grace and mercy. Let the sick and the dying receive from Thee most gracious assurances that their sins are pardoned through the blood of Jesus, and do Thou enable them to seek of Thee this great blessing. May they call upon Thee whilst Thou art near. Give them penitent hearts and a living faith in a Redeemer. We entreat Thee, Heavenly Father, to bless all the afflicted and distressed throughout the world. Let the saving knowledge of our Lord and Saviour fill the earth as the waters fill the sea. Let Thy kingdom come, Thy will be done on earth as it is in heaven, and let all flesh see Thy salvation. All these favors we ask Thee in the name of our dear Redeemer, Jesus Christ. Amen."

This prayer will show the kind of teaching the children received at that period. A newspaper, published many years ago, commented on that prayer in these words: " It will serve as a sample of the verbiage, contradiction and threatening horrors inflicted upon children educated at the public expense, even in the present enlightened generation. What a delightful frame of mind such a form of prayer is calculated to produce in the little ones, who, utterly unconscious of having committed any wrong or sin whatever, are compelled to say they have well merited eternal punishment. How can they reconcile such instruction with Christ's ' Suffer little children to come unto me, and forbid them not, for of such is the kingdom of heaven.' An evangelical hair splitter might attempt to do it; but to a simple-minded, light-hearted child, as to a man of common sense who has studied the life of Christ, the brimstone mixture of this so-called prayer has a noxious odor. The children of the Almshouse who are compelled to 'sit' under the Evangelical must be in a most pitiable condition."

In January, 1818, the managers received from the Board of Health a communication relative to a malignant fever which then prevailed in the Almshouse, and caused considerable excitement in this community. It was referred to Dr. James Rush, who was one of the attending physicians, and he made the following report on it:

"*First.* That the prevailing fever at present in Philadelphia Almshouse appeared there about the beginning of November last, since which time the number of patients admitted with it has gradually increased.

"*Second.* That the disease is of malignant type, and passes by the name of typhus fever. That the circumstances attending its introduction to the House, its extension there and all other points relative to a judgment upon the subject do not, in my opinion, warrant an inference that it is a contagious disease. But at the same time I wish to express my firm belief that the extent and direction of the disease and its mortality will be much influenced by the atmosphere around the patient, and that uncrowded rooms and free ventilation are, in this fever, among the important means for its relief and removal.

"*Third.* The whole number of patients who have to this date been under medical treatment is eighty-six. Of these sixteen have died, twenty have been discharged cured, and there remains fifty, fully one-half of whom are convalescent.

"*Fourth.* The gradual increase of the number of patients admitted, which has heretofore taken place, still at this date continues; nor does there appear anything connected with this disease that makes its future duration determinable."

The physicians differed as to the contagious nature of this disease, and it was deemed prudent to separate the fever patients from the other inmates of the House. The old sugar house was again used as a hospital, and extra nurses were employed to attend the sick. The fever panic lasted until April.

The managers passed resolutions of thanks to Mr. Inslee, the steward, and his wife, for "the fidelity displayed during the period of trial," and made each of them a handsome present in money. A number of nurses and others were rewarded in the same manner. Several medical students distinguished themselves at the time, while others resigned and left the institution.

In the summer of 1820 a malignant fever again prevailed in the Almshouse, and the medical students were charged with suppressing facts which should have been reported to the Board. The following preamble and resolution was adopted: "Whereas it appears that early in the month of May there were reported upon the returns made by the students of medicine and surgery in this institution sundry cases of malignant fever, and there have occurred during that month and all the months succeeding, many deaths in the hospital of this institution, of persons whose diseases were of the same character in all respects to those which had been previously reported as malignant, but that, at a period contemporaneous with the efforts of the Board of Managers to draw the attention of the Board of Health to those malignant cases, the students of this House have foreborne or neglected to report, as it was their duty to report, such cases as were malignant, although the cases in the sugar house were numerous and malignant, and bearing the worst features of malignant bilious fever, of which disease several of the nurses of the hospital have died, and it appearing to the managers that the omission to report these cases to the Board was a breach of duty on the part of the students and dangerous as a precedent, therefore,

"*Resolved*, That a committee of three be appointed to inquire into the motives or causes of the changes made in the medical reports and what measures it may be necessary to take to prevent any suppression of facts in the future."

The only reason given by the students for the falsification of the records was that "they wanted to prevent a panic."

The records do not show that any proper punishment was

inflicted, and it might be presumed that this accounts for the continual trouble the managers had with those gentlemen.

Mr. William Duane, who had been Secretary of the Treasury under President Jackson, was President of the Board of Managers, and Silas Yerker, Samuel Emlen, Henry Barrington, Joel B. Sutherland, Thomas D. Grover, John Wallace and Lawrence Shuster, all well known and respected citizen, were members.

A committee submitted an amusing and instructive report at the meeting in January, 1821, in which it was stated : " The committee have ascertained that the *well* paupers, when employed at work, said to be unusually laborious, are accustomed to receive more or less spirituous liquor through the day, a practice which it seems has been occasionally authorized by the visiting committee of the week. They believe this unnecessary, and recommend a prohibition of it, as it would take away one strong motive which keeps within its walls so many slothful inebriates, who are young, strong and able to maintain themselves outside by daily labor. The other persons using liquors in this House, so far as the committee have ascertained, are the visiting physicians, the Committee on Bastardy, the out-door Guardians, and other visitors, and the Board of Managers. The physicians and Committee on Bastardy only receive in their rooms malt liquors, such as porter and ale. The quantity used by them during the year could not be learned. The closet in the managers' rooms is supplied with brandy, wine and other liquors, but no record is separately kept by which the whole quantity used could be ascertained. The committee must state as their belief that there is a very unnecessary and very improper use of liquors in this room, and they respectfully ask the serious attention of managers to the subject."

The managers must have given the matter their " serious attention," as they requested the doctors to use as little liquor as possible.

In 1821 there was a reorganization of the Board having charge of the poor. The old Board of Managers was abolished, and Guardians (23) were elected by the city and districts, and the general management was given to them. They elected four of their

5

number to have the special direction of the Almshouse. The Guardians held regular meetings at the institution.

One of the important duties of the Board was the binding out of children. The uncertainty of the kind of persons who applied for them, and the difficulty of enforcing the rules and the observance of the indentures frequently caused the Board considerable anxiety. If mistakes were made they were rectified as soon as the facts became known.

The following preambles and resolution were adopted in February, 1822:

"WHEREAS, It is believed that the binding out of children is one of the most important trusts committed to the Guardians of the Poor, inasmuch as the future improvement of the condition of the poor must very much depend upon the education of youth; and,

"WHEREAS, It is important to place this interesting class of our fellow beings under the care of persons who are in good moral standing in society, and whose situation in life will enable them to bring up those destitute youths to habits of industry and economy; and,

"WHEREAS, The managers of the Almshouse have recently bound a promising colored boy, named David Jacobs, aged nine years, without the consent, and contrary to the remonstrances of his mother, Rachel Jacobs, to a certain Solomon Sloby, a black man, whose occupation was that of a wood sawyer, or day laborer, to serve the said Sloby for no less than twelve years, seven months, and eighteen days, to learn the art, trade and mystery of a house servant; and,

"WHEREAS, the said Sloby has, contrary to the terms of indenture, been driving him about the streets as a chimney sweep, of which the mother justly complains; therefore,

"*Resolved*, That a committee be appointed who shall, in conjunction with the solicitor of the Board, have the boy brought up before the Court on a *habeas corpus* for the purpose of having the indentures cancelled, so that the child may be either given up to his mother or placed under the care of a suitable master."

It was shown that this man Sloby had used a number of children in the same manner.

This was only one of a number of cases that were discovered by the Guardians, but they frequently had the master or mistress punished when it was shown that the children had been abused.

An association for the care of colored orphans, founded by some Quaker ladies, made a proposition to the Guardians to take the colored orphans under eight years of age from the Almshouse; to " furnish them with comfortable lodging, suitable clothing, cheap and wholesome food, and to train them in habits of industry; likewise to instruct them in school training and to give careful attention to their personal conduct and mental improvement, if fifty cents a week were paid to the association for each child." The orphans were to be kept in reach of the Guardians, and were not to be bound out without the consent of the Board. The proposition was accepted, and the children were better cared for than they would have been in the Almshouse.

The building on south Fifth Street near Carpenter, which had been rented for some time for a childrens' asylum was purchased by the Guardians from Mr. Thomas J. Wharton in November, 1822; it was intended to make it a permanent home, but the idea was subsequently changed.

A committee, appointed to consider complaints of citizens regarding the manner of burying the dead, made the following startling report : " The manner of depositing the coffins and leaving them slightly covered for a length of time is very improper and very offensive, and it is not at all surprising that the residents in the neighborhood have expressed their disapprobation of the proceedings on that ground.

" It is the custom to dig a number of pits, say about seven feet by four, at the opening, and nine feet in depth. These pits are wide enough to admit of laying two coffins in the bottom, which they cover with about two inches of dirt, until two more coffins arrive, which they place on top of those already there, when they fill the pit up. But it will be recollected that it takes a considerable time to get a sufficient number to fill a pit, *in consequence*

of the many visitors to carry off the corpses left there for interment.
It is from three to five weeks before they can cover these pits,
which certainly makes it very offensive to have all the corpses for
that length of time nearly exposed to the open air. Your committee are of opinion that the mode of burying ought to be altered,
and that each corpse should be put in a separate and distinct grave
of a good and sufficient depth, and that persons who are desirous
of having corpses ought to have some trouble to obtain them,
instead of having them placed above ground and inviting persons
to carry them away to save the trouble of burying them." The
same committee made another report at a subsequent meeting, in
which was stated : " We visited the ground on the 18th inst. A
coffin had arrived which was said to contain the corpse of a colored
boy. There were two pits open, one said to contain three bodies
and the other empty. The men said they were waiting for another
corpse, and then they intended to close the one pit up. The committee ordered that the corpse that was in the yard should be
placed in the empty pit, and that then both pits should be filled
up. This was done, but not until an examination was made of the
three coffins that were in the pit, and it was found that *one of them
was empty.*

" Your committee are of opinion that the persons who attend at
the graveyard have the whole charge of the same, *and make such
arrangements with the doctors as they please*, and are not accountable to any body."

The steward was censured for not carrying out the rules, but
the bodies were still to be had " through arrangements made with
the doctors."

The Board of Guardians authorized the erection of an addition to the west wing, for the accommodation of the sick and disabled. The large increase in the census of the House demanded
more room, yet the Board seemed to be adding on a little here and
some there, to get along economically, so that the institution looked
anything but handsome, and began to be considered an eye sore to
the neighborhood.

The question of what was the proper thing to do with bad

boys and girls was one that caused serious consideration at this period.

A committee of the " Society for Alleviating the Miseries of Prisons " had a conference with a committee of the Guardians of the Poor, in 1823, to discuss the evils that resulted from the imprisonment of boys and girls among hardened criminals. The result of the conference was the following suggestions :

"*First*—That a suitable place should be provided by the Guardians of the Poor for the reception of all minors who are taken up by the watchmen, others strolling about the streets, and some without homes, all of whom are now committed to the county prison, among the untried prisoners, who are charged with murder, arson, grand larceny and other crimes. By this system of imprisonment the minors become inured to vice in its most formidable shape. The place to be provided should be sufficiently strong for their safe keeping, until they can be bound out as apprentices to some persons residing at some distance from the city.

" *Second*—If any of the minors confined as thus suggested should become refractory that measures be adopted for placing them in solitary confinement.

"*Third*—That the Mayor and Aldermen be requested to refrain from committing such minors to the county prison and send them direct to the Almshouse, and also to request the Legislature to prevent the imprisonment of minors for misdemeanors."

The Guardians prepared a bill in accordance with these suggestions, and it was sent to the Legislature to secure the proposed reform. From the discussions upon this subject the establishment of the House of Refuge, an institution that has accomplished much good and reflected credit upon the city, was the ultimate result.

Another very serious question to be considered was the method by which the outdoor relief was distributed. The amount of money expended for that purpose had become so large that, after much discussion, a committee was appointed, in October, 1824, to " take the whole subject into consideration, and to inquire whether any plan could be devised to check that prolific source of pauperism."

The committee submitted an interesting report, in which it stated : " The average population of the City of Philadelphia and the districts included in this poor corporation, from the year 1800 to 1810, was 80,298. The amount of taxes for the same period was $773,000, being $77,300 a year, and 96¼ cents per annum for each inhabitant. In the same districts the average population from 1810 to 1820 was 102,905. The amount of taxes for the same period was $1,118,000, being $111,800 per annum, and $1.08½ per annum for each inhabitant ; this being an increase of poor tax, over and above the increase of population of 12¼ cents per annum. From 1815 to 1819, the average cost of supporting each pauper in the Almshouse was $1.24 ; from 1820 to 1824 this average was re- duced to 77¾ cents, while the great increase of the expenditures for out-door relief caused the poor tax to be much higher than it ever was before."

The committee believed that the system of out-door relief was so much abused, and had such an injurious tendency, that it ought to be abolished.

Resolutions were passed to " prevent unworthy persons from subsisting at the public expense," but it took a number of years to change the system entirely.

The Guardians had been very generous in their expenditures for relief, if it cost, as the report stated, $1.08½ per annum for each inhabitant of the district. If we consider the population of the city at the present time, say 1,300,000, and appropriated $1.08½ per annum for each inhabitant, it would amount to $1,410,500, which is about three times as much as was expended in any of the years of the last decade.

VINTAGE AVENUE, LOOKING NORTHEAST.

CHAPTER VI.

THE Guardians adopted the following preamble and resolution at their meeting in January, 1826:

"WHEREAS, It has been represented to this Board that Elizabeth Helm, widow of Peter Helm, deceased, is in necessitous circumstances, and believing that it would add to the comfort and happiness of said Elizabeth Helm to be placed in the 'Asylum for Indigent Widows and Single Women;' and, in consideration of the patriotic and disinterested services rendered by the said Peter Helm, during the prevalence of an epidemic disease in the year 1793, as set forth in a certificate of thanks to himself and others, presented at a meeting of the citizens of Philadelphia, at the City Hall, on the 28th day of March, 1794, and signed by Governor McKean ; therefore, be it

"*Resolved,* That the President of this Board be directed to make application to the managers of the Asylum referred to above for the admission of Elizabeth Helm, as soon as an opening may present itself, and that he be authorized to expend such sum of money as may be requisite to place her there in a situation to render her comfortable during the remainder of her life."

The resolutions were carried out, and the action of the Board was very praiseworthy and reflected much credit on the members. Peter Helm was the noble Moravian who volunteered his services, in connection with Stephen Girard, to take charge of the Bush Hill hospital, and to nurse the poor, afflicted yellow fever patients during the terrible times when the people were panic stricken, and all who were able fled from the city. Those two heroes remained, and they were justly entitled to be held in grateful remembrance.

The first practical movement looking to a decided improvement in the location of the Almshouse was made on May 24th, 1826, when Mr. Joseph M. Truman offered the following preamble with resolutions :

71

"WHEREAS, It is the prevailing opinion of many valuable citizens that the present location of the Almshouse and House of Employment has become a matter of deep interest, and it is believed to be materially injurious to private property within its immediate vicinity, and also very deficient in the necessary requisites for which it was originally intended, and believing that the location of the Almshouse and House of Employment ought to be on a farm, at a convenient distance from the city, and that the hospital department ought to be in a different location, within as short a distance as circumstances would admit; therefore be it Resolved, etc."

The resolution provided for the appointment of a committee to devise a plan for locating the institution on a farm, with power to advertise for proposals for ground, not exceeding one hundred and fifty acres, not less than one and a half miles from Broad and Market Streets; also for a lot, not less than five nor more than ten acres, to be located where the Board of Physicians, in conjunction with the committee, might think it most advisable. The committee to be authorized to employ an architect, at an expense not to exceed two hundred dollars, to draw the plans and make estimates of the probable expense. If the plans, etc., were adopted, application was to be made to Council and the districts for permission to proceed with the purchase of the grounds and the erection of the buildings.

The Board was not ready to take such action at that time; the resolution was laid on the table; was called up and postponed at several subsequent meetings, and was finally allowed to slumber. But the seed had been sown, and the results were seen in a short time.

In March of the following year the managers of the House sent a communication to the General Board, calling attention to the crowded condition of the institution and the great inconvenience and unsanitary situation of the sick wards, and recommending the erection of an additional building. A special committee was appointed to consider the subject, and the report made favored the recommendation of the managers.

The necessity of greater accommodations was acknowledged,

but the Board feared to take the necessary steps to secure them; it was a question of money, with the problem of how to get it to solve. A committee was appointed to visit the principal cities, to compare their systems of relief with that of Philadelphia, and it was discovered that it cost much more here than it did in any city in the country. The report of that committee brought the whole subject before the public and led to considerable discussion. It was well known that the Almshouse was entirely too small for its purpose, yet the fear of an enormous increase in expenditures was always prevalent and prevented the taking of proper measures to secure the necessary accommodations. Mr. Truman's project was looked upon as chimerical, as it was thought to mean an immense increase of taxation.

At this time considerable interest was caused by a fugitive slave case that had been brought to the attention of the Guardians of the Poor.

The committee appointed to investigate the subject made report stating the facts, which show that "The slave Nat or Nathaniel, who is now in the Arch street prison, ran away from his master and came to this city about two years since. Shortly after his arrival he became acquainted with a young colored girl and entered into an engagement to marry her; but from some cause or other they never were united in marriage, although they had a child in April last. In the month of August Nat was taken up as a runaway slave and carried before Judge Peters, who, after a hearing, granted an order of removal.

"On the same day Nat was committed by the agent of his master to the Arch street prison for safe keeping. Shortly after his incarceration, an application was made by the mother of the child to Alderman Badger, to arrest him for the purpose of compelling him to support the child, and under this writ he is now detained by the sheriff. In addition to this, it will be remembered that the mother, since the apprehension and confinement of the runaway, has made application to this Board, through one of its members, for the support of her child, and that a letter had been received by the said member from the United States District Attorney, threatening him with the penalties of the law for hindering the master from getting possession of his slave. Your committee are of opinion that the Board ought not to take any part or interest in the controversy. In this instance, the fact that the child was not sworn to until it was at least four months old, and not until the father was arrested as a fugitive slave, has satisfied your committee that the real object of the application to this Board is to induce an interference between the master and his slave, and not for the support of the child."

The Board refused to take any action in the matter, and left Nathaniel to the mercy of the court and his master. It seemed to be a very complicated affair, and the action of the Guardians was watched with a good deal of interest.

In the fall of 1827 the city hospital, generally known as the "Small Pox Hospital," was completed, and a number of patients was sent to it from the Almshouse during the winter. It was located on Bush hill, upon grounds which are now within the limits of the Fifteenth Ward. This hospital was considered as one of the best adapted for the care of contagious diseases in the country. It was torn down shortly after the consolidation of the city and districts in 1854.

The question of the removal of the Almshouse was again under discussion in 1828. All kinds of arguments were used on both sides. The main opposition was simply on the grounds of expense, but there was a number of influential men who believed that what is worth doing should be done right. They were opposed to the piecemeal methods of patching up continually to make things stretch out for the time being. If a change was necessary —and that was acknowledged—they favored the erection of buildings that would be a credit to the city and would furnish sufficient accommodations for the poor for many years. They approved of Mr. Truman's idea of buying a farm, and it has been stated that some of the Guardians determined, while the discussion was going on, to buy the ground at their own expense and risk, trusting to the intelligence and liberality of the city to re-imburse them.

They at length concluded to apply to the Legislature to

obtain the necessary authority for the selling of the old buildings, the purchase of ground and the erection of a new Almshouse and House of Employment. In compliance with their request an Act was passed March 5, 1828, and as that was the law under which the present Almshouse was erected, some of the sections are quoted entire, so as to give the principal features.

The first section of the Act provided: "That the Select and Common Council of the City of Philadelphia, the Commissioners of the incorporated district of the Northern Liberties, the Commissioners of the district of Southwark, the Commissioners of Spring Garden, choosing for the township of Penn, and the Commissioners of the Kensington district, choosing for the said district, and the unincorporated part of the Northern Liberties, shall meet on the third Monday of May next, each body in its own usual place of meeting at 3 o'clock in the afternoon, or as soon thereafter as may be, and shall elect and choose as follows, that is to say: The said Select and Common Councils, by joint vote, shall elect six respectable citizens, inhabitants of the city; the Commissioners of the incorporated district of the Northern Liberties shall elect two respectable citizens, inhabitants of said district; the Commissioners of the district of Southwark shall elect two respectable citizens, inhabitants of said district; the Commissioners of Spring Garden shall elect one respectable citizen, an inhabitant of Penn township; and the Commissioners of the Kensington district shall elect one respectable citizen, an inhabitant of said district, or of the unincorporated part of the Northern Liberties, to the Guardians of the Poor of the said city, districts and townships."

The Act provided for the organization of the Board, etc., and it was incorporated by the title of the "Guardians for the Relief and Employment of the Poor of the City of Philadelphia, the District of Southwark and the Townships of the Northern Liberties and Penn."

Twelve persons were to be elected, to be called the "Directors of the Poor Tax." It was their duty to meet at the Almshouse or such other place as might be designated by the Guardians of the Poor, and it was the duty of the Guardians of the Poor to make

and exhibit to the said Directors estimates of the probable amount
of money that would be required for the relief of the poor for the
year, and the Directors were instructed to make an assessment, not
exceeding fifty cents on the hundred dollars, at any one time, upon
the value of all the real and personal estate within the said districts and townships respectively, and not more than one dollar per
head on every freeman in any fifty-cent tax, and so in proportion
for every less rate on the county assessment, for the purpose of
defraying the expenses of the Guardians of the Poor.

The Directors, in laying the rates as aforesaid, were to be
guided by the county assessment made, or to be made, having due
regard to every man's estate within the district. The rates were
entered in a book and signed by the Directors. The book was
delivered to the Guardians of the Poor and a return made to the
respective districts, showing the amount of money required and
the assessments made. The Guardians of the Poor were authorized to employ collectors.

"SECTION 9.—Immediately after the election of Guardians
of the Poor, on the third Monday of May next, as directed by
the first Section of this Act, the Select and Common Councils
of the City of Philadelphia, and the Commissioners of the respective districts, as aforesaid, shall elect twelve respectable citizens within the bounds of their respective jurisdictions, who shall
be styled the ' Commissioners for the erection of buildings for the
accommodation of the poor.' The Select and Common Councils
shall elect six, the Commissioners for the incorporated district of
the Northern Liberties shall elect two, the Commissioners of Southwark shall elect two, and the Commissioners of Spring Garden and
the Commissioners of the Kensington districts shall each elect one,
and the said electing bodies shall, by their respective clerks, give
notice in writing, to each of the persons so chosen, within two days
thereafter, and the said ' Commissioners ' shall meet at the Almshouse on the fourth Monday of May next, at 3 o'clock in the afternoon, and respectively take an oath or affirmation, to be administered by any Alderman of the City, or Justice of the Peace of the
County of Philadelphia, faithfully to discharge the office of ' Com-

missioner for erecting buildings for the accommodation of the poor,' and to perform all the duties required by this act, truly and faithfully, to the best of his knowledge and abilities, and the said Commissioners shall there form a Board and appoint one of their own body President, to preside over their deliberations, and may from time to time make such rules and regulations for their government and the business and duties of the said Commissioners as they may think proper and necessary."

"Section 10. It shall be the duty of said Commissioners, having first obtained the approbation of the said Board of Guardians, to purchase a suitable site, not exceeding two miles from Market and Broad streets, the title whereof shall be vested in said corporation, for the erection of buildings suitable for an Hospital, Almshouse, House of Employment, and Childrens' Asylum, and to cause, as soon as practicable, the necessary buildings to be erected and constructed, upon such plan or plans as a majority of said Commissioners may think proper for the purpose contemplated; such plan or plans having been first submitted and approved by the said Board of Guardians, having due regard to the full and comfortable provision for all such poor persons as may require medical or surgical aid; and, also for such as may be unable, through age or other infirmities, to procure subsistence; and for the employment of all those who may be able to work; and also for the health, convenience and instruction of the children; to make all necessary contracts for material, &c., and, in the case of the death or resignation of any of the said Commissioners before the completion of their trusts, the electing bodies, within whose jurisdiction the vacancy may occur, shall fill the same, on notice thereof, in manner aforesaid, and each of the said electing bodies shall have power, from time to time, and at all times, to remove any of the said Commissioners appointed by such body, and to appoint another person or persons to fill the vacancy or vacancies thus occasioned. Provided, that should the Board of Guardians deem it necessary for the better accommodation of the sick, the said Commissioners are hereby authorized to purchase a site and erect an Hospital at some convenient place within the limits of Philadelphia, to the eastward of Eighth street from the river Schuylkill."

" SECTION 11. In order to carry the objects and provisions of the law into complete effect, it shall and may be lawful, and said Guardians of the Poor are hereby authorized and invested with full power to negotiate and contract for and upon the faith of the said corporation of the Guardians of the Poor, any loan or loans, from time to time, according to their discretion, not exceeding two hundred and fifty thousand dollars, upon the best terms and lowest rate of interest, payable half yearly ; and the said corporation of Guardians of the Poor shall receive the amount of said loans, and are hereby authorized and required to issue certificates of stock, duly attested by the President and Secretary of the Board of Guardians, under the corporate seal, for any sum or sums not less than one hundred dollars each, as may from time to time be necessary, in pursuance of the contract for such loans, which certificates shall be transferable on the books of the said corporation, in the same manner as the certificates of loans made to the corporation of the City of Philadelphia are transferable ; and it shall be the duty of the said Guardians to keep regular transfer books, and to adopt such proceedings, from time to time, in relation to such transfers as may be deemed advisable ; which loans as aforesaid, to be made, and the premiums, if any thereon, shall exclusively be appropriated to the purchase of the site and the erection of the buildings, as aforesaid, and for no other purpose whatsoever ; and the money arising therefrom shall be deposited in bank, in the name of the corporation of the Guardians of the Poor, and may, from time to time, be drawn out by checks signed by the President and at least two other members of the Board ; and attested by the Secretary, and paid over to said Commissioners for the purposes aforesaid, who shall keep regular accounts of all monies received and expended by them, and shall render such accounts, and produce their vouchers quarterly to the Guardians of the Poor."

" SECTION 12 authorized the Guardians of the Poor to sell the old Almshouse and lots and the proceeds of the property was appropriated towards the purchase of the site and the erection of the buildings."

In compliance with the act, the following named gentlemen were elected as "Guardians of the Poor:"

By the Select and Common Councils—Messrs. Thomas P. Cope, Abraham L. Pennock, Matthew L. Bevan, Thomas Rogers, Thomas Earp and John Hemphill.

By the District of Southwark—Messrs. Jesse R. Burden and John Keefe.

By the Northern Liberties—Messrs. John Kessler, Jr., and William Binder.

By the Kensington District—Mr. Michael Day.

By Penn Township—Mr. James S. Spencer.

The Board was organized by the election of Mr Thomas P. Cope as President, Mr. Geo. Heyl as Secretary and Mr. Abraham L. Pennock as Treasurer. John M. Scott, Esq., was elected as Solicitor for the corporation.

Agreeably to the act the following named were elected "Commissioners for erecting buildings for the accommodation of the Poor:"

By the Select and Common Councils—Messrs. John Moore, Elkanah Keyser, William Boyd, Nathan Bunker, Charles Johnston, and Isaac Roach.

By the Northern Liberties—Messrs. George N. Baker, and James A. Mahany.

By the District of Southwark—Messrs. William McGlensey and Thomas D. Grover.

By Spring Garden or Penn Township, Mr. John M. Ogden.

By Kensington—Mr. George Wilson.

The Board organized by the election of Mr. William Boyd as President, and the appointment of Mr. George N. Baker as Secretary *pro tem.*

On June 2d, 1828, Messrs. Boyd, Keyser, Baker, Ogden, Wilson and McGlensey were appointed as a "committee to inquire and seek an eligible situation suitable for the erection of buildings for the accommodation and employment of the poor, under the

Act of Assembly, by advertising or otherwise, and report to the Board "

Bids were advertised for, and on July 18th the Board met and "proceeded to view and examine the different lots of ground which had been proposed by the owners to sell, agreeably to the following schedule."

OWNER.	ACRES.	LOCATION.	PRICE.
Jeremiah Warden	30	N. W. from Center Sq., op. H. Pratt's seat	$12,500.
William Parker	45	Ridge Road, adj'g lands of H. Dixon . .	37,500.
John Gardiner, Jr. . . .	27	On 5th St. Road, S E. from Center Sq. .	11,000.
James Sharwood	27	N. W. from Dr. Turner's Lane	12,500.
George Harrison	30	Adjoining to Penitentiary	600 per acre.
Lewis Reineck	22	On Long Lane Neck	300 per acre.
John Lambert	29	Turner's Lane, adjoining Sharwood's . .	18,000.
John Evans	10	Stamper's Lane	10,000.
J. C. Fisher	21	Adj'g H. Pratt's and Schuylkill River .	25,000.
Caleb Griffith	32	Islington Lane	12,000.
Henry Pratt	82	W. of Schuylkill, near Hamiltonville . .	250 per acre.
Henry J. Williams . . .	10	Francis' Lane, E. Penitentiary . . .	1,000 per acre.
Henry J. Williams . . ·	15	South Penitentiary	3,000 per acre.
N. Nathans	49	Falls of Schuylkill Road	300 per acre.
Michael Pray	31	Inter. Turner's Lane	10,000.
Simon Gratz	71	Broad Street	10,000.
Samuel Keith	18	Ridge Road, near Turner's Lane	5,000.
T. Mitchell	24	Adjoining U. S. Marine Hospital	35,000.
T. Mitchell	25	South Side U. S. Arsenal	25,000.
Thomas Lieper, executor	33	Neck Land, Passyunk Township	200 per acre.
David Woelper	27	North Side Turner's Lane	12,000.
John Lambert	35	Ridge Road and Turner's Lane	27,500.
Geo. F. Randolph . . .	42	North end Broad Street	30,000.
Samuel Keith	10	Germantown Road	1,500 per acre.
N. E. Thomas	10	Adjoining above	2,000 per acre.
Joseph Jouett	12	Francisville and Ridge Road	9,500.
T. Camac	20	Camac Street, near Broad Street	1,000 per acre.
H. Nixon	30	Ridge Road	25,000.
Hamilton Estate	158	Adj'g Woodlands, W. of Schuylkill River	300 per acre.

After visiting the grounds offered, the Commissioners selected the piece belonging to the Hamilton Estate, and with the approval of the Guardians of the Poor it was purchased for the sum of two hundred and seventy five dollars per acre.

This ground possessed many advantages—plenty of fresh air and excellent facilities for drainage.

The deed conveying the property reads :

" THIS INDENTURE,

Made the first day of January in the year of our Lord one thousand eight hundred and twenty nine, between Henry Beckett of the city of Philadelphia merchant and Mary his wife of the one part and the Guardians for the Relief and Employment of the Poor of the City of Philadelphia the District of Southwark and the Townships of the Northern Liberties and Penn witnesseth that the said Henry Beckett and Mary his wife for and in consideration of the sum of Fifty one thousand five hundred and twenty eight dollars twelve and-a half cents lawful money to them in hand paid by the said Guardians for the Relief and Employment of the Poor of the city of Philadelphia the District of Southwark and the Townships of Northern Liberties and Penn at the time of the execution hereof the receipt whereof is hereby acknowledged have granted bargained sold released and confirmed and by these presents do grant bargain sell release and confirm unto the said Guardians for the Relief and Employment of the Poor of the City of Philadelphia the District of Southwark and the Townships of the Northern Liberties and Penn their successors and assigns all that certain Tract Plantation and parcel of land situate on the west side of the River Schuylkill in the Township of Blockley and County of Philadelphia in the State of Pennsylvania Being part of a certain larger tract of land known by the name of the Woodlands bounded and described agreeably to a resurvey thereof lately made by Enock Lewis, Esquire as follows Beginning at a Post on the margin of the River Schuylkill at low water mark in the mouth of a small creek and at the corner of land belonging to John Hare Powell and Edward S. Burd Esquire thence up the creek by the land of the said Powell and Burd north thirty six and two thirds of a degree West nineteen perches and one sixteenth of a perch to a post North fifty three degrees west twenty three perches to a post, thence leaving the creek but still along the line

6

of Powell and Burd's land north forty-nine and a half degrees, west one hundred and eight perches to a post on the southern side of the Darby road, south sixty-two degrees and a quarter west, one hundred and three perches and a quarter of a perch, to a corner of Thomas Fleming's land; thence by the said Fleming's land south twenty six degrees east, seventy nine perches and four tenths to a post in a small stream of water; thence south ten degrees west twenty one perches and five tenths of a perch to a post; thence south one quarter of a degree east, fifty one perches and seven tenths of a perch to the low water mark of the River Schuylkill; and thence up the said river, by the several meanders thereof, two hundred and sixty two perches, more or less, to the place of beginning, containing one hundred and eighty seven acres and sixty perches of land; being the same tract of land and premises which Jacob Strembeck Esquire, High Sheriff of the City and County of Philadelphia, by Deed Roll stated the eighth day of December last past granted and conveyed to the said Henry Beckett in fee seized and sold by virtue of legal proceedings issued out of the District Court for the City and County of Philadelphia as the property of William Hamilton, Esquire, deceased, at the suit of Margaret Hamilton as in and by the said recited Deed Roll duly acknowledged and entered among the records of the said Court in Book E page 231; and will more fully appear together with all and singular the buildings, improvements marsh cripple landings landing places ways waters water courses rights liberties privileges hereditaments and appurtenances whatsoever thereunto belonging or in any wise appertaining; and the reversions remainders rents issues and profits thereof, and all the estate right title interest property claim and demand whatsover of him the said Henry Beckett and Mary his wife as well at law as in equity of into and out of the same to have and to hold the said Plantation Tract and parcel of land hereditaments and premises hereby granted or mentioned and intended so to be with the appurtenances unto the said the Guardians for the Relief and Employment of the Poor of the City of Philadelphia the District of Southwark and the Townships of the Northern Liberties and Penn aforesaid, their suc-

cessors and assigns forever; and the said Henry Beckett for himself, his heirs, executors, and administrators doth hereby covenant
promise and agree to and with the said the Guardians for the
Relief and Employment of the Poor of the City of Philadelphia
the District of Southwark and the Townships of Northern Liberties and Penn, their successors and assigns in manner following: to
say that he the said Henry Beckett and his heirs, all and singular,
the hereditaments and premises hereby granted or mentioned and
intended so to be with the appurtenances unto the said the Guardians for the Relief and Employment of the Poor of the City of
Philadelphia the District of Southwark and the Townships of the
Northern Liberties and Penn their successors and assigns against
him, the said Henry Beckett, and his heirs, and against all and
every other person and persons whatsoever lawfully claiming or to
claim by from or under. him them or any of them shall and will
warrant and forever defend by these presents.

"In witness whereof the said Henry Beckett and his wife have
hereunto set their respective hands and seals dated the day and
year first above written.

"Sealed and delivered in
    the presence of   HENRY BECKETT, [L. S.]
"G. BARTRAM,   MARY BECKETT. [L. S.]
"A. W. JOHNSTON."

CHAPTER VII.

ON September 8th, 1828 the Commissioners were informed of the death of J. A. Mahany, Esq., one of their members. Daniel Groves, Esq., was subsequently elected to fill the vacancy.

The Guardians appointed Messrs. Thomas P. Cope, Thomas Rogers, Dr. Burden, Thomas Earp, and John Kessler as a committee to confer with Isaac Roach, Thomas D. Grover, E. W. Keyser, Daniel Groves and Charles Johnston, the Committee of the Commissioners as to the plans for the erection of the buildings, &c.

At the meeting of Commissioners, on October 6th, 1828, the committee appointed to confer with the Guardians submitted the following report:

"That in joint meeting the committees from the two Boards proceeded to obtain a census of the inmates of the Almshouse and Children's Asylum and the number of the out door poor to whom relief is at present afforded and from a careful examination of the contemplated system of employing the poor, they are of opinion that the following buildings will be required to be erected on the site of ground west of Schuylkill, say,

ALMSHOUSE PROPER.

"This building should be calculated to accommodate about 1250 paupers, and in the construction of it a complete separation of the sexes should be kept in view and a proper classification of the inmates; provision to be made for 80 married persons, also for the Steward's and Matron's families, students, clerks and other officers, rooms for the Guardians to meet in and offices for transacting the business of the institution, kitchen for the paupers, &c.

"HOUSE OF EMPLOYMENT.

"To be constructed with suitable apartments for workshops, etc., and for lodging about 500 persons in separate rooms. In this

84

house the sexes must be kept separate, so as not to have opportunity of communicating with each other; the whole of this establishment to be enclosed with a wall sufficiently high to prevent escape, and to take in space for large yard, kitchen, refectory, etc.

"Hospital.

"This building to be large enough to contain 600 patients, including lunatics, and to be divided into suitable apartments for the different descriptions of diseases; to have a lecture room sufficient to hold 500 students, an apothecary shop, a large room for storing drugs, a library room and a room for a laboratory (fireproof), a dead room and another for post-mortem examinations, etc. Special attention must be given to have every room in the hospital properly ventilated, one fireplace in each room, but the different apartments to be warmed with heated air as far as practicable, the sexes to be kept entirely separated; 100 cells to be constructed for the insane, and suitable rooms for the cell-keepers and assistants; the whole to be enclosed with a high wall or fence to prevent escape; kitchen, refectory, etc.

"Children's Asylum.

"This building to accommodate 400 children, with apartments for the matron and assistants, school-room, infirmary, etc., the sexes to be kept separated; large yards to be enclosed for the use of the children, kitchen, refectory, etc.

"A building for storehouse or some accommodations in one of the buildings for that purpose.

"Some one of these buildings to contain a commodious apartment or place for public worship."

William Dougherty was employed to open and examine the quarries on the new grounds, and report was made that "much valuable stone for the contemplated buildings will be obtained."

Plans for the buildings were advertised for October 23d, 1828, and a premium of three hundred dollars was offered for the "most approved plan of buildings, accompanied with estimates.

November 10th, 1828. The committee recommended the construction of a wharf opposite the termination of South street, and the Board resolved "that a wharf or landing, together with a road leading from the fast land thereto, be constructed as soon as practicable, and that the south line thereof be upon a line and in the direction of the north side of South street, extending into the river until it affords a depth of five feet at low water. The front to be sixty feet extending northward, and from there on the north side to the shore, at right angle with the front thereof."

The wharf was erected by Mr. Thomas D. Grover for the sum of three thousand six hundred and seventy dollars.

Plans and estimates were received from Messrs. William Strickland, George Sennef and J. Haviland. Due consideration was given them, and at the meeting held on March 6th, 1829, the following resolution, offered by Mr. George N. Baker, was adopted:

"*Resolved*, That the plan submitted by William Strickland, as to its form and general outlines, is such as to merit the approbation of the Board of Commissioners, and that such part or parts thereof may be altered or dispensed with as circumstances may require, and that the concurrence of the Board of Guardians be requested thereto."

The Guardians, "after deliberating for some hours on the plans submitted for their consideration, came to the resolution to appoint a committee consisting of Thomas Rogers, Thomas Earp and A. L. Pennock, to confer with the commissioners on the subject."

Sealed proposals for a five per cent. loan for $100,000 were advertised for on December 8th, to be opened December 29th, 1828, "the money to be applied towards the purchasing of grounds and the erection of buildings." A lien upon the property purchased and the buildings to be erected was given as security for the payment of principal and interest. Stephen Girard, Esq., offered to take twenty-five thousand dollars of the loan at *par*, and Thomas Phipps, one of the assignees of Harper & Gillingham, offered to take four thousand dollars of it on the same terms. Both offers were accepted.

In December, 1828, the Board of Guardians received notice that the House of Refuge had been opened for the reception of vagrant or delinquent juveniles. This information was a source of congratulation, as it solved the very serious problem of what was best to be done with that class of boys and girls.

The Committee of the Guardians appointed to confer with the Commissioners presented the following communication to that body:

"A plan of a suite of buildings for the accommodation of the poor" intended to illustrate some of the views entertained by the members of the Board was submitted at the last meeting.

"It is now resolved that our committee be directed to lay that plan before the Commissioners, together with the following communication, which is directed to be signed by the President and attested by the Secretary.

"The Guardians hold in respectful consideration the attention given by the Commissioners to the subject of buildings.

"It is under these feelings they have appointed a committee to confer with the Commissioners on the subject of the plans submitted by the latter, and to express the views which the Guardians have in relation to that plan, among which are the following:

"1st. The Guardians are of opinion that if the several Buildings to be erected are to have distinct Superintendents, their being grouped together as delineated in the Plan is not necessary, and so far as the arrangement would preclude the extension of any of the Buildings, or interfere with a suitable classification of the Inmates, it would be inconvenient.

"2d. But the Guardians are of opinion that a Judicious administration of the public funds, independent of other considerations of economy, would not permit the employment of more than one principal male and one principal female Superintendent. With this view it is important that all the females should be brought as near as conveniently may be to the Matron, and in the same manner all the males should be brought as near as possible to the Steward. With the best possible arrangement the duty of visitation will be arduous, but on the plan proposed it would be doubly so, from the manner in which the men and women are alternately located, requiring the Matron to pass through ranges of the buildings appropriated to the men and of the Steward a similar passage through the apartments of the women, or otherwise requiring them to pass considerable distances exposed to the weather.

" 3d. The Physicians of the house form necessarily a part of the Steward's family. The spaces they will have to traverse and their exposure to the weather in passing to and from the Hospital are important considerations, both as it regards them and the subjects under their care.

" 4th. A separation of the sexes is of great consequence. In our present establishment it is found impossible, and consequently great inconveniences arise from their too free intercourse, and therefore the Guardians are particularly solicitous of finding this object fully attained in the Plan which shall ultimately be adopted. Again, a proper classification of the different grades is scarcely of less moment. The Guardians do not perceive that their objects have claimed the due attention of the Architect, nor is it seen how they can be readily accomplished with the plan submitted to them.

" 5th. The Guardians are of opinion that so far as it can be obtained without too great an extension of the plot all long entries or passages ought to be on the side of the buildings, in preference to the middle, from the difficulty of preserving a pure atmosphere in long middle passages. By putting the passages on the side, Piazzas are rendered unnecessary, and more persons may beneficially occupy a room of given dimensions on one side of such a passage, owing to the purer atmosphere, than in a room of the same size on one side of a middle passage.

" 6th. The Hospital and House of Employment, instead of being contiguous, should be at remote points of the plot, that the sick may not be annoyed by the noise of the latter establishment.

" The Guardians suggest that the whole basement story should be *above ground*, with the exception of such apartments of it as are intended for cooking, or for furnaces of any description. These should be made fire-proof, and of course will have to be depressed to leave room for arching.

" The plans which the Guardians have instructed the Com-

VINTAGE AVENUE, LOOKING SOUTHWEST.

mittee to submit to the consideration of the Commissioners was prepared and is presented to the latter for the purpose merely of exhibiting some of the leading views which the Board entertains in relation to the great object to be obtained. The minor details of the plan have not as yet engaged the particular attention of the Board."

The plans were referred to the Physicians, and they made the following report, March 28, 1829 :

"The Committee of Physicians, to whom were referred several Plans for a new Hospital, report that they bestowed such attention as the importance of the subject requires. Of these plans the one proposed by the Guardians comes the nearest to what the Committee conceive should be the interior arrangement of a Hospital ; the others they are disposed to reject wholly as not applicable to the case in view. The remarks which they make are therefore intended for the plan of the Board of Guardians.

"The Committee think that the long entry or passage should be abandoned, and the space thus alloted to be applied to increase the size of the Wards. The Wards themselves should be enlarged by leaving out many of the partitions marked in the plan, as the present well-established experience in Europe is in favor of very large rooms wherever there may be sick people. The Committee also think that this plan would be much improved by a Piazza along one side of the building, which will answer both for communications between different parts of it and for exercise and exposure to open air for convalescents.

"Maniacs should be accommodated in a wing and above ground. The cellars should in every case be left untenanted, except as offices, for cooking, washing and store-rooms, for their unavoidable dampness in this climate is a radical objection on the score of humanity to their being used as permanent abodes. There are few animals, except the amphibious, which can bear constant immersion in an atmosphere of that kind without great prejudice to health.

"The Committee are fully satisfied that the space marked out on the plan will not accommodate more than 400, or at most 450 patients, and then they will be crowded and may generate pestilential effluvia. The opinion is founded on the following calculations, which may be applied to any number, great or small, of patients. Each patient should have alloted to him a space of six by ten feet with an elevation of twelve feet; by applying this simple rule to the plan it will produce the result stated, to wit: accommodations for 450 persons. But, in addition, some space must be conceded in every ward to tables, chairs and water closets; a very moderate concession to such articles would be one-sixth of the whole ward. The latter must therefore be enlarged or the number of the patients reduced proportionately.

" As the position of the new Hospital is yet to be determined on, the Committee deem it a suitable time to state as their opinion, and that of their colleagues, that the location of it out of town would be detrimental to its service, and in the highest degree injurious to the just reputation which Philadelphia enjoys for furnishing the best and most copious means of medical instruction in the United States.

" The Committee also believe that there are many important pecuniary interests of the citizens which would be materially injured by a measure curtailing the means of medical instruction, and thereby putting other cities of less note and advantage upon an equal footing with our own."

It will be seen that there was much diversity of opinion regarding the plans of buildings, and there was considerable thought given as to the advisability of erecting the Hospital on grounds " east of Eighth Street from the Schuylkill."

CHAPTER VIII.

REPORT ON LOCATION OF NEW HOSPITAL.

THE Guardians appointed a special Committee to consider the question of " location of hospital," and the subject was discussed thoroughly. After all parties interested had been heard, and their remarks duly considered, the Committee submitted the following exhaustive report:

" The Committee to whose consideration was referred the important subject of the location of the Hospital for the poor, have endeavored to give it the attention to which it is entitled, and they submit as a result of their deliberations the following report: ' Pursuant to that portion of the Act of March, 1828, which authorized the " Commissioners for erecting buildings for the accommodation of the Poor," with the approbation of the Guardians of the Poor first obtained, " to purchase a suitable site, not exceeding two miles from Market and Broad Streets, for the erection of buildings suitable for an Hospital, Almshouse, House of Employment and Children's Asylum," the Board of Commissioners on a unanimous vote of its own members, and the similar concurrence of this Board, purchased a tract of land on the western bank of the Schuylkill river, opposite the city, containing 187 acres.

" Of this tract about 60 acres are meadow or susceptible of improvement as such: the residue is upland. On a ridge of the upland is presented a position as favorable in every particular as could be reasonably desired for the site of buildings contemplated to be erected, and, as respects salubrity, no situation more eligible it is believed could have been obtained within the range allowed by the law.

" But the above act provided ' That should the said Board of Guardians deem it necessary for the better accommodation of the sick, the said Commissioners are hereby authorized to purchase a site and erect an Hospital at some convenient place within the limits of the City of Philadelphia to the eastward of Eighth street from the Schuylkill.'

"It therefore becomes the duty of the Board of Guardians to determine whether it will be proper to locate the Hospital on the site already provided for the buildings generally or on some lot to be hereafter purchased, within the limits prescribed by the provision of the act.

"At the threshold of this inquiry we are met by the consideration that a large additional expense will have to be incurred in the provisions of a site within the city limits, should such a purchase be resolved upon. This expense will not be confined to the procuration merely of a ground plot for the building but must embrace the possession of ample grounds around it to insure a pure atmosphere and free circulation of air. The lots appurtenant to our present establishment, with a sick population rarely exceeding 400 persons, embrace one entire and one-half square of our city plot. The Pennsylvania Hospital, which contains on an average of 140 patients under medical treatment and 100 insane, holds a space equivalent to three of our city squares, and the retention of grounds of this extent, unoccupied except by buildings for the sick, is deemed by its Directors to be essential to the well being and recovery of the objects of their care.

"A Hospital for the poor of this corporation ought to be adapted to the reception of at least 600 patients, that number having been actually, though inconveniently, under charge of our establishment at a former period. With the data above recited, it would scarcely be deemed prudent to estimate a city square as being sufficient for the purpose of this extended establishment. Your committee certainly presume that no judicious person would venture to assert that it would be safe to enter into possession of less than such a square for these objects; or that a lot of such dimensions, when surrounded by a compactly built city, and having within its circumscribed limits the exhalations of 600 sick persons, would present as pure an atmosphere as that belonging to the vicinity of a hospital located in the country.

"Assuming, then, that a city square is the least quantity of ground which it would be proper to apply to this object, the price of such a square east of Eighth street from the Schuylkill, and at the remote points of the city plot either north or south could not be estimated at less than $50,000, while in the vicinity of High or Chestnut streets it would probably amount to $100,000. Indeed, most of the squares within the prescribed limits being practically improved, it is doubtful whether a suitable site could be obtained for the average of the prices named.

"We may safely estimate the cost of the buildings for the accommodation of the sick, either in the city or at the site west of the Schuylkill, if built in an equally plain manner, as being about the same, but the extra buildings required for the officers and servants of the establishment, and nearly the whole expense of a wall to surround the City Hospital would have to be charged as an expense peculiar to the latter, the plan of the Almshouse affording sufficient accommodation for all the attendants of the hospital if connected with it, and requiring for its inclosure either with or without the hospital about the same extent of wall. The cost of the wall surrounding the present Almshouse and Infirmary was about $14,000, and a low estimate of the expense of the additional accommodations would be $7,000. Charging however for both these accounts $20,000, and adding this sum to $75,000, an average of the estimated cost of the site, it would make the extra first cost of the city establishment $95,000.

"But it is not as regards the site merely that an enhanced expenditure would attend such an establishment. Distinct male and female Superintendents, an additional number of subalterns, both officers and domestics and the waste of furnishing two establishments instead of one could not be estimated, it is confidently believed, at less than $2500 per annum, and would probably much exceed that amount. This sum added to the interest of $95,000 at 5 per cent. would exhibit the *extra* annual expenditure of the city location at $7,250.

"If, however, it can be made to appear that the comfort and recovery of the sick, which is the primary object of this institution, would be best promoted by establishing the Hospital within the limits of the city, your committee would regard it as false

economy to allow a difference of expenditure, however considerable, to induce a decision adverse to these objects.

" With this sentiment your committee have canvassed with great
attention an objection preferred against the site on the west side of
the Schuylkill, that a removal of the patients to that distance
would be attended with great injury, and in some cases would
prove fatal to them ; in support of which the instances of persons
brought to the present house, who have died on their passage to
it, and the probability of an augmented number in case the distance
is increased, has been urged. Your committee, however, believe
that could the facts be ascertained, many of the instances of persons attempted to be removed in the last stages of existence, and
who have died on their way to the present infirmary, have resulted
out of the too great contiguity to the Almshouse, and that a greater
distance from it would have prompted an earlier removal or dis-
couraged the attempt and thus averted the distressing catastrophe.
It is very obvious that with the increased distance a more cautious
proceeding will be observed, and that patients not fit to be removed
will be provided for in the way contemplated by the law, by furnishing them with every requisite comfort at their homes. Rarely
could the case exist in which it would be proper and safe for an
invalid to be removed to a city hospital, who could not be removed
with equal propriety and safety to the western site, the distance of
a few squares with an easy method of conveyance being very im-
material compared with the fatigue the patient experiences at each
end of the route—to wit : in descending to and entering the vehicle
and in being removed from it and conveyed into the infirmary.
These observations are made with reference to the probabilty of
such an improvement being made in the manner of conveying
the patients generally as will considerably mitigate all the inconveniences they at present sustain from the existing modes of conveyance. The ample provision made by the Pennsylvania Hospital
for the reception of cases of wounds and fractures within twenty-
four hours after their recurrence has precluded such from being
brought to our house. This class of patients would therefore be
unaffected by any site adopted for the Hospital. The diseases of a

considerable portion of our patients on admission to the house are chronic. The conveyance of such cases, except in the last stages of disease, involves no essential inconvenience. When acute cases present they would obtain from the out-door physicians and visitors that care which would also preclude difficulty. But supposing the possible, yet improbable fact, that the patient might *safely* be removed to an infirmary within the city limits who could not without danger be removed to one west of the Schuylkill, your committee would suggest that in so rare a contingency accommodations could be obtained for him as a *pay* patient at the Pennsylvania Hospital, and that an expenditure of this kind, comparatively trifling, would be far more judicious than that which would provide a Hospital in the city for the few cases of this character which would ever occur.

"It is probable that no location could be obtained, within the city limits, to which the same objection of distance would not be applied by some portion of the extensive district embraced by this corporation ; and it ought to be borne in mind that as the city is rapidly spreading on the eastern banks of the Schuylkill nothing but the narrow stream will shortly separate the western establishment from a dense population.

"Your committee would now call your attention to a portion of the poor whose interests in this particular have not been brought into view, and to whom the location west of Schuylkill will be absolutely important. We allude to the inmates of the Almshouse, comprising generally persons whose constitutions, from various causes, have been much impaired, for which reason they are dependent on the public bounty, and whose cases require frequent medical aid. By the theory of our law we are to suppose that the mass of persons obtaining regular aid will be found within the walls of the Almshouse and this will be strictly so after the necessary buildings are erected, so that the law may go fully into effect. To separate the Hospital from these would be attended with inconveniences far more onerous and insuperable than would be productive of benefit to the poor without.

"We suggested in the commencement of this report that no

position more salubrious could have been obtained within the range allowed by the law than that purchased by the Commissioners. This assertion was made on due consideration, and with the knowledge that an opinion had been advanced by respectable citizens that this site would of necessity be unhealthy from its contiguity to the Schuylkill. The winds ordinarily prevailing in summer and autumn are, however, supposed to protect the western banks of all rivers from these deleterious exhalations, which, wafted to their eastern shores, are the source of disease, and popular observation has confirmed this theory as regards the Schuylkill, or rather has established the fact of the general healthiness of its western shores, leaving it to science to form the theory.

"Seasons have indeed occurred of such general and severe visitations that no place, however reputed for its health, has been exempted from the approach of disease. If on these occasions the country west of the Schuylkill was visited with sickness in common with other districts reputed to be healthy much more did it abound in that portion of the city in which the Hospital would be located if built within the city limits.

"Of the general healthfulness of the west side of the Schuylkill we have the evidence of respectable and observing persons long resident in that section. Their testimony we consider as superior to all theory, and we have similar unequivocal testimony of the salubrity of the particular site purchased by the Commissioners from a family who were resident upon it for above fifteen years.

"We now arrive at objections to the location of the Hospital on the above site, of a character different from those which have preceded, in not having relation to the interests of the poor, but to other interests which it is supposed are entitled to attention in the decision of this question. A Committee of the Board of Physicians attached to this institution, in a report under date March 29, 1829, represent it ' as their opinion, and that of their colleagues, that the location of the Hospital out of town would be in the highest degree injurious to the just reputation which Philadelphia enjoys for furnishing the best and most copious means of medical instruction in the United States,' adding as their ' belief that there are many pecuniary interests of the citizens which would be materially affected by a measure curtailing the means of medical instruction.' Suggestions emanating from so respectable a source are entitled to profound attention, and such your Committee have endeavored to bestow upon them. In approaching the objection to the location implied in the above report your Committee are free to acknowledge that Public Hospitals ought to be *tributary* to the advancement of medical science, subject to the reasonable qualification that the benefit of the sick should be the *primary*, the other the secondary purpose of these institutions. On this principle the Infirmary of the Almshouse has very properly contributed to the promotion of medical science in the following particulars :

" 1st. As a school for a limited number of resident students, who, after a term of six months duty in that station, perform, during a further tour of six months, the duty of physicians in the House, subject to the supervision of the regular attending physicians of the establishment.

" 2d. As furnishing to a number of non-resident students the opportunity of witnessing the clinical or bedside practice of the house, thus enabling them to acquire, by direct inspection and observation, a practical knowledge of diseases, and, with the aid of such remarks and directions as are suggested by the physician on duty, an acquaintance with the most approved manner of examining cases and applying the proper remedies.

" In the first of these particulars the Infirmary has been eminently beneficial, by completing annually the medical education of eight physicians, who, instead of entering into the professional world with the theory only of medicine and the feelings of novitiates in practice, are enabled to commence their public career with all the confidence and skill which constant and complicated practice during a years' residence in the house may be supposed to impart to them.

" We understand the objections of the Physicians to a removal of that Hospital out of town, as applying in no respect to the first of these propositions, only in a limited degree to the second, but principally to the third of the series.

" Exhibitions of operative surgery which do not occur frequently

7

are always of that intersting character to the medical student that we can scarcely believe that the difference of a few squares in the location of the Hospital would present any obstacle to a young man's attendance on these occasions.

"We shall therefore proceed to the third particular, in considering which the practice which has obtained of bringing the sick into the operating room and there lecturing on their diseases, though not included in the limits of our proposition, must necessarily be brought into view.

"By the views of the University and possibly of the Jefferson College, a student, in order to graduate, is required to take a ticket to attend the medical practice, either of the Pennsylvania Hospital or Philadelphia Almshouse. One hundred and eighty-five tickets were taken last year to attend the practice of this Infirmary and one hundred and eighty-five appear to have been taken the present year. On inquiry we find that the number who attend the regular visitation of the sick during eight months of the year varies from 30 to 50, while during the period of lectures the most interesting cases being brought into the lecture room, attendance in the wards is not usual. The number attending at the operating room during this period is about 170 persons.

"The number of persons who can be really benefitted by attending the practice of the house is *limited*. It is even confined to a much smaller number than do attend, for it is only those who can approach the patients and observe by personal inspection and observation the symptoms on which the treatment is predicated who can derive any material advantage from it. This number is so small, compared with the total number of medical students, that a removal of the Infirmary would have but little practical effect on the medical school at large.

"We are aware that in a suitable building such an arrangement of the patients and division of the attending medical students might be made as would render an attendance on the practice of the house more extensively useful, but it is to the present condition and usages of the establishment that our remarks must be applied.

" To remedy the difficulty which presents to extensive clinical instruction in the wards, a practice not permitted in the Pennsylvania Hospital, has gained admission into this institution. We refer to the usage before noticed, of holding lectures in the operating room upon medical cases of particular interest, the patients being brought from their wards into the lecture room, and there detained during a lecture of 15 to 20 minutes. But except that the lecture is made more imposing by the subject of it being present, and possibly the student's attention to the case being *fastened* by the display, we know of no benefit which can accrue from it which would not equally result from the case being lectured, in the absence of the patient, on the notes of the physician, which form, in reality, the basis of the lecture.

" After what has been said on the subject in which benefit is derived from clinical instruction, showing the necessity of a near approach to the patient, the total inutility of bringing into the presence of one or two hundred students any case of disease, excepting a surgical one, must be apparent. An image of the patient would be just as efficient.

" Your committee, having found it necessary to introduce this practice to the notice of the Board, feel it due to the medical gentlemen attached to the institution to say that they have not discovered that many instances of material injury to the patients have resulted from it. Great care has been taken to avoid such a consequence; at the same time the attendants of the sick speak of this display as a source of anxiety to the invalid previous to the lecture, and your committee would suggest that, particularly to the delicate and timid, this exposure must be a trial of no small magnitude.

" Upon the whole, your committee are of opinion that the advantages which have accrued to the medical students *generally* by the Almshouse Infirmary have been overestimated in any estimate which would make its removal ' highly injurious ' to the Philadelphia School. We consider its advantages to be inestimable to those who gain admission into it as resident students and physicians, and we believe it greatly useful to those who can avail themselves of an acquaintance with its surgical and medical practice. Beyond this, the medical school does not appear to be benefitted.

" Let the institution, however, have all the credit for usefulness which, for the purpose of this argument, its medical friends might choose to assign to it, we do not perceive how its removal " will impair the reputation which Philadelphia now enjoys for furnishing the best medical school in the United States." It is true the circumstance of its location being a few squares different from its present one may occasion some inconvenience to the attending students. This inconvenience, however, is susceptible, as we shall show, of some remedy; while it is greatly overbalanced by the advantages which will be presented by an Infirmary erected on a plan combining all the modern improvements which science and art have suggested as promotive of the health, comfort and convenience of its inmates.

" So far, then, from the effect predicted being the result, the converse of it must ensue from the removal to an establishment constructed with particular reference to a classification of the sick, so important to their proper treatment ; and with such an arrangement of its rooms that, by a suitable division of the attending students into classes, assigning to each class a ward, practical clinical instruction may be imparted to upwards of two hundred pupils in each day's course of visitation, *without injury to the sick.*

" The inconvenience of the attending students resulting from the greater distance of the Almshouse would find, it is believed, a natural remedy in the selection which medical students desirous of attending the Almshouse practice would make in their boarding-houses, so as to fix them between the Almshouse and university or college. Another remedy is found in the facility and cheapness with which conveyance by carriages or stages can be obtained. We have stages running which convey an individual to Frankford or Germantown for twenty-five cents, or about five cents per mile, and we have only to create a demand for such a conveyance to the Almshouse and it will be readily afforded at a reasonable rate.

" Suppose, however, that medical instruction to non-resident pupils was totally to cease at the Almshouse Infirmary in consequence of its removal.   In such event, by no means probable, the income of this institution would be diminished $2,000 per annum; which, taken from the statement made in an early part of this report of the extra annual cost of a city hospital, would still leave a large balance in favor of the country location.

"But what other interests would be affected by it? The Pennsylvania Hospital would gain the sale of additional tickets; the private schools of instruction would also be possible gainers.   Philadelphia has these decided advantages for medical improvement that the withdrawal of the Almshouse Infirmary from the system would only brighten the other institutions.   The remaining means of instruction are so various that no other city can boast an equality of advantages, and to the existing opportunities for professional observation a United States Marine Asylum is to be added.

"A conclusive argument in favor of the foregoing reasoning is to be found in the fact that the number of students who attended the University of Pennsylvania previous to the Almshouse being made a school for clinical instruction was even greater than have attended at any period since; thus showing that admission to the practice of the house has had no effect whatever to increase the number of students coming to this city for medical instruction.

"We see, therefore, that no pecuniary interests are likely to suffer by the location of the hospital west of the Schuylkill.   On the contrary, in looking forward to the period, by no means remote, when our city plot will be generally filled by buildings for commerce or residence, the existence of a large infirmary within the city for diseases of a promiscuous character would be received with great distrust, as a source whence disease and pestilence might possibly arise.   Whether such fears would be chimerical is not for us to pronounce.   They would most certainly exist, and would derogate much from the value of all property in its vicinity, besides impairing the general confidence in the purity of an atmosphere which is now inviting citizens of wealth and enterprise from all parts of our Union to a residence among us.   From the operation of such fears, combined with the inducements which may arise to dispose of the city possessions, resulting either from their increased value or a desire to diminish the public burdens, your committee have no hesitation in believing that half a century would not elapse ere another removal would be demanded and accomplished.

"For all the reasons above assigned, your committee are of opinion that the proper site for erecting a hospital is that already provided by the Commissioners.

"Which is respectfully submitted."

The report was signed by Messrs. A. L. Pennock, Thomas Rogers, Thomas Earp, John Keppler, Jr., Michael Day and L. Paynter.

These gentlemen were not of the kind to jump at conclusions; they considered every suggestion carefully, and thus formed their opinions. They believed that the public supported the institution for the care, treatment and cure, if possible, of the poor unfortunates under charge, and that medical instruction was *secondary* to that grand object. They were deep thinkers; their conclusions were not influenced by glittering generalities, but were based on what they regarded as facts, "cold, stubborn facts."

After a lapse of seventy years it is interesting to note how their predictions have been verified. The section of the city in which the institution was located is now one of the most prosperous, and there are, probably, more houses west of the Schuylkill River than were in the entire city at that time.

That report settled the question; the Hospital was erected on the Almshouse site and is one of the departments of that great establishment.

Its reputation is world-wide and of the best; medical books are full of descriptions of cases treated in the Philadelphia Hospital—Blockley, as it is familiarly called—and many physicians have found it to be the stepping-stone to high honors in their profession.

CHAPTER IX.

MESSRS. WILLIAM BOYD and Charles Johnson, members of the Board of Commissioners, tendered their resignations, and Messrs. A. Cuthbert and J. W. Linnard were elected by the Select and Common Councils to fill the vacancies. The Commissioners elected Mr. D. Groves as their President.

The entire lack of discipline and the incompetency of the Steward of the House is shown by a report of the committee, which stated:

" The Committee of the House have been under the necessity of inquiring into the circumstances of an alarming and disagreeable quarrel which occurred at the Steward's table on the 5th inst., and, in the prosecution of the inquiry, have discovered other instances of disorder, all of which they deem it proper to exhibit in the following report.

" ' About three months since an affray took place at the table between some of the physicians and Mr. Hutchinson, the Superintendent of the manufactory, in consequence of the observation of Dr. Mott, in relation to Free Masonry, which Mr. Hutchinson took up as a designed affront to himself, though no such design appeared. Some high words ensued. The contents of a tumbler were thrown in the face of Mr. Hutchinson, and he was forcibly expelled from the room by the others. This altercation became the subject of a legal inquiry, and the persons by whom the assault on Mr. Hutchinson was committed were subjected to a very moderate fine for the offence, which the Recorder considered was much mitigated by the manner and conduct of the individual assailed.'

" The Guardians, to whom this altercation was known, hoped that with the decision of the Court would have terminated all controversy, and no order was taken upon the affair by them. It appears, however, that in a single instance, subsequent to the trial, Mr. Hutchinson improperly remarked at table that he had heard the doctors were unable to raise the money to pay their costs, while very frequent occasions have been sought by the other side to irritate his feelings by using idle and indecorous speeches having allusion to him. Dr. Jones, one of the resident physicians, admits that fact, and that he has frequently made remarks with respect to Mr. Hutchinson, with a view to compel his absence from the table, and he justifies this by referring to a communication which the physicians submitted to the Board on the subject of Mr. Hutchinson's presence at the table, but on which no order was taken by the Board. Dr. Hunt, the prominent party in the recent quarrel, admits also that since the remark was made by Mr. Hutchinson regarding their not being able to pay the costs he has assailed him himself, and taken frequent opportunities to satirize him.

"All the testimony received evinces that, prior to the first affray, and subsequent to it, with the exception of the remark we have noticed, the conduct of Mr. Hutchinson was decorous and unexceptionable, while the persevering remarks and taunts of the physicians above named were annoying in the extreme, and to have resisted the feelings they were bound to excite, must have called for much self-command on the part of Mr. Hutchinson.

"Thus goaded, Mr. Hutchinson expressed to some individual a determination to chastise Dr. Hunt should the latter persevere in taunting him at the table. Shortly afterwards Dr. Hunt heard of the declaration, and, on the 5th inst., at the dinner table, renewed his attack upon Mr. Hutchinson, first saying, in relation to a celery glass, that it would make a good hog-trough, the term hog being understood, by previous inuendos, to designate Mr. Hutchinson. The doctor then inquired of Mr. Stockton, the Steward, whether he had heard of any threats of vengeance declared against him, adding that he feared no threats uttered behind his back; none but cowards made such threats and they did not execute them. Mr. Hutchinson now replied that these remarks were made for him; that he would no longer bear them, and that if Dr. Hunt persevered he would thrash him and give him a pair of black eyes, accompanying the threat, it is alleged, with profane language. Dr. Hunt now seized a tumbler and projected it at the head of Mr. Hutchinson with a force that would have resulted in incalculable injury had it struck the intended mark. Mr. Hutchinson, seizing another tumbler, hurled it at his assailant, after which missiles of a similar nature were thrown by Dr. Hunt. The doctor was about to seize a poker from the fireside when he was arrested through the interference of the family.

"The Committee omits all comment upon the scene, but it is due to Mr. Hutchinson to add, in relation to the alleged profanity of his language, that the testimony is, he is not in the habit of using profane language, which is, unfortunately too much used by the individuals making the allegation."

"On the last 'Board night' all the physicians absented themselves from the Steward's table. It appears to be the practice of the House to furnish the physicians with luncheon at 11 o'clock and supper at nine. On this particular evening Dr. Clarke, taking a plate from a servant, declared, without examining it, that the meat was spoiled. He then placed the meat on the floor, near the threshold of the door, when Dr. Jones kicked it several yards into the passage.

"On the next day a piece of meat was served in the same manner by Dr. Hunt, whose excuse was that he suspected the meat was the same that was kicked over the floor on the preceeding day.

"It is proper to add that the allegation of Dr. Clarke of the meat being bad is without the shadow of a foundation, and the testimony is that Mrs. Piersol, who has charge of the table, is very ambitious to have everything very nice in relation to it."

The physicians complained of were very young men, and the Board took that into consideration; and, while some of the members were in favor of dismissing them, it was deemed to be sufficient punishment to reprimand them, and "they were warned that their continuance in the institution depended upon their conducting themselves in a more decorous manner." There does not appear on the records anything to show that the incompetent official in charge was dismissed or even reprimanded for allowing such disgraceful conduct to continue to bring its mismanagement so prominently before the community.

The indiscriminate distribution of out-door relief had grown to such alarming proportions; such a long list of pensioners, as they were termed, being supplied with money, as well as provisions, etc.; the cost had arrived at such figures; and, the abuses of the system had become so glaring that a general demand was made to stop, or at least, check it.

An act was passed by the Legislature, in compliance with the request of the Guardians.

At the next session a bill was introduced to repeal that act. The Guardians obtained information of the proposed action and sent the following memorial, which received the full vote of the members of the Board:

" To the Honorable the Senate and House of Representatives of the Commonwealth of Pennsylvania in General Assembly met.

" The memorial of the 'Guardians for the Relief and Employment of the Poor of the City of Philadelphia, the District of Southwark and the Townships of Northern Liberties and Penn,' respectfully sheweth.

" That your memorialists have seen with deep regret a Bill No. 81, on the Senate files, which proposes to change in very material features the existing system for the management of the Poor in this District and your memorialists beg leave most respectfully to state their entire dissent from all the features of that Bill.

" It must be in the recollection of many of the members of your Honorable Bodies that the system now in progress was adopted upon the earnest demand of the people of the City of Philadelphia and the adjoining Districts and Townships, it was called for by them loudly; they complained, and had long complained of abuses resulting from the former system. They at last rose in their Primary Assemblies in Town Meeting and declared by acclamation that their grievances must be redressed. They referred the subject to intelligent and experienced men from the City and County. The plan which these men, after long and anxious reflection proposed was hailed with universal approval, it was submitted

HOSPITAL GATE.

to and approved of by the Councils of the City, by the Board of Commissioners of the Northern Liberties, of Southwark, of Kensington and of Penn Township and by the former Board of Guardians, consisting of fifty citizens from all parts of the District. It was presented to your Honorable Bodies supported by numerous memorials in its favor. It was at your last session fully examined, debated and finally adopted and passed into a Law, and is now in the progress of execution and experiment. What, then, your memorialists would ask, can have occurred to render an interference with this Law necessary ; before its operation has been tested, before its principles have had an opportunity to unfold their results ? Does the public voice call for this interference ? Your memorialists have not understood that it does ? on the contrary they believe the feelings and wishes of the community to be all enlisted in favor of the act now in force. They cannot believe otherwise without imputing fickleness of sentiment to that public, who are equally the constituents of your memorialists and of the members of your Honorable Bodies.

"Your memorialists beg leave to remind you that one great subject of general complaint was, what is generally called the *outdoor system of relief*, the practical operation of which was the establishment of a regular and constantly increasing ' List of Pensioners,' who fed upon the public purse without check or control and demanded as a right, and received as a right the produce of the labours of the industrious classes. There was no end or limit to this evil, it had attained an alarming magnitude. To arrest its course required the strong arm of the Law ; it was interposed and the evil has been stayed, and the people were thankful.

"Yet the first section of the Bill against which we remonstrate is intended once more to launch against us this engine of destruction. Your memorialists pray your Honorable Bodies to recur to the Petitions of the last sessions and to adhere to the course of policy then adopted and predicated upon those petitions. They beg leave to suggest that the Law, as it now stands, permits *temporary relief* to the sufferer in his family, but to be administered in food, clothing, fuel, medicines and all the necessaries and comforts of life, while it forbids the baneful grant of pecuniary Pensions.

"Your memorialists are also averse to that part of the Bill which *compels* them to erect a Hospital within the bounds of the city. Allow them to ask why *they* should not be entrusted with this question. Are not your memorialists like yourselves elected to discharge the duties belonging to their station? Are they not responsible for the violation of these duties? Do they not act under the sanction of a sacred obligation, are they not members of the community most interested in the matter under discussion? Do they not themselves contribute by payment of Taxes, to the creation of the fund? Why, then, shall they not be permitted to exercise the functions thus cast upon them, and in which they have so deep an interest? Why must your Honorable Bodies be appealed to, to superintend, check, control and pass upon each and all their acts?

"If the people call for your interference, your memorialists admit the case for interference would then arise, but while they are not dissatisfied, your memorialists submit that such intervention would be equally unjust to them and burdensome to you.

"Again it can only require to be mentioned, it need not be insisted upon, that the establishment of a Hospital at a distance from the Almshouse would be for many reasons impolitic and imprudent; cruel to the tenants of the latter place, and by the process of removal and its consequences fatal to Individuals and offensive in cases, perhaps dangerous, to the public. An establishment for the reception of those who may suffer from sudden accident, or from illness which cannot be properly attended to in their families may become desirable at a future period within the city, and will then be erected; but your memorialists respectfully submit that the people of this District, and the public bodies of this section of the State are competent to Judge of the proper time and occasion for such an erection. At this moment it would be burdensome, expensive and inconvenient.

"Allow your memorialists also to respectfully ask whether they are not entitled to Judge of the *Rules* which should govern their mode of transacting their own business? Must they be driven on all occasions to recur for assent and approbation to other authorities, to Judges and Attornies-General? What other corporation is so restricted? Why are not the members of this Body to be entrusted with their own government? Will the City of Philadelphia, the District of Southwark, the Townships of the Northern Liberties and Penn—will they depute men to the performance of this trust who are not worthy to be permitted to enact their own rules? Do not the principles of our government forbid this supposition?

" And allow us to ask, can the authorities referred to in Section 3 be competent Judges of the necessity, or of the mode of operation of these rules? Can any Body of them except those who witness their effects?

" In conclusion, your memorialists respectfully pray that they may be allowed, without change or alteration of any kind, at least to give a fair experiment to the system now in operation, demanded as it was by the acclamation of the community and granted by you in consequence of the acclamations, which hardly yet ceased to resound through your Halls.

" With these observations, your memorialists most respectfully remonstrate against the passage of any Bill which may change the existing Laws for the relief and employment of the Poor in the City of Philadelphia, the district of Southwark and the townships of the Northern Liberties and Penn.

" By order of the Board.

" THOMAS P. COPE, *President.*

" Attest: GEORGE HEYL, *Secretary.*"

It was thought at the time that the parties who were instrumental in having the bill introduced were interested in having the hospital built where it would be more convenient for them, and as it was generally known that the Board of Guardians had decided upon its location, this measure was intended to frustrate their plans. If such was the fact, the scheme miscarried, the memorial had the desired effect and the Bill was not passed.

The Commissioners for erecting the buildings were anxious to employ the architect to superintend the building of them. Mr. Strickland was a very busy man, and it was deemed advisable to communicate with him, and, if possible, secure his services.

In reply to their communication, they received the following:

"PHILADELPHIA, October 25th, 1829.

"*Sir:* As it will be entirely out of my power to give my exclusive attention as architect to the building of the new Almshouse, and as I can only devote that time which may be unemployed under my present engagements, I take the liberty of proposing for your consideration the following terms upon which I can agree to superintend the Building : To make all the drawings necessary for the workmen and to give the building generally a proper attention whenever my other duties will permit, for the sum of $800 per annum.

Should this proposition meet with your approval, I shall be happy to serve you.

With great respect I am, sir,

Your obed't serv't,

"WILLIAM STRICKLAND."

The terms were accepted, and it was ordered that the salary should be started at once.

Mr. Tracy Taylor, commissioner for erecting buildings, tendered his resignation, and Mr. P. Deal, Jr., was elected by the commissioners of the Kensington district to fill the vacancy.

Several conferences were held by the committees representing the two Boards, to endeavor to agree upon the plans for the buildings. The architect was called into these consultations, and, on January 11th, 1830, the committee representing the Board of Guardians reported to that body that they had agreed upon the plans, which were submitted for approval.

" The plans were approved and the committee was instructed to wait upon the Commissioners and to *verbally* give their assent to the plans submitted."

It was now thought that everything had been arranged satisfactorily to all parties, and the work of erecting the buildings could be started.

A committee was appointed to advertise for proposals for the material that may be wanted to construct the walls, etc.

It was "*Resolved,* that in the erection of the buildings the stone work be done by the perch, mason's measure, except the dressed stone which shall be set by the superficial foot, measureing the face only. The bricks shall be laid by the thousand, including jobbing and other extra work. The carpenter work, as far as practicable, shall be done by measurement."

Proposals having been received, in compliance with advertisements, contracts were awarded: To Lane Scoffield for foundations, cellars, etc., at the rate of 14 cents per cubic yard; to J. and J. Snyder, and others, for 1,300,000 bricks at $6.37½ per thousand; to Samuel Davis and Jon'a Wentz for 80,000 bushels of lime at 21 cents per bushel; to Lehigh Co. for 60,000 feet 2½-inch plank at $10.00 per M., and 300 poles, not less than 40 feet, at $1.40 each; to Hugh Scott for 20,000 feet of chiseled dressed stone at 60 cents per foot, and to Robert P. Crosby for 11,000 perch of building stone at $1.05 per perch, measured in the wall.

It was agreed to divide the mason's work into two, and the carpenter's work into five parts.

The Commissioners elected Messrs. Corlies & Cowperthwaite and Thomas Eastlack as masons, and George Senneff, John Bishop, H. L. Coryll, John Gilder and G. R. Harmstead as carpenters.

It was agreed that the Center Building, Almshouse, be denominated No. 1 and assigned to H. L. Coryll; northeast wing, No. 2 ,to G. R. Harmstead; southwest wing, No. 3, to John Bishop; Hospital, southeast wing, No. 4, to George Senneff; and northwest wing No. 5, to John Gilder, and, that all of the general jobbing work required previous to the commencement of the new buildings be given to George Senneff, under the direction of the architect. Mr. Harmstead declined and P. Deal & Co. were elected in his stead. Mr. W. Govett was elected Superintendent. On motion of Mr. W. Wagner "the Superintendent was authorized to purchase three rafts of white pine boards, 30,000 feet sap boards and one raft of oak scantling, and that W. Wagner and G. B. Baker be a committee to direct and advise him in said purchase, and that an order be drawn in favor of W. Wagner for $1,000 to pay the bill."

Mr. D. Groves, President of the Commissioners, resigned, and Mr. W. Wagner was elected in his stead. The Board selected E. W. Keyser, Esq., as President of their body.

Another change in the plans was called for. The Superintendent of the New York Almshouse, Mr. Arthur Burtis, had sent several letters to the Board of Guardians relative to separate dormitories. These were transmitted to the Commissioners "with information that this Board will cheerfully concur in any modification of the plan adopted for the new Almshouse, which, on consideration, may be found necessary, useful and expedient."

The architect subsequently reported "that he had accommodated the plans of the new buildings, as far as regards separate dormitories, to meet the views of the Board of Guardians."

E. W. Keyser, Esq., President of the Board of Commissioners, laid the corner-stone of the new Almshouse on May 26, 1830. He delivered an appropriate address, which was listened to with much interest by those present. The ceremonies were witnessed by Messrs. Moore, Wagner, Deal, McGlinsey and Bunker, of the Board of Commissioners, nearly all of the members of the Board of Guardians of the Poor, and a number of other persons.

Although the Board of Guardians had approved the plans that had been adopted for the buildings, it soon became apparent that the members were not satisfied. There was a constant friction between the two Boards. Whenever the Guardians thought that they were not entirely pleased, and that seemed to occur very frequently, they wanted to stop all proceedings. This, of course, was very annoying to the Commissioners, and led to loss on the part of the workmen. Contracts were made in accordance with plans that had been adopted, and when the work was partly done the Guardians managed to discover that it was not what was wanted, and called for a change. This interfered very materially with the progress of the work and added to the cost.

Instead of working together harmoniously the two Boards drifted apart. The Guardians adopted the following: "Whereas it is highly important to the welfare of the Poor and to the interests of the public that the buildings for the accommodation of the former should be erected on such plans as shall combine comfort and economy; and Whereas, this Board (to which the Law has given an approval of the plan) is not satisfied with the arrangements of the Buildings as now progressing, and feels assured that a little delay will result in harmony and in the adoption of a more perfect plan; therefore,

"*Resolved*, unanimously, that the Board of Commissioners be respectfully requested to arrest the progress of the buildings until such period as the committees of conference in joint meeting may deem advisable.

"*Resolved*, That the Committee of Conference be instructed to wait on the Commissioners and submit to their consideration the plans for separate dormitories now before this Board.

"*Resolved*, That the said committee be instructed to suggest to the Board of Commissioners the necessity of constructing the walls of the Buildings in such manner as to admit the most approved mode of cleaning and ventilating the apartments.

"*Resolved*, That the Committee of Conference be instructed to meet the committee appointed by the Board of Commissioners at stated periods in order that the state of the Buildings from time to time may be known, and that the interior arrangements may be so found as will best answer the purposes for which the buildings are designed."

Messrs. Isaac Roach and J. W. Linnard resigned, and the Select and Common Councils elected Messrs. John W. Fraley and John Moss to fill the vacancies. The friction regarding the plans caused a cessation of the work, and the changing of some of the interior called forth a letter from Corlies & Cowperthwaite, contractors, in which they said: "The change in the plan of the Building makes a very material difference to us in executing the work, in addition to which we have been obliged to stop and discharge all hands for one week; this has occasioned considerable loss and

8

inconvenience, besides being idle for a week. Three or four weeks before we had no chance to push the job, for reasons you are doubtless acquainted with. Under these circumstances we confidently expect that you will not hesitate to make good the contract by paying us the difference in building the dormitories; to be assessed by two persons to be appointed by the parties. The alterations, such as taking down and re-building, to be measured and valued."

Mr. George N. Baker resigned, and Mr. Edward Shotwell was elected Commissioner to fill the vacancy.

The Commissioners concluded to purchase some materials without advertising for bids, as the minutes show: "The Building Committee are authorized to purchase 100.000 ft. oak plank on the best terms they can, not exceeding $10.00 per M.; the committee are authorized to purchase nails, &c., on the best terms, &c."

Philip Raybold was awarded a contract November 1st, 1830, for 1,500,000 bricks at $6.00 per M. Contracts were also awarded for stone, lumber, &c., as the work progressed.

CHAPTER X.

THE Select and Common Councils sent a communication to the Commissioners January 16th, 1832, requesting information as to the amount expended and likely to be required to complete the contemplated buildings. In reply thereto the following statement was transmitted:

Cost of Farm containing about 188 acres	$51,716 94
Present cost of the two buildings, each 500 ft. in front by 65 ft. deep	195,303 00
Cost of constructing a wharf on the Schuylkill, with a road leading to the Buildings	4,517 00
Estimated cost to complete the present Buildings, Almshouse and Hospital	85,000 00
Estimated cost of two other Buildings, which are intended as House of Employment, Children's Asylum and Women's Apartments, which are to be built in conformity with present buildings	215,000 00
Total	$551,536 94

Contracts were awarded for plastering, painting and glazing of the center building on February 20th, 1832. The Committee of Conference of the Guardians of the Poor and of the Commissioners reported, March 5th, 1832, that they had unanimously agreed upon the plans for the additional buildings.

An advertisement for proposals was inserted on March 13th, 1832, reading: "Sealed proposals will be received by the Board of Commissioners for erecting the new Almshouse on the west bank of the River Schuylkill until the 19th inst., for doing the masons' work of the Women's Almshouse and House of Employment. The former to be built on the dormitory system, similar to the Men's Almshouse already erected, except that one-half of the dormitories are to be double and the other half single. The partition walls of the latter to be stone. The work to be done in a substantial and workmanlike. manner. The stone work by the perch, mason's measure. The brick work by the thousand, brick maker's count, and the chiseled dressed stone, say, sub-basement and belting courses, coins, heads and sills by the superficial feet when

115

laid in the walls only, and no allowance to be made for bed or joints; all jobbing of every description to be included." The advertisement also called for bids for the carpenter work, for 1,500,000 bricks and for chiseled dressed stone.

The work was divided in the same manner as the other had been, and bids were received from the same carpenters to do the work, at a deduction of forty per cent. from the old prices. Their propositions were accepted. The proposal of Joseph L. Atkinson for doing mason's work, etc., viz: for stone work at 55 cents per perch, brick work at $2.29 per thousand, and laying chiseled dressed stone at 10 cents per foot was accepted, and the Women's Almshouse was allotted to him. The proposal of Henry Reeves for stone work at 58 cents per perch, brick work at $2.18 per thousand, and laying chiseled dressed stone at 9 cents per foot, was also accepted, and he was given the work on House of Employment.

The contract for furnishing 1,500,000 bricks was awarded to Philip Reynolds & Son at $6.25 per thousand.

Mr. Wm. Wagner resigned his seat as a Commissioner and Mr. Jonathan Johnson was elected to fill the vacancy.

Messrs. Moss, Ogden and Deal were appointed as a committee to " purchase lumber generally."

The following communication was forwarded:

" PHILADELPHIA ALMSHOUSE, July 30, 1832.

" *The Commissioners for Erecting New Almshouse :*

" GENTLEMEN—The Board of Guardians of the Poor having decided upon the immediate removal of a considerable portion of paupers from this House to the New Buildings over Schuylkill, we respectfully request that you will instruct the architect to have immediately erected a temporary apparatus sufficient to cook for five hundred persons. Until this is effected the removal cannot take place, and it is a matter of necessity that the paupers should at once be removed. It is also requested that carpenters be directed to prepare slats for the dormitory and to do such other work as may be immediately required for the accommodation of the paupers." Referred to Joint Committee.

On August 23d, 1832, the following resolution was passed:

"*Resolved*, That the Board of Commissioners for erecting the New Almshouse be requested to furnish the names of all persons under salary, how they are employed, and the amount of salaries respectively; the names of all persons with whom they have contracted for materials or work, stating the kind of materials and work. The names of persons who have supplied material or done work without contracts; a copy of the different contracts entered into for material and workmanship."

The Commissioners replied as follows: "That the following persons are employed by this Board at annual salaries, viz.: Wm. Govett, Superintendent, $900; Wm. Strickland, architect, $800; John Diehl, clerk, $800; George Meyers, $600, as blacksmith, in lieu of working by the piece.

" The copies of *all* the contracts called for by the Guardians being very voluminous would require much time and labour, to avoid which, and at the same time to meet the views of said Board, the Commissioners respectfully invite them to examine, through the medium of a committee, the written contracts, books of minutes and such other documents as may be required to accomplish the objects of their inquiry." The yeas and nays were called on the motion to send the above information and were: Yeas, Messrs. Keyser, Fraley, Deal, Johnson and Bunker. Nays, Messrs. Moss, Ogden and Grover.

On July 7th, 1832, the following communication was received: " Special meeting of the Board of Physicians and Surgeons was held at the Philadelphia Almshouse. Present: Drs. Neill, Hodge, Horner, Barton, Randolph and Morton. On motion,

"*Resolved*, That the Medical Board recommend to the Board of Managers the propriety of prohibiting the introduction into this house of any case of cholera.

" *Resolved*, That it also be recommended to the Managers to make provision for such cases of cholera as may occur within the limits of their administration, and that said accommodations be located as near as practicable to this infirmary."

(Signed)   S. G. MORTON, M. D., *Secretary pro tem.*

The following preamble and resolution were received from the out-door physicians:

"WHEREAS, The experience of Europe has shown that the removal of patients attacked with cholera to hospitals remote from their places of residence is attended with injurious effects; therefore,

"*Resolved*, That the Board of Guardians for the Relief and Employment of the Poor be recommended to establish, under the superintendence of the out-door physicians, temporary hospitals for the reception of such cases as it may at the present period be deemed inexpedient to admit into the Almshouse.

D. F. CONDIE, Chairman.

These were the warning notes of the approach of the disease that afflicted the people of the city and caused so much fear and misery. Every measure that could be suggested for relief was tried by the Guardians of the Poor. A special meeting of the Board was held on Sunday July 29th, 1832, "to consider what measures ought to be adopted in consequence of a case of malignant cholera having occurred in the Almshouse." The following preamble and resolutions were adopted:

"WHEREAS, A case of cholera morbus of a highly malignant character has occurred in the Medical Ward of the Almshouse, this day, and we have every reason to believe that the disease will progress unless immediate measures be taken to remove the population; and, as in every place where an epidemic has made its appearance, its progress has been checked as soon as the inhabitants have been removed from the infected district, and few, or no new cases have occurred among the persons so removed therefrom. To protect the lives of the inmates of the Almshouse and to prevent the cholera from obtaining a favorable spot for the infection of Philadelphia.

Resolved, That measures be taken for the immediate removal of all healthy paupers from the Almshouse to the new buildings over Schuylkill or to some other suitable place, except those whose services are required for the sick.

"*Resolved*, That the sick persons be so distributed in the wards as to afford all the advantages of ventilation and cleanliness.

"*Resolved*, That a committee be appointed to carry the foregoing resolutions into effect and organize the place provided."

Messrs. Woolf, I. Cope, Lippincott, Hansell, Ryan and Burden were appointed on the committee.

By request of this Committee the mayor sent a letter to Commodore Barron asking him to place the Naval Asylum in possession of the Committee, with permission to remove into it some of the paupers from the Almshouse. A reply was received from Dr. Connors, the attending officer, " declining to comply, not feeling authorized to allow the admission of paupers into it, or its occupation by the civil authorities for any other purpose than as a hospital for cholera patients.

The mayor was chairman of the Sanitary Committee of the Guardians of the Poor and consulted with that body. It was suggested that the Board of Health be requested to take possession of the Naval Asylum, and to allow the Guardians to occupy the City Hospital near Bush Hill.

The Committee was instructed to erect sheds at the " new buildings over Schuylkill " for a hospital for the sick of that building, and the Committee of the house was authorized to employ two resident physicians for the " house over the Schuylkill."

The Board of Health declined to act upon the request to take possession of the Naval Asylum.

Dr. Burden reported, August 13, 1832, that by direction of the Committee of the house, he had " made application to the Rev. Mr. Hughes for the aid of some of the ' Sisters of Charity,' and that eight of them had arrived and were engaged in attending upon the sick in the house."

A report from the Committee of the house, under date of August 27, 1832, gives an idea of the conditions at that time. It reads as follows :

" When cholera made its appearance in the different wards of the Almshouse, and led to the belief that the atmosphere of the whole institution was infected, the nurses and attendants became clamorous for an increase of wages, and after their demands were gratified, such was the appalling nature and extent of the disease, that fear overcame every other consideration, and it was found impracticable to keep the nurses to their duty or to obtain, at a reasonable price, proper persons to attend to the sick.

" In a disease which requires unremitted attention from nurses, those employed in the wards (a few excepted) were by no means suitable. In several cases where the doctors had succeeded in raising patients from the collapsed state, and when there was well grounded hope of recovery, death resulted from the carelessness and inattention of the attendants. In one ward where the disease raged in all its horrors, where one would suppose that the heart would be humbled and the feelings softened at the sight of distress, the nurse and her attendants were in a state of intoxication, heedless of the groans of the patients and fighting over the bodies of the dying and the dead.

" The Committee, in their daily visits to the wards, used every exertion to preserve decorum and to cause proper attention to be given to the sick, but without success. The few good nurses were broken down by loss of rest and by fatigue, and the remainder abandoned the sick from fear of disease or resorted to intoxication, the means for producing which being necessarily at their disposal.

" Under these circumstances the Committee came to the determination of soliciting the Sisters of Charity at Emmetsburg to take charge of the wards, and for this purpose they applied to Bishop Kendrick, to whom they were introduced by the Rev. Mr. Kiely. The application was received by him in the spirit of Christianity and kindness. The Rev. Messrs. Donahue and Hughes likewise favored the views of the Committee.

" Two hours after the receipt of Bishop Kendrick's letter, the Sisters were on the road to Philadelphia. On their arrival the Committee prepared accommodations for them in the eastern tower, and they immediately entered upon the dangerous duties assigned them.

" The Committee cannot express the feelings of respect and admiration which they entertain for the conduct of the Sisters. It requires no common exercise of courage for persons to remain in the chamber of sickness, to administer relief, even to relatives and friends, during the prevalence of pestilence. These ladies, however, left a healthy home to visit an infected city, to encounter a dreadful disease, to live in an atmosphere dangerous in the extreme, to watch by the bedside of strangers, of the friendless, of the outcast, of those who generally had proved themselves unworthy of kindness.

"Nothing but a high sense of duty and a disinterested love of their fellow creatures could have induced the Sisters to take charge of our wards.

"Since their introduction to the house the Committee has given them the sole control of the female department, and are much gratified with their mode of government, as it will not only contribute to lessen the expenses of the institution, but will cause an improvement in the morals and discipline highly desirable.

"As nurses their services are valuable; guided by no mercenary motives, refusing all compensation, sustained by principle alone; kind, intelligent and cheerful, their attentions will contribute to the success of the physicians. The patients will find in them friends indeed and 'Sisters of Charity.'

"The Committee believe that if the Sisters can be prevailed upon to remain, the Hospital department of the Almshouse will afford greater opportunity for the recovery of the sick than any other institution in the United States. The Committee submit the following resolutions:

"*Resolved*, That the Sisters of Charity have charge of the Female Department of the Almshouse, and of such medical and surgical wards of the Male Department as they may consent to.

"*Resolved*, That they be requested to remain permanently in the institution.

"*Resolved*, That the Committee of the House be directed to have the Hospital department put in as favorable a condition for the comfort and attendance of the sick as the construction of the wards will admit of.

"*Resolved*, That the thanks of the Board be tendered to

Bishop Kendrick and the Rev. Messrs. Kiely, Hughes and Donahue for their Christian-like and gentlemanly conduct in procuring
the aid of the ' Sisters of Charity.'

Respectfully submitted by,

J. R. BURDEN,
JOHN L. WOOLF,
LEWIS RYAN,
WM. S. HANSELL,
Committee.

The resolutions were unanimously agreed to.

The Guardians applied for the schoolhouse at Twelfth and
Locust Streets, but could not obtain it. They rented a building on
Broad Street near Vine and fitted it up for the reception of patients.
Dr. Thomas Mackie Smith, one of the resident physicians at the
Almshouse, was appointed Physician-in-Chief of the Broad Street
Infirmary, and Dr. Benjamin Neill as Assistant. Under their
direction, the Hospital was opened on July 30th, 1832. It was
closed September 3d. The Committee said there was no further
occasion to continue it, as " the cholera had almost entirely disappeared." During the time it was in operation there were 44 males
and 21 females treated; of which 4 died, 38 were sent to the Almshouse, 19 discharged cured and 2 eloped; one was sent to cholera
hospital and one to Bush Hill.

On September 20, 1832, the Committee of the House was
directed to remove the paupers from the new Almshouse over the
Schuylkill to this house. Dr. Samuel G. Morton was paid $100
for professional services " over the river during the prevalence of
cholera," and Mr. William O. Kline was paid $100 for services as
steward, " over the river."

The Guardians were very anxious to remove to the new Almshouse, and on November 12th, 1832, a report was made by the
" Committee of the Whole," " that, after a full examination, they
were of opinion that the buildings would be fit for the accommodation of the inmates of the House on or before May 1st, 1833." A
committee was appointed to make arrangements for the removal,

and another to prepare a plan for the sale of the Spruce Street property."

Dr. T. Mackie Smith was paid $75 for services rendered in the Almshouse Infirmary " during the prevalence of the cholera." Notwithstanding the anxiety of the Guardians, the buildings were not ready to be occupied at the time stated, and on April 29th, 1833, the Committee on Conference was requested to " inquire as to the progress made in the new buildings over Schuylkill, the probable time when they will be finished and the sum which will be required to finish them." The Commissioners were requested to proceed as early as possible to finish the two buildings already erected, so that they could be in condition to be occupied.

Mr. Woolf gave notice " that at the first stated meeting in July he should move for the removal of the paupers to the new buildings west of the Schuylkill.

A special meeting of the Guardians was held on May 17th, 1833, to consider a communication from Rev. John Hickey, Superior of the Sisters of Charity, in relation to their removal from the Almshouse. The following extract gives the reasons assigned for recalling them :

" Being now on the spot, and having made all the inquiries necessary to determine my judgment, I feel it my duty, gentlemen, to advise you that I do not consider their longer stay in the Almshouse to be the department of charity in which they can be most usefully employed.

" With all the good will and kindness which you gentlemen have manifested in their regard, I do not perceive that, consistently with the principle on which the institution is founded, supported and governed, it is in your power to secure to them those opportunities of practicing the duties of their state of life according to their rules ; that protection of their feelings from the rude assaults of such persons as are necessarily in your institution, and regard it as their own, whilst they look upon those who minister to their comfort as servants, paid for doing it; or that security from misrepresentation of motives and action to which a few retiring and timid females are necessarily exposed, laboring amidst such a population of paupers.

" Besides, in every case of legal provision for the poor, the expenses of attending them are included; the places occupied by the Sisters might afford employment to others who stand in need of it, for the sake of the emolument, which enters not into the motives that influence the Sisters or their superiors. Consequently the poor would be attended to in your institution, whilst the Sisters could be employed in other departments of charity, where the unhappy sufferers have to depend upon a more precarious support; where the orphans will look upon them as mothers and the sick as sisters; where theirs will be the task to plant the seeds of virtue and of education in the minds of poor children, where poverty and wretched parents sometimes conspire to deprive them of both, unless such facilities be afforded."

Mr. Woolf presented the following preamble and resolutions, which were unanimously adopted, and, together with the letter of Rev. Mr. Hickey, ordered to be published:

" WHEREAS, A written communication has been received from Rev. John Hickey, Superior of the Sisters of Charity, intimating, for reasons therein stated, that it is his intention to recall the Sisters now in the Almshouse, as soon as the Board shall have had time to supply their places, and

" WHEREAS, It is proper that some testimony should be borne to the zeal, fidelity and disinterestedness which these amiable philanthropists have exhibited; therefore,

" *Resolved*, That this body entertain a deep, lasting and grateful sense of the generous devotedness, the sincere and Christian kindness, and the pure and unworldly benevolence which have prompted and sustained the Sisters of Charity attached to this institution during the trying period of pestilence and death, and afterwards in the midst of constant suffering and disease.

" *Resolved*, That the invaluable services of these amiable women have been productive of lasting benefits to this institution, in the admirable and energetic measures which they have introduced for the relief and comfort of the sick and afflicted, and entitle

them to the warmest thanks and gratitude of the whole community which have been benefitted by their labors.

"*Resolved*, That this body, in parting from the Sisters of Charity, regret that the rules and habits of the order, to which the Sisters belong, do not admit the acceptance of any reward, as it would give them pleasure to bestow such a testimonial as might serve partially to express the grateful feelings which they entertain.

"*Resolved*, That in permanent testimony of our feelings in this regard, the above resolutions be recorded in the minutes of the Board."

On May 27, 1833, the following replies to inquiries proposed by the Committee of Conference to the Building Commissioners were read:

"1st Query—The two buildings, in all probability, will be ready to receive the paupers by the 1st of October. There remains yet to be completed the portico, culverts, privies, tanks and forcing pumps and apparatus for cooking generally.

"2d Query—The two now erecting, have on their second floor of joist and the work is progressing rapidly. Expended up to this period $107,072.78. Sum necessary to complete these two buildings, $175,000; they will be finished in course of next season.

"3d Query—The sum required to finish the entire establishment being $200,000.

"4th Query—Contracts yet to be made for the two in progress are plastering and rough-casting, both copper and coppering, painting and glazing."

These answers do not appear to have satisfied the Board, as a motion to negotiate another loan of $100,000 caused considerable discussion, and when passed it '*provided, however, that no money shall be paid to the Commissioners for the erection of the new Almshouse until said Commissioners furnish a detailed statement in writing of the money already expended, the names of the Contractors, the names of Agents and Superintendents, with their respective salaries, and the probable amount of money required to complete the buildings respectively.*'"

June 3, 1833, the Commissioners sent a communication, showing the amount of money expended to have been $482,358.60, and that the sum required to finish would be $200,000, of which $150,000 would be required in 1833. A list of contracts for furnishing materials and prices of work, together with the names and salaries of persons employed, was also furnished.

CHAPTER XI.

OCTOBER arrived, but the buildings were not in condition to be occupied. On the 21st of that month, in reply to an inquiry of the Guardians, the Commissioners stated that it would require $170,000 more to complete the buildings, and gave notice that they had drawn on the Board for $50,000.

The Guardians requested the Commissioners to furnish them with the original estimates of the cost of the buildings, the amount expended and the sum required to finish them. The Commissioners replied, November 4th, that the original estimate for the erection of the buildings was $320,000.00 ; the amount expended was $579,829.46, and the amount yet required to complete them was $170,000.00.

The Guardians gave notice that they would remove all the paupers to the new Almshouse between the 1st and 10th of April, 1834. The visitors of the poor districts were directed to report the names of their out-door paupers who now receive regular relief, designating those who are willing to go into the new Almshouse and those who refuse to go.

A committee was appointed to consider the propriety of establishing two omnibuses to run between the Exchange and the new Almshouse, and also to inquire from the Bridge Company as to what arrangements, with regard to toll, could be made with them.

April passed, but the paupers were not removed. On June 16th the Guardians again asked as to the time required to finish the buildings and whether arrangements could be made to hasten their completion.

On June 23, 1834, Mr. Hemphill made the following report, which was accepted :

" Agreeably to the resolution of the Board, passed on the 15th inst., the Treasurer makes report in relation to the loans as fol-

127

lows: 'The *first* proposal for a loan of $100,000 was published in 1829, but brought forth no offers, except a private letter to the Treasurer from Stephen Girard, Esq., who offered to take $25,000 at par, which was accepted by the Board, and the money was received in January, 1829. Of the residue of this loan $44,000 were sold at par, $5,600 at 1 per cent. premium, and $25,400 at 3½ per cent. premium, making principal $100,000, premium, $945; total, $100,945.00. This loan is redeemable in 1836; interest payable January and July at 5 per cent., $5,000 per annum.

"The *second* loan was for $150,000, redeemable in 1840; it commenced in 1830. Proposals were advertised for, but with little effect, as only $25,000 of it were disposed of, and at par, up to July, and it was not until October, 1831, that the loan was filled, different amounts having been disposed of at intervals until the close, at 4 per cent. premium. Thus there was at par $25,000, at 4 per cent. premium $125,000; premium, $5,000; total, $155,000. Interest payable January and July, at 5 per cent., $7,500 per annum.

"The *third* loan was disposed of by the Finance Committee to Thomas Biddle & Co. at 10 per cent. premium, between March and August, 1832, redeemable in 1850 for $100,000 at 10 per cent. premium, $110,000. Interest payable January and July, at 5 per cent., $5,000.

"The *fourth* loan was commenced in August, 1832, and was disposed of to Thomas Biddle & Co. at 10 per cent. premium, and was received in various amounts as required between that period and April, 1833. It is redeemable in 1860. The principal is $100,000; premium, $10,000; total, $110,000. Interest payable January and July, at 5 per cent., $5,000 per annum.

"The *fifth* loan was for $100,000, and was disposed of to different persons, in 1833, at a premium of 8 per cent. It is redeemable in 1863. Principal, $100,000; premium, $8,000; total, $108,000.

"The *sixth* loan commenced later in the year 1833, and was designed to be for $100,000. Of this sum, however, only $75,000 have been actually disposed of, the residue being considered as appropriated to meet the note given to Mr. Trotter, due about this time for copper. Of the $75,000, $42,500 have been disposed of at par, and $32,500 at 1½ per cent. premium, $32,987.50. Reserved to meet the note of Mr. Trotter, $25,000. Total, $100,487.50. This loan is redeemable in 1865. Interest payable in January and July, $5,000 per annum.

RECAPITULATION.

Loan No. 1 . .	Redeemable	1836 . . .	$100,000	Premium, . . .		$945 00
" " 2 . .	"	1840 . . .	150,000	"	. . .	5,000 00
" " 3 . .	"	1850 . . .	100,000	"	. . .	10,000 00
" " 4 . .	"	1860 . . .	100,000	"	. . .	10,000 00
" " 5 . .	"	1863 . . .	100,000 . . .	"	. . .	8,000 00
" " 6 . .	"	1865 . . .	100,000	"	. . .	487 50

Total Loans	$650,000	$34,432 50
Total Premiums	$34,432 50	
Total	684,432 50	

" The interest already paid or accruing, to be paid on the 1st of July next :

On No. 1	1836	$24,510 38	
" " 2	1840	24,213 85	
" " 3	1850	12,125 00	
" " 4	1860	10,000 00	
" " 5	1863	2,500 00	
" " 6	1865	1,595 61	
Total interest to July, 1834			$74,944 84
Less the sum received from Thomas Biddle & Co. for interest while sums were in their hands			$3,820 12
			$71,124 72

" The semi-annual payment of interest will be, after the 1st of July next, $16,250.00.''

Respectfully submitted,
JOHN HEMPHILL, Treasurer.

June 23d, 1834.

On June 30th, 1834, the following preamble and resolution were passed by the Guardians :

" WHEREAS, The Board of Commissioners for the erection of the new Almshouse have failed in making their quarterly statement, required by law, therefore,

9

"*Resolved*, That this Board will not authorize any further loans until a satisfactory statement be given for the omission."

On July 7th, 1834, it was resolved that the Furnishing Committee be requested to have the manager's and steward's apartments of the new Almshouse fitted up during the present week. It was also

"*Resolved*, That we commence moving on Monday next, at nine o'clock.

"*Resolved*, That a Committee of the whole Board be a Committee to oversee the removal.

"*Resolved*, That the Commissioners be requested to inform the Board at what time they will be able to deliver for occupancy the Almshouse, (eastern building) Hospital and Outhouses."

Dr. Harlan appeared before the Board and presented the following resolutions of the Board of Physicians.

"*Resolved*, That in the opinion of the Medical Board, who recently visited the New Almshouse, it is expedient to remove, as soon as practicable, the occupants of the present house to their future abode, the latter being fully prepared for their reception ; and further,

"*Resolved*, That they highly approve of the project to devote a portion of the extensive grounds attached to the New Almshouse to the establishment of a Medico-Botanical Garden, and would suggest that in order to make it practically useful to the students, the patients and the profession generally, it will be necessary to place its permanent superintendence in the hands of a scientific Botanist, who for a moderate annual salary would furnish occasional practical lessons to the students attending the practice of the house."

At a special meeting, held July 16th, 1834, Mr. Hemphill, of the Finance Committee, reported that they had an offer from Messrs. Biddle for $25,000 loan at sixty days with interest, at par, and that the Bank of United States had agreed to discount a note for $10,000, on a deposit of stock, which was approved.

The following resolutions were adopted :

"*Resolved*, It is expedient that the order of removal adopted by this Board on Monday last be so amended as to give discretionary power to the Committees on Removal to make such alterations as they may deem necessary.

"*Resolved*, That the Board be and is hereby divided into three committees of four members each, to be denominated Removal Committees, two of which go off each day, the two that have been on the previous day to divide themselves, so as one of each will be at each house.

"*Resolved*, That no permits for liberty be granted during the time taken up in removing, and that no discharge be granted to any of the inmates of the house that are known to be of intemperate habits.

"*Resolved*, That previous to the removal of any Ward twenty-four hours' notice shall be given to the paupers, that they may make preparations ; the Steward or Matron (as the case may be) shall take care that the paupers shall have their breakfasts before they start and every arrangement shall be made for their reception in the New Almshouse in such way as to give them beds and their regular meals.

"That the hours of removal shall be between 6 o'clock A. M. and 12 M., and that not more than 100 shall be removed in one day.

"That two cooks shall be detailed for service in the new house.

"*Resolved*, That the Matron remove to the New Almshouse to-morrow."

The committees were :

1. Messrs. Fraley,	2. Messrs. Day,	3. Messrs. Hemphill,
Hansell,	Woolf,	Keefe,
Earp,	Lancaster,	Keyser,
Burden.	Jones.	Smith.

July 28th, 1834, it was

"*Resolved*, That the President of the Board inform the County Commissioners that after Saturday next the Board will cease to occupy the office on Chestnut street.

"*Resolved*, That the office of the Board of Guardians shall be established at the Spruce Street Almshouse."

"*Resolved*, That the President cause public notice to be given in the daily papers of the occupancy of the New Almshouse and the removal of the office."

"Adjourned to proceed over Schuylkill to meet in the New Almshouse."

The first regularly organized meeting of the Board in the New Almshouse, was held on the 28th day of July, 1834, four years, two months and two days from the time of laying the corner stone. The census of the house at time of removal was 604 men, 407 women and 70 children, a total of 1081.

At the meeting held August 18th, 1834, notice was received of a legacy of $5000 from Mrs. Esther Waters and the Finance Committee was directed to invest the amount in such manner as was deemed best.

It was ordered that the Almshouse on Spruce street should be opened to receive " those of the colored population who have left their homes in consequence of the riots in the lower parts of the city and districts."

On complaint of a member of the Board and the Steward against Dr. John B. Calhoun for a violation of the rules of the house in relation to the examination of the dead, the doctor appeared before the Board, and, after he was heard, the following resolution was adopted:

" *Resolved*, That Dr. John B. Calhoun be requested to tender his resignation to the Board as one of the resident physicians of the Almshouse."

On September 8th, 1834, it was

" *Resolved*, That a road in as direct a route as possible shall be laid out and opened immediately from the landing to the Almshouse and from the Almshouse to the Darby Road, and the Committee of the House be requested to attend to the construction of said road."

The Children's Asylum was not ready to be occupied, and as the old building in which they were quartered would require extensive repair, the Guardians urged the Commissioners to finish the building intended for that purpose as quickly as possible.

On September 29th, 1834, it was resolved that the Board would offer for sale the materials and buildings on the Spruce street grounds at public auction, on the first Monday in November, and will offer for sale the square bounded by Spruce and Pine streets and by Tenth and Eleventh streets, on the second Monday of November next, at public auction, notice to be given in the public papers.

On the day appointed the Committee on Sale of Lots reported the terms of sale: "One-third cash, one-third in one year, and the remaining third in two years, secured by bond and mortgage in the usual way, with interest. If required, after the first payment is made, sixty feet front, running from Spruce to Pine streets, will be released to purchaser, possession to be given in all in February. The buildings and wall to be excluded from the sale of the ground."

Mr. Smith moved to limit the price to be taken for the lot to $115,000. Mr. Day proposed $120,000 and Mr. Hansell suggested $125,000. Mr. Hansell's sum was agreed to.

The ground was knocked down to Mr. Richard Smethurst for the sum of $126,000, but he failed to pay the first installment. Mr. Charles I. Wolbert was the auctioneer who conducted the sale.

After much deliberation it was determined to again advertise the lot for sale, upon the same terms and conditions as the former sale.

When the committee called upon Mr. Wolbert to instruct him to advertise and sell the lot, they learned from him that if the ground was not sold at the second sale he should expect commissions on the first sale from the Guardians, but if it was sold at the second sale he would ask but one commission. The committee referred the matter to the Board for further instructions. In their report they said: "After due consideration of your committee they were at loss to know how to act without further instructions. If the lot is offered and we become the purchasers the question then arises whether we do not release Mr. Smethurst, and if sold for a less price than last time then the question is, whether we can get the difference from Mr. Smethurst. In either case we are liable for the commissions."

Mr. Hemphill moved that the committee wait on Mr. Freeman and arrange with him for selling the lot. Mr. Keyser offered as a substitute that the committee wait on Mr. Wolbert and " say to him that the Board is ready to pay him the commission whenever he hands over the purchase money."

No definite action was taken until February 19th, 1835. It was then resolved " that the terms of sale should be one-quarter cash in ten days, one-quarter payable January 1st, 1836, one-quarter payable January 1st, 1837, and one-quarter payable January 1st, 1838, secured in the usual way, or, if more convenient to the purchaser, any sum not less than $20,000 will be received at any time on account of the Bonds, upon giving fifteen days notice to the Board of Guardians.

"*Resolved*, Unanimously, that the lot be limited to $128,000."

The committee reported that the lot was offered for sale on 19th instant at the Philadelphia Exchange, but was not sold.

It was resolved that a committee of three be appointed who shall be authorized to dispose of the Almshouse Square at a price not less than $130,000.

On March 2d, 1835, the committee reported that the lot had been sold to Mr. A. D. Cash for $130,000. Mr. Cash paid $30,000 and gave the bond of Charles F. Lex and John Gregg, payable to the order of the Guardians of the Poor for $100,000, with a mortgage to secure the payment on January 1st, 1836.

The Commissioners for Erecting the New Almshouse passed a resolution, on April 27th, 1835, to notify the Guardians of the Poor that they " now surrender to them the entire possession of the House of Employment and Women's Almshouse," together with the policies of Insurance.

Notice was given by the Guardians that in accordance with the act of May 5th, 1828, that from and after the 1st of July, 1835, no relief, other than temporary, shall be granted to the out-door poor, and said relief be confined entirely to fuel, provisions, clothing, medical attendance and medicines.

Mr. Wolbert, auctioneer, was paid $714.00 for commissions and expenses attending the sale of the old Almshouse lot.

Mr. Thomas Mitchell bought the old Children's Asylum on Fifth street for $15,000, June 17th, 1835, and the children were removed to the new Almshouse.

The Commissioners had erected four distinct buildings at right angles with each other, inclosing a space of about 700 feet by 500 feet. They were located near the southern line of the property, at about 1,500 feet from the river. The main building fronted on a road, now known as Vintage Avenue, which runs northeast and southwest. This location secured plenty of air and a beautiful outlook.

Scharff & Westcott's history says: "The main building contained a portico 90 feet front, supported by eight columns in the Tuscan order, built of brick and rough cast, and was flanked by two wings, each 200 feet in length. The portico, being elevated on a high flight of steps rising beyond the basement story to those of the principal story, gave to this group of buildings a commanding appearance."

Early pictures show steps extending across the whole front of this portico, similar to those on the United States Custom House on Chestnut Street. That would make it appear as though the main entrance was on the second floor. It will be noticed that the description quoted speaks of the lower story as the "basement," and the second as the principal story. It is not so now, as the porch extends to the front and makes room for an entrance and two offices on the first floor. There are two lines of steps, one on each side of the offices.

The Men's Almshouse was located in the wings of this building, the center being appropriated for dining rooms, clothes room and offices on the first floor, and for the offices of the Board and Superintendent on the second. The Doctor's dining-room, kitchen, etc., are located in the rear of the third. The rest of that floor, together with the attic, is used as apartments for the Superintendent and the domestics required in that part of the House.

The Women's Almshouse was directly opposite the department for males, running parallel to it on the northwestern side of the quadrangle.

At right angles to these buildings, starting at about 100 feet beyond the ends of them, were located the Hospital on one side and the House of Employment on the other. The four main structures were about 500 feet in length and 60 feet in depth. Stone walls connected the buildings, so that the interior space was inclosed. Streets, walks, courtyards, etc., were provided within the inclosure, for the accommodation of the inmates, and the departments were separated by walls supplied with large gates, on the line of the streets, to admit of the passage of wagons, carts, etc.

The interior of the Almshouses was arranged to have two tiers of small rooms or cells in each ward, so that each inmate would have a private sleeping room. This was the dormitory plan that was recommended by the steward of the New York Almshouse and which caused much discussion, the altering of the plans, the halting of the work and additional expense for construction.

These little "cubbies" were built on the side of the wards, one tier over the other; were only about six feet deep and five feet wide; were not properly ventilated, became dirt holes and had a decidedly foul smell after a few years' use.

A ferry was established to carry passengers across the Schuylkill from South Street on the City side to the wharf on the Almshouse grounds. A large batteaux was used for this purpose and a small fare was charged for the service. This was a great convenience for the down town people, as it saved the trip up to the bridge at Market Street.

A bank had been constructed around the river front to protect the meadow land; sluice gates were placed in the bank, to be opened at high tide in the winter season, to flood the meadow for the purpose of obtaining a crop of ice for the use of the institution.

The grounds were inclosed by a wooden fence, and the main entrance was on Darby Road (now Woodland Avenue). A small house was erected close by the gate, in which the gatekeeper resided.

The graveyard was located in the northeastern portion of the grounds. It was inclosed and was under the charge of the ferryman. It was the cause of much scandal in connection with the history of the Almshouse and the " Board of Buzzards," as the Guardians were at one time termed.

The large stone barn and farm house were erected on a high plot of ground in 1836, at a cost of $10,000. The farm house has been used as a children's asylum for a few years, while the old barn had to be removed to accommodate the University of Pennsylvania a short time ago.

A school room was fitted up in the southeastern end of the Hospital building for the use of the children. It was upon the plan of the infant schools of the city; teachers were employed, and the reports say : " The children have made as much progress in learning as could reasonably be expected from pupils under similar circumstances."

On February 6th, 1837, the Commissioners informed the Guardians that they had actually paid on account of the erection

of the new Almshouse, ...	$845,088.30
Paid for the Farm, ...	51,716.94
" on account of Guardians during Cholera, .	1,166.32
" Interest on Copper Bill, . : . .	2,016.44
	$899,988.00
Yet due on Bills rendered, ...	2,182.10
	$902,170.10

They could not state the amount that would be required to finish the work.

The first steward of " Blockley," as the institution was generally called, was Mr. William S. Stockton. In November, 1836, the Board advertised for applicants to fill the position, but they did not succeed in finding a suitable person; so Mr. Stockton was retained, although he was not satisfactory to the Board. Mrs. Sibbert was the first Matron elected.

The name Blockley Almshouse was usually applied to the establishment. There are many people who do not know that it took that name because it was located in Blockley Township. An old woman went to the House, under the influence of liquor, one evening a few years ago. She wanted to be admitted to the Hospital, but the doctor who examined her found that she did not require any medical treatment and refused to assign her to the sick wards. She became very indignant and exclaimed very loudly, " I'd have you to know that Mr. Blockley left his money for the benefit of us poor people and not for a lot of you d—— doctors and the white caps." She applied the term " white caps " to the nurses in the Hospital, and it is evident that she thought that " Mr. Blockley " was a man something like Stephen Girard.

CHAPTER XII.

HOW BLOCKLEY GOT ITS NAME.

IN connection with the name, it may be of interest to state how the township got the name. An article published in a newspaper many years ago stated:

"The first white settler west of the Schuylkill and within the limits of the present city of Philadelphia was Mr. William Warner. This gentleman was a captain in the army of Oliver Cromwell. He was a zealous and devoted friend of the Lord Protector and particularly obnoxious to the royalists. After the death of Cromwell in 1658 and the restoration of the Stuarts, Warner was compelled to fly from his native country in order to save his head. The American wilderness was then the principal refuge of the hunted lovers of liberty, and hither the Puritan captain was glad to escape.

"Before the arrival of Captain Warner, the only white settlers who had penetrated to the region of the Schuylkill were the adventurous Swedes. Warner pitched his tent on the west bank of the Schuylkill, in the vicinity of the present Girard Avenue bridge or a little north of that locality. The precise spot cannot now be determined; but it is certain that the Captain obtained possession of an extensive tract of land in that beautiful "wild," to which he gave the name of "Blockley," in memory of the happy home in England which he was compelled to desert. Twenty-four years elapsed after the arrival of Warner before the emigrants who came to settle Pennsylvania under the grant to William Penn reached the vicinity of the Puritan soldier's cabin. Two years afterward (1684), William Penn confirmed the title of Captain Warner to the land he occupied.

"For twenty years the old soldier was alone in the wilderness, or, rather, he was the solitary white man who resided there and communicated to the Indians ideas of the races and civilizations beyond the sea.

"It is to be regretted that we have no record of his mode of life, his adventures, and his strange experience in his woodland home before the advent of the Quaker colonists.

"Subsequent to that event Captain Warner became possessed of great wealth and obtained social and political influence. He took an active part in organizing the first provincial government of Pennsylvania, served as a justice of the court and was elected a member of the first Assembly chosen under the rule of Governor William Penn.

"Captain Warner died at his residence in Blockley in the year 1706, and was greatly lamented. He retained and exercised the stern virtues of the Puritans throughout his career, was energetic and determined in the maintenance of his convictions and commanded respect by the strength and purity of his character.

"During the latter part of his life he expressed his approval of the peace principles of the Society of Friends.

"A number of the descendants of the captain still reside upon the land which their ancestor acquired, but few or none of them bear his name. Some of his descendants may be found in Bucks County. If the material for a full biography could be collected the life of the pioneer of the Schuylkill would be a most remarkable contribution to our local history. Our sketch is merely to explain the origin of Blockley."

When the new Almshouse and House of Employment had been erected at such cost it was deemed necessary to utilize the pauper labor at the earliest moment, and arrangements were made accordingly. The Committee reported in August, 1836, that the profits of the factory during a single quarter reached the sum of $549.20. The report further said: "Your Committee would remark, that if their exertions to compel all males and females in this institution to work, who may be capable of working, were seconded by the Hospital and House Committees, as well as by the steward and matron, the just expectations of the public, of producing beneficial results by the establishment of an extensive House of Employment will not be disappointed, and our lazy, intemperate vagrants and paupers will become convinced by experience that an

Almshouse is no place in which they will any longer be permitted to indulge their idle, vicious habits, and that it is just as easy to work in mechanics' shops in the City and Liberties and enjoy their liberty, as it is to be confined within these walls and be compelled to work in our factory."

At this time the question of dependent foreigners was a very serious one; the Almshouses throughout the country were burdened with them, and the United States authorities attempted to correct the abuse. Hon. Levi Woodbury, Secretary of the Treasury, communicated with the Boards of Guardians and Overseers of the Poor in reference to the deportation of paupers from foreign countries.

The Guardians, through a committee, made a thorough examination of the inmates of the Almshouse and endeavored to get some proofs to substantiate the charge that they had been sent to this country by the authorities of their homes.

That is a useless task. It is impossible to get a pauper of that kind to tell the truth about the matter. They are afraid of being sent back. It was the case then, is so now, and probably will always be so.

In reply to his inquiries the Board sent to Mr. Woodbury the following report, made to the Guardians by their committee, under date of November, 1836:

"Your committee report that, having caused an examination to be made of the foreign paupers in the House, they have not been able to ascertain that any had been sent to this country or to the British provinces by Overseers of the Poor in England or elsewhere, or had received any aid from any parish to enable them to emigrate.

"The only information having any relation to the subject of inquiry derived from their examination is, that the practice of sending away paupers chargeable to parishes, by *parochial aid*, is quite common in England, and that many have been sent in that way. This practice, however, as far as they profess to be informed, is confined to emigration to the British settlements.

"Your committee would here remark that there is great difficulty in procuring from a pauper any information which might affect himself, and that, should there be in the House any person who had been sent, either to this country or the British settlements, by parochial aid, the apprehension that he would be discharged from the House upon the fact being known, would induce him to conceal it. The reports of the Poor Law Commissioners of England furnish some information as to the deportation of paupers from that country. In the instructions of these Commissioners to their agents in different districts, the attention of those agents is particularly directed to emigration as one mode of relieving the parishes of their superabundant poor population, and thereby reducing the poor rates. They speak of emigration generally, and do not confine it to the British settlements.

" So, in some of the reports made by these agents to the Commissioners, deportation of paupers, by means of parochial aid, is mentioned as having taken place, without naming the country to which they have been sent.

" In some reports the British provinces in North America are mentioned as their places of destination, and from one report it appears that four families had been sent from the parish of Rye to New York.

" These reports comprise but few of the parishes of England and Wales, not more than two hundred parishes out of fifteen thousand; and therefore, while they establish the fact that paupers have been sent from England to the United States, as well as to the British settlements, they do not show the extent to which this practice may have prevailed in that kingdom.

" From the examination made of the inmates of the House, the committee have ascertained that one guinea was paid to each of the paupers brought by one vessel to Quebec, upon their landing at that place; that in some instances one hundred acres of land were offered to each of the paupers, which offer the majority of them declined. In other instances no provision was made for their support, and they subsequently found their way into the United States.

" Among the paupers in this House there are several persons who have been pensioners of the government of Great Britain,

COURT YARD OF MEN'S OUT WARDS.

and their being in this country is attributable partly to the agency of that government."

The conditions in those days were about the same as they are now. There have always been more foreigners supported in the Almshouses than Americans, and so long as the passage costs less than the continual support, just that long will other countries endeavor to dump their paupers on American shores.

The Board of Guardians consisted of Messrs. George W. Jones, John Hemphill, William S. Hansell, John Price Wetherill, Isaac N. Marselis, Peter A. Keyser, John L. Wooly, Michael Day, John Keefe, Isaac Collins, Bela Badger and Joseph B. Smith.

These were all well known citizens and commanded the respect of the community.

It is very pleasant to find that after all the misunderstandings and fault-finding, the labors of the "Commissioners for Erecting Buildings for the Accommodation of the Poor" ended in the most pleasant manner, on the 28th day of August, 1837, and the records show the high regard that the two Boards entertained for each other.

Mr. E. W. Keyser, President of the Commissioners, sent a communication to the Board of Guardians informing that body that "They had fulfilled the duties of their appointment in the erection of the Buildings for the Accommodation of the Poor, and to the best of their ability completed everything delegated to them under the Law whence they derive their power.

"That they hereby resign their functions and have agreed to dissolve the Board, not, however, without expressing the hope that they have the entire approbation of the Board of Guardians of the Poor for their best endeavors.

"That the accounts and vouchers they most cheerfully submit for the examination of the Board at any moment they may desire them.

"That he is further instructed to return the thanks of the members to the Board of Guardians of the Poor for their cordial co-operation at all times during the progress of the work, and for the gentlemanly deportment experienced at their hands."

After the communication was read at the meeting of the Guardians, it was unanimously resolved "That the President of this Board be requested to notify the Commissioners that their resignations are accepted, and also to convey to the said Building Commissioners the thanks of this Board for the attention they have bestowed to the duties entrusted to them."

The Commissioners had performed their labors; they had been in existence nine years, although many changes had taken place in its membership since its organization. Only four of the original twelve remained on the Board, one having died and seven having resigned.

No suspicion of jobbery or peculation was ever attached to the proceedings of the Commissioners; no desire was ever expressed for their abolition. They did their work on a grand scale, and Philadelphia received, as the result of their labors, one of the best and most commodious Almshouses that could be found in the United States at that period.

When it is considered that these buildings were erected to accommodate the people of only a portion of the county of Philadelphia it will be seen that they were sufficiently large for the purpose.

The other districts and townships in the county were compelled to rely upon the Overseer system of relief, or else build almshouses for their own use. Several districts pursued that course.

"The Directors of the Poor and of the House of Employment for the Townships of Oxford and Lower Dublin, of Philadelphia County," were given authority under the Act of April 11th, 1807, to establish an Almshouse, and a farm of 145 acres was purchased and buildings were erected for the purpose.

A corporation was created in 1809, entitled "The Managers for the Relief and Employment of the Poor of the Township of Germantown in the County of Philadelphia."

A lot of ground containing 20 acres was purchased and an Almshouse was established.

The "Guardians of the Poor of Bristol Township" were incorporated in 1823, with authority to purchase ground and to erect a "Poorhouse."

The Township of Roxborough was authorized to build a
" Poorhouse " in 1837.   The Borough of Manayunk was united
with the Township, and the Almshouse grounds embraced 20 acres.

Moyamensing also established an Almshouse, in the early part
of the century, on Irish Tract Lane, below the present Fitzwater
street.   The buildings were of brick and several acres of ground
were enclosed.

The report of the Auditing Committee showed :

Amount paid to order of Commissioners		$909,733 38
" expended—For purchase of ground		51,716 94
" " " erection of buildings		857,969 75
" of total expenditures		909,686 69
" Unexpended balance returned		46 69
Stone quarried by paupers—		
5741 cubic yards, used on roads, @ 75		4,305 75
1500 perch, used in Barn and Walls, @ 88		1,320 00
Stone used for other purposes, valued at		1,500 00
Total valuation		$7,125 75

The collection of " Head money " on arriving emigrants was
an important item of the receipts of the Board of Guardians.   This
was collected under the authority of Law, and was, in a manner,
an insurance against the emigrants becoming dependent upon
charity.   Prior to 1832 the amount collected was $2.50 per head ;
it was then reduced to $1.50 on each one arriving.   The owners
and consignees of the ships that brought them frequently endeavored to evade the payment of this tax, and suits were entered
against them in consequence.   One case that caused considerable
discussion was that of " The Guardians of the Poor *versus* The
Master, Owners and Consignees of the ship St. Cloud."   A writ
was issued, claiming $14,100 as the amount of penalties due to the
Board, and the Sheriff took possession of the ship.

The consignees entered bonds, signed by Samuel Grant, Dex-
ter Stone and George Fales, for the payment of any penalties that
might be adjudged against them.

The testimony showed that the ship was entered at Wilmington, Del., although no part of the cargo was intended to be delivered there, and a portion was intended for and consigned to a mer-
10

chant in Philadelphia. The ship without actually entering the port of Wilmington, breaking bulk, or securing the duties on the cargo there, proceeded to Philadelphia.

The "Head money" on 188 passengers was paid to the Trustees of the Poor at Wilmington, and a license given to land the passengers at that place. All the passengers, however, were not landed; neither were they at any time in Wilmington or its vicinity; they were received on a steamboat from the ship lying in the Delaware River.

They were then taken to Quarryville, a place on the river a few miles from Wilmington, where they stopped a few minutes, and were then transported to Philadelphia. The steamboat was unable to take all of the passengers upon the one trip; the remainder were taken on the down run and conveyed to Wilmington, not for the purpose of landing them, but to remain a short time, so as to run them up to Philadelphia and land them at *night*, as the others had been landed.

The consignors proposed a compromise, which was accepted by the Board, and the case was settled.

The records showed the amounts collected were:

For year ending May, 1829,			. . . .	$6,457.50
"	"	"	1830, ...	4,217.50
"	"	"	1831, ...	9,544.50
"	"	"	1832, ...	9,129.50
"	"	"	1833, ...	5,248.50
"	"	"	1834, ...	3,988.00
"	"	"	1835, ...	4,635.00
"	"	"	1836, ...	2,533.50
"	"	"	1837, ...	3,174.50

Making a total in nine years $48,928.50

John Sergeant, Esq., Solicitor, was asked for his opinion as to the construction of the Act of Assembly in regard to the "Head money" on foreign emigrants. He replied that he thought the "Guardians could elect between imposing a tax of two dollars and a half upon each passenger and taking security that such passenger would not become chargeable."

The minute books show some very queer cases that were referred to the Board of Guardians for consideration. In fact,

women would " throw themselves on the Guardians of the Poor "
for satisfaction and redress under some peculiar circumstances.

The following report of one of the committees will serve to
illustrate the character of some of their little schemes.

The communication of John Enhart, charged by Eliza Worl
with being the father of a child of which she had been delivered,
had been referred to a committee, and the report said : " The said
Eliza Worl is a married woman, with a family of children and a
husband in the United States service, and who was at that time
stationed at the Lazaretto, and who was in the constant practice of
coming to see her, all of which facts she states herself; and your
committee are of opinion that it would be very difficult to convict a
man of being the father of a child by a married woman under such
circumstances ; and that it would be improper at all times to take
any action that would encourage married women to charge other
men than their husbands of being the fathers of any children they
may have ; and that this Board ought at all times discourage all
proceedings that would bastardize the children of married people ;
and inasmuch as Eliza Worl has acknowledged that her husband
was in the habit of visiting her, the child is as likely to be his as
any other person's."

The Board declined to take any action in the matter. As there
is nothing said of any movement on the part of the " injured husband," it might be inferred that he was in a conspiracy with his
virtuous wife to extort money from the victim of the plot.

The panic of 1837 reduced thousands of persons from affluence
to poverty, and but for the Almshouse and the relief extended by
the Guardians of the Poor, many would have starved. Workmen
could not obtain employment and much suffering was the result.
The charitable nature of those who could assist by contributions
was again made manifest, and many were helped without the cases
being made public.

On July 2d, 1838, the Board of Guardians received a communication from the Commissioners of the Township of Moyamensing, expressing the opinion of that Board, " That any arrangement the parties interested can agree upon, by which the Poor laws

of the County of Philadelphia can be made general, equal and uniform, and the poor of this Township be united with those of the City and the Districts interested in the Almshouse at Blockley, would be greatly beneficial to the Township and to the citizens of Philadelphia generally." They notified the Guardians that they had appointed a committee to wait upon them to arrange for a conference in relation to the subject.

In August, 1839, it was discovered that it cost no less than $10,000 per annum to maintain the table for the Steward and the Resident Physicians. The Guardians were astounded, and resolutions were adopted to abolish that expensive supply and to make an addition to the Steward's salary of $500 per annum in lieu thereof. The Resident Physicians paid the sum of $250 for the privilege of serving in the Hospital for the term of one year. It was now changed to $125, and to pay for their board $50. They were compelled to board outside of the institution for a short time after the discovery of the cost was made.

A committee was appointed to inquire into the manner in which meats had been issued during the year, under the supervision of the Steward, and it was found that no less than fifty-four thousand pounds of meats were unaccounted for.

The committee reported: "That, after a tedious and careful examination of the Steward's statements, and making the most liberal allowances that could reasonably be claimed, by adding the largest number of men, at the longest period that said men were employed, the whole amounting to 704 persons, who were 1310 days receiving extra rations, and, if deducted from the true census, leaves 622 persons entitled to ordinary rations. The accompanying account current, made from above statement, shows a deficiency of 54,523¼ pounds of meats for the past year, after deducting four per cent. for draft, amounting to 10,657 pounds, allowing for bones, sixty pounds per week, or 3120 pounds per annum.

"The committee further report, that in the statements number 3 and 4, it is shown by the Steward that 9795 pounds of meat were used more than were used during the preceding year, and the committee are satisfied that the population was 112 less than during the previous fiscal year.   They take the census from an examination of the books.   The above 112 persons, by an equal average, would be entitled to 13,104 pounds of meat during the year, which being added to the 9795 pounds, makes the aggregate of 22,899 pounds, this being the excess of meats used during the last over the preceding year."

Shortly after this report was made, the time to elect the Steward and other officials arrived.   Six members voted for the re-election of Mr. Stockton, as Steward, and it seemed as if they were determined to sustain him whether he was right or wrong.

A number of ballots were taken, and, as no person received a majority of the votes, it was found to be impossible to elect a Steward at that meeting, and the old Steward was instructed by a resolution to continue to perform the duties of the office until a successor could be elected.

The gentlemen who voted for Mr. Stockton were John Price Wetherill, Peter A. Keyser, William S. Hansell, John Keefe, Michael Andress and John Hemphill, and as they were all citizens of standing in the community there must have been some reason for their action, although it was not explained in the minutes. Mr. Stockton continued to serve four years under the resolution, notwithstanding there was strong opposition to his continuance during all that time.   The Guardians did not succeed in electing a Steward until 1843, when Mr. Daniel Smith was chosen for the position.

CHAPTER XIII.

A SUPPLEMENT to the Act entitled " An Act for the Relief
and Employment of the Poor of the City of Philadelphia,
the District of Southwark and the Townships of
Northern Liberties and Penn," was passed and approved
January 15th, 1840.

This repealed so much of the act as prohibited the granting
of outdoor relief in money, under certain conditions. It also repealed the act relating to the appointment and defining the duties
of Directors of Poor Tax, and the Guardians of the Poor were
authorized to " borrow money and levy a poor tax for as much as may
be necessary; provided, that such tax or assessment shall not exceed
the amount now laid for the relief and employment of the poor."

President J. B. Smith called a special meeting of the Board of
Guardians on January 30th, 1841, at which he made the following
statement: " From an examination of the receipts of emigrant
money, it appears that Mr. Alexander Wentz, the Secretary of this
Board, has neglected to pay over to the Treasurer more than six
thousand dollars received by him during the years 1838, 1839 and
1840; that he had not paid upwards of $500, admitted by him to
have been received from the sale of tickets to the clinical lectures
about the first of last December; that it had also been discovered
on that very day, that the Secretary had presented to the Bank
and received the money for three checks drawn by the Treasurer,
and left with the Secretary to be delivered to the persons in whose
favor they were drawn. The checks were: One for $600, drawn
payable to the order of John Friend; one for $195.25, drawn pay-
able to the order of John Price Wetherill; and one for $151.co,
also drawn to the order of John Price Wetherill; that he had called
the meeting at the earliest moment after the discovery of these
things for the purpose of taking into considerarion the deficit and
determining upon what measures should be adopted."

150

The Board directed the solicitor to bring suit forthwith against Mr. Wentz and his surety; and summoned the Secretary to appear before the Board at 9 o'clock on the next morning.

Mr. Wentz appeared as requested, and was asked to explain the deficit that appeared on his books; to inform the Board as to the manner he had disposed of the money he had neglected to turn over, and which he had drawn from the bank; and what amount he had in his possession or under his control. Mr. Wentz made a statement which appeared to the Board to be false and contradictory, and the sheriff was instructed to execute forthwith the capias in his hands. Arrangements were made for pressing the suit against Mr. Wentz and his bondsman, Mr. John L. Wolf, the solicitor being assisted by William M. Meredith, Esq. New orders were drawn for the payment of those persons whose checks had been used by the Secretary, and the official was turned over to the Court.

Shortly after this occurred it was discovered that the trusted Treasurer of the Board was more than $26,000 short in his accounts. Suit was immediately entered against him and his surety, and eventually the Board secured almost the entire sum of his defalcation.

It appears that even in the "good old days" some men who could not resist temptation fell by the wayside.

The increase in population in the Almshouses was a subject of much thought and discussion. It was thought that if the causes of pauperism were known some steps might be taken to check it, at least, if it could not be entirely halted. To arrive at a full knowledge to enable those persons interested to successfully grapple with the subject, communications were sent to the various Boards of Guardians and Overseers of the Poor, requesting such information as they might be able to furnish. In order to make the proper reply to the inquiries propounded the Guardians instructed the House agent at "Blockley" to secure certain data for them, and in compliance with the order he submitted the following instructive report to the Board on August 2, 1841:

"In obedience to the resolution of the Board of Guardians 'making it the duty of the House agent to ascertain and report the number of paupers who have been brought to misfortune by intemperance and vice,' the agent respectfully reports that he has attended to the duty assigned him, and has devoted all the time he could spare from other duties to a personal examination of the Inmates of the House, throughout the different wards, that he has availed himself of all the information on which he could rely, has collected every fact within his reach, and has endeavored to condense the whole, and now presents the following summary which he believes to be substantially correct :

" 'The population of the House may be taken at about 1400, of which 550 are adult males (not including Lunatics), 470 females, 150 children, 90 Insane males, 98 Insane females, 23 Epileptics and 24 Idiots.

" 'To commence with the Hospital : Respecting the men's surgical and syphilitic wards, which together number 86 patients, it may be said that there is not one temperate person in them, and that lewdness and intemperance have pauperized them all.

" 'Of the men's medical wards, containing 56 adults, 40 are now, or have been, intemperate, and are here for that cause. The remaining 16 are temperate at present.

" 'Of the women's surgical and syphilitic wards, containing 40 patients, only 10 are believed to be temperate. Of the remainder it may be said that lewdness and intemperance have brought them to the House.

" 'Of the women's medical wards, containing 60 patients (including the colored wards) only one-half are temperate, and of the others it may be said that habits of intemperance formerly indulged in, either by them or their husbands, have caused their poverty.

" 'It follows, then, that out of 242 adults, male and female, sick in the hospital, only 56 can be set down as temperate, and that habits of lewdness or intemperance, or both, were the causes of their poverty and suffering.

MEN'S AND WOMEN'S ALMSHOUSE.

" ' The various wards of the men's Almshouse, containing 410 adults, have only 48 who can be put down as temperate in their habits, leaving 362 who *are* or *have been* intemperate, and whose destitution may be traced to that cause.

" ' The women's Almshouse contains 184, of whom 40 can be set down as temperate. It has been ascertained that at least 20 of the remaining 144 are *opium eaters*, and the rest are intemperate. Of many of these it should be stated that they are, or have been, mothers of illegitimate children. Lewdness and intemperate habits, therefore, may have been the cause of their impoverishment.

" ' The old women's Asylum numbers 150, the great majority of whom are at *present* decent and orderly, of temperate habits and correct deportment. It has been ascertained, however, that they have not always been orderly and temperate, their moral condition having been greatly improved during the last few years, while in this House. The causes of their misfortune also may be traced either to irregular habits in themselves or others with whom they were immediately connected in former years. There are, no doubt, some exceptions, but their number is not easy to determine. At present it is believed that 50, or one-third of the whole, are temperate, and that the remainder and at least one-half of the others owe their present destitution to the causes above stated and 25 to unavoidable misfortune. This is decidedly the best part of the House.

" ' The men's Lunatic asylum contains at present about 90, one-half of whom are believed to be temperate.

" ' The women's Lunatic asylum number 98, and about the same, if not a greater proportion, are and have been of temperate habits.

" ' Respecting the 150 children in different parts of the House, it may be said that they are generally the offspring of dissolute and intemperate parents, who in very many cases were sent to the county prison while their children were sent to the Almshouse, or they are orphans, made so by the premature deaths of parents, occasioned by following vicious courses.

" ' In conclusion—If the preceding statements are correct, it follows that, of the entire adult population, only 330 persons have any claim to be considered temperate, and that more than one-half of them have only recently become so, if, indeed, they are reformed.

" ' The moral character of the inmates of the House has, however, been gradually improving for the last few years.

" ' The friends of temperance have been exerting a salutary influence among them, and the amount of moral and religious instruction, now almost daily afforded, has greatly increased. A religious association, formed in the house about two years since, is still in existence and flourishing. It numbered at first about 80 members, one-half of whom left the House and gave proof of their reformation by maintaining themselves out of it, not having returned.' " The report was signed by William H. Stewart, Agent.

That document did not speak very highly of the character of the paupers of that period. It could not be believed that the inmates of the Almshouse at the present time are of as low a grade, taken as a whole, as those described, although there are many just as degraded.

The utter lack of discipline and the mismanagement of the institution were very apparent during the time that Steward Stockton had charge. There was not a proper supervision of the internal affairs and the subordinate officials seemed to be allowed to do as they saw fit. If the Steward possessed the authority he should have had, and it is to be presumed that he had, the abuses that existed could not have continued if proper vigilance had been exercised. There appeared to be entirely too much dependence placed upon men who were unworthy of it.

Certain discoveries of mismanagement or worse were made in 1842, which, upon investigation, brought forth a report from the committee, from which the following extracts are quoted:

" Your Committee regret to say that they have found much to censure and condemn. It appears from an examination of Mr. A. S. Hutchinson, Superintendent of Manufactures, he makes no entry whatever whenever anything is sold by him for cash, but puts the money in his pocket. A pass is given by him to the person purchasing, to take the goods out, and, after a lapse of one, two or three weeks, as the case may be, he takes up the passes, and then makes an entry in the books himself or directs Mr. Ross, the clerk, to make one.   He (Mr. H.) then destroys the passes.

"The Committee may further remark that the general management is, in many cases, loose and unjustifiable, and calls loudly for a more efficient system.

"It appears, from the testimony before the Committee, that the Superintendent is in the habit of drawing his supplies of flour, cornmeal, potatoes, tinware, shoes, hard and soft soap, tubs, buckets, carpeting, towels and feed for a large stock of chickens and pigeons, and sometimes goats, and in some instances such articles as bedspreads and muslin, from the supplies belonging to the institution, all of which the Committee supposed to be contrary to the agreement made with him.   On his examination, Mr. Hutchinson first admitted only that he received flour for pies when there was good flour in the mill, but afterwards, on a close examination, he admitted that he drew all his flour at all times from the mill, when there was any flour in it, stating that he believed he had been authorized to do so by Mr. Keefe, and also believed that it was done with the knowledge of the present Committee.   He also stated that he bought his potatoes, except that he might have received a peck or a half-peck or some small quantity of them. This assertion he reiterated on the question being put to him a second or third time, so that he might fully understand its import.

"The Committee are constrained to say, from the testimony of Captain Kelly, who has charge of the potatoes, that Mr. Hutchinson is in the constant habit of receiving from him his supplies by the bag full whenever there are potatoes for distribution in the House.   This is confirmed by three other witnesses who have knowledge of the deliveries.

"Finding Mr. Hutchinson so uncandid in his denial of a fact so well established before the Committee, they have little confidence in his denial of many other things which have been well established before them, and they are induced to believe, from the general tenor of the evidence, that he obtains his supplies generally, for the use of his family, from those belonging to the institution."

The Board notified Mr. Hutchinson that his services would be dispensed with. The clerk was also discharged.

An Act was passed in May, 1844, providing "for the admission of the Township of Moyamensing to participate in the advantages and privileges of the institution at Blockley."

The management, or rather the lack of it, in the medical department of the institution was the cause of much dissatisfaction on the part of the Guardians in 1845. One of the reports of the Hospital Committee said, "That the existing conditions do not in many respects meet the approbation of your Committee." It referred to the rules providing for four physicians, four surgeons and two accouchers who served gratuitously, and further said, "Nearly all the gentlemen at present holding these situations are connected with the medical schools of the city as Professors or Lecturers, and for about four months of the year attend regularly at the Hospital, for the purpose of lecturing to their classes." The sick patients were taken from their wards to the lecture room to "undergo examinations for the purpose of furnishing subjects for the lectures." None of the patients are exempt from the liability of being thus exposed. This connection of the Almshouse Hospital with the medical schools, in consequence of the facilities it affords for clinical instruction, interesting surgical operations and post mortem examinations is, no doubt, of no small value to the schools, but as our interests in them do not predominate over the interest we feel in the discharge of duty towards the poor, as their legal Guardians, we cannot admit the propriety of the connection.

"Without attaching any censure to the skilful and learned gentlemen who officiate in this capacity for anything wrong in the *manner* of performing these duties, we nevertheless hold that our sanction of the thing itself is altogether unjustifiable. There are rights possessed even by the recipients of charity which should be guarded, and feelings which should be respected.

"At this time there were eight young resident physicians on duty for one-year terms. They were supposed to be under the directions of the Visiting Staff, and under the rules they were not allowed to prescribe, unless in a case of emergency. It was said that the rules were not complied with, and that the residents, recently from school and anxious to practice, often rather unduly elated with the first honors of the Doctorate, are placed at once, and while totally inexperienced, in situations of the highest responsibility, in charge of a Hospital often containing 500 patients, subject only to such limited control as the attending physicians see fit to exercise; or rather such as the residents themselves are willing to submit to.

"Whether it is consistent with our duty towards these unfortunate inmates of the Hospital to place them in charge of mere novices who never had a case before entering its wards, may be questioned."

This report caused much thought, and before a final conclusion was arrived at, another report from the Committee showed the unruly spirit of the resident physicians and brought on a change in that department. The report stated that the "Resident Physicians had relinquished their charge of the sick in the Hospital, without having given any previous intimation of their intentions." The reason assigned was that they would not board with the steward, as required by the rules. The sick in the wards were thus left without medical attendance, which might have proved fatal to some of them.

A resolution was adopted by the Board dismissing Doctors Keating, Higginbottom, Porter, Jones, Farquharson, Sherrard, Mason, Brent and Haines from the institution, and authorizing the Hospital Committee to make temporary arrangements to secure medical attendance for the patients.

A special meeting was held on the following day when a communication was received from the offending physicians, in which they announced their readiness to perform the duties of their positions, and stating that they only desired redress of their grievances in regard to the steward.

The steward, the dismissed physicians and the nurses were summoned to appear before the Board, and an investigation commenced.

The steward, Mr. Daniel Smith, who had succeeded Mr. Stockton, made a statement, and Dr. Keating gave his version of the difficulty.

It appeared that a lady who ate at the same table with the steward and doctors complained of the deportment and language of the physicians, after the nuisance had become intolerable, and they were rebuked for their violations of propriety. The doctors attempted to represent the steward as being a man of offensive manners and meddlesome inclinations, but they did not succeed.

Those who knew Mr. Smith spoke of him as " being always amiable and gentlemanly in his intercourse with those connected with the institution."

The Board declined to re-instate the physicians who had been dismissed.

The doctors who had been discharged published a statement in the *Ledger*, in which they not only attempted to justify their actions, but assailed the Guardians, and insinuated charges impeaching the integrity and moral character of some of the members of the Board. The vacant positions were soon filled.

Another report from the Committee said:

" A building is provided as a depository during the interval between death and interment. An official is constantly stationed to guard it, and rules of the most stringent character have been adopted for the safe keeping of the bodies and to preserve them unmutilated in cases where the friends of the deceased can be found. A messenger is always dispatched forthwith to inform the relatives or friends of the deceased, in order that they may have an opportunity of removing the body ; and it has always been enjoined on the Resident Physicians and students never to make any examinations, unless with the express permission of the friends. In other cases, where there are no known friends, or where they cannot be found, although there are no rules prohibiting the examination of the bodies, yet it has been well understood that such examinations should not be made oftener than necessary, and always with a strict regard to decency and propriety. A recent instance might be cited to show the little heed given to the first injunction and the utter disregard to the second will be sufficiently established by mentioning the fact that within a few days, two members of the Board happening to enter an unfrequented, and, as they supposed, an unoccupied part of the building, discovered the mutilated remains of a human body, in a condition too revolting to be described. Appearances indicated that the remains had been there for several months, and we suppose they had been overlooked."

The conditions described by these reports called for immediate action; the committee recommended the election of a Chief Resident Physician and Assistants, to be paid for their services, to reside on the premises, and to have entire charge of the Medical Department of the House.

The recommendation was adopted, and Dr. H. S. Patterson was elected Chief Resident Physician, at a salary of $1800 per annum.

The following consultants were also chosen: Dr. Wm. Byrd Page, Consulting Surgeon ; Dr. Meredith Clymer, Consulting Physician ; Dr. N. D. Benedict, Consulting Accoucher. They were each to receive $100 a year for their services.

CHAPTER XIV.

A PROTEST, signed by six members of the Board, regarding the graveyard, was presented on November 10th, 1845. In it the statement was made that "the practice of taking the bodies from the graveyard to the Lecture rooms had prevailed for years."

In reply to the argument that the schools must have bodies and that obstacles placed in the way of their procuring them would be injurious to the interests of science, the protest said: "This should have no weight with us, inasmuch as the duties of the Board are limited to the relief and employment of the poor, the Board sustaining the same relation to the people under its charge that the head of a family does to the members of it. That the same kind, if not the same degree of care should be exercised, and that it has no right to seek the promotion of other objects which interfere with the proper performance of these duties."

It had been said that "as paupers are of no use to society while living, there is no wrong done in making them useful when dead." The protest answered that by saying: "If the basis of this argument was true, the inference would be shocking. What then should be said of it in the face of the fact that many of them during the principal part of their lives, and until old age or sickness overtook them, supported themselves and families, often under the most difficult and trying circumstances, in a creditable and respectable manner, who have been useful members of society and who have as keen sensibilities in regard to decent interment and safety of their remains as any other people. But we are not willing to admit that even in the case of the most depraved, the Board would be excusable in conniving at any violations of the grave. Few, and perhaps none, are so deadened in feelings as not to desire the rites of Christian burial, for who would not revolt at the idea,

160

GARDEN IN CENTER OF COURT YARD OF MEN'S OUT WARDS.

if they were consulted on the subject, of permitting their bodies to be exposed in the lecture rooms, cut to pieces for the benefit of the schools and then thrown into a pit containing the remains of hundreds of others.   All look to the Guardians for protection; no distinction is practical or expedient.

" To trifle with or disregard these feelings is a cruelty altogether unjustifiable.

" If the advancement of medical science be a sufficient plea for this, why might it not be as well applied as an apology for the infliction of bodily torture, for it is questionable whether that would be a serious cruelty, compared with the goading of the mind to agony by the horrible apprehensions of such a fate to await the body after death.

" That it occasions dread and anxiety in the minds of some of the inmates of this House, is a well known fact.   They are fully aware, or at least many of them are, that burial here, during the lecture season, is a mockery, and to be buried elsewhere is sometimes asked as the last and greatest favor.

" It is not to be supposed that these fears and exciting anxieties do not produce evil effects on the sick and often diminish the chances of recovery, for they haunt them until the last hour of life and increase in terror as the moment of dissolution approaches.

" And may not this anxiety to have the remains cared for and protected after death be partly produced by the idea that the spirit may continue to be cognizant of what is done to the mortal part ? *That death does not mean a total disconnection ?*

" The evils complained of and the wrong done admit of a remedy which should be instantly applied.   Justice and common humanity forbid that the bodies of the poor should be treated in a manner which the law allows only in the cases of the worst felons.'·

This subject was the cause of much discussion, but no immediate action was taken, as the majority of the Board of Guardians contended " that the colleges must have subjects," and that if the supply from the Almshouse was cut off, the bodies would be stolen from the cemeteries; and that it was better that those who died without friends or relatives to mourn for them should go to the

11

dissecting rooms than that the doctors should have the graves, in which so many living persons felt an affectionate interest, *robbed of their contents.*

This question was not settled for many years, and was the cause of much scandal. Certain people, who had an *interest* in the *bodies*, spoke of the sentiments embraced in the protest as "mawkish sentimentality," but the community at large did not agree with them.

A nurse named Welsh left the institution in 1848 under peculiar circumstances, and a committee investigated the matter. The report stated "Nurse Welsh left her duties on Saturday, August 15th; came on the afternoon of Monday, 17th, and a case of labor occurring at that time was attended to by her. She left again that same evening, and returned on Wednesday, the 19th. She received her month's wages from the Steward, which he paid her by order of Mr. William Abbott, a Guardian, although it was not due. She took away from the House with her two loads of goods, one of which the Steward saw. He found that it contained a box, a part of a bedstead, some chairs and four or five trunks, the contents of which were unknown. The other load he did not examine, as he was relieved of that duty by the pass of Mr. Abbott. Neither the Steward, Matron or Doctor knew anything of Nurse Welsh's intention to leave until the Saturday afternoon she left, when Mr. Abbott mentioned it to the Matron as he was passing through her department. There was no nurse or competent assistant left in charge of the ward, and as there were at least four patients there requiring constant and special attention, they must have suffered considerably from neglect. Several flat irons are missing, and a large box containing bed clothing cannot be satisfactorily accounted for. The Steward, at the request of Mr. Abbott and some other members, took down the bedstead that Nurse Welsh took away.

"Your Committee have therefore come to the following conclusion: that the rules and practices of this Board have been grossly violated, not only by the nurse who left her duties prematurely, without giving proper notice to the Committee, and at a time when her services were much needed, but also by the member who assisted her in getting her goods from the House, without the possibility of the Steward or the Matron knowing who the said goods belonged to."

The Board dropped the matter, much to the relief of Mr. Abbott.

To show the character of Nurse Welsh, it need only be said that she was afterwards sent to the Penitentiary for throwing vitriol in a young man's face and destroying his sight.

This Mr. Abbott was soon mixed up in other affairs which did not reflect much credit on him, to say the least.

John Wistar, an inmate of the House, died, and Mr. Abbott, without consulting his colleagues, notified the Coroner that the death occurred under suspicious circumstances, and asked for an inquest to be held.   The newspapers took the matter up and reflections were cast upon the management of the institution and the Chief Resident Physician, Dr. Benedict (he having succeeded Dr. Patterson) in particular.

The Board thoroughly investigated the matter, and adopted the following preamble and resolutions, which were published in the daily papers in November, 1848:

" WHEREAS, The Board of Guardians was apprised by the certificate of the Coroner and by certain publications in the newspapers that an inquest had been held on the body of John Wistar, late an inmate of the Almshouse, who died in the drunkards' ward of that institution ; and

" WHEREAS, The several publications alluded to, and the certificate of the Coroner, contained severe strictures upon the rules for the government of the institution, and upon the conduct of its officers ; it was, on motion,

" *Resolved*, That this Board do proceed to make a full and careful examination of everything connected with this matter ; and,

" WHEREAS, This Board has been made fully acquainted with all the circumstances of the case, by a careful examination of all the persons who had any connection with the said deceased, after his last return to this House, and is satisfied that great injustice has been done to the institution and its officers by the publications and certificate; therefore, it is deemed proper for the Board to state fully the conclusions to which it has arrived, viz.: That there was nothing in the condition of John Wistar, at the time of his return to this House; nor in his confinement of forty-eight hours; nor in his sickness; nor in his death in this House, which in the slightest degree justified Mr. William Abbott, one of the members of this Board, in sending for the Coroner.

"That this Board cannot but view with serious regret and disapprobation the examination by the Coroner, which, to say the least of it, was limited, and extraordinarily limited, inasmuch as he declined to examine the Chief Resident Physician, who attended the case, although notified that he was in waiting in an adjoining room, and permitted the jury to make up their verdict from an examination of the Steward, Doorkeeper and Cellkeeper, neither of whom pretend to know anything about the cause of Wistar's death, and extraordinary as it resulted in a statement of 'death from inflammation of the bowels,' without any consultation with the attending physician, or post mortem examination.

"That the statement in one or more of the newspapers that John Wistar had been confined in the lock-up thirty-six hours longer than the usual time of punishment is untrue. He was confined but forty-eight hours, and after that time had the freedom of the Ward, halls and yards, as all the other patients had. His punishment was by order of the Steward, who alone has the power in such cases. That the evidence conclusively shows the death of Wistar to have been caused by an excessive debauch of seven or eight days, operating upon a constitution broken down by long-continued intemperance. That this Board do declare that they have not been able to discover the slightest ground for censure against the Medical Staff or any other officer of the House."

Dr. N. B. Leidy was the Coroner at that time, and he subsequently sent a note to Dr. Benedict, in which he said, "The certificate contains a small portion of the cause of death."

Dr. Benedict paid no attention to this half apology.

This was the same Mr. Abbott who was connected with the singular departure of Nurse Welsh. After the Board had so generously overlooked his actions in that affair he certainly did not show any gratitude for their leniency. It was very small, on his part, to raise all this trouble and scandal about nothing.

An old newspaper, in speaking of this gentleman, said : " With the entrance of Mr. Abbott into the Board of Guardians commences the degeneracy of the management of the Almshouse. From that time various individuals were elected Guardians, who, without attending to any private business, or receiving any *legal* emoluments, contrived to make a living out of it."

Here commenced the scandals which ultimately resulted in the reorganization of the Board upon a better basis.

The arrangements for heating and ventilating the Insane Department were very poor in 1849. Stoves were used for furnishing heat, but they did not accomplish the object. The poor unfortunates in that part of the institution suffered severely with the extreme cold. No one could imagine the effect it would have on them to be confined in wards where the temperature was below the freezing point; it certainly would not assist in their recovery. Feeble, demented creatures, whose bodies were not always properly covered with suitable clothing, could not endure it as well as the strong, healthier people, although it must have been very trying to all in the place.

The Board instructed Dr. Benedict to make tests with thermometers and to report the results. In February he presented a statement, in which he said : " On the first floor of the west wing of the Women's Lunatic Asylum, at about 9 o'clock A. M., found that a towel which a nurse was using to wipe one of the patients, in one of the cells, had frozen. The patient was a very delicate woman, and altogether unfit to be placed in such a temperature.

" This morning one of the patients was found under the bed, on the floor, wrapped up in the bedclothes. All water in the room was frozen. The thermometer then stood at from 13 to 18 degrees. On the same day, at 2 o'clock P. M., the thermometer stood at 27 degrees in the cells, and 24 degrees in the open air. In the cell nearest the stove, and with the door standing open, within three or four feet of the stove, the thermometer indicated a temperature below the freezing point. The bed clothes upon which water was spilled were constantly frozen during the severe weather."

What a horrible condition. In these days if the thermometers registered below 70 degrees reports of insufficiency of heat would soon be made, and would be remedied immediately.

The committee recommended a plan for heating that part of the House by steam, and the Board promptly approved it, and took the proper steps to introduce the improvement.

The Board appeared to be afflicted with certain members who did not appreciate the courtesy due to their colleagues, or were ignorant of the proper course to pursue to accomplish their objects. Mr. Thomas Stewart was evidently one of that class, as the action taken by the Guardians on a resolution offered by Mr. Gilpin, on April 9th, 1849, would seem to show.

The resolution as presented read :

" *Resolved*, That our fellow member, Mr. Thomas Stewart, foreman of the late Grand Jury, who made their presentment on the 27th of March last, be requested to present to this Board a plan for the better government and employment of a class of our inmates, alluded to in said inquest, said class being designated as a 'number of strong, healthy and able-bodied persons, of both sexes, without employment, idly lounging away their time throughout the premises ; and also in the factory are to be seen a large number of the same description of men, employed in picking oakum, earning from two to five cents per diem.' "

Mr. Fell moved to add the following :

" And if, as he stated, the above suggestions were made in a respectful manner, what is the explanation of the following paragraph, which occurs in the presentment alluded to? 'And in place of devoting their time and energies, and, as it were, warping the institution to serve particular selfish ends of a doubtful policy, at variance with its general principles, economy and usefulness, and that have a tendency to distract the harmony, efficiency and united action of their own body.' "

The Board adopted the resolutions and agreed to make reply to the Grand Jury's presentment. Mr. Stewart had no plan to suggest, as he had been requested to do.

To take advantage of his position as Foreman of the Grand Jury to impeach the conduct of his colleagues, was, to say the least, a display of very bad taste.   If he knew of anything that was wrong in the management, it was his duty to call the attention of the members of the Board to the facts and endeavor to have it improved.   His method not only brought discredit upon the Board, of which he was a member, but was a reflection upon himself and a proof of neglect of duty.

The Board made the following answer to the Grand Jury's presentment.

" The Grand Jury for April session in their presentment say : ' The Hospital Building, erected with especial regard to the necessities of the sick, with airy and pleasant apartments, opening on a cheerful garden, has been converted into a receptacle for a comparatively small number of idiots and generally incurable lunatics, while the great mass of the sick are crowded into apartments in the factory buildings and elsewhere.   None of these rooms on the first floor have sufficient ventilation, opening on a few feet of barren yard, and a blank high wall.   It is certainly desirable that the insane should have every necessary comfort and convenience, but not at the expense of human life, and the sacrifice of the original intention of the institution.'

" This language distinctly charges that the patients in the lunatic asylum are comparatively a small number, or *one-thirtieth* of the sick ; that, for the accommodation of the former, the latter have been removed from their airy and pleasant quarters and *crowded* into other places, and that the change has been made at the expense of human life   The Guardians, in refutation of these allegations and without commenting on the reckless ignorance or active malevolence which alone could have prompted them, submit a few facts.   In the first place, the number of persons of unsound minds in the lunatic department, instead of being small in comparison with that in the hospital—instead of being *one-thirtieth*, as averred in the presentment—is in fact greater, the number in the insane department being 390, while that in the hospital is 349.

"In the next place, these 349, or whatever number may at any time require medical or surgical aid, instead of being crowded, as the presentment alleges, by the change of their apartments, have had their accommodations extended and their means of comfort proportionately increased. In the building formerly occupied by the sick there were 12 wards, each 44x40 feet, or 1,760 square feet each, containing 228 beds; 6 wards, each 22x40 feet, or 880 square feet each, containing 56 beds; 1 attic, containing 40 beds—making a total of 324 beds. The present hospital consists of 11 wards, each 47x44 feet, or 2,068 square feet each, containing 220 beds; 9 wards, each 47x22 feet, or 1,034 square feet each, containing 90 beds; 6 wards, each 32x25 feet, or 800 square feet each, containing 42 beds; 2 attics, containing 80 beds—making a total of 432 beds.

"Thus, in the opinion of the Grand Jury, the patients were amply provided for in the old hospital, where in the wards less than 93 square feet were allowed each bed; but are crowded at the expense of human life in the new hospital, where more than 104 square feet are allowed for the same purpose.

"The classification of the insane was not the only object proposed to be accomplished by this change, the proper treatment of the patients also required it. Before any change had been effected, the building used as a hospital for the sick, from the increase of patients, had become totally inadequate for the purpose, and from a necessity which was regularly increasing other and better accommodations for them had to be provided.

"To effect this, either the interior of the large buildings forming the wings of the old hospital, which had been arranged at a heavy expense for the use of the lunatics, must have been entirely remodeled to fit them for the sick, and other and costly arrangements made elsewhere for the lunatics, or the present more economical, and in all respects the more suitable plan, adopted.

"It appears, from the statement before given, that by the change of the hospital for the sick the Guardians have been enabled to increase the number of beds precisely one-third, and have effected this not by the sacrifice of space or room, but, on the contrary, have greatly increased it.

"It will be perceived that the wards in the old hospital contained but 26,300 square feet. The present hospital has 36,854 square feet in the wards, and in addition it has 16 rooms 32x16 feet, used as operating rooms, bath rooms, nurses' rooms, dining rooms, kitchen, etc. The former and present hospital are parallel to each other, forming the opposite sides of a hollow square, and consequently have the same exposures. The second and third stories are very pleasant and airy, and command a fine view of the city.

"The ventilation of the first floor is little, if any at all, obstructed by the wall inclosing the yard. The removal, however, of the sick and dying from the former quarters, where they were in the immediate proximity of raving maniacs, whose howls and screams rang in their ears by day and by night, more than compensate for minor inconveniences, even if such exist. That the change complained of was made 'at the expense of human life,' or even of the discomfort or inconvenience of the paupers is therefore utterly untrue.

"The Guardians cannot forbear expressing their deep regret that men, acting under the responsibilities of their oaths or affirmations, should have been induced by any influence to make representations so evidently groundless that even the slight opportunity afforded by their short visit, if properly improved, would have prevented them from making.

"Although not directly required by any remarks of either of the grand juries, it may be well, as explanatory of the difficulties which the Board has had to encounter, and of the probable influences which produced these presentments, to refer briefly to the history of the lunatic asylum. The buildings originally intended for lunatics were constructed upon plans adopted by commissioners appointed for the purpose, and approved by the then existing Board of Guardians. In those days it seems to have been considered that humanity discharged its whole duty to these, the most unfortunate of her family, when she prevented them from inflicting injury upon themselves or others, and cells, high walls, straightjackets, tranquilizing chairs, ring-bolts, fetters and manacles were the favorite preventatives. With these views, and having reference to the number of this class, then a charge upon the public, the commissioners, no doubt, thought that they made sufficient provisions when they caused 120 cells to be erected for their accommodation. In 1834, when the cells were first occupied, there were 92 persons to become inmates of them. But when more correct and benevolent views of their condition and their demand upon society prevailed, when it became more generally understood that no matter to what extent they were bereft of reason, that they were neither wild beasts to be caged nor felons to be chained, but human beings, having claims upon our sympathies and care in proportion to their afflictions, susceptible of treatment and not unfrequently of cure; then the apartments provided were found entirely inadequate.

" The number of these patients since 1834 has been constantly, greatly and ever fearfully increasing. In 1834 the number of new admissions was 68; in 1841, seven years afterwards, the number had increased to 202; and in 1848, after another period of seven years, the new admissions amounted to 287. On the 16th of July, 1834, when the asylum was opened for their reception, the number under care and treatment was 92; on the 1st of January, 1849, it was 375. It is therefore obvious that the limited buildings constructed upon the principle designated were not merely useless, but positively injurious. This great number, until recently, were from necessity thrown together, without regard to the peculiar character or producing cause of their fearful malady, the raving maniac with the weak-minded and partially insane, the confirmed and incurable with the recent and probably temporarily deranged. Any attempt at classification was defied, treatment was helpless and cure impossible.

" In reference to these evils the Grand Inquest for March, 1845, says: 'The system is a dreadful one, and a brief residence among the uncontrollable mad may alone suffice, sympathetically or from fear, to establish forever the disorder in one, who, differently situated, might be restored to health and reason.'

" Thus this and other Grand Juries, in 1845, and earlier, were earnestly pressing the changes that a Grand Jury in 1849 has thought proper to condemn.

" The Guardians, however, needed not the promptings of a Grand Jury. They had seen and deplored these evils, but there were difficulties to encounter and obstacles to overcome before a remedy at all commensurate with the necessities of the case could be carried into execution. The opposition of some who were slow to believe that a mind diseased could be administered to, or that a disordered intellect might be restored to its healthy exercise, and of others who balanced the removal of any amount of human suffering against the possible increase of a poor rate, for a time retarded the adoption, and has since attempted to harrass and perplex the execution of a remedy urgently required by humanity and sanctioned by enlightened economy.

" The Board will no longer conceal that at every step they have encountered the opposition, degenerated at last into personal hostility, of an active and untiring minority. That of this minority the gentlemen who were Foremen of the two last Grand Juries form part, and the presentments of these Juries are but weak dilutions of the tirades that for a time amused, until their repetition disgusted the Board.

" The Grand Jury for February recommended, ' That all labor, nursing, attendance, etc., that is required in and about the establishment should by all means, so far as is possible, be done by the inmates of the house." So far as it is possible, and at the same time be *consistent with decency*, this at the present time is the practice. In but one department—that of the lunatic females—has pauper attendance and nursing, to any extent, been dispensed with with, and the recommendation of the Grand Jury can have no other meaning than that the Board should, in this department, return to the practice that formerly prevailed.

" It may be premised that pauper labor is little to be relied on, even with the most careful and continued supervision, and for nursing and attention to the sick should not be employed. It is true that poverty, disease, age and decrepitude bring to the Almshouse some who merit much better provision than public charity affords, but from these nurses and assistants can seldom be taken. The duties of these persons require health and strength to discharge, and they are necessarily taken from those who have been cured of diseases brought on by their own vile and vicious habits. These, for the most part, are persons whose companions are the most abandoned, whose haunts are the most degraded, and whose lives are about equally divided between those haunts, the Almshouse and the prison. They are detained against their will, they work reluctantly without hire, they are insensible to praise and have no fear of punishment. They perform no labor which they can avoid, and do nothing right that is easier to do wrong.

"The female lunatic department was formerly under the charge of a male superintendent, assisted by two male paupers from the class above described, who slept among the female patients, and by several female paupers, perhaps still more degraded and abandoned than the men. The duties of the men were among the most violent patients, who destroyed their clothing and stripped naked their persons, and whose ablutions, when performed, were done by the men.

"Some of the patients, even in their madness, shrunk from this rude handling, and raved with increased fury at their indecent exposure. Revolting to decency as this practice was, it was not without difficulty and only by degrees that it was abandoned. At present no males are employed in the female lunatic asylum. The patients are classified, having a hired female superintendent over each division, with female inmates of the house as assistants.

"The substitution of these paid superintendents for male paupers to take care of these wretched and helpless women is what the Grand Jury desire should be abolished, and upon the ground of economy recommend that the paupers should again be employed as the only nurses and attendants. Even on this ground the Grand Jury are mistaken. The whole increase of salary consequent upon the change is $650 per annum; which is more than compensated for by the saving from waste, destruction and plunder of pauper labor with imperfect supervision. We must assure the Grand Jury that we cannot adopt their recommendation. If the public desire a return to the former barbarous management of this department, they must procure other agents, if they can, for the accomplishment of their desire.

"We do not believe, however, that, even among the members of this Grand Jury who have been so imposed upon, more than one can be found willing to aid them.

"The Grand Jury of February was much surprised at seeing so many strong, healthy and able persons of both sexes without employment, idly lounging away their time throughout the premises.

"In reply to a resolution of the Board calling upon the Steward for information on this subject, he makes report 'that there are very few able-bodied men in the institution. Persons not intimately acquainted with the inmates would, upon a casual observation, suppose that there were many such; but upon a close examination it will be found that nearly all are afflicted in some way or another; that the cooks, bakers, butchers, woodmen, coal carriers, messengers, ward-keepers, etc., all have their several duties to perform, which does not occupy all of their time, yet so much of it as to prevent them from being engaged in anything else. When their work is done they assemble in groups in different places.'

"This also leads to the impression on the minds of such casual observers as the Grand Jury that they are a number of healthy, able-bodied men and women unemployed. It is but justice, however, to add that the Grand Jury visited at a season of the year when the House is crowded with the most improvident if not the most vicious, who seek shelter from the winter. But very few of them are acquainted with any mechanical occupation at which they can be engaged, and at this season of the year it is difficult to find continuous employment for such a number upon the farm and grounds. This also may have contributed to lead the Jury into the error of saying what they did.

"All persons, however, able to work are provided with employment suitable to their condition. That which is the most profitable or useful to the institution is of course selected. If the ability or condition of the pauper does not qualify him for such employment, then the least expensive is resorted to, and rather than suffer any one to be idle, they are put to picking oakum, of which this very Grand Jury complains.

"It appears that there were at the time 756 male paupers, 449 of which were patients in the hospital, lunatic asylum and incurable wards, and 67 were nurses, assistants, etc.; leaving 240 as a balance. There were 162 of these employed as farmers, gardeners, carpenters, weavers, tailors, shoemakers, etc., and the other 78 worked around the kitchens, store-rooms, etc.

"The Guardians may here be permitted to remark that if the Foreman of this Grand Jury, who is also a Guardian of the Poor, and sworn or affirmed diligently to perform his duty as a Guardian, knew or believed that the presentment, written by himself in this particular was true, it was his duty to have brought the matter before the attention of the Board, who alone could rectify the abuse, if any existed. Since the publication of the presentment the Board has, by resolution, in a very respectful manner, and with perfect sincerity, requested him to submit a plan of more economical government of the institution, and of a more profitable employment of the labor of the inmates. From want of leisure, disposition or ability, he has not complied with this request.

"The Guardians believe that the Grand Inquest for April had been imposed upon, when they say 'from facts which came to their knowledge, they are convinced that persons confined in the cells (for punishment) suffer for want of medical attendance.' It seems strange that such facts should have come to their knowledge during one short visit, and yet have entirely escaped the observations of the Guardians, who, either as a Board or in committees, are at the Almshouse three times in every week.

"The Guardians have no doubt that these pretended facts are the allegations of the Foreman of the Jury, which had been faithfully investigated by the Board, and ascertained to have no other foundation than his implacable hatred to an officer of the institution, by whose suggestions and under whose direction many of the most humane and important improvements have been accomplished.

A conclusion the Grand Jury would have arrived at, had it the means and opportunity of making an investigation.

"The Board of Guardians would be gratified by, and invite the attendance of the municipal authorities of the city and the districts embraced in this corporation, and of all citizens who feel an interest in the many difficult, onerous and important matters committed to the management of the Board."

Published by order of the Board.

WM. G. FLANAGAN, *President.*

SAMUEL J. ROBBINS, *Secretary.*

CHAPTER XV.

PHILADELPHIA was again visited by cholera in 1849, and, as a consequence, something like a panic prevailed among all classes. The first three cases occurred on the 30th of May.

One of the victims was an Irish emigrant, who arrived in New York from England a few days before. The disease had been raging in Europe in 1848, and probably the man contracted it there. The other two were men employed on a canal boat at Port Richmond. They all died on the day they were attacked.

Owing to the prevalence of the disease in Europe, the Board of Health endeavored to place the city in a favorable condition to avert, as much as possible, the consequence of an epidemic. Particular attention was paid to cleansing, sewerage and the removal of all nuisances; the gutters were flushed constantly with a free use of water, and the School Controllers were requested to give a vacation to the children during the epidemic, and to give the use of some of the school buildings for hospitals. They refused both requests.

The city hospitals were opened in Cherry, Pine and South streets; in the county at Bush Hill, Moyamensing, Southwark, Northern Liberties, Kensington, Richmond and West Philadelphia.

The number of cholera patients admitted to these hospitals was 344, and the deaths numbered 111. The whole number of deaths in the city and county from the 30th of May to September 8th, was 1012.

There were no cases in the Almshouse until June 27th, about four weeks after the disease broke out in the city.

A special meeting of the Guardians was held on the 13th of July, at the request of the Mayor; ways and means were discussed at length, but as the members of the Board had confidence in the ability and fidelity of the Medical Staff they declined to accept the services of additional physicians. The mortality in the Almshouse was much greater than elsewhere, as the most of the persons attacked were generally of broken down constitutions, or weak or feeble.

The death-roll of one week reached the alarming figures of 100 in a population of 1,546; all kinds of exaggerated reports were circulated, and it was feared that it was even worse. During the following week the deaths were 99 in a population of only 1,358. The ravages of the disease diminished rapidly from that time, and during the week ending August 7th there were only 58 deaths in the Almshouse.

The medical men, nurses and most of the persons employed at Blockley worked hard and intelligently, and the speedy mastery of the disease can be attributed to their efforts.

The city at large did not suffer as heavily as was anticipated, owing to the prompt and wise measures of the Board of Health.

In the following December the special committee made a complete and interesting report, in which it was stated: "That the epidemic first appeared in the institution on June 27th. A colored man, named William Jones, was admitted into the black men's medical ward from the city on that day and died with the disease before night. The next case was that of Isaac Wood, also colored, who was brought in from the city on the 29th following, and died on the same day. There were nine other cases in different parts of the House previous to the 1st of July, at which period a hospital was opened in the second story of the building known as the washhouse. At that time the disease became quite alarming, and it is believed that for six or seven days no regular record was kept of the admissions into the hospital.

"On the 7th of July the register begins and gives an account of 99 males admitted, 12 of whom were cured and 87 died. In the female department 101 cases were admitted, only 11 of whom were cured. On the 13th of July the Medical Board recommended that two temporary hospitals should be erected outside of the buildings. They fixed upon a site near the gate on the Darby road. By the 20th these buildings were so far completed and furnished as to be deemed fit for the reception of patients, and they were accordingly

12

occupied on that day.   By the registry there kept, it appears that 20 male patients were admitted, of whom three were cured.

" In the female department eight were admitted, of whom five were cured. On the examination of the ' death book ' and the registers, the committee find a number of cases and deaths of the various kinds of cholera, which it is believed are not included among those already mentioned. `Adding these, the aggregate of cholera cases and deaths would be 307 cases and 229 deaths.

" About the 30th of August the disease entirely diappeared from the institution, when the committee gave directions to have the outer hospitals taken down. The population of the House upon the breaking out of the cholera was 1,546, and at the period of its disappearance 1,397, being a decrease of 149 in eight weeks.

" This difference is partly in consequence of many of the inmates being removed from the House to the city or districts and there supported until the epidemic disappeared.

" The whole expense on account of this visitation of the cholera at the Almshouse is stated at $4,982.60."

This committee of Guardians, including Michael Day, William P. Bolton, Reese D. Fell and Thomas Stewart, were warmly thanked by their colleagues for their labors in connection with the Medical Board during the ravages of the epidemic.

Dr. N. D. Benedict, Chief Resident Physician, resigned in November, 1849. The Board passed a fine eulogium upon his character as a man and his skill as a physician. The doctor deserved it, as he had shown himself to be one of the best that had ever been employed in the institution.

A number of improvements which he suggested at the time he tendered his resignation were subsequently adopted. Dr. William S. Haines was elected to fill the position, and the salary was raised to $2,000.

Miss Sarah Adamson, a graduate of medicine, made application to the Board for " such a situation in the Blockley Hospital as will afford me the opportunity of seeing its practice to such an extent and under such conditions as may comport with the proper regulations of the institution."

BIRD'S EYE VIEW OF COURT YARD FROM HOSPITAL FIRE ESCAPE.

The committee, to whom the request had been referred, reported favorably on the 25th of May, 1851, and a resolution was adopted by the Guardians requesting the Chief Resident Physician to "assign her to such position as will best enable her to obtain the knowledge she desires without detriment to the institution."

Dr. Adamson was the first female physician employed in that capacity.

A contract had been made for apparatus for heating and ventilating the Hospital and Insane Departments. It was not satisfactory and the Board refused to pay the contractors. Suit was entered for the amount the contractors claimed was due to them, and a long and expensive litigation followed, which was finally settled by a compromise.

Although the Guardians had agreed to the settlement they were determined to go on record, and the following resolution was adopted:

"*Resolved*, That in compromising the suit of Birkenbine & Trotter it is understood that it is not an expression of their approval of the manner in which the heating and ventilating apparatus was constructed in the Hospital and Lunatic Asylum, but adopted as a means of economy and to save further loss to the Board."

The Board purchased the building on North Seventh street above Zane, now Filbert street, in August, 1851. It has been in constant use since that time as the City Office, where application for relief is made and all the outdoor service is performed.

One of the Resident Physicians of the Almshouse is in attendance on the mornings of the week days to examine applicants and to render such assistance as may be needed.

Rumors had been circulated and much discussion indulged in by the community at large regarding the manner in which supplies had been purchased for the Almshouse. Serious charges had been made which reflected upon certain members of the Board in connection with these purchases, and it became necessary for the reputation of the Guardians that certain facts should be ascertained.

To accomplish this Mr. Alexander Cummings moved "that a special committee be appointed to investigate the manner in which blankets and tobacco had been purchased during the past year."

The committee appointed under this motion made two reports.

The majority stated that "Four bales of blankets had been purchased of different parties at different prices, the said blankets appearing to be identical in quality; that the tobacco furnished, and charged at fifteen cents per pound was pronounced by disinterested experts not worth seven cents per pound and utterly unfit for use; that the committee had before them no evidence that any member of the Board had been interested in or benefitted by the high prices charged for goods submitted to them, but they thought that the members purchasing had neglected to give proper attention to the quality and price of said goods." They recommended a resolution making it the duty of the House and Store Committees to examine all goods purchased and report to the Board when the price was considered too high.

The resolution was adopted. That report was signed by Alex. Cummings, Robert P. King and A. I. Flomerfelt.

Mr. Thomas made a minority report, stating that the blankets were believed to be purchased at second hand; that the tobacco was unfit for use, and a better article had been substituted, and that a supply of tea had been purchased in the same manner as the blankets. The minority report made no charge against any member of the Board, except that of neglect to purchase articles of regular wholesale dealers.

As might be expected, public opinion was not satisfied with the action of the Board; it looked too much like "whitewashing," and it was thought that the responsibility for such reckless, if not corrupt purchases should be put upon certain individuals.

The Committee of Investigation, having been continued, made a further report on the 3d of June, 1853, which stated:

"The committee appointed on the 2d ult., to inquire into certain alleged abuses in relation to the purchase of supplies for the House, respectfully further report: that they find by an examination of the books, that, in October last, a bale of blankets, consisting of 147 pairs, was purchased, and the bill rendered to the Board in the name of George Mustin at $3.00 per pair. The purchase was made for this Board by D. S. Beideman and the bill endorsed by him and marked correct.

"Upon inquiry we find that George Mustin is not, and was not, at that time, engaged in any regular business, and has no means of supplying such an order. In pursuing our inquiry, it was ascertained that these blankets were procured by Mustin from the firm of Watson & Co., a respectable and responsible importing house, as he alleged at the time, for the Almshouse, at $2.45 per pair, less five per cent., in payment of which they received the note of D. S. Beideman at thirty days for the identical blankets charged to us at $3.00. Yet he endorsed the bill to us as correct. In addition to this it appears on the order book that Mr. Beideman drew the money from our treasury for the blankets, and so far as the record appears, here the transaction stops.

"Two months after this, in December, another bill of blankets was bought by Mr. Beideman, and the bill rendered to us in the name of E. Vanhook. It is well known that Mr. Vanhook does not deal in such articles, being engaged in a business of a totally different nature, nor does it appear at all clear how his name became connected with the transaction. He did not allege that he ever had anything to do with it; on the contrary, all the evidence within the reach of the committee goes to show that he was an entire stranger to the whole affair, except so far as his name is connected with the bill, and why it was used it is impossible for us to tell. He never owned the blankets in any way, and did not sell them to us. Our inquiries have elicited the following information with regard to this strange transaction: The blankets were sold by Lewis & Co., a very respectable importing house, to D. S. Beideman, at $2.30 per pair, and sent directly from their store to the Almshouse, and charged to D. S. Beideman, and paid for with his note. These goods are charged to us, as before stated, at $3.00 'per pair.

"Your committee makes no comment on these strange facts;

it is their business, by instructions of the Board, merely to present this statement; the conclusions belong to the Board.

"With regard to the tobacco purchased last year, the quantity appears to be unusually large, the whole amount being between eight and nine thousand pounds, and nearly all purchased by William Abbott and sold to us under the name of Charles R. Abbott. Upon inquiry we find that Charles R. Abbott is engaged in the occupation of a clerk in an iron establishment in Richmond, and in no way connected with the tobacco trade. In several instances the orders for the tobacco were procured by Mr. Abbott from other members of the Board under the allegation that his son was engaged in the tobacco trade, and was, at the time, in the receipt of invoices which he wished to dispose of. The orders on our treasurer for the payment of all this tobacco are receipted for by William Abbott, and the only connection that Charles R. Abbott seems to have had with the transactions is in the use of his name in making out the bills to us. He had no tobacco to sell, and, so far as your committee could learn, had no facilities at his command to fill these large orders; and the only imaginable reason that can be given for the use of his name is that he or some one else might be enabled to pocket a profit at our expense.

"The quality of the tobacco has been complained of during the whole year, and that on hand at the time of the appointment of your committee the Board has already ordered to be returned, and the money paid for it to be refunded.

"These statements are submitted to the Board in the hope that something may be done to preserve its character and to vindicate the integrity of its members. Accompanying the report are tables showing the quantities and prices of blankets and tobacco purchased during the last year, with names of the purchasers and persons selling."

This report was signed by Mr. Thomas, in addition to Messrs. Cummings, King and Flomerfelt.

The minutes of the meeting at which the report was presented state that Messrs. Beideman and Abbott both made personal statements concerning their connection with the transactions referred to by the committee, but the secretary failed to state what the nature of the statements was. The report was laid on the table and the committee discharged from the further consideration of the subject.

It is not to be wondered at that the community looked upon the Board with suspicion. When such a report as that can be made and no action taken upon it it certainly looks as if the majority were not the kind of men to be trusted.

Mr. Beideman appears to have been a veritable Wilkins Micawber in his use of notes, and Mr. Abbott will be remembered by his connection with the leaving of Nurse Welsh and other questionable transactions.

Mr. Alexander Cummings appears to have been determined to prosecute the case, as on the 13th of June he offered two resolutions to the effect that William Abbott and D. S. Beideman, having been found guilty of speculating on the treasury, be expelled from the Board.

As was to be expected, the resolutions were simply read and laid on the table, and the accused members were virtually acquitted by the Board.

CHAPTER XVI.

THE scandal connected with these infamous transactions brought the matter before the Board again, in September, 1853. It was stated that the accused had been given no opportunity to defend themselves or to explain their connections with the purchases before the Investigating Committee. Another committee, consisting of Messrs. Smith, Potts, Gay, Flanagan and Cummings was appointed. On October 31st a report was submitted which stated: "The committee appointed on the 19th ult. to inquire into the official conduct of Messrs. William Abbott and D. S. Beideman, in connection with certain alleged abuses, in the furnishing of tobacco and blankets for the Almshouse, respectfully report: ' That they have received from Messrs. Abbott and Beideman certain affidavits, etc., hereto annexed. The committee further report that through their chairman they invited Mr. Charles R. Abbott to meet the committee, but he declined to do so, and also refused to submit to the committee the bills from the parties from whom he procured the tobacco furnished in his name. The committee ask to be discharged from the further consideration of the subject.

There is nothing in the minutes to show the character of the affidavits referred to, which is unfortunate, as there is no reason given for the Board's action. Resolutions to expel were again voted down, and the Guardians were willing to condone the offence and stand by the offenders.

The tracks were laid for the Philadelphia and West Chester Railroad in 1853. The road passed through the grounds of the Almshouse on a line with Thirty-first Street. Trestle-work several feet high was erected to raise the track up to grade, as the meadow land of the Almshouse was much lower than the ground to the north and to the south. After the tracks were laid, the ground was filled in to the established grade. The company paid $5,955 as damages for the land taken.

184

Reports of cruelty to one of the children bound out from the children's asylum were received, and after an investigation it was decided to appoint a new officer to be known as "visitor of children."

His duties were to be to visit at least once a year all the children bound out from the institution, to inquire into their condition and treatment, and to see that the terms of their indenture were faithfully fulfilled. This officer went on duty in March, 1854, and the appointment proved to be wise, as it checked the abuses that by common rumor had been quite frequent.

On the 2d day of February, 1854, the Act known as the "Consolidation Act" was passed by the Legislature. This was in many respects the most important Act that was ever enacted. It abolished all of the governments in the districts, boroughs and townships in the county, and turned them all over to the government of the city of Philadelphia. The districts of Southwark, Northern Liberties, Kensington, Spring Garden, Moyamensing, Penn, Richmond, West Philadelphia and Belmont ceased to have corporate existence. The boroughs of Frankford, Germantown, Manayunk, White Hall, Bridesburg and Aramingo lost their franchises; and the townships of Passyunk, Blockley, Kingsessing, Roxborough, Bristol, Germantown, Oxford, Lower Dublin, Moreland, Northern Liberties (unincorporated), Byberry, Delaware and Penn were abolished, and all the franchises and property of these governments were transferred to the city.

The enlarged city was divided into twenty-four wards, and the Act provided for the election of the proper officers to transact the business of the municipality.

The management of the Poor department was entirely changed, not only in the mode of selecting the Guardians, but in the curtailing of their powers and authority.

Prior to the passage of the Act, the Board virtually levied, collected and expended the money for the relief of the poor; it collected head money from arriving immigrants, amounting to as much as $16.000 in one year; and a number of fines, imposed for various offences, was paid over to the Board. In fact, it was almost a government within itself.

This Act revolutionized that.   One member of the Board was
to be elected from each ward ; the Guardians thus chosen were to
create the department, and it came under the same rules and regulations as the others.   Councils would levy all taxes, including
that for the support of the poor, and would appropriate what they
thought was necessary to maintain the Almshouse and supply the
other needs, to the Guardians of the Poor.

This caused considerable friction and much strong personal
feeling ; the Guardians claimed that Councils were penurious,
while the Councilmen, in many cases, charged the Guardians with
extravagance and profligacy.   It took a number of years to bring
the two bodies into harmonious working.

The Act consolidated all the business in the county except
that for the relief of the poor.   It does seem inconsistent to find
the schools, police, fire, highways, water and other important departments under the city management, and at the same time see
the separate poorhouses managed by district trustees or overseers,
as they have been since they were established.   Councils do not
levy the poor tax in those districts, although in all other respects
they come under the same government as the other parts of the
city.   So far as the system of poor relief is concerned, the Act of
Consolidation does not consolidate.

The first election, under the new act, was held on June 6th,
1854, and the following gentlemen, whose names are given accord-
ing to the number of their wards, were elected Guardians : James
G. Peale, John L. Hamelin, L. L. Crocker, G. W. Cross, F. M.
Adams, John Price Wetherill, Robert P. King, J. Buchanan, Joseph
B. Smith, T. S. Crombarger, J. I. Mathias, L. Schrimick, Townsend
Smith, Wm. F. Potts, L. Henley, Frederick Reel, J. Fallon, J. H.
Bringhurst, Oliver Evans, Edward Dingee and J. N. Marks.

Dr. Joseph D. Steward, Chief Resident Physician, died, and
Dr. Archibald B. Campbell was elected to succeed him.

On May 29th, 1854, Mr. Cummings presented the following :

" WHEREAS, Various rumors are in circulation as to one of
the members of this Board having been found spending the night
in the Women's Department of the Almshouse : and,

" WHEREAS, Such a practice must give rise to suspicion of improper conduct; therefore,

" *Resolved*, That a committee be appointed to inquire into the circumstance of this case and report to the Board."

The President called Mr. Flanagan to the chair and took the floor; he opposed the appointment of a committee to try him in secret, being conscious, from rumors, that he was the person referred to in the resolution, as asking that a fair and impartial trial might be had in the matter by the Board itself, acting as a committee.

Mr. Evans moved to strike out all after the word resolved, and insert that " when we adjourn, we adjourn to meet on Wednesday afternoon next, at 3 o'clock, when an investigation into the matter contained in the preamble may be made, that witnesses may be present to give evidence thereof."

This was adopted, and when the Board met in accordance with it, Drs. Budd, Mitchell, Woodward and Eastman of the Almshouse were present.

They were separately examined as to " whether they knew of a member of the Board having been found spending the night in the Women's Department of the Almshouse." Drs. Budd, Mitchell and Woodward testified that Mr. Townsend Smith, President of the Board, had spent a night in the Physicians' Room, located in that portion of the building known as the West Centre, and that there were no women there. They further testified, as did Dr. Eastman, that they never knew of any immoral conduct on the part of Mr. Smith at any time. This closed the investigation, and a resolution was offered and carried by a large majority, which exonerated Mr. Smith from all blame.

It was thought that the rumor which caused this investigation was nothing but spitework, as Mr. Smith was, for many years, a useful and active member of the Board, and had served as its Treasurer.

The new Board organized on the 3d of July, 1854. Mr. F. M. Adams was chosen to preside, and S. Snyder Leidy was continued as Secretary. Daniel Smith, the experienced Steward, was re-elected.

A request was sent to Councils for an appropriation of $5,000 for the immediate use of the Board. Nearly $100,000 was asked for to pay the expenses of the department during the balance of the year.

The new Board had hardly started in, when charges of negligence and corruption were made against some of the members. The new President, Mr. Adams, who was charged in the newspapers with purchasing *sour* flour, demanded an investigation.

After the examination of witnesses, the Board passed a resolution which completely exonerated him. This was but the beginning, and it did not look as though the community had much confidence in the new administration.

The cholera again made its appearance in the Almshouse on July 7th, 1854. Some few cases of it appeared as late as the beginning of November. Most of the cases were treated in the Smallpox Hospital near the gate on Darby Road, and in a small building adjacent to it. There appears to have been about 300 cases of the disease, of which about one-half proved fatal.

It did not take long to start more scandal. Rumors connecting the name of Mr. George W. Cross, the representative of the Fourth Ward, with speculative purchases, etc., were freely circulated. A special meeting of the Board was held, " To inquire into abuses alleged to have been made in the purchase of flour within four months."

Mr. Anson Gray, a member of Councils, certified that Mr. Cross had purchased 100 barrels from his brother, Mr. Wm. H. Gray, for the Almhouse. The price was $8.75 per barrel, or 12½ cents advance on the cost of the flour, which was bought from James Steele & Co.

Mr. Gray said that Gray & Brother charged the Guardians the same as other parties could purchase the flour for, and no more; he fully exculpated Mr. Cross from the suspicion of defrauding the public by making a profit on the flour.

Mr. Gray further stated, that a member of the old Board had intimated that if he did not go to see the Controller the bill would not be passed. This he declined to do.

The other parties mentioned appeared and corroborated Mr. Gray's statement.

The Board passed a resolution exonerating Mr. Cross, and "expressing regrets that slanderous and unfounded rumors should be circulated reflecting upon the Guardians and respectable business men with whom they dealt."

Mr. Cross was not so fortunate later on.

An application was made to the Board in December, 1854, for the admission of 150 paupers into the Almshouse, they having been brought in a body from New York to Philadelphia.

The Guardians refused to admit them, but to supply their immediate necessities a small appropriation was made.

The conduct of the New York authorities in their attempt to throw these people on the tax payers of Philadelphia, called for expression of much indignation on the part of the press and the community at large. It is a common way of getting rid of undesirable burdens, and is practiced even up to the present time, but not so openly as this was.

Mr. Cross was again brought to the front, and he did not come out with flying colors as he did before.

At the meeting of the Board, held on April 16th, 1855, the President stated " that an editorial appeared in the *Pennsylvanian* on Friday, reflecting seriously on the conduct of a member of this Board for passing ' poor orders ' in payment of his own private debts." A committee was appointed to inquire into the matter and report. " As one of the members of that committee, I have to say that Mr. Hamelin and myself called at the office of the *Pennsylvanian* and saw Mr. Rice, the proprietor, who informed us that they had the orders, and if we would call at 3 o'clock we would learn more in relation to them." Mr. Adams said that " after leaving the office, he met Mr. Edward G. Webb, who is represented as being connected with the *Pennsylvanian*, and after some conversation, Webb exhibited two ' poor orders ' for one dollar each, drawn in favor of certain persons, and passed to the credit of one Patrick G. Coyle, a gardener. The said poor orders were signed by G. W. Cross, a member of this Board."

At a hearing of the case Mr. Patrick G. Coyle was called, and he stated "that Mr. Cross had owed him $1.25 for trimming some vines, etc., in his garden; that he made a bill for the same, sent it to Mr. Cross' house for collection, but without success. He (Mr. Coyle) finally called on the 31st of March to get payment for the bill. Mr. Cross said he would call and see him, which he did; he asked for pen and ink, and inquired if I knew Mr. Quigley, the grocer. I answered that I did. He (Cross) then filled out an order for a dollar's worth of groceries, and threw it on the table, and I asked who the order was for. Cross answered 'for you.' I said, I'm no pauper and don't need it; I work for my wants. Cross then filled another order for the same amount, threw it on the table and left. I again sent to collect the bill, when Cross said, I've seen Mr. Coyle, and thought it was sufficient."

After the article appeared in the papers, Coyle having given the poor orders to Mr. Webb, Cross called on Coyle and asked him whether he had seen the publication. Coyle said that he had not, but supposed it was all true. Cross wanted the orders and said there were men quite as good and better than Coyle, who received these orders. Coyle also testified that "Cross acted as though he was sailing under a heavy press of whiskey."

Mr. Cross made a short speech, in which he disclaimed any intention to defraud the city.

At another meeting of the Board, after the committee's report was submitted, the following very curious preamble and resolution were adopted without a dissenting vote:

"WHEREAS, The Board of Guardians, after a deliberate and patient investigation of the charges made against George W. Cross, a member of this Board, to the effect that the said George W. Cross had given away orders for groceries intended for the relief of the poor, in payment of his own private debts, this Board are of the opinion that the testimony of the witnesses produced to substantiate said charges is not of itself sufficient to justify any decisive action; yet taken in connection with the admissions of Mr. Cross, particularly as to his having been, at the time of the occurrence of the transactions complained of, in a state of intoxication, and incapable of explaining the same satisfactorily, they are compelled to consider the charges proven ; therefore,

" *Resolved*, That George W. Cross be, and he is hereby expelled from the Board."

It could not be expected that the action of the Board and the exposure of such contemptible business, would raise the reputation of the Guardians very much in the estimation of the public. Such transactions are calculated to bring odium on all connected with them.

At this time there was considerable comment about certain members who were in the habit of taking large numbers of their special friends to the Almshouse on Sundays, and drinking freely of intoxicating liquors. Liquor was at the command of the Guardians, and some of the best members tried in vain to correct the abuse of it. The expulsion of Cross, and the denunciation of the Sabbath sprees in the newspapers in a manner checked it somewhat.

CHAPTER XVII.

GUARDIANS OF THE POOR KNOWN AS BOARD OF BUZZARDS.

THE Guardians elected in the spring of 1855 took their seats in July. A majority of the old board had been re-elected. Joseph B. Smith was chosen President, S. Snyder Leidy, Secretary and Treasurer, and Daniel Smith was unanimously elected Steward of the Almshouse. Dr. Robert K. Smith was elected Chief Resident Physician, in place of Dr. A. B. Campbell. This change caused considerable feeling; Dr. Campbell charged that his personal and professional character had been impugned and threatened suit against some of the members of the Board.

At a meeting on the 9th of July the following resolution was adopted :

"*Resolved*, That a committee of three be appointed to gather testimony as to the neglect and inefficiency manifested on the part of Dr. A. B. Campbell as Chief Resident Physician, to be prepared to meet any action he may bring against this Board, as referred to in his communication."

Dr. Campbell remained in the institution and declared that he would continue there, notwithstanding the election of Dr. Smith.

The difficulty was adjusted, however, without any legal proceedings, and Dr. Smith went on duty.

The feeling entertained for the Board of Guardians was clearly shown when Councils took up the appropriation bills in the fall. The newspapers had frequently commented upon the alleged " enormous expenditures and the extravagant manner in which the business of the Board was carried on." Councils refused to make the appropriations asked for. All kinds of charges were made against the Guardians, and the Board referred the whole subject to a committee for consideration. At the meeting of the Guardians held on September 17th, 1855, Mr. Bringhurst presented the following preamble and resolutions as a report from the committee, and they were adopted as a reply to the charges made.

" WHEREAS, The Board of Guardians of the Poor of the City of Philadelphia, though they have been aware that there had appeared in some of the newspapers, from time to time, in different forms, most gross and unjustifiable statements and imputations in respect to the management of the department under their care, originating, as was supposed, from some sources entitled to but little consideration and prompted by unworthy motives, have forborne to publicly notice them, trusting that both the character and motives of the professional fault-finders would be appreciated as they deserved.

" But as these statements and imputations have been echoed in the City Councils, and have been indorsed by members with additions, as appears by the published proceedings of the Common Council on Thursday last, and as forbearance to notice them from this source might be considered as an admission of their truth, it is deemed proper, in vindication of themselves, to characterize these allegations in respect to this department as being, in the mildest sense they deserve, gross and untrue exaggerations; and, as preliminary to the connection of the matter referred to, it may be well to notice that, since the Act of Consolidation went into effect, the members of the Board of Guardians of the Poor became such by virtue of election by the same constituency that placed members of Councils in positions they occupy, except as to those whose constituents have no direct interest in the department, and who, though they are not taxed for its support, are allowed a control in its affairs through their representatives; thus exhibiting the anomaly of representation without taxation. And it is fair to assume that as much respect was had by their constituents in the selection of men who, from their intelligence, public spirit and fidelity to the public interests, are as much entitled to public confidence as they selected and elected to other positions. They also bear their full share of burthen of this community with their fellows, in or out of office.

" One member of Councils is reported to have said that the expenses of the Almshouse had doubled within a year or two, and attributed the cause to the inefficiency of this Board. As the alle-

13

gation itself is not a fact, the conclusion has no support. The actual total expenditures of the Guardians for the support of the House, and on account of the manufactory, farm and in and about the premises, from the 20th of May, 1853, to the 20th of May, 1854, was $136,606.56. There were during that time provisions, clothing, medicines, medical attendance, nurses and attendants for the insane and sick, with their board, beds, bedding and all other necessaries furnished for an average of 1,828 inmates, consisting of 400 lunatics, 400 sick and diseased, the aged, the infirm, the maimed, the blind, the idiotic, the deformed, the ruptured, the incurable and others hopelessly addicted to habits which wholly unfits them for self-maintenance, making a cost of $1.44 per week for each; while the total expenditures for the same purposes from July 2d, 1854, to July 2d, 1855, was $189,502.17, for an average population of 2,147 of the same description, making a cost of $1.69 per week for each.

"The total cost of the House has been increased by the increase of population, and the increase of cost of each article of supplies during the past over the previous year, as all house-keepers, at least, have ample proof, by extra draft on the pocket. In view of these facts the expenditures of the Board, under the present organization, compared to that of former Boards, works no disparagement to the present is clear to a demonstration.

"The increase of population, too, can be be accounted for upon facts which can not have failed to present themselves to all reflecting minds, which ought to excite, did excite, and brought into active and effective operation the sympathies of the community during the past year, viz : the general depression of business, the lack of employment for the mechanics and the laboring people—male and female—the low price of labor when obtained, and the high prices of almost every necessary, reluctantly compelled many who had aged, infirm, blind, crippled or sick dependents upon them for support to send them to the Almshouse, as a relief to themselves, from a burthen they were unable to bear; for the same reason, too, in connection with the high price of fuel of all kinds, the out-door expenditures were greatly increased during the last winter over previous years.   But these are at present at as low a point as they have been for years, and further reduction, it is believed, will tend to swell the population of the House.

" A little reflection on the subject and a little trouble to obtain information, which was at all times obtainable, and a discreet use of both, would have saved the member from the position he has placed himself in, of an accuser of the present Board of Guardians of " inefficiency," in the absence of facts to support the accusation.

" In respect to the alleged fact that persons go to the Alms-house, get married, and have children there, the present Board have no knowledge, and presume that if such things ever did happen there (and it is presumed that such cases are rare at any time) it was previous to the connection of any of the present members of the Board under its present organization.

" AND WHEREAS, Another member is reported to have said : ' That he could lay his hand on some $8,000 which had been expended for segars, brandies, etc., and how much more he was unable to say, in banqueting at the Almshouse.'

" If the allegation is intended to be understood as meaning an actual expenditure (and it seems to be a fair inference from the statement that it was so intended) under the present organization of the Board, for banqueting by the Guardians, in which they participated, or were accessory to, he has placed himself in the position of having determined to ' go it blind ' in assailing the official acts, integrity and moral standing of men who can boldly challenge an equal degree of the respect and confidence of the community at large for all the qualities, including that of fidelity to public trust, which constitute good citizens, as the member himself.   One thing is certain, a much longer residence in this community has afforded the people greater opportunities for scrutinizing and forming an opinion of them.

" Charity, however, dictates the conclusion that ignorance of the subject, as evinced by his allegation, and a forgetfulness, in his case at least, of the respect due from a gentlemen to his equals, had led him to make the assertion that he could lay his hand on what has no existence in point of fact, and in attempting to do which he would discover that he would be in the condition of the Irishman and the flea—it would be absent.

" The allegation is too monstrous for even the more gullable to swallow as a fact, and is dismissed with the suggestion that if the gentleman would act upon the homely but wise rule, ' Be sure you are right, then go ahead,' and not upon that of go ahead, whether you are right or wrong, he would not be so likely to commit acts of injustice and wrong against others.

" AND WHEREAS, Another member is reported as having commented upon the same subject in condemnation of the Guardians, closing with an insinuation as to the paternity of some of the children born in the Almshouse, which may have been intended as a joke, and if so he is welcome to enjoy it, but if otherwise intended it might be thrown back with propriety upon himself. One thing is a serious fact, and that is that the locality he specially represents has its full share of representatives in the Almshouse in the shape of babies.

" The delay of Councils in making an appropriation for the use of the Guardians in support of the department is working in direct increase of expenditures far exceeding any made in the way in which some of the members are so flippantly eloquent in complaint of, from the fact that purchases cannot be made in view of the present condition of affairs from less than from 8 to 12 per cent. advance upon prices at which they could be obtained under a more favorable one.

" That supplies must be furnished at the House is an imperative necessity demanded by every sentiment of humanity. To permit the unfortunate creatures herein described to suffer cannot, and will not, be tolerated in a community whose people are ever ready, voluntarily, to send thousands and tens of thousands of dollars to relieve the sufferings of the destitute in distant communities, therefore,

" *Resolved,* That the assertion that brandy, wine or other spirituous liquors are used by the members of this Board, or have been since its organization, is maliciously false in every particular,

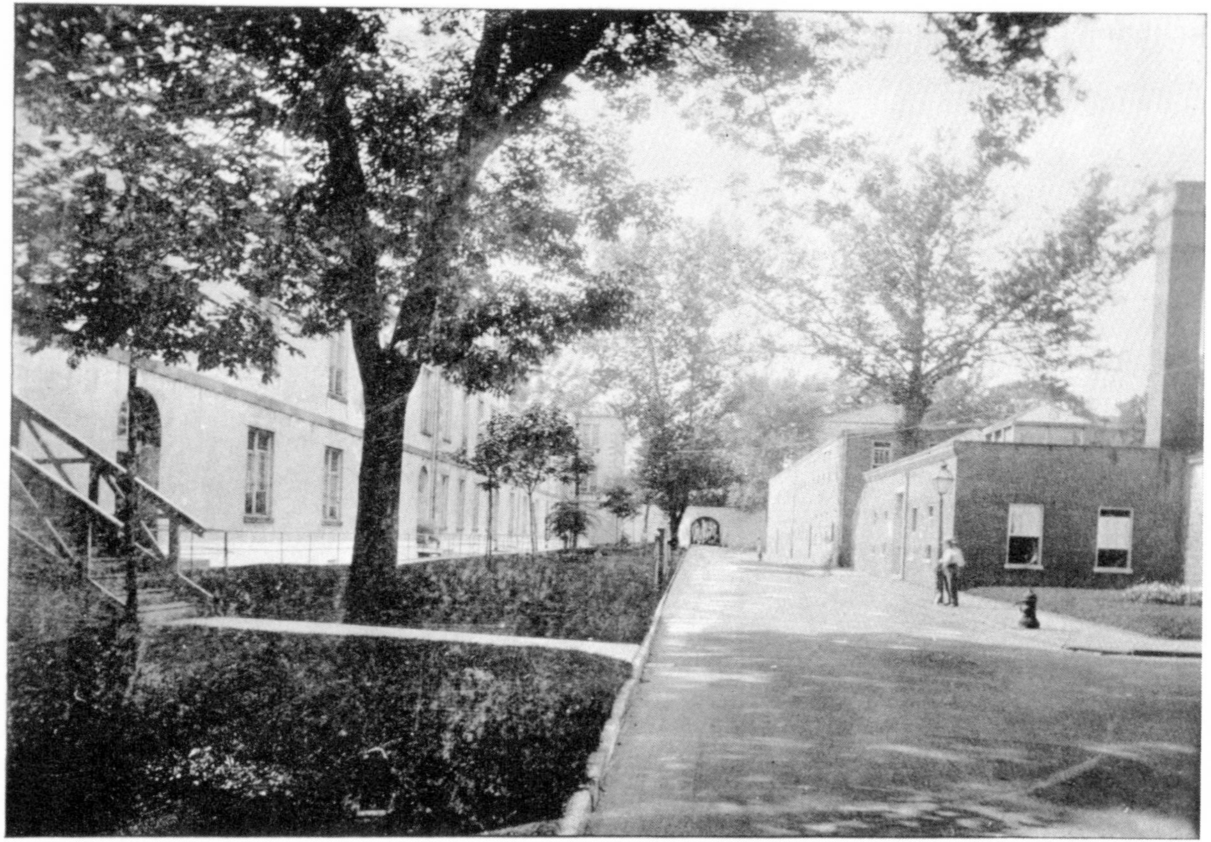

STREET IN FRONT OF INSANE WARDS.

and those who made such assertions must have known this or possessed no knowledge of what they were speaking.

"*Resolved*, That dinners are not furnished this Board, nor ever have been since its existence.

"*Resolved*, That the delay by the Councils to make the necessary appropriation to draw warrants upon, by this Board, is attended with no other results than of injury to the credit of the Board, causing a higher price to be paid for such goods as they are compelled to buy, thereby increasing the taxes to that extent, which the citizens have to pay."

This shows the feeling that existed between the members of Councils and the Board of Guardians, and one can form an opinion as to the character of the men of both bodies. It did not have any effect on the Councilmen, and the appropriations were still kept back. The credit of the city at that period was not very high, and the Guardians were compelled to get along as well as they were able under such circumstances.

Hon. Robert T. Conrad, Mayor of the city, in his annual message to Councils, in February, 1856, referred to the management of the Department of the Poor in very strong language, and said: "The call made upon this department has remained unanswered. There is, perhaps, no branch of the government in relation to which there is so ample scope for improvement and reform. The attention of Councils is respectively invited to the recommendations made on this subject in a former message. An enlightened and prudent revision of the present system, in all its details, would be attended with important results and advantages, not only by checking the present inordinate expenditure, but by the discouragement of idleness and pauperism."

Of course this was answered by the Guardians, and they adopted resolutions in which they expressed their regrets "that the misrepresentations to which this Board has been subjected are being continued; and they invited Councils to appoint a Special Committee of Investigation to inquire into the details of the policy pursued by the Board."

The Guardians subsequently concluded to discontinue all out-door relief, except in cases of sickness. Even after the appropriations were made for the year 1856 the Board found that it could not continue its system of out-door relief on such an extensive scale.

On the 7th of July, 1856, a new Board was organized by the election of Mr. Oliver Evans as President, and F. A. Server as Treasurer. Dr. A. B. Campbell was reinstated in his old position of Chief Resident Physician of the Almshouse. As Mr. Daniel Smith did not desire to continue any longer as Steward, Mr. Charles Murphy was chosen to succeed him.

The Board consisted of Messrs. John F. Heishley, Wm. T. Lafferty, A. R. Kauffman, Robert Selfridge, John R. Angney, William Riddle, F. A. Server, John Hartman, N. R. Moseley, Charles Taylor, James D. Brown, John Dunlap, Marshall Henzey, William F. Potts, Andrew Hackett, James Smith, James Lloyd, John H. Bringhurst, Oliver Evans, Isaac M. Post and Alex. C. Garvin.

The majority of them were elected by the Democrats. They made an effort to reduce the expenditures, but very soon after they assumed the management of the Department they were called the "Board of Buzzards," and were known as such for many years.

After Hon. Richard Vaux had been inducted into office as Mayor, he requested a report from Dr. Campbell, as to the conditions existing in the Almshouse. The following extracts from the report of the Chief Resident Physician show a terrible state of affairs, and reflect no credit upon any one connected with the management of the institution. The doctor said:

"I have the honor to state: This institution, usually called the Almshouse, comprises within it a smallpox hospital, a lunatic asylum, a children's asylum, a lying-in department, a nursery, a hospital for medical, surgical, venerial and mania-a-potu cases; besides the Almshouse properly so called, which is in reality an infirmary for the blind, the lame, the superannuated, and other incurables so decrepit as not to be able to earn for themselves a livelihood.

"The number of able-bodied men and women, although to the eye of the casual observer apparently large, is really comparatively small and consists chiefly of those vagrants who spend their lives in alternating between the low down dens of vice throughout the city, the county prison and this institution.

"These are the ones who disgrace themselves and humanity, and by their presence bring a stigma upon the afflicted and the unfortunate, who are compelled here to seek relief and support, which would not attach to them if this place was in name, and, in the opinion of many in the community, what it is in reality, a hospital. These constitute the proper subjects for a House of Correction, which is so urgently required.

"This building, although it covers an area of sixteen acres of ground, is even now too small in many of the wards to furnish accommodations for the sick ; and, from its construction does not permit encroachments to be made from the men's side of the different departments upon the women's side. So that while the men's side of the lunatic asylum and the women's side of the hospital still have nearly room enough, the women's side of the lunatic asylum requires now one-third more room for the present number ; in the open wards many sleep on the floor, and in each of the cells, 80 in number, which should be used by one alone, have to be occupied by two, and in some cases by three at one time ; and the men's side of the hospital would require the whole wing now occupied by the children's asylum for its accommodation.

"On the third floor, men's medical wards, the wards are full, and there have been 100 sick crowded into a long garret, about 7 feet high by 18 feet wide, with no ventilation, and no means of discharging the impure exhalations arising from the bodies and breaths, but the sliding windows, one pane of glass in height, the draft from which being over the heads of the beds, was as dangerous almost as their fœtid emanations. There are only a few patients at this moment in these garrets, but the season approaches when they will be more fully occupied. On the second floor white men, with diseased eyes, occupy one side, and black men with surgical and venereal diseases, boys and men indiscriminately mingled, occupy the other side of the same ward ; and, at the same time, the beds are too numerous in the other wards.

"The effect of this over-crowding is, that all the cases are much longer in recovering than they would otherwise be, and in many instances men remain blind who under more advantageous circumstances would have recovered their sight.

"But the most disastrous results from crowding and want of ventilation occur on the first floor. For years past there has not been a bed unoccupied, and sometimes there is a patient sleeping on the floor for every one on a bedstead—once even when the *hall* was filled with bedsteads. The result is an erysipelatous and gangrenous atmosphere pervades them in spite of my most strenuous efforts. I have everything taken out of each ward at a time. It is whitewashed, and the floors and windows are scrubbed; the bedsteads are scrubbed and varnished, and when dry replaced; every article of bed-clothing is fresh from the wash-tubs, and the bedsacks are filled with fresh straw; but this infection lingers, though in a lighter degree.

"The consequence of this has been, that if a patient is brought in with his throat cut, although the wound is not mortal, he dies of gangrene. If an amputation be performed, the man, who should recover, dies in a week of gangrene in the stump. If a minor operation be done, erysipelas attacks the wound, and it is much longer than it should be in healing.

"The unfortunate condition of things on this floor might be, to some considerable extent, remedied by transferring the adjoining ward from the children's asylum to the men's surgical wards.

"This room could be spared from the children's asylum, with some inconvenience it is true, but without serious detriment to the interests of that department. That transfer, however, would be but temporary relief, and to a very limited extent. It might, and would probably, aid in removing the hospital gangrene.

"But the hospital now requires the whole of the children's wing, and every year the aggregate number of patients increases.

"Not only the wants of the hospital, but humanity and philanthropy demand that an asylum for the children should be provided elsewhere than within the walls of the Almshouse.

"It admits of a question, as to each one of the grown persons, whether the misfortunes which have brought them to this place have been altogether the result of the agency of other people ; but as to the helpless orphans, for they are all orphans or worse off, who are thrown upon the city for support, education and protection, they are innocent of any agency in their own unhappy lot.

" Not only our duty to God, but a wise economy demands that they be brought up away from the pernicious influences which must operate on them, and will reach them in spite of all precautions, within this building. They may be educated to become useful members of society, or they may be trained to prey upon the community which has neglected them.

" Why not, if possible, save the future from the opprobrium of ever having been the inmate of an almshouse? This object especially commends itself to the heart of every benevolent citizen.

" The women's side of both the lunatic asylum and the hospital are heated by steam and are well ventilated. The air is admitted into the chambers in the cellars, where it is heated by coils of steam pipes, and is delivered into each ward near the ceiling ; while the vitiated air is drawn from the rooms through openings near the floor, and is carried off by flues, which conduct to a shaft rising many feet above the roof of the building.

" By this means the wards are at the same time warmed and thoroughly ventilated.

"A similar arrangement is required on the men's side of both buildings, for sanitary purposes as well as to avoid the danger of setting them on fire, particularly on the lunatic side, where the men congregate around the stoves, and annually destroy large quantities of clothing by scorching it, and from the filthy habits of many of them, often make the atmosphere redolent with bad odors. It is a matter of astonishment that the house has not long since been burnt down.

"A conflagration in a place where there are so many helpless lunatics or disabled sick would be terrible, beyond the power of language to describe.

" None but those who occupy the house or pass through it after nightfall can appreciate the difficulties, annoyances and vexations which arise from the use of oil in small hand-lamps. The building is the embodiment of gloom. The patients, in their desire to increase the quantity of light, constantly, although every effort is made to prevent it, have the lamps smoking. The smoke irritates the lungs of the consumptives and others afflicted with diseases of the air-passages, and they are wearied out with coughing until, exhausted, they fall asleep; it also soils the walls and the clothing.

"The introduction of gas would aid the assistants in the administration of medicines and in performing their offices for the sick, and would prevent much rascality, pilfering and eloping. Gas is so much cheaper than oil that within three years the cost of its introduction would be made up by its use and ever after be a saving to the city.

"A laundry is very much needed; the expense of feeding and clothing the large number of washerwomen necessary to wash the clothing of from two to three thousand persons, together with the bedding of so large a hospital, would more than pay for such an establishment. The washing would be done better, quicker and more economically, because the clothing would last longer and there would be less of it stolen and lost.

"There is not a water closet in the hospital; the want of such an essential arrangement is productive of great annoyance, inconvenience and injury, particularly in wards having no ventilation, and adds greatly to the labors of the house.

"Convalescent patients are compelled to go from the highest and most distant wards and cross a yard at all seasons, and through the rain and snow to reach the offices. On the men's side there is but one bath tub, which is altogether insufficient for the uses of the sick. Bathing should be one-half the curative agency in the treament of many diseases.

"On the women's side of the Lunatic Asylum there has been put up and nearly completed a series of water closets, baths and sinks as good as, if not superior to any other in the country. A similar arrangement should be constructed in several other parts of the house."

The doctor certainly painted a horrible picture, and it is to be hoped that there were no other wants that he overlooked or forgot to mention. Things were very different then from what they are now.

CHAPTER XVIII.

MEMBERS OF BOARD CHARGED WITH SELLING DEAD BODIES.

THE Board of Guardians sent the following communication to the Select and Common Councils on September 1st, 1856:

"The Board of Guardians of the Poor feel constrained to again make application for an adequate appropriation for the remainder of the present year, for the purpose of out-door relief to the poor of the consolidated City of Philadelphia.

"In doing so, we deem it proper to give such explanation of the operation, character and necessity of this kind of relief, as may serve to correct erroneous impressions in regard to it, and will also relieve those who immediately preceded us from the charge of a lavish and improvident expenditure of the amount appropriated to the out-door account.

"Before we proceed further, it may be proper to say (as you may see by answers we have given to certain interrogatories addressed to us lately) that to the out-door account is charged the salaries of Secretary, Out-door Agent, Visitors, Out-door Physicians and Apothecaries, rents of offices and expense generally outside of the Almshouse, in addition to the proper relief given to the poor.

"To show that the sum appropriated for the present year for this item has not fallen short through extravagance in its expenditure, but because of the refusal of the last Councils to furnish an adequate sum for the purpose, we need only refer to the amount heretofore expended for the same purpose.

"By the published statements, which are accessible at any time, it will be seen that the account for out-door relief for the year ending May 20, 1854, the year preceding the consolidation of the city, reached the amount of $67,442; of this sum $33,986 was expended for fuel, and over $20,000 in groceries and money to the poor.

"The winter of 1854–1855 having been one of unusual distress among the poor, there was an increased demand for out-door aid, and we accordingly find that the amount expended in the year 1855 reached the sum of $102,998, of which $52,580 were for fuel, $27,395 in groceries and $4,640 in money. It will thus be seen that over $84,000 were expended during the year 1855, outside of the Almshouse, in proper relief for the distresses of the poor.

"As required by the act of consolidation, an estimate of the amount required for the expenses of the Almshouse for the current year was furnished to the late Councils, divided into different heads, under which our statements are detailed. For the out-door account the sum asked for was $83,950, $19,000 less than was expended in 1855. Much effort having been made during the last winter to reduce the out-door account expenditure; it had been so successful that a reduction of nearly 20 per cent. was thus proposed in this item. But this was considered as great a reduction as it could bear, and it was not supposed that Councils would for a moment think of still further reducing this sum.

"But in fixing the appropriation they, in their eleventh-hour zeal for economy, and with a view of keeping down the rate of taxation, saw fit to reduce the amount for this item—although the Finance Committee reported in favor of $73,950—to the sum of $53,950; that is, thirty thousand dollars below the sum deemed requisite by the Board of Guardians, and but little more than half the amount expended the preceding year for the same purpose.

"By referring to our statements it will also be observed that the cost of fuel constitutes nearly one-half of the out-door expenses, and it is to be remembered that this expenditure is confined to the winter months. Hence it was, that, in accordance with the usual custom, contracts were made before the commencement of winter for the supply of coal and wood, for the greater portion of it was distributed to the poor last winter before Councils fixed the bill of appropriations for the Almshouse for the present year.

"And although there was a large reduction in the amount of fuel distributed the last, in comparison with the previous winter, this item was enough to consume some three-fifths of the whole amount appropriated to the out-door account, and was required to be paid immediately at the close of winter.

"It will thus be seen that when, in addition to this sum for fuel, we deduct the other charges to this account for salaries, rents, bonded and support cases, etc., etc., there remained but little to relieve the distresses of thousands who have been or are to be aided in being kept out of the Almshouse by a little seasonable aid in groceries, and, to a small extent, in money.

" Upon the propriety and necessity of out-door relief in certain cases, but a word, we think, is necessary.   Is it not better to give 25, 37 or 50 cents a week to a poor person in distress, for a short or a long time, than to send them to the Almshouse to be supported at an average cost of $1.50 per week ?   And second, is it not more consistent with the requirements of humanity to render this little aid to the unfortunates, who are striving still to help themselves, and can yet claim their little home, than, by refusing, to consign them at once to the wards of a house, in which, however diverse may have been their former condition, all must be placed on one common level.

" The assistance of persons in distress, outside of the Alms-house, is a custom of long standing.   It had its origin, doubtless, in the benevolent consciousness that there are poor outside, as de-serving as those inside of the Almshouse, and that it would be doing a wrong to such, to force them into the house, if a small amount of assistance would prevent it.   Laws, too, regulating this form of relief, were enacted long before our days.   Their force, we presume, is in no respect lessened by the Act of Consolidation ; and their propriety, we consider, as enjoined alike by the dictates of humanity and the principles of sound economy.

" But it is to your bodies we must now look for the means requisite for the performance of our duties in this matter.   With those in whom resides the power.will rest the responsibility of a failure to provide the means for the necessary expenditure.   If your predecessors have, as we believe, inordinately and capriciously cut down the amount to be expended for out-door relief, we do not believe that it will either meet the approbation of your own judg-ments, or the approval of our citizens, to perpetuate this wrong.

" It has been and is our constant aim to keep down the expenditures of the department under our control, and make it as little as possible a burden to our heavily-taxed community, and we think that an examination and comparison of its expenditures will compare favorably with any other similar institution.

"In respect to the character of those receiving outside assistance—if many become its recipients because of imprudence or improvidence, still when they become sick or afflicted, with no friends to support them, we think it better to give them a little outside aid, and discourage their entrance into the Almshouse as long as possible as a matter of economy, as well as with a view to cherish that remnant of pride against becoming a public charge in a public institution ; for when once this habit is acquired, it is difficult to eradicate.

"But there is also a large class—those who have enjoyed brighter and better days, but whom misfortune has visited with a heavy hand in their old age—to whom the thought of the Almshouse is more terrible than death. This is the class by whom the little pittance that we give is most thankfully received, and serves, when joined perchance with a little gained by some light labor or with the assistance of some early friend, to eke out a scanty existence.

"Now, if the door of relief is to be shut for the remainder of the year upon those who have been supported in the past by us, it will easily be seen that, while it will be the cause of vast suffering, it will also greatly increase the expenses of the house. While many will only enter the Almshouse at the last extremity, a large proportion of those whom we have aided outside, probably one-half, often with children or decrepit friends depending upon them, will be forced into the Almshouse, and instead of twenty or twenty-five dollars per annum, they will cost the city three or four times as much."

This document was signed by Oliver Evans, President.

There appears to have been rumors of all kinds in circulation about the action of some of the members of the Board or officers of the house, and the newspapers published some of this town talk. The Guardians were much annoyed and occasionally felt compelled to take some notice of these reports.   The records show that Mr. Potts offered the following preambles and resolution at a meeting of the Board held in the latter part of the year:

"WHEREAS, An article appeared in the *Daily News* on Tuesday last, charging upon a member of this Board the infamy of prostituting his office to his own personal profit in making merchandize of the bodies of deceased paupers; and

"WHEREAS, The odium of this mercenary and sacreligious imputation rests equally upon us all, inasmuch as the editorial failed to publish the name of the offending party; therefore

"*Resolved*, That a committee of three be appointed to call upon the editor of that paper, obtain his authority for the statement, ascertain the name of the guilty member, investigate the facts of the case and report to the Board at the next stated meeting."

The preambles and resolutions were adopted, and Messrs. Potts, Garvin and Dunlap were appointed as the committee.

The chairman and a member of the committee called upon the editors of the paper, and, after stating their business, requested the name of the member implicated.   He stated several reasons for refusing to give the name, but said that he would give such information as, if properly investigated, would prove the truth of what he had asserted.

In pursuing the investigation, the chairman procured a copy of the deaths from the officers of the House and the registry of burials from the graveyard, for the use of the committee.   On such a reported copy he presented a partial report, in which he stated that there is a discrepancy of twenty-one bodies between the deaths and the number of burials, which deficiency was admitted at the time by a member of the committee, but which admission was based on the presumption that he was acting with high-minded, honorable men, and that information received from them was reliable.

The majority of the committee reported: "These gentlemen went on to show that no account was kept at the graveyard of the number of burials, and the only records were the small pieces of paper tacked on the heads of the coffins, on which the names, etc., were written, and are liable to be removed from various causes before the coffins reach the graveyard, and your committee has been informed that such notices have been found and frequently picked up on the grounds of the institution."

That was the way the majority accounted for the discrepancy; "the papers may have been lost from the coffins, and then there would be nothing to show that the bodies had been buried." Mr. Potts was censured for his conduct in pursuing the investigation, and the report concluded by recommending that the House Agent and the Superintendent of the graveyard be furnished with suitable books to keep records of deaths and burials.

Mr. Potts, the chairman, presented a minority report, but the majority of the Board would not allow it to be read or to be entered on the minutes.

The newspapers denounced the majority of the Board for their action in stifling the investigation. The name of Dr. Mosely, a member of the Board, was freely mentioned as being the principal one connected with the sale of bodies, and it was charged that the majority made themselves accomplices.

It is not surprising that they were known as the "Board of Buzzards."

It is very evident that Councils had but little confidence in the Board as a body; while there were some reputable gentlemen connected with it, the majority did not command much respect in the community. Their communications to Councils did not seem to have much weight, and but little attention was paid to them. Reductions in the amounts asked for were made by wholesale. The minutes of the Board record another appeal, which was sent on November 24, 1856, in which occurs the following choice language: "The Board of Guardians of the Department of the Poor of the City of Philadelphia, having submitted their annual estimate for the year 1857, and having learned from some of the members of Councils that the items are too high, we candidly and sincerely appeal to you as men, as representatives of this great metropolis, to weigh well the interests of this department. Before your biased minds take charge of your better judgment, we most cordially and sincerely solicit your honorable body to pay us a flying visit, examine the institution in all its branches and judge for yourselves of the aged, the blind and infirm who are withering out their existence upon the charity of our generous citizens in this enlightened and Christian community. Let us once more plead to you again to look back for half a century and examine any one institution in this commonwealth, and then say what takes better care of those who are poor and needy than Philadelphia.

" Our department can boast, and years of toil can vouch for it, that it is one of the best governed institutions in America for cleanliness, comfort and sustenance; always making it an ornament to this great city, and which makes the hearts of the aged and fatherless rejoice, praising the Maker of the Great Universe that it is far better to be poor and needy than to serve out a life of career in your *prisons*. Christian hearts and hands are always open and more ready to give than to receive. How many poor are there in this vast metropolis whose pride buoys them up, and they go begging from door to door to keep them from being compelled to enter the Almshouse as public paupers ? "

Here followed an argument for outdoor relief, similar to previous ones sent, after which the paper reads : " Examine well and see that the poor tax laid for the year 1855 is but 13 cents on the hundred dollars, while the other departments are of still greater character and for what benefit? Years of experience have attested the wise legislation of our City fathers, and has proved the sagacity of their conduct, by being just to their constituents. To railroad companies, of private interest to these representatives, the public justly attribute the cause of our bankruptcy. By robbing the poor and needy, who are dependent on the cold charity of our citizens. How many millions of dollars have been squandered away by these knavish transactions and unjust intrigues of corporate powers? We again ask you to remember the poor. The cold and cheerless winter is coming on us again; many, very many of the wretched and miserable creatures who have no homes, no friends to cherish them in their feebleness and old age, devoid of sound intellect, lame and blind, go dragging out their pitiful existence over

14

our thoroughfares, begging from door to door, and die upon our streets or in some miserable hovel, or are cast into the Almshouse, where pride withers and the body wastes away in dark oblivion.

"Our estimate, as presented to your honorable bodies, has been carefully examined by the Committee of Accounts, and we find, by the items and costs of this year (1856), thus far is as low as can be made. The rapid increase of persons being admitted into the House, now 168 more than the same time last year, and averaging at this rate, by the 1st of February, 1857, there can be no doubt there will be upwards of 2500 persons within the walls of Blockley Almshouse, at a cost of $1.50 per week, and all this increase has been brought on by cutting off this out-door relief from those who are still able and willing to support themselves in some light work. Does not reason and sound sense admit, that if $50,000 will relieve those asking alms on the outside of the institution and keep them from going to the Almshouse, where should they be consigned through unwise legislation, it will cost the city over $150,000 at $1.50 per week; and, while there, should sickness overtake them, they will be compelled to go under medical treatment, averaging at least 30 to 50 cents per week for medicines, nurses, etc. Take all these things into consideration before you decide. You will perhaps say to yourselves our taxes are too high, they must be reduced. Yes, gentlemen, let us tell you your taxes were less when the old corporations were in existence than at present with the consolidated powers. Look at them and contrast the difference, where are they squandered away? Look at your High-way Department, your Police system and Railroad Knavery, and then do not say it is in the Poor Department. These are weighty measures, which we trust your honorable bodies will take into due consideration. Leave not the credit of this institution be swept away and suffer, while we are compelled to look to your august bodies to bear out its reputation.

"One word before you decide; let us again as a body, a Board of Guardians, solicit your Committee on Poor, (*not your poor committee*) to visit this institution in general and duly examine it in all its various branches; view it carefully; let not prejudices sway

your feelings toward the unfortunate, for it is not those on the out
side who know the wants of those within the walls of the Almshouse better than they who are daily connected with it, and if we
wisely err let us assure you it is not of the heart but of the head,
and we are always ready and willing to serve our constituents
towards the unfortunates, who are generously and liberally supported by the citizens of Philadelphia."

This appeal was signed by Oliver Evans, President.

There is a marked difference in the reports of the conditions
in the institution as presented by the Guardians and as represented
by Dr. Campbell. They certainly did not look at things through
the same glasses. The doctor reported that everything was wrong
and in a horrible condition ; the Board, on the contrary, say, " it is
one of the best governed institutions in America, for cleanliness,
comfort and sustenance; always making it an ornament to this
great city, which makes the hearts of the aged and fatherless
rejoice, praising the Maker of the Great Universe, etc."

After making this assertion they insist upon the Councilmen " visiting the institution and inspecting it in all its various
branches." This did not look as though they feared an examination of the conditions.

It would puzzle one to form an opinion under these circumstances ; probably both sides exaggerated, and if it were possible
to arrive at a " happy medium," one might get near to the truth.

CHAPTER XIX.

DR. JAMES McCLINTOCK ELECTED—VISITING PHYSICIANS RESIGN—
RESIDENT PHYSICIANS LEAVE—VISITS OF STUDENTS
STOPPED—GAS INTRODUCED.

IN June, 1857, Dr. A. B. Campbell, Chief Resident Physician, resigned his position, and Dr. James McClintock was elected to fill the vacancy. This selection caused considerable excite. ment in the medical fraternity. The resignations of the members of the Visiting Staff were tendered to the Board of Guardians, and were simply "laid on the table" by that body. Six of the Resident Physicians resigned and left the institution; these vacancies were filled by the election of others in their places. A complete change in the management of the medical department took place, and the visits of students were stopped.

The principal objection to Dr. McClintock was that he manufactured some medical remedies, the contents of which he would not divulge. Consequently the medical gentlemen denounced him as a "quack doctor," although his knowledge and abilities as a physician were unquestionable.

A panic occurred in the winter of 1857–1858, which threw a large number of working people out of employment and caused great suffering. Relief Committees were formed in every ward and they distributed the necessaries of life to many of the sufferers.

The census of the House for January, 1858 shows a population of more than 3000 inmates and the Board was compelled to refuse admission to a great many applicants. The out-door relief distributed by the Guardians in one month comprised $2,504.84 worth of groceries, 1,571 tons of coal and 351 cords of wood. The number of persons assisted in this manner was 3,556.

A contract was made with Samuel Sweeton & Brother, in March, 1858, to introduce gas pipes, etc., into the institution, for the sum of $5,992.35. The work appears to have been done satisfactorily, as the Board passed a resolution to that effect, and recommended the contractors as first-class mechanics.

At the meeting of the Board held on March 15th, 1858, an affidavit was read, which was signed and sworn to by seven women and two men, in which they testified that "they had severally called on James Mackin, Visitor of the Guardians of the Poor, at his office, No. 1347 North Front street, and solicited relief, of which they are severally in want, and received for answer, 'there is nothing here for the Dutch.'"

The matter was referred to a special committee for investigation, but there is nothing to show that any action was taken to punish the official.

The Board elected to serve for 1858–1859, consisted of Messrs. A. J. Preall, J. L. Hamlin, James Armstrong, Hugh Gamble, Jacob C. Freno, C. C. Overbeck, Wm. Budd, E. E. Smith, J. F. McClelland, R. W. Kensil, James D. Brown, A. H. Dunlap, Marshall Henzey, George Huhn, Joshua Kames, J. S. Riehl, Edward Sherry, John A. Fisher, George P. Oliver, J. J. Allison, William Dawson, Oliver Brownell and J. J. Hoopes.

Dr. George Huhn was elected President, John A. Fisher, Treasurer; Marshall Henzey, a member of the Board, Steward of the Almshouse, and Dr. R. K. Smith was reinstated in his former position of Chief Resident Physician.

The following letter was read *after the election had taken place :*

"To the Board of Guardians of the Poor :

"*Gentlemen*—On the 8th of June, 1857, the Chief Resident Physician resigned his place here, and I was elected to fill the vacancy, and commenced my duties on the 20th of the same month. In July I was re-elected.

"In seeking the position I looked upon it as a professional station, and not a political place. I requested and received votes from gentlemen of both political parties then on the Board.

"I have faithfully discharged the duties of the place, and by economical management of the department under my care, in which I was greatly assisted by Charles Murphy, Esq., Steward, I have saved for the public a sum much greater than my salary.

"If you, gentlemen, view the place a professional station, I would be pleased if you will retain me, and I shall discharge the

duties faithfully, as I have heretofore done; but if you have deter-
termined to make it a political place, and a man whose qualifications no one doubts or denies, is to be proscribed because he is a
Democrat, I am perfectly willing to be displaced.

"I am, gentlemen, very respectfully yours, &c.

"JAMES McCLINTOCK,
"*Chief Resident Physician.*"

On the 19th of July, 1858, at the instigation of Dr. Smith,
Mr. Preall offered a resolution which stated "that as all objections
have been removed which prevented the medical gentlemen from accepting office of this kind in the institution, and the medical profession of Philadelphia are desirous of re-establishing the relations
which formerly existed between the profession at large and Blockley
Hospital," and provided for the election of a consulting staff. This
brought on a stirring debate. The obstacles or "objections that
had been removed," were recognized as referring to Dr. McClintock,
and some of the members of the Board intimated that Dr. Smith
required assistance in the performance of his duties." The resolution was finally "laid on the table."

Dr. Smith appeared to be mixed up in a number of the scandals
that was put in circulation. On the 30th of August, 1858, Dr.
Oliver offered the following:

"WHEREAS, Rumors are being circulated that one of the officers of the Medical Department of the Almshouse has been recently engaged in the nefarious business of selling a number of
the bodies of the inmates who have died in the institution, and as this
course (if tolerated) is calculated to destroy that confidence which
the community have reposed in the members of this Board, and
annihilate the prospect indulged in by them of that anticipated
reform in this particular, the hope of which led to the success of
the present and the demolition of the power of the former Board.

"And as from this traffic (even if warrantable) no revenue accrues to the institution, the proceeds being entirely appropriated to
the use of those engaged in this outrageous transaction, it therefore behooves the members of this Body that they should show their

MALE INSANE EXERCISING YARD, SHOWING PART OF WARD BUILDINGS.

constituents that they have no participation in, or give countenance in any way, to such illegal proceedings; therefore,

"*Resolved*, That a committee of three be appointed to ascertain the truth or falsity of these rumors, and report to the Board at its next meeting."

Messrs. Oliver, Kensil and Kames were appointed. They reported that they had made a careful examination and found that there was no foundation for such report. They said: "That no medical officer of the House has been engaged in any such transaction or in anything calculated to lead to the suspicion of such transaction.

"Dr. Smith, the Chief Medical Officer, admitted that he had preserved two dead bodies for the purpose of obtaining two rare specimens of diseases, and claimed that by so doing he was only in the pursuit of a legitimate and proper privilege, one which he had a perfect right to exercise for the advancement of medical science.

"The evidence showed that Dr. Kelly, one of the assistant physicians, was anxious to obtain the fractured arms of a female who had died of consumption. Dr. Smith was equally anxious to obtain them as valuable specimens of morbid anatomy. After Dr. Smith's trouble in preparing the body to prevent decomposition, some other physician, outside of the institution, procured them. The disappointment of Dr. Kelly was to a great extent the origin of this investigation, and the result of it proves absolutely nothing."

This was indeed a wonderful report. It showed the great *care* that was taken of the bodies. It was certainly too bad that Dr. Kelly should be disappointed, especially when he was so anxious; but there was Dr. Smith, who had taken the trouble to preserve it, and then to think that "some other physician outside of the institution procured them!"

Who was this other physician, and how did he procure them? The committee failed to state whether this "other physician" took them out secreted in his vest pocket, or how he *did* take them. Possibly the body walked out.

It was outrageous that any one should have the temerity to insinuate that there was anything wrong with such excellent management, and it is to be hoped that Dr. Oliver's constituents were pleased.

Councils managed to appropriate just enough money to keep the Board's finances in a very straightened condition.

On the 27th of September, 1858, the Guardians adopted a series of resolutions begging for sufficient money to maintain the institution, in which they stated: " We therefore respectfully urge upon Councils the necessity of prompt and immediate action in supporting this department. The article of flour, which always commands cash, is now nearly exhausted, and in a few days the inmates will be without bread.

" Now nearly all of them are without sufficient clothing to protect them from the approaching cold weather, and there is not one cent left to purchase shoes for the barefooted men and women who are compelled to leave their wards and work within the institution.

" The Hospital supplies are also in the same condition, and all of the medicine for the sick have thus far been purchased upon the responsibility of the members of the Board, without a dollar of appropriation to meet the bills."

This was truly a deplorable condition to be placed in. Political feeling was very strong in those days, and seemed to enter into the management of the departments. It was even hinted that some of the *Guardians* intended to do some " crooked " work, but the following preamble and resolutions, which were *unanimously* adopted at the meeting of the Board, held on October 11, 1858, proved that the rumor was untrue. Of course no one would go on record as voting against them. The resolutions said:

" WHEREAS, We are now upon the eve of an election, the importance of which cannot be overestimated, when we will be called upon to deposit our votes to say who shall represent us in the various offices to be balloted for; and,

" WHEREAS, The right of the elective franchise is dear and religiously sacred to every American citizen, whether native or adopted, and as the price of liberty is said to be eternal vigilance, and as the inviolability of the ballot-box lays at the foundation of the perpetuity of our Republican institutions, we must view with the utmost abhorrence, and punish with the utmost severity, those who would in any way seek to perpetrate a fraud upon the sacred right of freemen in this matter ; and,

" WHEREAS, It is rumored that the majority members of this Board have been seeking to perpetrate a gross outrage, not alone upon the citizens of the 24th Ward in particular, but also upon the rights of every American citizen, by forcing upon them, as qualified voters, the paupers who reside in the Blockley Almshouse, that are supported by the taxpayers of the city of Philadelphia, who have therefore no moral right to be turned out on the day of election for the purpose of neutralizing the legal votes of an equal number of American citizens.   Therefore,

"*Resolved,* By the Board of Guardians of the Poor of the City of Philadelphia, that we disown having any part or lot in this matter whatever, either individually or collectively.

" *Resolved,* That any member of this Board or officer connected with the House or Board, who shall be proven guilty of aiding or abetting, in any manner whatsoever, either preparing for or assisting to deposit, on the day of election, the vote of any pauper, shall be considered guilty of misdemeanor in office, and shall be dismissed forthwith."

This must have relieved the public mind and set at rest all wild rumors.

The appeals to Councils for more money did not appear to have the desired effect, and the members of the Board began to get impatient and to assume a more belligerent attitude.   On the 25th of October, 1858, Mr. Kames offered the following :

" WHEREAS, This Board has appealed for the past three months to the City Councils for an appropriation sufficient to meet the deficiency of last year's expenditures, for which this Board is not at all accountable, which appeal has so far been disregarded ; and,

" WHEREAS, The appropriations for almost all articles necessary for the support of the inmates is exhausted, and the only method left to carry on the affairs of the institution is for the members of this Board to make themselves individually responsible for such purchases as are required; that we have done already to a a large extent; and,

"WHEREAS, Councils have neglected to appropriate that portion of the public funds raised by taxation off our mutual constituents, thus leaving the Board without money to purchase necessary supplies for the support of the inmates of this institution, and without funds for the purchase of raw materials for the employment of the various mechanics now under the Almshouse roof, thus involving the city in a loss since the first of July last, already exceeding $10,000, and now daily increasing, partly in consequence of the additional prices charged for all articles bought on credit, without any prospect of an appropriation to pay for the same. And this Board, being unwilling to be instruments in the hands of Councils for such mismanagement and waste and loss of the public funds and credit, over which we have no contol; therefore,

"*Resolved*, That no article be purchased for the use of this institution after the first day of November next, unless an appropriation be first made by Councils sufficient to meet existing demands, and that a committee of five members of this Board, to confer with Councils to set forth the necessity of prompt action on their part and urge an immediate appropriation of a part of the public money raised expressly for the support of this institution, be appointed.

"And that, in case Councils shall continue, as they have been for the past three months, indifferent to the public interests, and should fail to act as the emergency demands, that then the said committee be requested to solicit donations from public-spirited citizens for the support of the lunatics and children's asylum, and that the adult paupers be forthwith discharged and recommended to the mercy of the City Councils."

The preambles and resolutions were adopted.

The action of the Board did not have the desired effect, and Councils continued as they had been "for the past three months." There is nothing to show that donations were asked for or that the adult paupers were discharged and recommended to the mercy of City Councils.

Mr. Hoopes gave vent to his indignation by the introduction of the following preambles and resolutions at the meeting held on the 8th of November, 1858:

"WHEREAS, This Board, influenced by a desire to guard the interests of the city and to economize the means placed at their disposal for the maintenance of the poor of Philadelphia, applied to Councils for an appropriation to enable them to make available and profitable the surplus labor within the walls of the Almshouse; and,

"WHEREAS, The appropriation, amounting to but $2,400, to be used in purchasing material for the construction of a building and the purchase of tools for the employment of this labor, has been stricken from the ordinance by the arbitrary and factious opposition of a few members of Councils, prominent among whom is the member of Select Council from the Thirteenth Ward, it behooves the members of this Board to make a plain statement of the motives that governed them in their official relations; the necessities that required such action; the impediments which have retarded an economical and proper administration of their trust, and the ignorance and recklessness which has marked the opposition arrayed against this Board and the true interests of the city by the individuals who have controlled it.

"No Board of Guardians have ever been elected who entered upon their duties with a firmer determination to administer honestly and faithfully their trust than the present one.

"With this determination they had scarcely entered and taken their seats than they discovered that the year's appropriations for most of the important items of necessity were exhausted; that debts to the amount of more than $8,000 had been contracted; that the institution had been stripped of supplies in all its departments and left in so deplorable a condition as to require the means at that moment to maintain its vitality, and that the labor unappropriated around the institution was an evil that demanded an immediate remedy.

"These were the motives and these the necessities which influenced this Board in the application to Councils for the money absolutely indispensable for the welfare of the institution.

"And appealing, as they believed, to honest, intelligent and honorable men, bound by every pledge of duty to the interests of the city, they anticipated neither difficulty nor delay in the accomplishment of their object, nor did they suppose that the Council chamber would be made the theatre for abuse or the arena for a display of ignorance and the promulgation of falsehood.

" The course pursued by this small faction in Councils is manifestly the offspring of malevolence or is the result of still less worthy motives.

" The great interests of the city are lost sight of and bartered away for the gratification of personal feelings, and Councils are entertained with the antics, vulgarities and hypocrisy of a political harlequin.

" By the published proceedings of the Select Chamber, it will be seen that one member at least asserted that the members of this Board were dishonest; that their official conduct was tainted with fraud, and that his opposition was not to the department, but to the Guardians of the Poor.

" This member was the Select Councilman from the 13th Ward, a man sent to legislate for the interests of the city, and not to take advantage of his official position for the gratification of his personal malice.

" This man knowing, or at least having been informed, of the whole character of the legislation necessary for the welfare of the department, knowing that the ordinance for the support of the House for six months, from July 1st, was one thing, and the ordinance to pay the debts of the old Board was another, professed that the whole thing was a riddle, and endeavored, from the beginning, to stigmatize the Board and induce the people to believe that its members are profligate squanderers of the public moneys.

" These slanders are on a par with the ignorance thus exposed. The Board asked for $2,000 to put up a building which by contract would cost $10,000, and yet these gentlemen arrest this important work and destroy the whole object to be attained by introducing a proviso that the work shall be done by contract, thereby preventing the employment of these very men whose labor we desire to make profitable. It is therefore with a desire to test the relative powers of the Councils and the Board of Guardians of the Poor, and the right of Councils to retard and injure the interests of this department that the following resolutions are offered:

"*Resolved*, That a committee of three be instructed to cause the question of the relative powers of the City Councils and the Board of Guardians of the Poor to be thoroughly investigated and adjudicated by the Courts of Justice.

"*Resolved*, That this Board do tender the services of 200 able-bodied men to the Select and Common Council to be employed as their wisdom may direct."

During the discussion which ensued on the motion to adopt the resolutions, Mr. Brown said that he disapproved of the erection of the building, and asserted that he had used his influence in Councils to defeat the appropriation therefor, and from other remarks made the following protest from the Chief Resident Physician was presented and read:

"I protest against Mr. Brown, or any other man, connecting my name with any act for which I am not responsible, and this man Brown shall not falsely, through motives of malevolence, involve me in any act with which I have no connection."—R. K. SMITH.

The vote on the passage of the preambles and resolutions was 21 in favor to 1 in opposition, "this man Brown" being the only one opposed to their adoption.

On the morning of December 22, 1858, a fire occurred in the clothes room, which was located in the second story of the bake house; it was the cause of considerable fright, and for a time looked quite serious, but was fortunately extinguished without any loss of life.

The Board passed a vote of thanks to Mr. Henzey, the Steward, for "his indefatigable exertions and for the untiring zeal with which he labored to extinguish the conflagration which at one time threatened the Almshouse with entire destruction."

The fire caused great inconvenience, as there was no surplus of clothing at the best of times. The Steward notified the Board on January 3, 1859, "that in consequence of the fire they did not have sufficient clothing to furnish inmates on their discharge from the House. There are a great many who would have been discharged but for the want of clothing."

The religious character of at least a few of the members was shown by the following preamble, which preceded a resolution to authorize the purchase of hay :

WHEREAS, Owing to a dispensation of Providence the grounds kept for haying purposes were overflowed during the past harvest, and consequently almost our entire crop of hay was destroyed, therefore," etc.

Mr. Hoopes offered the following : " WHEREAS, The taxpayers of the city are paying to support at least 1000 able-bodied men and women, and the Guardians of the Poor have no means of employing them, therefore,

" *Resolved*, That a committee be appointed to use their influence with members of the Legislature to procure the passage of a bill to authorize the sale of a portion of the Blockley Almshouse property sufficient to raise means to build a suitable House of Correction."

CHAPTER XX.

D R. SMITH is again brought to public notice. His name had been associated with that of one of the female nurses, and caused considerable gossip. The matter was discussed informally by the members of the Board, and a resolution was offered to expel or suspend him until an investigation could be made. This called forth the following characteristic letter from the Doctor:

" *Gentlemen*—At your meeting on Wednesday evening a resolution was offered to suspend me from my duties for the present, until certain charges against me were settled.

" If charges exist I should like to know what they are, for I am ready for any investigation that may be started. I am responsible to the Board of Guardians for a faithful performance of my official duties, among them is the respectability, so far as it rests upon me, of the departments under my care.

" If I have been guilty of any dereliction in any of those particulars I am answerable to you, and I claim it as a man and a public officer that the charges be plainly, specifically and publicly made under a responsible name, that I may have an opportunity to vindicate myself before the public, where I have been so deeply injured.

" As a citizen I can stand erect before the world, conscious of my own integrity, and am ready to answer to any immoral act that either by stealth or stratagem my enemies have endeavored to fix upon me.

" Apart from my office there is a higher tribunal than the Guardians of the Poor to decide upon my moral conduct, and a more impartial one than the Sunday papers, but I shrink from nothing into which you may choose to look, and as I have been publicly traduced and calumniated I invite you to fully and freely investigate anything and everything with which my name has been so unfairly connected.

"I ask then that some one who complains shall make his charge openly and fairly, and that you appoint a committee to investigate.

"Respectfully yours,

"ROBERT K. SMITH."

The committee appointed made a report on March 28, 1859, in which it was stated: "We have had repeated meetings and have notified all parties in any way connected with the scandalous rumors to be present and make charges or produce evidence, and as no charges have been made of any sort to implicate the Doctor in any improper transaction, and as all the evidence adduced was entirely calculated to liberate him from anything wrong, your committee regard the whole of these rumors as the offspring of malice."

The troubles of the Board were augmented when Mr. Armstrong, one of the members, made a statement regarding flour transactions, and said that 690 barrels of it had been stolen by members of the Board. As might be supposed this bold charge caused consternation as well as indignation, and a committee, consisting of Messrs. Armstrong, Allison, Gamble, Hoopes and Smith, was appointed to investigate and report.

Mr. Armstrong was alone. The other members of the committee made report on February 2d, 1859, and, after reciting the mode of procedure and the evidence, showing statement of the books, etc., they concluded by saying: "There is therefore indubitable evidence that neither fraud nor dishonesty has marked the conduct of any man connected with the institution in these flour transactions, and the charges are gratuitous, false, slanderous, and only manufactured for political effect.

"Your committee therefore offers the following resolutions and ask for their adoption:

"*Resolved*, That James Armstrong be and is hereby expelled from the Board of Guardians of the Poor, and from this day his seat be declared vacant.

" *Resolved*, That the Secretary officially informs Councils that a vacancy exists in the Third Ward and ask them to elect a member to fill it.

" *Resolved*, That James D. Brown deserves the censure of his colleagues in sustaining Mr. Armstrong in his course, and that he be required to make to the Board a public apology for the wrong he has perpetrated.

" *Resolved*, That the members of this Board regard themselves disgraced by their official connection with Mr. Armstrong and every other public defamer and calumniator."

When Mr. Preall moved the adoption of the resolutions, Mr. Armstrong took the floor, and after he had spoken more than an hour the previous question was called and the motion to adopt the resolutions was carried unanimously, while Mr. Armstrong was continuing his remarks.

Mr. Armstrong paid no attention to the expulsion, but attended the next meeting as though nothing had happened.

The vote on the adoption of the resolutions was reconsidered and Mr. Armstrong presented a minority report, in which he stated : " Your committee agree in all the statements of which you will find a printed copy hereto annexed, with the exception of two bills, one for 150 and the other for 200 barrels.

" The objection is that they were not passed until the meeting of December 27th.

" I admit they were not passed until that meeting, but I do contend that they were charged respectively on the 15th and 20th of December, 1858.

My charge ends on the 25th, but I contend that the flour was delivered on and previous to the 25th. The baker makes his returns on Saturday evening. This Saturday referred to was the 25th. The 26th was Sunday, and, of course, no flour was delivered on that day. The bills passed the Board on the following day.

" Now, when was the flour delivered ? Is it pretended that there was no flour delivered from the 15th to the 26th ? "

" The report of the majority of the committee is equivalent to this. Now let us admit this for the time, and say that it was delivered

15

on Monday, before the meeting of the Board. Let us refer to the
baker's statement, received from all sources, including all the following week, 140 barrels, and baked, say 117, which is the same as
the preceding week. How does the statement stand?

Whole amount received and bills passed	2,854
Amount on hand July 3d	70
Total barrels	2,924
Whole amount baked to January 1st, 1859	2,584
To be accounted for	340

" Does this, after giving all that you ask, make the matter
straight? Now I insist that there was not a barrel of flour delivered at the House from the 25th to the 27th of December when
the bills were passed."

Councils appointed a committee to investigate the flour transactions and the Board dropped the matter, so far as Mr. Armstrong's charges were concerned.

At the same meeting Mr. Kames offered the following:

" WHEREAS, Upon an examination of the books of this department, it appears that in the six months elapsing from the 1st of
January to the 5th of July, 1858, inclusive, there is a deficiency of
510 barrels of flour, that has been paid for more than was delivered,
by the Board in power previous to this; therefore,

" *Resolved*, That a committee be appointed to investigate the
matter and report to this Board."

Messrs. Kames, Gamble and Smith were appointed, but no
report from that committee appears on the records.

Mr. Armstrong called attention to the manner in which meats
were furnished and distributed, and a committee was appointed to
investigate. A long report was made, in which it was stated
" That Councils, with a false view of economy, refused to appropriate
sufficient to pay salaries to competent clerks to keep the accounts.
. . . The officers of the institution are appointed in a great
measure as partisans and removed solely on party grounds. Certain
of the positions for but a single year, they cannot be expected to

feel that interest in the institution which they would if their situations were permanent, as in New York, during good behavior." The report concluded with the recommendation of a system which, the committee said, " would render any scheme of fraud impossible."

Mr. Armstrong, not wishing to associate with the Board any longer, and feeling that he had started enough worriment to last for some time, tendered his resignation, which was accepted; no doubt it was received with joy.

More troubles awaited; charges of corruption came from all quarters; the Controller referred to Councils bills for muslin purchased by Messrs. Freno and Preall, members of the Board, and they asked for an investigation.

The Committee appointed reported that the muslin could have been bought for less than the amount charged in the bills to which the Controller objected, but acquitted Messrs. Freno and Preall of any intention to make anything out of the transactions.

The Committee of Councils appointed to investigate the flour transactions submitted a long report; there was no whitewashing indulged in, as the following extracts from it show:

" The Committee met at the Almshouse on February 22, 1859, and proceeded to examine the books of the institution.   We examined the book kept by the Almshouse clerk to the Board of Guardians, in which a record is made of all bills passed by the Board, the date of each bill that is bought, the articles bought, the prices paid, the names of the person or persons selling to the Almshouse, the names of the Guardians making the purchases, the dates the Board passed the bills and the numbers of the warrants drawn for the payment of the bills.

" We examined the book kept by the storekeeper of the Almshouse, in which a record is made of the purchases for Almshouse.

" We also examined the book kept by the Steward of the Almshouse, in which a record is made once a week of the flour received, the amount consumed and the amount on hand. This record is kept by the Steward from reports made to him by the baker.

"These three books were examined from January 1st to July 3, 1858, which embraces the first part of this report. Secondly, they were examined from July 3, 1858, to February 17, 1859, relative to the flour transactions of the Board of Guardians from January 1, 1858, to February 17, 1859.

"The Committee find upon the examination from January 1st to July 3d, 1858, that the Board passed bills for flour to the amount of 2,615 barrels that was bought between January 1st and June 28th, 1858. The bill of June 28th was the last purchase made by the old Board and was passed by that Board on July 5, 1858. This is as the clerk's book shows.

"The storekeeper's book shows that he has given a credit for 2,485 barrels of flour as received into the institution between January 1st and July 3d, 1858.

"The Steward's book showed that he received between January 1st and July 3d, 1858, inclusive, 2,597 barrels of flour. The last receipt of flour by him was July 3d. These three statements show the following results: That the Board passed bills for *130 more barrels* of flour than the storekeeper has any record of on his books. The bills which the storekeeper has no record of and the Board have passed are as follows, viz: for 30 barrels purchased of Peter Maloy, April 1, 1858, purchased by Hugh Gamble; R. H. Baker's bill for 50 barrels, bought June 28th, by Mr. Heishley, and T. E. Lukens' bill for 50 barrels, bought June 28th, by Mr. Heishley. These bills have been paid.

"And the books show that the Board passed bills for 18 more barrels of flour than the Steward's book shows he received *as the figures stand upon his book.*

"If you take the amount as was originally entered in writing and figures before any erasures were made, it would show then that the Steward had not received as much flour by 164 barrels *as the Board passed bills for.*

"The Steward's book shows that five alterations were made from January 1st to July 3d, 1858. The alterations are: January 23d, 1858, the entry in writing and in figures is for 157 barrels, the figures have been altered to 125 barrels.

"May 17th, entered in writing and in figures for 90 barrels; figures altered to 70 barrels.

"May 27th, entered in writing and in figures for 150 barrels, the words 'one hundred and' have been erased, and the word sixty has been written over the word fifty, and the figures 150 have been altered to 60.

"May 29th, entered in writing and in figures for 139 barrels; altered to 135.

"June 26th, the amount entered in writing is entirely erased.

RECAPITULATION OF ALTERATIONS.

" As originally entered.	As altered to.
June 23d, 157 barrels	June 23d, 125 barrels.
May 17th, 90 "	May, 17th, 70 "
May 22d, 150 "	May 26th, 60 "
May 29th, 139 "	May 29th, 135 "
June 26th erased.	
Total . . 536 barrels	390 barrels.

making a difference between the alterations and the original entries of 146 barrels. Now if the original entries were correct, then there was a loss to the institution of 146 barrels.

"The amount of flour entered on the Steward's book as baked March 6th, in writing and figures was 125 barrels; the figures were altered to 105. Now if this original entry was correct there was a saving of 20 barrels, which should be deducted from the 146 barrels, which leave, according to original entries, 126 barrels to be accounted for.

"The committee examined the books of the clerk to the Board, the Storekeeper and the Steward from July 3d, 1858, to February 17th, 1859, which have been kept under the present Board of Guardians.

"The clerk's book shows that bills have been passed by the Board for 3,204 barrels of flour.

"The Storekeeper's book shows that he has received 2,854 barrels.

"The Steward's book shows that he has received 3,159 barrels, or the baker has so reported to him.

"These books therefore show that the Board passed bills for 350 barrels more than the Storekeeper has any record of on his books; they also show that bills have been passed for 45 barrels more than were reported to the Steward to February 12th, 1859, at which time the baker made his last report to him.

"Now the great difficulty of the committee is to account for the 160 barrels that were reported to the Steward by the baker on February 5th and 200 barrels on February 12th. As the last purchase was made on February 1st, 1859, of 100 barrels, bought of J. K. Tyson, and the bill passed the Board on February 14th, and the entry of 100 of the 160 barrels of February 5th is easily accounted for by the purchase of February 1st of J. K. Tyson, which could not have been reported to the Steward before the 5th; the 200 barrels reported to the Steward as received, which was entered upon his book of February 12th, and 60 barrels of the entry of the 5th, making 260 barrels excess, after the last purchase of February 1st.

"Your committee have not been enabled from all the testimony before them to ascertain where it came from; whether it was in the institution previous to February 1st, and withheld from the Steward, or whether it had been supplied after February 1st to make up deficiencies by some parties unknown to your committee. If such was the fact, then a gross fraud was attempted upon the city, and your committee think that every person who takes the trouble to read the records and testimony taken in this investigation must come to the same conclusion, and that the flour was in the institution before February 1st, or it has been sent in since to make up deficiencies. The question then naturally arises, if supplied since February 1st, how far the city is liable for its payment.

"The storekeeper, George Jeffries, was examined under oath, and said most emphatically, 'No flour was delivered between the 1st and 12th of February, except the 100 barrels bought of J. K. Tyson on the 1st.

"Now, if the testimony of the books kept by the Clerk of the Almshouse to the Board of Guardians, the testimony of the storekeeper, sixteen members of the Board of Guardians, including the

House Committee for the month of February, comprising both sides of politics, twelve different parties who have been in the habit of selling flour to the Almshouse, is to be believed, no flour was purchased between the 1st and 12th of February, and this 260 barrels, which is entered on the Steward's book as received on the 5th and 12th of February must be included in the deficiency bills.

"Whether this flour was delivered before or after the bills were passed, one important fact is established, that no person can collect a bill for the flour entered upon the Steward's book of February 5th and 12th, except the 100 barrels bought of J. K. Tyson on February 1st.

"If frauds have been attempted to be committed, then this investigation has frustrated the designs of those making the attempt."

The Committee recommended the reorganization of the Poor Department, and an entirely different system of making purchases for the Almshouse.

The testimony taken by the Committee was submitted to Councils, and some of it was very interesting, showing, as it did, the very loose, if not criminal manner in which the business of the Board was conducted. Upon the examination of some of the members of the Board of Guardians, some very queer answers were elicited. Mr. Kames especially became noted for some of his answers. In reply to one question he said, "I do not know of any member of the Board of Guardians receiving commissions for the purchase of flour. Various members have been charged with fraud. We have all been charged with fraud, and with being thieves."

When he was asked, "Have you, either directly or indirectly, been connected with the flour transactions, in which you have received a bonus or an interest?" he declined to answer, because, he said, "I consider the question impertinent."

He said that the entry of a bill for 200 barrels of flour, upon the Storekeeper's book, purporting to have been purchased December 28th, of A. Harvey, was investigated by a committee appointed for that purpose. Among the parties before the committee was

Mr. Fisher, a member of the Board, who stated that he had ordered the bill entered on the book, for the purpose of having the matter in shape for passing when the flour was delivered His reasons for so doing were that the parties were friends of his, and as he was about leaving the city for Harrisburg, the parties of whom he had purchased were fearful that, if neglected, it might be left over. The reason given for not delivering the flour at the time of the alleged purchase was " there was not room for it."

It is somewhat strange to see that flour was purchased that could not be delivered because " there was not room for it," when we remember that, but a few months previous to this investigation, this same Mr. Kames introduced a series of resolutions at a meeting of the Board of Guardians, in which he denounced the members of Councils for " leaving the Board without money to purchase necessary supplies for the support of the inmates," and threatening to solicit donations from public-spirited citizens for the support of the lunatic and children's asylum, and to discharge the adult paupers," and recommend them to the mercy of Councils.

Now it seems that conditions have changed. The Board appears to have more money than can be properly expended, and when any of the members are about to leave the city, they order a couple of hundred of barrels of flour, so that no time need be lost, and the flour merchant can wait until enough of the surplus stock is used to make room for his delivery. It is not to be wondered at that no two of the books agreed, or that bills were passed for more than had been received. To term such methods as being " loose " is more than moderate; *criminal* would be nearer to the proper name.

CHAPTER XXI.

REORGANIZATION—LIBERAL OFFER OF HOMŒOPATHIC PHYSICIANS.

THE community at large had lost all confidence in the Board, and when the Legislature, in compliance with the general request, passed an act changing the mode of selecting Guardians of the Poor, it met with a hearty welcome by the public.

Under the new law, the Supreme Court appointed George Williams, Rowland E. Evans and Joseph M. Linnard; the District Court, Conrad S. Escher, William P. Cresson and Frederick A. Server; the Court of Common Pleas, John M. Maris, Elhanan W. Keyser and John Robbins; the City Councils, James N. Marks, Mahlon H. Dickinson and John D. Lentz.

The character and reputation of these gentlemen were closely looked into. Three of them, Messrs. Williams, Server and Marks, had been on the Board, and knew the details of the institution and its management.

The others were mostly men of means, who could afford to give the time to attend to the duties. At this period there was strong political feeling and antagonism between the People's Party, a large majority of whom became Republicans, and the Democrats, or Loco Foco's, as they were then termed.

The following editorials, quoted from the papers of that time, will show something of the feeling existing. One said: " The gentlemen who have received these appointments are, so far as we know them, reputable and upright business men ; but we regret to notice that the Supreme Court has set the example in their selections, by taking from the many intelligent and retired gentlemen of this city, only those who are active Loco Foco politicians. This act does not suggest the conclusion that the future Board is to ignore politics in their organization. Judges Ludlow and Sharswood, profiting by this example, have made similar appointments ; whilst, on the other hand, the Judges of the lower Court, who are said to sympathize with the People's Party, have selected gentle-

233

men who have in a great measure been unknown in the political arena, and such men as would doubtless administer their trusts regardless of any political influences.

"That the existence of Judge Read, the only Judge whose life has been passed among us, and whose interests have always been identified with the City of Philadelphia, should have been entirely disregarded as an appointing power in the Supreme Court, was a sufficient reason why those other Judges of the same politics should have provided against the possibility of a Loco Foco organization of the Department.

"The Councils in their election have not been unmindful of the interests of the city. They have taken for the three years' term Mr. James N. Marks, who passed a great portion of his life in the service of the institution over the river. As a Guardian upon a former occasion, he was one of the most efficient and faithful the city ever possessed. His independence and determination during that service cannot be denied, and no man is able to truthfully say that he has feasted at the expense of the city, or had taken the value of a penny that did not belong to him. He neither broke public bread, smoked a cigar, nor took from the garden even a bunch of flowers. And yet he is one of the first of the new appointments to be assailed by the Loco Foco papers.

"The object of the assault is apparent to every man. The design is unquestionably to detract from Mr. M. any influence he might possess as an upright, intelligent and honest man, one thoroughly acquainted with the wants of the institution, and his official duties.

"Messrs. Dickinson and Lentz are both good appointments. We believe them to be discreet and honorable gentlemen, and that they would not perpetrate a wrong, either public or private, in their official capacity. The same may be said of every one of the gentlemen who belong to the People's Party, appointed by the Courts. We would not be willing to believe that the appointments of the Loco Foco Judges differ from them in this respect. We only regret that they should be such decided politicians, and fear that their influence may be covertly exerted to serve party purposes.

FEMALE INSANE EXERCISING YARD, SHOWING PART OF DINING-ROOM BUILDING.

" It is certainly proper that this new Board should be governed by their own experience in making changes in the department; but we earnestly counsel them to avoid hasty action.

" Public clamor and newspaper scandal should never deter fearless and honest men from doing their duty, nor should it force them to do an injustice to the institution or its officers.

" We therefore caution this Board against all improper influences. Let them enter upon their duties determined to eradicate every evil they may discover to exist; but let them see and know by their own observation that changes are proper and ought to be made.

" It is not very likely that a large majority of the Board can understand the true character of the important trust they have assumed, in the beginning of their career, and as the public expects much from these gentlemen, it will be well for them to exercise much caution in the outset.

" These we know are the views of the mass of the people, and we are entirely disposed to endorse them. An injustice done in the beginning will start an opposition at once which it will be difficult to arrest."

Another paper, after giving the names of the members elected by Councils, said:

" Mr. Marks, the first on the list, is one of the particular friends of Dr. R. K. Smith, the present Almshouse physician. He was formerly a member of the Board, and during the term of his office, in 1855, had as good an opportunity to keep fast horses at the public crib as almost any one else. We cannot regard his appointment as a promising one in any light. Mr. Dickinson is a reputable citizen of the Sixteenth Ward, and last year represented his ward in Common Council. Mr. Lentz is a gentleman of good standing and strict business habits. Both of these, we believe, will serve the public faithfully.

" The tickets circulated among the Councilmen were, with the exception of the names of Messrs. Dickinson and Marks, made up of those of the present Board of Guardians. Among the candidates were: E. E. Smith, (P. P.); J. L. Hamelin, (distributor of coal contracts) ; J. J. Allison, (vindicator of Buzzardism), and A. H. Dunlay (the silent and sly). The names were conveniently arranged, so that, whoever was defeated, Mr. Marks, who was on all tickets, would slide in. He appears to have been the special favorite of the present Board, and, unless we are mistaken, will be regarded by them as their representative.

"Those chosen for the Board of Health are, with the exception of Dr. Jewell, hardly as well fitted for the position as the gentlemen named by the Courts. But they are, perhaps, as good as could be expected from a partisan body.

"The new Boards are now filled. Mr. Williams, we understand, intends to hold on to his appointment to the Poor Board, notwithstanding the opposition manifested everywhere to it.

"Robert Ewing has signified his intention of resigning. He did not seek the position, and his appointment was a tribute to his personal worth. He has every qualification to fill the office honorably, and we trust he may reconsider his intentions.

"Elhanan W. Keyser, it is stated, will also resign his position, in consequence of ill health. This intelligence will be received among all good citizens with sincere regret.

"The Guardians of the Poor have a Herculean task before them. They should at once, upon organizing, institute a searching investigation into all the affairs of their predecessors. They owe it to themselves, no less than to the public, to ascertain the whole amount of purchases made, how much of these have been delivered at the Almshouse, what quantity of fuel, clothing and supplies of every kind remain on hand, what proportion of the annual appropriation has been spent, what sum is to the credit of the department, and so on.

"This inquiry and a general publication of the result, are essential and should be immediately made.

"They should proceed to clear the institution of the *fungi* therein. In the first place they should elect a capable, discreet and gentlemanly Resident Physician in the place of Dr. R. K. Smith. To do otherwise would awaken general indignation. The affairs and the conduct of the officials deserve and should receive a rigid inspection, and especially the Steward's and the Storekeeper's departments. In a word the community expects the new Board to start fairly and squarely, with a candid exposition of Almshouse affairs and a thorough clearance of every officer who has in any way departed from an honest discharge of duty. We shall see what they will do."

The last meeting of the old Board was held on the 4th of July, 1859, at the Almshouse, for the purpose of closing up the business of the year, previous to final adjournment.

The annual report of the Visitors contained the following information : " Sent to the Almshouse during the year, 4,495 ; doctors' orders, 2,602 ; funerals, 58 ; coffins, 138 ; tons of coal distributed, 4,510 ; cords of wood distributed, 1,062½ ; cash paid for relief, $275.81 ; incidentals, $341.22 ; groceries distributed, $14,188.87.

The Out-door Agent collected $2,852.00 for immigrant tax. A resolution was adopted appropriating $100 to the Out-door Agent for services rendered in collecting this tax.

Dr. Oliver offered a resolution " returning thanks to the officers of the House for the efficient manner in which they have conducted the affairs of the institution," which was adopted unanimously.

Mr. Hamelin offered a resolution of thanks to the President of the Board, for the satisfactory manner in which he had discharged his duties, which was also unanimously adopted.

The President returned his thanks to the members and said that he and his colleagues separated with the kindliest feelings. He suggested that the retiring Board receive the new Board in a suitable manner, and not treat them as he and his colleagues had been treated—when they entered the House by one door, the old Board went out by another, and left them to get along in the best way they could.

A resolution was adopted requesting the Steward to introduce the new Board in the meeting room ; after which the old Board adjourned *sine die*.

At 10 o'clock the members of the Board reassembled, when the members of the new Board were introduced by Mr. Henzey, the Steward, and were welcomed by Mr. Kensil, the retiring President, who stated the willingness of himself and his colleagues of the old Board to render any information to the new Board that might be desired.

The old Board then vacated the seats, and the members of the new Board were sworn by Alderman Beitler to support the Constitution of the State and of the United States, and to perform the duties of the office of Guardians of the Poor with fidelity, after which the Board was organized by the election of Mr. E. W. Keyser as President.

Mr. Keyser, upon taking the chair, made the following brief speech :

"For the honor you have thus conferred upon me I return my sincere thanks. I pledge myself to perform the duties of the office with fidelity and impartiality. What can I say more ? "

Mr. F. A. Server was elected Treasurer, Mr. Henzey, Steward, and nearly all of the subordinates of the institution were retained, so it will be seen that the Board did not act upon the advice to make a clean sweep.

This is an account of the meeting as it appears on the minute book. The papers of that time went more into details and published the proceedings in their own style. One of the newspapers contained the following under a heading styled " The dying words of the doomed."

" The Board of Guardians of the Poor gave up the ghost on the morning of July 4th, one thousand eight hundred and fifty-nine. An event so important to tax payers, who have been fleeced so completely by the majority of the twenty-four, deserves a special record, and we accordingly transfer to the columns ' the dying words of the doomed.'

" After the consideration of a few reports and a resolution voting one hundred dollars extra pay to somebody in office and likely to go out,

" Dr. Oliver offered a resolution of thanks to the officers of the institution, and of the Board, and especially the Steward and the farmer, for their uniform capability, diligence and integrity in the performance of their duties.

"The President remarked that with one exception, and this one he would not name under the circumstances, all of the officers of the Board had done their duty in a manner that should command the respect of everybody.

"Mr. Brown said that to the ability of Mr. Henzey, Steward, and Mr. Myers, farmer, he owed the duty of bearing the strongest testimony. The ability and efficiency of both were above praise.

"Mr. Budd also said that he fully endorsed the comments of the gentlemen who had preceded him. With one exception every officer of the Board had done his duty. That one person he should not name, but he had entailed upon this Board and upon the Almshouse a stigma which could not be wiped out. With this exception he would heartily endorse the resolution, and hoped it would pass unanimously.

"Mr. Kames 'wouldn' make *any* exception whatever. He knew the person referred to, but thought he was more sinned against than sinning. The bills of mortality during the past year,' added he, ' show that as a physician this man has done his duty as well as any man that ever occupied the position. If he does anything outside of that its his own business.' The President: 'No name has been mentioned.' Mr. Kames: 'No, but everybody knows who is meant. I go in for covering up all animosities at a time like this. There is no use killing a man after he's dead.'

"Mr. Freno said that in leaving the Board he wished to thank his associates for all their uniform courtesies to himself and the officers of the Board and of the institution for their unvarying gentlemanly deportment to everybody. He would heartily support the resolution. The resolution was unanimously agreed to.

"Mr. Hamelin offered a resolution of thanks to R. W. Kensil, the President of the Board. It was adopted unanimously, and the President responded gracefully and feelingly in reply.

"Mr. Kames seemed to have died harder than the rest. He seems to have almost wept over his fate, and ' at a time like this ' was ready 'to cover up all animosities.' With keen and cutting memories still clinging to his susceptible heart, he couldn't help thinking, and that aloud, that 'there was no use killing a man after he's dead.' Alas, and has the paragon to whom Mr. Kames referred no other praise than this! How are the mighty fallen, when such a saint as Dr. Robert K. Smith, of Fagan fame, has none so poor as to do him reverence, who must be passed by because 'there was no use killing a man after he's dead.' Alack! one short month ago it was not thus. One month hence it will not be as it now is. Amen."

One of the first of the important subjects to claim the attention of the new Board was the reorganization of the medical department. From the manner in which it had been managed and the very decided opposition to the continuance of Dr. Smith as Chief Resident Physician, it was thought that the best solution of that question would be the abolition of the office and a return to the old system.

A resolution to that effect was offered and referred to a committee. Two reports were made to the Board on July 18th, 1859, the majority report favored it, while that of the minority opposed the proposition. In the latter report it was stated:

" The Guardians of the Poor, under its present organization, exists by virtue of a recent law, extorted from the Legislature by the force of public opinion founded on the belief that much corruption and extravagant expenditures existed in the Department, oppressive to the taxpayers and injurious to the prosperity of the city. The great object of the Board, therefore, is to proceed at once to the performance of the duties for which it was created, those of investigating and removing the abuses alleged to exist in the management of affairs, and not to waste the time of the members here and in committees in discussing subjects with respect to which two-thirds of them are wholly inexperienced.

" As the model system of the world, that of the Hospitals of Paris ought not to be overlooked. In considering this question it may be well to observe here that in them all the medical officers, from the highest to the lowest, receive salaries, and that by abolishing the office of Chief Resident Physician the Board will be departing wholly from the principles of this model, and removing the only paid and responsible officer who can assist them in the performance of a most important part of their duties."

" Action was postponed for the present."

The physicians of the Homœopathic Medical College were very anxious to practice and teach in Blockley Hospital, and on the 8th of August, 1859, they presented, through Mr. Linnard, the following very liberal proposition :

" We, the subscribers, Physicians of the City of Philadelphia, and Professors of the Homœopathic Medical College of Pennsylvania, propose to the Guardians of the Poor, as Directors of the Blockley Hospital, to take entire charge of the medical department of that institution, to carefully, punctually and faithfully examine and prescribe for all cases that shall be sent to the wards of the Hospital, we, ourselves, bearing the expense of all the medicines which may be necessary, and we pledge ourselves that for one year from this date the institution shall be at no expense for the same, thus saving the city the sum of $12,000 for the year."

This was signed by Doctors Charles J. Hempel, John Redman Coxe, J. W. Ward, Jacob Blakely, W. Ashton Reed, M. Semple and Thomas Moore.

The Board was not prepared to consider such an important measure at that time, so the proposition was laid on the table.

The office of Chief Resident Physician was abolished, to take effect on the 15th of September, 1859. " Dr. Smith was notified to vacate and surrender possession of the premises now occupied by him at the Almshouse."

This did not suit the doctor, and he ignored the notice until he found that "discretion was the better part of valor." He sent the following communication to the Board on October 11, 1859 : " I am willing at this time to deliver up possession of the house I now occupy. My self-respect dictates that I should not remain when the Board wishes me to go ; and I therefore relinquish all my legal rights." He strongly denounced Mr. Linnard, a member of the Board, as the author of the proceedings against him ; he

16

said that he incurred the enmity of Mr. Linnard by suspending a relative of his (Mr. L.'s) from the Medical Department nearly a year before.

After the reading of the letter, Mr. Linnard said that "there was not a word of truth in the assertions of Dr. Smith."

Whatever may have been the abilities of Dr. Smith, he seems to have been a man of such temperament as to make himself disliked by a large number of those with whom he was brought in contact.

Much feeling and comment were caused by the omission of a bid for furnishing the Almshouse with meat, which was sent to the office of the Board by Mr. John Palmer.

Mr. Palmer swore that on the 31st of July, 1859, he handed to Mr. Seultzer a proposal in writing to furnish the Almshouse with beef for $4.95 per hundred pounds, which proposal he believed was withheld from the Board after it was handed to Mr. C. M. Derringer, the Secretary of the Board.

Mr. Seultzer swore that he handed the proposal to Mr. Derringer on the 1st of August, and Mr. Charles B. Miller swore that he was present at that time and saw Mr. Seultzer hand two papers enclosed in envelopes, which he believed to be proposals for beef, to Mr. Derringer ; he said the Secretary looked at them and said that the endorsements were correct.

Messrs. Server, Marks and Dickinson were appointed as a committee to investigate the matter. Messrs. Server and Marks made a majority report, in which they stated : " Your Committee are of opinion that the contract with Mr. Hunt is a fortunate one.

Mr. Jones states in reference to it that the expectation was in offering it that, if things should continue in *statu quo* for two months, some two hundred dollars could be made on the contract, and that by reserving the choice pieces for the regular trade and furnishing the Almshouse the rough pieces called for in the advertisement. But he also stated that within two months the state of the market might so change that an immense loss might result, even several thousand dollars. The profit, quad rupled on the amount stated above, would not be unreasonable, your Committee think, in the face of the risk incurred, if the above statement is made upon possible changes in the beef market.

"Your committee was not charged to inquire whether Mr. Hunt's contract should be abided by; but since Mr. Palmer in his petition asks that the present award be set aside and his proposal accepted, your committee take occasion to remind the Board that your advertisement was for proposals from responsible parties, and it may very properly be questioned whether, under the testimony and statement exhibited, the public interests would be subserved by a change.

"Your committee conclude that the question 'the accident, mistake or neglect' by which the proposal of Mr. Palmer was lost, is a matter between that gentleman and Mr. Seultzer, and not between this Board and its Secretary. It seems quite probable that Mr. Palmer's bid would never have been heard of had Mr. Hunt's bid been $5.22, or Mr. Seultzer's $5.16.

"Fully exonerating Mr. Derringer from all complicity or neglect, your committee would conclude by expressing their confidence in his faithfulness as an officer, and respectfully submit the following resolution :

"*Resolved*, That the committee be discharged from the further consideration of the subject."

Mr. Dickinson submitted a minority report, which stated "that, upon inquiry, he had ascertained that the gentlemen who testified in relation to the facts of the alleged proposal having been made by Mr. Palmer, are gentlemen of standing and entitled to belief; and he felt constrained to give full credit to all they had sworn to relative to the alleged missing proposal submitted to the Board, and which, from all the testimony adduced, he believed, must have been lost or purloined from the Secretary's desk."

The majority report was agreed to and the committee discharged.

The newspapers of that period commented upon the action of the Board, and one of them had this editorial :

"The Almshouse Beef Contract."

"One of the most disgraceful proceedings that has lately occurred in any public body, was enacted in the Board of Guardians of the Poor on Monday last.

"The details of the beef business are familiar to most of our readers, but the manner in which the proposal of Mr. Palmer was purloined or suppressed is likely to remain unknown only to the guilty parties. No one doubts, or can doubt, that John Palmer made a proposal in a proper manner to the Board ; and, according to his testimony and that of another important witness, his bid was lower than that of any or all of the others competing with him. Messrs. Server and Marks, however, notwithstaning Mr. Palmer offered to supply the Almshouse with beef at $4.95 per hundred weight, consider the city quite 'fortunate' in being obliged to pay Mr. Hunt $5.20; and they have the boldness to say that this conclusion of theirs was brought about by a statement of John H. Jones, the late beef contractor of the Almshouse and brother-in-law of this very man Hunt.

"The figuring of these apologists for fraudulent transactions is really deserving of attention. They say that Hunt, at the present rates, will reap a profit of $100 per month, and yet they consider that another party could not afford to supply the institution for $80 per month, or five per cent. less than the profit above stated. They are not willing that the Board shall pay an advance of one thousand dollars per year to one person, but they are willing that another shall receive forty-eight hundred dollars for the same service.

"They think, even, that this would not be at all 'unreasonable.' It may appear right enough to Messrs. Server and Marks thus to squander thirty-eight hundred dollars, but the public will hardly agree with them or indorse such folly.

"But what right have the gentlemen to assume that Mr. Palmer would not fulfill his contract as faithfully as Mr. John H. Jones' brother-in-law?

"He is, as far as we can learn, a man of equal respectability, quite as honorable in his business transactions, and perhaps a little better able to carry out a contract in all its requirements. It is a bold assumption, therefore, on their part, because wholly unwarranted, and because it has added to the expenses of the Almshouse management, without any justification whatever.

" Mr. Dickinson, whose minority report was more fair and just in all its conclusions, has entitled himself to public approval for his course on this subject; and, indeed, his career throughout is in marked contrast with that of Messrs. Server and Marks, who were members of the Board in former years, and whose appointment cannot but be regretted. Had such experienced hands been excluded from appointment and men of Mr. Dickinson's stamp only chosen, no whitewashing like that which has taken place would in all probabilities have occurred. As it is, the President should hereafter exclude Messrs. Marks and Server from committees of investigation, for the reason that they are utterly unfit to honorably discharge the duties imposed."

At this meeting the House Committee presented a statement showing that they had on hand three barrels of whiskey purchased from Bispham & Son, which the committee, after having the quality and price tested, considered of inferior quality and exorbitant price.

The article was said to have cost 62½ cents per gallon, although the bill had not been presented for consideration.

The question of returning the whiskey to Messrs. Bispham & Son, together with the bill of James Elliott for whiskey and port wine, were brought before the Board for action upon them.

A long discussion ensued, and the quality of the whiskey furnished by Mr. Elliott and Messrs. Bispham was discussed, during which much temper was shown by some of the members of the Board. Mr. Maris asserted that the whiskey furnished by Mr. Elliott was not worth more than 70 cents per gallon, for which he had charged $1.50. This was a portion of the liquor purchased by Mr. Bender, the apothecary, a brother-in-law of Mr. Marks. On the other hand Mr. Marks denounced the whiskey bought of the Bisphams as " vile trash," not fit for external application, and demanded that it be returned. This was purchased by Mr. Maris, who also favored its return as, he said, Mr. Bispham could get 75 cents per gallon for it.   As most of the members declared that they were "no judges of the article," it was finally agreed that the bill of Mr. Elliott should be paid, as the whiskey had been used in the institution.   The Board refused to return the whiskey to Messrs. Bispham & Son, and the matter was dropped.

CHAPTER XXII.

PATHOLOGICAL MUSEUM—STUDENTS ADMITTED FREE—BAKE-HOUSE
ERECTED.

THE large number of vagrants and drunkards supported in the Almshouse was a subject of much concern to the Board of Guardians, and which was the best way to abate the nuisance was a question that was continually under discussion. Mr. Dickinson showed the opinion he entertained when he offered a resolution on the 11th of October, 1859, that a committee of three be appointed to confer with a similar Committee of Councils and Prisons, to consider the initiatory steps to be taken for the erection of a House of Correction. Messrs. Dickinson, Robbins and Marks were appointed.

A new bake-house had been erected at a cost of $1,932.12, but the bread furnished the inmates was not entirely satisfactory to everybody. Considerable complaint was made in some quarters, and the press took up the subject. An editorial appeared in the *Daily News* on Thursday morning, October 27th, 1859, which read as follows:

"GOD HELP THE POOR.

"We were shown, a few days since, a sample of the bread which is now doled out to the poor paupers of the Philadelphia Almshouse, under the new reform regime of Messrs. Linnard, Robbins, Marks & Co. If we kept a horse, we should consider him but moderately fed with the stuff which was cut from one of the loaves in the storehouse of this institution, and which now lies on our desk.

"We are impelled to the belief that the men who will so far forget the purposes of their appointment, would be well placed by changing positions with those over whom they have been appointed as Guardians.

"The history of this institution, as far as we can discern, never before presented so deplorable and humiliating a spectacle as at this moment. There are paupers there, and little children, as we are informed, absolutely clamorous for bread, that which is provided for them, as before suggested, being entirely unfit for use. The appetite that could master such diet must be voracious indeed, and this is the kind of bread they give the sick and the children. It is made from wheat middlings, which the baker said is purchased for $3.75 per barrel, and is the only kind of bread now used in the institution.

"But this is not the worst feature in the case; even with such diet furnished them, the quantity has been reduced to the starvation point by orders of the Committee on *Economy ;* and the matron of the Children's Asylum was found in tears a few days ago because she could not supply the wants of those committed to her care without disobeying orders and subjecting herself to the possibility of a loss of her situation.

"We are informed by a visitor that the old, infirm and sick who have friends visiting them and leaving their little contributions of money to purchase necessaries that are calculated to make them more comfortable, now send out their money to buy bread! Can this be possible? Will it be tolerated in the city of Philadelphia? Have the people of this great city the disposition to aid three or four men in their efforts to show a reduction of twenty or thirty thousand dollars in the public expenditures at the sacrifice of every principle of humanity and the neglect of every Christian duty?

"The new order of things has been established to convince the people that money can be saved in managing the Almshouse, and under the operation of this system we have no doubt it can. But there is something more intrinsic than the money it costs. Complaints from that institution come in thick and fast; everything there seems to be anarchy and confusion, and the present majority, made up as it is by men who have sought the sympathy and assistance of the Loco Foco party, seem to have but a single idea and a single object, and that is to show at the end of their term a saving of *money*.

"It is the appointment of such narrow, miserable men as these to public office that brings disgrace upon the city, and it is from just such men we would expect starvation. One of the members of the Board, who as we are informed is on the *Screw Press* Committee, whilst curtailing the appetites and cutting off supplies at the Almshouse, takes very good care to pasture his cows upon the public grass, and it is, therefore, fair to suppose that he has more sympathy for a dumb brute than for a human being, provided that brute is a cow and his own, and the fellow-being a pauper.

"As there is such an extraordinary disposition to economize in the Board of Guardians, we suggest to members that they should inquire into this pasture business of Mr. Linnard. It is a very small matter, truly, but then this is the day of small things at the Almshouse, and therefore it is a proper subject of inquiry."

A meeting of the committees to consider the subject of a House of Correction was held at the Almshouse on December 21, 1859.

During the discussion of the question, Mr. Dickinson, one of the Guardians of the Poor, stated that they had recently put to work between 80 and 100 men at one of the quarries on the Almshouse farm, "getting out stone" to be used in the construction of work shops which it is proposed to commence in the coming spring, or to be sold for the benefit of the institution. The men thus set to work are those who have heretofore idled their time away in the inside of the hollow square of buildings, smoking pipes and conversing together.

"This class comprises those who claim that they 'cannot support themselves; they would work if they could get it to do, but not being able to obtain employment, they are forced to go to the Almshouse, in preference to starving.'

"The Guardians taking them at their word, have given them work to do in the mode described and the result is there is a decrease in the population of the House of nearly one hundred, compared with the same time last year.

"The lazy class who frequently winter at the Almshouse, finding that they will be put to hard work inside, with considerable personal restraint, have wisely concluded to find work outside, where they have more liberty.

"There are still a number of mechanics, carpenters, shoe-makers, tailors and others, who, although able to work cannot be profitably employed at quarrying stone, which would disable them so much that no advantage would result from putting them to work at it. 'Many of these are usefully employed at repairing in the House, and if Councils should authorize the construction of new workshops, there is little doubt that all who are able would be profitably employed, and the Almshouse become in reality an insti-tution for the relief and employment of the poor, as specified in the Act of incorporation.' As a result of the conference it was decided that the Departments of the Poor and of Prisons should each petition Councils to appropriate sufficient sums to enable the Guardians to erect suitable workshops at the Almshouse, and the prison authorities to purchase more ground south of the prison and to construct the necessary buildings for the accommodation of prison uses and work shops.

"On the 3d of January, 1860, Mr. Dickinson offered a resolu-tion that provided for the 'immediate removal of the cells in the vaults of the Lunatic Asylum.'

"Mr. Dickinson, in speaking in favor of its adoption, said: 'That since learning of the death of a lunatic in the cells of that department, the Committee had visited the vaults referred to, and to their surprise found that there were cells in them, and that shortly before the present Board assumed control, these cells were used for the confinement of prisoners.'"

The resolution was agreed to.

"The subject of the abuses of the out-door system of relief was one that caused considerable discussion. It was an evil that was very hard to eradicate; much could be said on both sides, but it seemed as though the evils destroyed the good that was intended. 'Poor orders' were given to persons having a 'pull,' and supplies were furnished to those who were not entitled to them, and were amply able to do without such gifts. There were always frauds in the world, and as neither modesty nor principle predominated in their make up, they frequently succeeded in getting what was intended for more deserving people.

" The subject was ventilated at a meeting of the Board, held on January 16th, 1860, when Mr. Maris offered a resolution which provided that a ' supply of bread should be placed in the offices of the Visitors of the Poor, to be delivered whenever practicable, to applicants for relief, in lieu of orders for groceries.'

" Mr. Maris, in the course of his remarks on the subject, said that he had given some attention to this matter and he was satisfied that there was a very great amount of abuse practiced daily.

" It has been ascertained that not a few of the applicants for orders had obtained such luxuries as green tea, oranges, lemons, fruit, white sugar, and other luxurious articles on them, instead of the good solid necessaries of life. I have found upon close examination, that the list of names of persons who obtained aid from the visitors of the poor, are recorded on many, if not all of the charitable organizations of the city. We have the sick, the aged, and the infirm, whose every day wants should be supplied, and on the other hand we have a good-for-nothing set of lazy, idle loafers, who work in the warm weather, and spend their money in rum drinking, and then depend upon the Guardians of the Poor, and other charitable institutions for support. I am well aware of these facts, but am not prepared at present to take final action. The subject will certainly have my earliest consideration, and I hope that of the members of the Board also.

" By cutting off the lazy, improvident set of rum-drinking loafers, we would have a better opportunity of giving to the deserving poor, of which we have many in our midst."

Mr. Linnard desired to corroborate what Mr. Maris had said, and after some further debate, the matter was " withdrawn for the present."

The Committee on Manufactures reported on January 30th, 1860, that Councils had appropriated $5,000 to construct a workshop; the Committee was instructed to proceed with its erection on the plans adopted.

Another subject that claimed considerable attention at this period, in the community at large, as well as in the Board, was the report, frequently repeated, of the robbing of the graveyard of the bodies deposited there.

The ferryman, who had charge of this part of the institution, appeared to have been a man of very low character, and several attempts were made to dispense with him; but he seems to have had enough influence to retain his position.

One of the papers of that time contained the following editorial, which shows some of the feeling that existed regarding this matter:

" MODERN BODY-SNATCHING.

" In the personnel of the Almshouse are two officers between whom there exists an irreconcilable antagonism. The one is the estimable Mr. Linnard, of the Board of Guardians, and the other is a genius who occupies a position whose incumbent is termed the " ferryman." Mr. Linnard is in some respects a queer fish, while the ferryman is an equally queer fish in other points of view. Mr. Linnard bears a strong likeness to many of the portraits of George Washington, and being a hard-shell Baptist deacon, wears a voluminous white neckcloth, with fastenings hid from human vision, and supposed to be lying perdu somewhere about the spinal column. The ferryman isn't particular as to what *he* wears, and in personal appearance is suggestive of a cross between George Munday and a ghoul. The duties of the ferryman, now that the ferry is abolished, are to supervise the engine by which water is pumped into the buildings, to take charge of the banks of the river, to boss the paupers in the quarry and to attend to the duties of the graveyard. The latter is an institution of which few people except medical students and professors have any knowledge. Medical students during the winter season are charged from ten to fifteen dollars for each human subject for the dissecting tables, and a brisk business is done during the terms of the college lectures in the corpses of those who die at the Almshouse and whose bodies are not claimed by friends. Of revenue to the city not a single cent inures by the sale of these bodies; and as the ferryman has the sole control of the matter, the inference that the ferryman's position is a paying one is certainly admissable.

HOUSE FOR NURSES

"A spicy debate occurred at the last meeting of the Board of Guardians from this especial cause. Mr. Linnard, in the sincerity of his purposes, objects to this traffic in human corpses, and especially when the proceeds do not inure to the benefit of the city. He is plain and blunt in his address, is Mr. Linnard, and significantly said that he preferred to see bodies openly carried away from the graveyards by medical students, to seeing the pockets of the Superintendent surreptitiously lined by the auriferous traffic. Mr. Linnard's resolution to abolish the office of Superintendent of the Graveyard failed only by a tie vote. If renewed at some future time it will be likely to carry, for some of the members who voted in the negative voted under a misapprehension of the case.

"We are not the foe of science. For this reason we cannot oppose the relinquishment to the medical colleges of the bodies of those who die at the public charge, without friends whose feelings might be lacerated by the circumstances.

"But it is right and proper that whatever revenue accrues from this source should be paid into the treasury of the Board, to aid in defraying the heavy expenses for the support of an army of paupers, and of whom three-fourths are of foreign birth. If Mr. Linnard with his characteristic pertinacity in whatever he believes to be right, should still adhere to his movement, we think he will accomplish it, and that the wisdom of his policy will be vindicated by the removal of the present ferryman, and the abolition of modern body snatching as practiced at the Almshouse."

A singular circumstance occurred in July, 1860. It seems that certain parties made a bet, over which a dispute arose. The Guardians of the Poor entered suit to recover the amount of money involved in the bet, and obtained a judgment of $800 against each of the wagers. A communication was received from the City Solicitor enclosing one from Thomas Greenbank, attorney, offering as a compromise for both suits the sum of $1,000. The City Solicitor advised the settlement, and the Board followed his advice.

At the meeting on the 16th of August, 1860, Mr. Dickinson offered the following:

" WHEREAS, The buildings at present appropriated to the use of the Insane Department of the Almshouse are overcrowded and improperly arranged for the judicious classification and proper treatment of the patients, thus thwarting, in a great measure, the efforts of the Board of Guardians to place those under their care in the best possible condition by the influence of properly applied disciplinary and medical treatment, to insure their restoration to reason, and to relieve the public of the burden of their support; and,

" WHEREAS, The number of admissions in this department is steadily increasing, and thus constantly adding to the existing difficulties and demanding the serious consideration of this Board; therefore, be it

" *Resolved*, That a committee of five be appointed to examine the buildings at present appropriated to the use of the epileptic, idiotic and insane patients of the Almshouse; also the buildings occupied as general hospital; and to report for the consideration of this Board plans for rearranging and altering or extending the same, in order that the patients therein may be better accommodated, and such other matters appertaining thereto as they may deem of interest."

This called forth a lengthy discussion, during which Mr. Maris, who was elected President upon the death of Mr. Keyser in February, stated that he thought the inquiry of the Committee should be extended so as to consider whether a House of Correction could not be erected on the Almshouse grounds. He said " that in five or six years the insane department would be entirely overcrowded. At present there are 450 inmates, and in a year or two there would doubtless be 550, which would be beyond the limits of the present buildings to accommodate. It has been suggested by old members of the Board, that, by making certain changes in the buildings, a portion of the premises might be used for a House of Correction, which would save $150,000 to the City."

The resolutions were adopted and Messrs. Dickinson, Server, Erety, Brown and the President were appointed.

The following was presented at the meeting on September 24th, 1860 :

" *Gentlemen.*—The Committee on Hospital and Insane Departments, to which was referred the communication of the Medical Board suggesting the propriety of establishing a museum for the preservation of pathological and other specimens to aid in the investigation of diseases, respectfully report: That they have given the subject much thought, and are of opinion that a museum of the kind contemplated would be a valuable acquisition to the Medical Department of the Hospital and Almshouse; and can be collected and arranged at a comparatively trifling expense to the institution."

Respectfully,

M. H. DICKINSON,

J. M. LINNARD.

The Committee was authorized to make the necessary arrangements for establishing a museum; provided the expense would not exceed at any time the appropriation for that purpose.

At this same meeting it was decided "that hereafter the students attending the Medical Colleges, would be allowed to visit the hospital free of charge, and not be compelled to purchase tickets of admission, as they had previously been compelled to do."

CHAPTER XXIII.

MR. DICKINSON, Chairman of the Committee on Manufactures reported, "That they had erected upon the site of the old wooden workshop, a substantial stone building 160 feet long, 50 feet wide and two stories high. The lower story of the building will be appropriated to the use of the carpenters, wheelwrights and the fire apparatus belonging to the institution. The second-story will be occupied by the shoemakers, tailors and weavers, the Superintendent of Manufactures, and storeroom for the use of that department. The building formerly occupied by the weavers has been converted into a blacksmith shop, with the necessary furnaces and forges for doing all the work appertaining to this branch of industry.

"The entire cost of the building, exclusive of the material obtained from the quarry and sand banks on the premises, the greater portion of the labor having been performed by the inmates of the Almshouse, was $4,348.16."

The erection of this building gave great satisfaction, and as a proof that the work was well done one need only look at it at the present time, as it is still in use for the purposes for which it was erected.

In connection with this subject one of the papers of that date said : "Heretofore, the Almshouse was a sort of caravansera for able bodied but lazy men and women. Under the old Board, especially, stout and hearty loafers found comfortable quarters at the public expense, their only service in return, being performed at the polls when this political vagabond or that desired preferment. Under the present *regime*, with the prospect of work before them, this class have kept aloof and it is to be presumed that, with the successful prosecution of the manufacturing system there, the House will become what it was intended to be—a refuge for the suffering and deserving poor.

" With the details of the Committee's plans for the future we have not as yet been made acquainted, though it is stated that carpenters, cabinet makers, turners, wheelwrights, coopers, painters, tin and sheet-iron workers, shoemakers, tailors and weavers are to be kept steadily employed. It is presumed, however, that they will be compensated, as they should be, for their labor, over and above what it costs to maintain them. Such a policy would be a just and encouraging one. It would conduce to greater industry and inure to the benefit of the city as well as to the paupers themselves. Many of the latter are illy fitted for life's struggles in the broad world, and, unrestrained, are of no service to society or themselves. Such, by an encouraging system of compensation, could be induced to remain where temptations do not beset them and where they may be enabled to lay by something for future years of effort. At any rate, they should be paid for the labor they render beyond the actual cost of their support and management.

" To the operations of this workshop we look with more than ordinary hopefulness. It will, if properly directed, lead to what is generally desired—in the establishment of a more extensive House of Employment for petty offenders of all grades.

" The necessity of an institution of the kind is universally admitted, not alone as a matter of mere monetary economy, but as a conservator of the peace and morals of the community. There are thousands of instances occurring every year which demonstrate the policy of an early and earnest movement in that direction ; and arguments in its favor have been and are presented weekly and daily, either by grand juries, the proceedings of our courts, the records of our prisons or the hearings before the police magistrates.

" Petty offenders are not necessarily criminals as the term is generally applied. They are not as a general thing wilful in their acts. Idleness and vagrant habits have far more to do with their offenses than their moral status; and with class employment and restraint—not in prisons, but in Almshouses—can effect much in the way of reform. A helping hand and cheering words do more in raising the fallen than the felon's brand or the common curse ; and the sooner society is made to understand and act upon this

17

truth, the greater will be the safeguards around both person and property."

An editorial in another paper at that time brought a phase of one of the abuses of outdoor relief into view in commenting upon the action of the Board in adopting a resolution to check the fraud. The article said:

"A Needed Regulation.

"At the last meeting of the Guardians of the Poor, at the instance of Mr. Dickinson, a resolution was adopted, by which the coal contractors are required to take receipts for all the fuel they deliver, and present such receipts as vouchers for their bills. In former times there were many irregularities, to use no harsher term, in the delivery of fuel to the suffering poor. In many instances, well-to-do favorites of the Buzzards were supplied with winter warmth from the public bin, and in others charges were frequently made where no deliveries had taken place. Of course, there was no remedy. Under this resolution, however, it will be easy to ascertain who receives the fuel and in what quantities; and should false charges be made, forgery will be added to dishonesty. The offenders can, therefore, be readily reached."

It looks strange to see in a minute book a record " that Mr. Williams presented a communication from the nurses and others in the Almshouse, asking if some means could not be devised by which they could get their pay for the last four months, not having even received warrants, which they would be willing to sell at a discount."

Good service could hardly be expected under such circumstances, and there was mismanagement somewhere, when employees were treated in that manner.

Councils, acting under the advice of the Board of Health, directed that the Small Pox Hospital should be closed after 1st of April, 1861.

The Guardians of the Poor notified the Board of Health that " in future no more small pox patients will be received by this Board on the Almshouse grounds."

A communication was received from the Board of Health in reply to the notice, saying that the same was unbecoming and out of place for a department that provides for the pauper population, etc.

On motion of Mr. Marks, " this very *becoming* communication " was laid on the table by the Guardians.

Messrs. George Williams and James Marks tendered their resignations as members of the Board on March 11th, 1861. They were accepted.

The Visitors reported that they had relieved 9,453 persons at a cost of $4,178.83. The nativity of those relieved was : 335 Germans, 1,606 Irish, 147 English, 5 Welsh, 32 Scotch, 2 Italians, 13 French, 645 Philadelphians, 421 Pennsylvanians, and 600 from other parts of the United States.

The House Committee reported the average population of the House for the last quarter to be an increase of 235 over the same period of the previous year. The population on March 6th was 2,745 ; same time of previous year it was 2,386, an increase of 359.

This was just previous to the commencement of the war of the rebellion. There were large numbers of worthy people thrown out of employment, and thousands of families suffered for the necessaries of life. The Guardians of the Poor were kept busily engaged in the distribution of out-door relief. All of the charitable organizations were also doing the same kind of work. All kinds of calls for contributions were issued, and it was stated that " There never was a greater need of aid than now, nor objects more deserving of Christian charity."

Mr. Mahlon H. Dickinson tendered his resignation as a member of the Board. Mr. Linnard said he hoped an inducement would be held out to Mr. Dickinson, in order that the Board might not lose so industrious a member. Mr. Brown spoke in very high terms of the energy, zeal and experience of Mr. Dickinson. He regretted that the resignation had been sent in.

It was generally acknowledged that Mr. Dickinson was one of the most valuable members of the Board, and so, without doubt, he was. After much persuasion the resignation was withdrawn, and Mr. Dickinson rendered good service for several years after.

A resolution offered by Mr. Erety to establish an asylum for foundlings brought out a lengthy discussion. The President stated "that the deaths of foundlings in the House were 95 out of 100. The cause of this mortality was owing to the foul air in the wards. The deficiency of food was also another cause. A mortality of 95 per cent. is awful; there is a great necessity for doing something. At present the little children do not get enough to eat! This statement is alarming but true. A number of women could be obtained, anxious to nurse the children. I favor the establishment of a separate ward for the foundlings. If that will not decrease the mortality list, something else must be done."

Mr. Brown was inclined to think that the deaths were not so many as stated. During a late visit, he said, the children presented a healthy appearance. He was not opposed to any means by which the condition of the children could be ameliorated. He also stated that two children had been taken from the House and confided to the care of the Sisters of Mercy at Tacony.

Mr. Erety eulogized the Sisters of Mercy for thus coming forward in the discharge of a high and meritorious calling. He was willing that this fact should be known. For the Christian charity which they manifested let them have credit. Is there any other denomination who would come forward in the same Christian spirit?

Mr. Cresson said " other denominations take care of *old* people. This denomination has *an object* in taking little ones. I am opposed to giving the children to any such people."

Mr. McGrath defended the Sisters from the imputations sought to be cast upon them by the language of the previous speaker. The denomination to which they belong are always anxious to do the best in their power for young and old. He alluded to the proselyting attempts of the Beggar detectives, by which young children were stolen away and taught to forget the faith of their parents.

The matter was finally referred to the Hospital and Children's Committee.

On the 22d of April, 1861, the House Agent was dismissed for "Applying public money belonging to the City, that has come into his hands as an officer of this Board, to his own private use, contrary to Law," and his accounts were placed in the hands of the City Solicitor for "such action as he may deem proper to take."

Several attempts had been made to have an Act passed to authorize the sale of some of the Almshouse property. Different reasons were advanced as to why this should be done, the principal one being that it would furnish the means to build a House of Correction. Whatever the reasons were, the interested parties succeeded in having an Act passed and approved, May 1st, 1861, just as the rebellion broke out, when the public mind was so absorbed that no notice was taken of this legislation. After events clearly show that the erection of a House of Correction had but little place in the minds of those who had the Act passed. This important Act reads as follows:

"SECTION 1.—Be it enacted by the Senate and House of Representatives of the Commonwealth of Pennsylvania in General Assembly met, and it is hereby enacted by the authority of the same, That the City of Philadelphia, is hereby empowered to make private or public sale, and convey in fee simple or reserving ground rents, the present Almshouse grounds, or any part thereof, situate in the twenty-seventh ward of the city, containing one hundred and eighty-seven acres, more or less, and the buildings thereon erected, subject to the following conditions:

"1. That the City of Philadelphia shall reserve a part of said ground, not exceeding forty acres, to be laid out and maintained as an open public place forever, for the health and recreation of the people.

"2. That the said City shall also reserve at Pine and South Streets, on the river Schuylkill, pieces of ground sufficient, in the opinion of the Chief Engineer and Surveyor of said city, for abutments and approaches thereto, for a bridge or bridges, which may be lawfully authorized to be erected at either of said streets.

"SECTION 2.—That the City of Philadelphia is hereby authorized to purchase land and erect thereon an Almshouse or Poor House (with or without a house of correction and employment, as may be deemed expedient), and in payment thereof to create a loan which shall be exempt from State tax.

"SECTION 3.—That the proceeds arising from the sale of grounds and buildings specified in the 1st Section of this Act shall be specifically applied to and pledged for the purpose of payment of the loan authorized by the Second Section of this Act; and if ground rents shall be reserved, or mortgages taken in payment, the same, when sold or paid off, shall be applied to and for the same purpose."

The firing upon the American flag at Fort Sumter fired the blood of the people of the North, and men from all the walks of life volunteered by the thousands. All kinds of encouragement was given by employers to their workmen who desired to enlist; promises of assistance to the families of those who went to the field were freely given, and every inducement was held out to get volunteers for the Army and Navy. The Guardians of the Poor were not behind in that line, as the records show that Mr. McGrath offered the following resolution, which was adopted:

"*Resolved*, That the place of any officer connected with this Board, who may enlist in the service of his country, in defence of the national flag, shall not be vacated, and the salary of such officer shall be continued and paid as usual during the absence of such officer."

At the meeting held on the 13th of August, 1861, Mr. Dickinson offered a resolution "that the Committee on Hospital be instructed to inquire into the expediency of employing the services of Homeopathic physicians for such persons as require out-door relief, that may desire that kind of medical treatment."

Mr. Server was opposed to having two kinds or classes of physicians employed.

Mr. Linnard thought the majority of out-door cases would prefer the Homeopathic treatment. If this resolution would pass, it would be a preparatory step to test the merits of both kinds of treatment. He advocated the Homeopathic system, if for no other reason than that it would be less expensive to the Board.

Mr. Brown said he would be glad to see the Medical Department of the Almshouse equally divided between the Allopathists and the Homeopathists. There was no good reason why it should not be so. In other countries such a system prevails, and works admirably.

Mr. Server replied, "Introduce such a system and we will have endless discussions, quarrels and bickerings. Why·not allow, also, the Botanic and Eclectic systems to be introduced?"

Mr. Linnard said, "Give them all a chance. If science, in its onward march, revolutionizes long established systems, it is generally for the better, and we should not be resisting the tide of progress. The old physicians would, a few years ago, drug a patient with doses, the quarter of which they would not dare to administer to-day. Homeopathy has opened the eyes of the old practitioners, and the results are every day seen. I have all my life been under Allopathic treatment until recently.

The President said, "The gentleman has certainly attained a good old age under that treatment."

Mr. Whitall said it was unnecessary to send the matter to the Hospital Committee, for they would negative it. For myself, he said, "I would not give Homeopathic treatment to a sick dog."

The resolution was amended so as to refer the subject to a Special Committee, and was then adopted. Messrs. Dickinson, Erety and Taylor were appointed as the Committee. At the next meeting of the Board two reports were made. Messrs. Erety and Taylor declared it was inexpedient at this time, and asked to be discharged from the further consideration of the subject.

Mr. Dickinson presented a minority report, saying that "many of the poor will need such treatment, as they would rather be treated in the manner in which they have most faith." A resolution attached to the minority report provided for the election of four homeopathists.

The majority report was adopted. One of the newspapers of that period said in an editorial article:

"The Guardians of the Poor have decided that if the out-door recipients of the charity of our city don't choose to swallow the medicines administered by the allopathic physicians, they may remain sick. An application to permit the administration of homeopathic remedies, where the patient prefers that treatment, was voted down. This decision is not at all creditable to the intelligence or liberality of the Board."

Again, the scandals of "graveyard robberies" had become so clamorous that some notice had to be taken of them. Mr. Server offered a resolution making it "imperative on the Farm Committee to allow no persons to enter the grounds unless having a properly authenticated permit, setting forth their business."

Mr. Dickinson offered a substitute, as follows :

"WHEREAS, It is manifestly the duty of this Board to secure to the unfortunate persons who die in the Almshouse the rites of Christian burial, and to extend to their remains after interment the same care and protection as is given to those who have friends and relatives to watch over and guard their last resting places ; and,

WHEREAS, From the isolated position of the unguarded graveyard attached to the Almshouse, there is no security against the disinterment of the bodies deposited therein; be it therefore

" *Resolved,* That the Committee on Farm and Garden be instructed to select a site suitable for the purpose and estimate the cost of erecting thereon a safe and substantial receiving vault wherein to deposit and keep the remains of those who die in the Almshouse, until removed by their friends or their graves rendered secure from violation by reason of the partial decomposition of their bodies." This was agreed to.

On September 19th, 1861, the new Clinic Room, erected in the rear of the Drug Store, at a cost of $2,765.05, was formally inaugurated. Dr. J. L. Ludlow delivered an able address on the occasion. The old clinic room, in the Insane Department, was floored over and divided into doctors' offices, lecture room, etc.

CHAPTER XXIV.

CONSIDERABLE anxiety was caused in the latter part of the year 1861, by the return to the County Prison of the insane prisoners sent from that institution to the State Insane Asylum at Harrisburg. Under the act which established the State Asylum the several counties were authorized to send to that institution such criminals as were declared insane. A subsequent act changed the system and it was made a curative establishment, the officials being authorized to send back to the counties such persons as might be declared incurable. Six of those sent from Philadelphia were returned to the County Prison in November, and the lack of accommodations in that institution compelled the officials to request the Guardians of the Poor to receive them in the Almshouse.

The names of those returned were Ephraim Gear, Louis Durow, John Jennings, John Logue, George Auble and Jane Glazier.

Gear, who was an old man, made an attempt to shoot Jonas P. Fairlamb as he was stepping from the door of the Court of Quarter Sessions into the grounds of Independence Square, about nine years previous. The Court was in session at the time, and the occurrence caused much excitement. Gear was immediately arrested and the Judge committed him for trial. He was acquitted on the ground of insanity, but was confined in the county prison about two years; after which he was kept in the State Asylum seven years.

Durow was a Prussian, who had been transferred from the debtor's apartment to the county prison several years before, for attempting to cut the throat of one of the inmates. While in the prison he made several attempts to murder persons before he was sent to the Asylum, where he spent several years.

John Jennings was an old man, and but little was known of him at the prison. He spent a number of years in the Asylum.

John Logue was a notable character. He was known as the "Man with the Military Walk." He would disappear at times; then appear on the main streets with high-top boots and buckskin gloves, and strut along in true military style. For a time he was simply amusing, but finally he became troublesome and was arrested for assault and battery. He was pronounced insane and sent to the Asylum.

Auble was a German, forty years old, who killed an inmate of his cell by hitting him with an iron plate. He was acquitted on the ground of insanity, and the Court committed him to the Asylum.

Jane Glazier had been a resident of Kensington. She had been arrested on suspicion of killing her husband and became insane in consequence of it. She spent several years in the State Insane Asylum.

At a meeting of the Board of Guardians, Mr. Erety offered the following:

"*Resolved*, That a committee of three be appointed to examine and report on the probable number of insane, epileptic and idiotic patients it will be necessary to provide for in the Insane department of the Almshouse, in contemplation of the insane patients from Philadelphia now in the State Hospital at Harrisburg being returned to Philadelphia, and together with the insane now in the Philadelphia County Prison, being thrown for support and maintenance on the Guardians of the Poor."

The resolution was adopted, and Messrs. Erety, McGrath and Server were appointed as the committee.

Mr. Dickinson discovered that the Resident Physicians were in the habit of punishing the patients under their charge by the use of a shower-bath and otherwise. He offered a resolution to prevent it. Mr. Server offered an amendment, striking out all after the word "*Resolved*," and inserting "That no authority has been delegated by the Board of Guardians to the Resident Physicians for the infliction of punishment upon patients under their charge, either by commitment to the cells or by means of the shower-baths, and any infraction will subject the offender to immediate suspension by the Hospital Committee." This was agreed to.

The needs of the Army for the suppression of the rebellion were recognized at that time, as will be seen by reports to the Board. The Matron submitted a communication on the 13th of January, 1862, which shows, "with the sanction of the committee, have made, by the women in this department, and furnished to the Pennsylvania troops on the Potomac, 1000 pairs of good woollen stockings and 100 pairs of cloth socks."

Mr. Dickinson offered the following:

"*Resolved*, That the Steward be authorized to loan to the United States Government, for the use of the military hospitals in this city, the hospital tents belonging to this department; and, if desired, on the part of the Government, he is further authorized to grant permission to have them set upon the farm attached to this institution."

The resolution was adopted.

The census showed a decrease of more than 300 in the population of the house, in comparison with the previous year. A great many of the men who generally spent at least part of their time in the house had gone into the service of the country.

Mr. Maris called attention to the reduction made by Councils in the estimates furnished by the Board for the expenses of the House for 1862. The item for flour had been reduced from $27,600 to $25,000, and the item for beef and mutton from $28,000 to $25,000. He said that it used to cost, with the present population, for beef and mutton, $61,000. He regretted the action of Councils, because it had been done without any examination, and was the first evidence shown by them of a want of confidence in the present Board. He thought it would be reconsidered and corrected.

The Committee on Outwards made report of the bad condition of the roofs of the buildings, and instructions were given to obtain estimates for new coverings. The roofs at that time were covered with copper. Estimates were received and it was decided to take off the old copper and put tin on instead. The copper was sold for

$35,070.78, and as the new tin cover cost $12,496.28, there was a balance of $22,574.50 which was used on the children's asylum.

It was common talk for years that "the 'Board of Buzzards' stole the roof off of the Almshouse," but this statement refutes the assertion.

The Committee to whom was assigned the duty of erecting a vault for the reception and safe keeping of the bodies of those who died in the institution, reported—"That in accordance with instructions, they had a vault erected in the Almshouse grounds, at a cost not exceeding $100."

The receptacle was twenty-five feet long and twelve feet wide, and was fitted to hold forty-two coffins. The substantial manner in which it was built and its close proximity to the residence of the outside watchman, made the Committee feel confident that the bodies deposited therein would remain undisturbed until they were no longer desirable for the dissecting table.

A resolution was adopted which directed the Committee on Hospital "to place the receiving vault under the care of one of the officials of the House, who shall be held responsible for the safe keeping of the bodies deposited therein, have them removed and properly buried when danger of disinterment no longer exists, and no sooner; and also see that the objects of the Board in having the vault constructed be strictly carried out."

One of the inmates of the Insane Department succeeded in committing suicide by drowning. The matter was investigated and the Committee made a very singular report, in which it was stated: "The suicide of Mrs. Jenkins was unavoidable, she having drowned herself in the bath tub, the room door being open to allow the patients to wash, at the time."

The report was accepted.

One would think that ordinary care for the insane would have suggested the necessity of having an attendant on duty in the bath room at the time "when the patients were allowed to wash." That precaution would have prevented that poor woman's sorrowful end and the odium which is produced by such criminal carelessness.

The matter of providing separate apartments for foundlings was again called up in April, 1862. Mr. Maris said, "The little ones in the Almshouse positively do not get enough to properly sustain life. I called the attention of a member of the Board to a beautiful little blue-eyed baby, six or eight months old, that would have adorned the parlor of any gentleman here, or been the well-spring of pleasure in any home in the world. This was only a short time ago. But a few days since I saw that innocent baby; its blue eyes had begun to fade, its eyelids were red, and certain other indications plainly evidenced that it was afflicted with marasmus. This was the result of not feeding the baby properly.

"On asking the nurse why she did not feed it better, she replied: ' I can't, for I haven't milk enough for my own baby.'

" Are you going to let this little strange baby die for want of proper nourishment ?

" ' Well, I can't help it, I haven't any more milk than will supply my own.' This is a fair sample of the condition of the foundlings in the Almshouse."

Mr. Brown said " that not long since a ' pair of twins ' were left at the Almshouse, and the ' Sisters of Mercy,' who have a home at Tacony, have taken charge of them, and say they are ready to take charge of all the foundlings.

" The Sisters of Mercy have an office at Fourth and Franklin Streets, where little foundlings may be left, instead of being placed on sundry door steps, sidewalks and in alleys, as has been too often the case during the past year or two. The door steps of the Sisters of Mercy's office are said to be wide and handy."

The subject was referred to Committee with power to act.

Notwithstanding that a vault had been erected to protect the bodies of those who had died in the institution, it appears that the " traffic " continued, as the minutes of the meeting of the Board, held November 3d, 1862, show that Mr. Dickinson offered the following: " *Resolved*, That the Steward be instructed to have the bodies of those who die in the House placed in the receiving vaults, there to remain as provided for by the rules of the Board."

A motion was made to postpone, but was not agreed to.

Mr. Erety said that there was a report published in the New York papers that the House had been closed against medical students. Therefore, the New York medical colleges were making capital out of these statements, and they were having a damaging effect upon our medical colleges."

Mr. Dickinson thought "there should be a law passed in this State similar to the one in New York. In the latter place the colleges are entitled to the bodies of paupers, and get them without pay; while here there is a regular traffic in dead bodies, which the Board is anxious to stop. This business has been going on all summer. As soon as the burying of bodies in the graveyard was begun, the colleges commenced to steal them. The speaker had been informed by the watchman on the bridge that every night bodies were taken over, and he supposed they were from the Almshouse. About three weeks ago a body was found lying near the fence of the grounds, and it is supposed that the resurrectionists had been disturbed in their work."

The resolution was laid on the table. This action called forth comments in the newspapers, and one of them had this editorial:

" BUZZARDISM REVIVED "

" Some time ago the Guardians of the Poor, in order to put an end to the Buzzard practice, had a vault built for the reception of the dead bodies of paupers, in which they could be kept until claimed by relatives, if called for in a reasonable time, or until decay had so far progressed as to render the bodies useless for purposes of dissection. This regulation, if strictly carried out, would have put an end to the 'Buzzard' practices which have excited so much attention in connection with that institution. It was a wise and good arrangement. At a recent meeting of the Guardians, however, a retrograde movement was decided upon. It was resolved that during the warm weather the reception vault should not be used for purposes of interment as formerly. What might be considered 'warm weather' and how long the warm weather was to last, were left unexplained. This action, however, opens the gates for the medical schools completely. Theoretically the

ISOLATING BUILDING,

bodies of the paupers who died at the Almshouse were always interred in the burying ground, but practically they were not. The summer is the great season for the medical schools, the bodies being prepared to keep by proper injections in the veins and by preserving them in whiskey, ready for the commencement of lectures at the colleges in the fall. Are we therefore to understand that the Guardians of the Poor have determined to reopen this traffic, notwithstanding the pretence of opposition to it which the erection of the receiving vault was supposed to signify ? "

A communication was received from Councils in reference to the erection of a Municipal Hospital for cases of contagious diseases.

Messrs. Dickinson and Haines were elected Commissioners to superintend the building of the Hospital, in connection with the committees appointed by Councils, the Board of Health, the Prison Inspectors and the Mayor.

The House Agent's report showed that the number in the House was 2,869; at the same time, in 1861, there were 3,275 inmates. This decrease of 406 was probably caused by the enlistments for the army or navy.

At the meeting of December 15, 1862, the following communication was received:

" The Junction Railroad Company have located their line of Railroad through the City Almshouse property, alongside of and immediately adjacent to the ground now occupied by the West Chester Railroad Co., and at a meeting of the Board of Directors, held December 10, 1862, the following resolution was adopted:

" ' Resolved, That the Engineer and Secretary of the Company be, and they are hereby authorized to make application in form to the Board of Guardians of the Poor to enter upon and take possession of such property belonging to the City as may be necessary as right of way for the construction of the Junction Railroad, and to further arrange, if possible, with said Board for such Jury or Board of Viewers as may be necessary to fix upon the value of property so used, and to perfect title to the Railroad Company.'

" The undersigned would respectfully request the appointment by the Board of Guardians of some person or persons with whom they can confer on this subject and make the proper arrangements in accordance with the above resolution at as early date as possible.

"JOHN A. WILSON, Eng'r.
"JOSEPH LESLIE, Sec'y."

The matter was referred to the Committee on Farm, in connection with the President.

The amount assessed for the valuation of the ground required was $10,000, and it was paid by the Company in 1865.

An ordinance was passed and approved December 31, 1862, which provided for sending the feeble-minded children from Blockley to the Training School at Media. This was a very wise and charitable movement; it was a great relief to the officials of the institution, as it was almost impossible to care for these poor unfortunates in a proper manner there. The term feeble-minded is very elastic, and it has been stretched to cover a large number of different kinds of mental and nervous ailments. Special treatment is required for these various diseases, and it seems to be wise to send these cases where the proper treatment can be given.

Twelve children were sent in 1863, and since then the number has been increased, from time to time, until now there are more than one hundred and sixty in that institution, for whose maintenance the City of Philadelphia defrays the expenses.

Councils appropriated money to commence the heating of the buildings by steam in 1863. The Committee on "Ventilation and Warmth" was instructed to procure a plan by which ventilation and warmth would be secured in all the buildings connected with the Almshouse, and "directed to proceed with the work and complete as much thereof as can be done with the appropriation made by Councils for that purpose."

As so many of the able bodied men connected with the institution had entered the United States service, Mr. Taylor offered a resolution on June 16, 1863, with a proviso which read:

"WHEREAS, There is not at present in the Almshouse a sufficient number of able-bodied men (paupers) to perform the necessary work, the Committee on Manufactures be authorized to make arrangements with the Board of Prison Inspectors to transfer from the prison to this institution such male vagrants as can, in the judgment of the committee, be made useful to the public by laboring in and about these premises."

At the same meeting a committee of five was appointed to confer with the Committee of Councils in reference to the starting of a House of Correction.

The drafting of men to fill the quota for the army took four of the six resident physicians in July and another in August, 1863.

President Maris retired from the Board, and Mahlon H. Dickinson was elected in his stead October 6, 1863.

Mr. Lee offered a resolution, on February 9, 1864, which instructed the "committee to inquire and report whether it is advisable to invite applications from soldiers who may be disabled in the field to be employed in the various offices under the charge of the Board."

Four boilers for heating purposes were contracted for, to cost $1,400 each.

Mr. Dickinson resigned May 17, 1864, and Mr. George Erety was elected as President to fill the vacancy.

18

CHAPTER XXV.

ON the morning of July 20th, 1864, at about six o'clock, the foundation of a pier, which was the central support of a series of arches which upheld a chimney-stack and walls, on which rested the joists of the second, third and attic stories of a tier of wards in the transept of the women's portion of the insane department, gave way, and without any warning, the whole division wall and chimney-stack fell in with a crash, burying many of the patients in the ruins. Of these fifteen were killed outright or died very soon after they were extricated, and twenty-five were more or less severely injured, of whom two subsequently died. The wards in which the accident occurred were 45 feet by 48 feet in size, and the wall that fell divided them through the centre.

The ward on the first floor was occupied on one side of the arches as a sitting-room for the epileptic and idiotic patients, about sixty in number, and on the other as their dining-room and that of the colored patients, about thirty in number. Breakfast was just being prepared, and if the accident had happened fifteen minutes later, there could hardly have been less than seventy-five killed on this floor alone. As it was, there were but three killed, one of whom was an assistant nurse, and a few slightly injured.

Those in the sitting-room were protected by the joists of the second floor, which fell in the centre, but rested against the outer walls. The patients were left in the angle thus made, mostly unharmed.

The ward on the second floor was all used as a sitting-room for eighty patients, a large portion of whom were carried into the vortex, and several were killed and others wounded.

The ward on the third floor was used as an infirmary, and was occupied by about twenty-five sick and infirm women, many of

274

whom were in bed. Nearly all of these, with the nurse in charge, were precipitated to the first floor, and a large proportion of the killed and wounded belonged to this ward. The nurse escaped most miraculously, with a few bruises. The nurses on the lower floors had fortunately just left their wards.

The attic floor was occupied as a sleeping-room by the washer-women, scrubbers, etc., and they had just gone down. It is remarkable that so few were killed and injured.

In 1849 a contract was made with Birkenbine & Martin to construct a heating apparatus. In performing this work in the basement, the centre piers and chimneys were cut entirely through a width of six feet, leaving eight inches on one side and four on the other to support the pier above.

The condition of the walls under the piers had not been noticed until within a few weeks previous to the accident, when workmen were engaged in making a different arrangement for heating. As soon as it was noticed, workmen were employed to strengthen the foundation, and were so engaged on the day preceding the accident, a temporary wooden upright had been placed under the pier that fell, and preparations had been made to build a solid wall under this pier.

The Coroner's Jury, after investigation, said: "There is no doubt whatever in the minds of the Jury that the cutting away of the piers was the cause of the accident. It is possible, however, that the preparations made the day before may have hastened the catastrophe. Independently of this, the pier must have soon given way, as the Jury noticed a settling of floors opposite to all of the piers similar to the one that fell. It is only a matter of surprise that it did not happen long before. The Jury cannot but condemn in the strongest terms the reckless manner in which the alterations were made in 1849. No care whatever appears to have been taken to examine into and preserve the strength necessary to support the weight of the walls, piers and floors above."

The verdict of the Jury was: "That on the 20th day of July, 1864, the victims of the disaster came to their deaths by reason of injuries inflicted by the falling of the division walls already noted, together with the floors resting on said walls, the primary cause being the careless manner in which the walls under the centre pier were cut away, in constructing and introducing heating apparatus in the year 1849."

It will be remembered that at the time the work was done it was not at all satisfactory and the Guardians refused to pay for it. The contractors entered suit and it was settled by a compromise.

There was considerable discussion, at this period, about the large number of deaths in the Children's Asylum, which led to the appointment of a Committee of Councils to "investigate and report what the average population of the Asylum was during the two years dating back from June 1st, 1864, together with the mortality during that period; also the two years dating back from June 1st, 1862, together with the mortality during that period."

The Committee reported that the information had been obtained and a report from the Guardians of the Poor, enclosing a voluminous statement from the Medical Board, was presented to Councils. President Erety, on behalf of the Guardians, said: "To have furnished a mere statement of the number of inmates and number of deaths in the Children's Asylum, during those four years—without giving some other items of information in explanation of what might have appeared a very high rate of mortality—would have scarcely answered the spirit and design of the inquiry. In order to afford to Councils all the light upon the subject within our control, the Board of Guardians requested the Medical Board of the Almshouse to supply them with the statistics, as well of the Children's Asylum of the Almshouse, as also of such other kindred establishments elsewhere as they had knowledge of, and also with such other information as they might think useful to Councils, or to the public, upon the inquiry presented.

"The latter report is hereto annexed, and reference thereto requested, as presenting the statistics called for, and the material facts necessary for a proper understanding of the causes which produce the large proportion of deaths in the inmates of the Children's Asylum.

"These causes may be reduced to the following heads:

" I. The very low physical condition of one class of the inmates at the time of coming into the Asylum—viz.: the Foundlings.

" II. The defects of the sewerage and ventilation of the Almshouse building used for the Children's Asylum.

" III. The proximity of the Asylum to the Surgical and Medical Wards of the Almshouse.

" The first of these causes no effort on the part of this Board or its Medical Officers can remove. It is the history of all establishments receiving and caring for foundling children, that a very large proportion of them die in infancy, by reason of the diseased constitutions they have inherited from their parents ; it seems so ordered by Providence. Even with the utmost care and attention which can be afforded by good medical attendance and nursing, this result is certain to follow, as the facts detailed in the medical report will demonstrate. Yet, our duty is plain, to sustain and preserve these lives, feeble, imperfect and diseased as they may be, by all means and efforts within our reach.

" The second of these causes, this Board, through its Committee having charge of the Children's Asylum, have done and are doing all that lies in their power to remedy, with the means at their command for the purpose. When it is borne in mind that no other location for this Asylum was open to the Board than one of the Wards of the Almshouse, which in its original construction was deficient in the important items of proper sewerage and ventilation, Councils can well understand that though subsequent alterations may make some improvement, this Board cannot, while occupying their present quarters for the children, properly provide in these respects for the wants of the inmates as they could in a separate building designed exclusively for these objects of the public care, with the improvements which modern science and present experience have proved to be necessary for supplying an abundance of fresh air and proper drainage.

" In respect to the third cause, as above stated, this Board have long since been impressed with the conviction that no alteration of the apartments in the present Almshouse building, now used for the Children's Asylum, will ever render them suitable for the purpose for which they are now used, and that the health of the children can only be properly provided for in a building separate and apart from the wards now occupied by the sick and infirm adults. Acting under this conviction, this Board heretofore applied to Councils for authority to construct such a building.

" This authority was granted by an Ordinance passed the 19th day of April, 1862, upon the terms therein prescribed, and a special appropriation of the surplus realized on the sale of the old copper roofing (after defraying the cost of a new roof) was made towards the construction of such building.

" The Board of Guardians, after the passage of this Ordinance, proceeded to have plans matured and prepared of a plain, substantial building, of a capacity suitable to the wants of that particular portion of the Almshouse population, the estimated cost of which was, at that time, $50,000. The work was actually commenced, so far as with the labor at our command from the inmates of the house, to grade and prepare the site and to quarry the stone to be used in the building. But when the time arrived for the purchase of other materials and the employment of skilled mechanics, the prices had advanced to such a point as to deter us from further prosecution of the work, as the cost of the building would probably have reached nearly twice the original estimate.

" While the Board have refrained, under present circumstances, from pressing upon the attention of Councils the great want felt for this new building, they still express the hope that the time will soon come when an adequate fund can be placed at their disposal to ensure its completion, and that the claims of these children upon us can be met and discharged in a manner worthy of our city, which has won a name for its efforts to relieve the poor and the helpless, in which the citizens take a just pride.

" It is proper, in conclusion, that the Guardians should add that as to the care and treatment which the children receive at the hands of the medical attendants, matrons and nurses, they appear to be as well provided in those respects as they can be while occupying such apartments in the Almshouse as it is in the power of the Guardians to at this time devote to their accommodation."

The Medical Board's report, in giving the statistics, said:

" It will be right, however, to remark, in anticipation, that the principal mortality in the asylum is due to the presence of foundlings, and these foundlings were not admitted to the wards until the 10th of August, 1861, hence the ratio of deaths in 1860 differs in so marked a degree from that exhibited in the following years.

"The following table will show the relative population and mortality in the Children's Asylum:

YEARS.	POPULATION.	MORTALITY.	OF WHICH WERE FOUNDLINGS.
1860–61	352	28	00
1861–62	462	79	37
1862–63	460	91	33
1863–64	486	111	36

" It might, perhaps, be proper here to state, as explaining the great mortality exhibited by these figures as occurring among the foundlings, that these children come into the institution under the most unfavorable circumstances. They are generally the children of the vicious and diseased, and the constitution which they inherit from their parents is such as to make their early death unavoidable.

" But in addition to this large class of foundlings, others are admitted reduced to the lowest extremity by many other causes, such as starvation, exposure, improper clothing and the free use of narcotic poisons; most of these are dying when admitted, few survive one month, notwithstanding the utmost care.

" Statistics of infant mortality show us, that of all the children born one in three dies before the completion of the first year. It is easy to understand, therefore, that the mortality among infants in an institution devoted exclusively to their care must necessarily be very large, even under the most favorable circumstances. But when we bear in mind that these infants, instead of being placed in our care under the most favorable circumstances, are brought to us under conditions the very reverse, we can easily perceive that the rate of mortality must be greatly increased."

This report contained statistics of the mortality in other countries and States : " The proportion of deaths at Turin is estimated at 75 per cent. of the total admissions. At Moscow the admissions during ten years averaged 5,255 annually, and the deaths 3,471. During the ten years from 1822 to 1831 inclusive, 39,114 children were received into the hospital at St. Petersburg, and 31,799 died. It was stated that 317 died out of 417 who were admitted into the hospital at Arch-Angel.

" At the close of the last century, the mortality of foundlings during the first year was, at St. Petersburg, 40 per cent.; at Paris, 80 per cent.; at Florence, 40 per cent.; at Marseilles, 90 per cent.; at Barcelona, 60 per cent.; and at Dublin, 91 per cent.

" In the Foundling Wards of the Blockley Hospital the whole number of admissions into the Children's Asylum up to June 1st, 1864, was 154, of which 126 died, or nearly 82 per cent."

The report spoke of the defective sewerage and ventilation and suggested some improvements. It expressed the hope that when the heating apparatus, then in course of construction, was completed, if connection could be made with proper flues, great improvement in the ventilation might be anticipated.

The reports appeared to be satisfactory to Councils, and the committee was discharged from the further consideration of the subject.

When we consider the feeling that had existed between the members of Councils and the Board of Guardians of the Poor, extending over a period of many years, it is very refreshing to read the report of a special committee, appointed to investigate certain charges made against the management of the Almshouse, presented by Dr. Uhler, chairman, at the meeting of Councils held on the 27th of October, 1864. The report said : "After a full and thorough investigation of the matters confided to us, in which we have received every facility, as well from the Guardians as from the officers of the institution, your Committee is satisfied that not the slightest foundation exists for the charges made in Councils, and they cannot refrain from expressing their regrets that so serious a charge against one of our most important public institutions should have been made upon no better authority than mere idle rumor, set afloat most probably by some gossiping old woman."

The report was accepted and the committee discharged.

The annual report of the Visitors showed that the total number who received out-door relief during the year 1864 was 60,651; of whom 20,657 were white adults, 31,795 white children, 3,399 colored adults and 4,800 colored children. Of the whole number, 10,740 were Americans, 13,316 foreigners and 36,595 children.

A communication was received on November 27th, 1865, from Dr. S. D. Gross, resigning his position as Surgeon of the Philadelphia Hospital, a post to which he had been annually re-elected for the past seven years. President Erety remarked that he greatly regretted the resignation of Dr. Gross, which he understood was caused by the great increase of his practice, and he suggested to the Board the propriety of creating an Emeritus position, which could be conferred on eminent medical practitioners on their resignation from offices held under the Board, so that they could, without fear of being accused of interference, give aid and advice at the Hospital during the prevalence of epidemics.

The resignation was accepted and Dr. F. F. Maury, of the Medical Staff, was subsequently elected to fill the vacancy. Dr. Garvin was elected to fill the vacancy on the Medical Staff.

The falling off of the population of the House during the years that the Rebellion lasted shows clearly how it was affected by the War. The largest number of inmates during the year 1861 was 3,299. In 1862 it fell to 2,881, in 1863 it was 2,746, while in 1864 it was only 2,683. In 1865, after the close of the War, it increased to 3,015, and it was reported that on Christmas Day in 1865 the number in the House was 651 more than were there on the same day in 1863.

The new Municipal Hospital for the treatment of contagious diseases, which had been erected on the grounds at Twenty-second Street and Lehigh Avenue, was formally opened on April 18th, 1865. It was expected to relieve the Almshouse by caring for cases of small pox, etc., from that institution, and was much needed.

After ineffectual attempts had been made at a number of the meetings of the Guardians to elect a Chief Physician for the Insane Department, Dr. D. D. Richardson was selected on November 13th, 1866, to succeed Dr. Butler who had been in charge there since September, 1859, when it was separated from the hospital and made a department by itself.

In answer to an inquiry the Board informed the Governor of the Commonwealth that, on March 5th, 1867, there were 182 Pennsylvania soldiers in the Almshouse, of whom 152 were white and 30 colored. Of these eight were in the Insane Department.

On April 17th, of that year, General Wagner offered the following in Common Council:

"WHEREAS, The rapid progress of improvements in the Southern, Western and Northwestern portions of our city will necessitate the early removal of our prisons and Almshouse; and,

"WHEREAS, An economical management of our penal and reformatory institutions require their concentration as well as their location on ground not accessible to general improvement; therefore,

"*Resolved*, By the Select and Common Councils of the City of Philadelphia, That a Joint Committee of three from each chamber be appointed to consider the feasibility of acquiring possession of Treaty Island, commonly known as Petty's Island, or such other suitable location, for the purpose of erecting thereon our County prison, penitentiary, Almshouse, houses of correction and refuge, as they may be removed from their present location from time to time."

The resolution was passed and the Committee appointed, but, as no action was subsequently taken by Councils it can be assumed that it was found to be impracticable, as Treaty Island is within the Jurisdiction of the State of New Jersey.

George Erety, Esq., President of the Board of Guardians died on August 11th, 1867. Mr. John M. Whitall was elected President to fill the vacancy.

Dr. D. Hayes Agnew resigned his position as Curator, October 15th, 1867, and Dr. William Pepper was elected in his place.

CHAPTER XXVI.

W E now come to the sale of the first piece of Almshouse ground to the University of Pennsylvania, and, as that was the entering wedge, the matter is reported in full.

On the 13th of May, 1869, the Chairman of the Finance Committee reported favorably upon a bill entitled "An Ordinance to sell a tract of land situated in the Twenty-seventh Ward, belonging to the City of Philadelphia."

"Section 1—The Select and Common Councils of the City of Philadelphia, do ordain, That the following described real estate, belonging to the City of Philadelphia, situated in the Twenty-seventh Ward, of said City, bounded and described as follows, viz.: Beginning at a point in the middle of Thirty-fourth Street, continued, where the same is intersected by the Northeastern line of the Blockley Almshouse farm; thence southward along the middle of said Thirty-fourth Street, crossing Locust and Spruce Streets continued, about eleven hundred and twenty-three (1123) feet to the middle of Pine Street, as proposed to be continued, sixty feet in width; thence eastwardly along the middle of said last mentioned proposed street, crossing Thirty-third Street continued, about seven hundred and seventy-eight (778) feet to the middle of Thirty-second Street as proposed to be laid out, sixty-feet in width; thence continuing northeasterly, along the middle of said last-mentioned street, about five hundred and eight (508) feet to the middle of Spruce Street, continued; thence eastwardly, along the middle of said Spruce Street, about two hundred and five (205) feet to a point in the northeastern line of the Blockley Almshouse farm aforesaid, and thence northwesterly along the said northeastern line of the said Blockley Almshouse farm, crossing Thirty-third Street and Locust Street, about fourteen hundred and forty (1440) feet to the middle of said Thirty-fourth Street and place of beginning, con-

283

taining together and included in said bounds nineteen acres and sixteen one-hundredths of an acre, more or less, be and is hereby sold by the City of Philadelphia to the Trustees of the University of Pennsylvania, their successors and assigns, for the price or sum of eight thousand (8000) dollars per acre, payable in cash at the time of the execution and delivery of the deed; "*Provided, however,* That the proceeds of said sale shall be paid to the City Treasurer and form part of the sinking fund of the City of Philadelphia.

"*And also*, That the said Trustees shall, when requested by Ordinance or the Survey Department, duly dedicate to the City of Philadelphia for public use as streets and highways all the ground covered by the streets or parts of streets which shall or may pass over said tract of land.

"*And also*, That they, the said Trustees, shall at the time of the execution of the deed, enter into a sufficient agreement with the City as to require them, without expense to the said City, to open, grade, pave and curb said streets and parts of streets and intersections thereof, at such times and manner as may be deemed necessary by the authorities of said City.

"*And also*, That said Trustees shall, at the same time, enter into an agreement with the City that said property or improvements to be made thereon shall not be exempt from taxation, except that portion thereof as is actually in use for University purposes, and that even such exemption shall not be claimed until such time as all the other real estate owned by said University become liable to taxation.

"*And also*, That the terms of sale mentioned in this Ordinance shall be accepted and fully complied with by said purchasers within six months from the date of its passage, and said purchasers shall pay all expenses for stamps and conveyancing.

" SECTION 2,—That the Mayor of the City be and is hereby authorized to affix the corporate seal of the City to such deed or deeds as may be necessary to convey the said tract of land to the said purchasers in accordance with this ordinance."

The bill passed Common Council on that day and was sent to the Select Council for concurrence. It was called up for consideration on June 11th, and, after some discussion, it was indefinitely postponed.

Nothing appears to have been done until November 4th, at which time Mr. Cattell moved "that the Chamber do now resume the consideration of the bill," which was agreed to by a vote of 16 to 12.

An amendment was offered to the first section to strike out the description of the property proposed to be sold, and inserting in its place the description of a tract in a different location. After the reading of the amendment it was moved that the further consideration of the bill be postponed, and that it be made the special order for the next stated meeting, at 4.30 P. M. The motion was agreed to.

At the meeting on November 11th, Mr. Cattell moved "that the Chamber do now proceed to vote upon the motion to reconsider the vote indefinitely postponing the bill, the proceedings as to this bill at the last stated meeting being informal and erroneous."

This was agreed to by a vote of 14 to 11.

It is hard to understand how a motion to reconsider a vote that had been taken five months previously could be entertained, but it was acted on by Select Council.

The motion to indefinitely postpone the further consideration of the bill was then declared to be before the Chamber. It was not agreed to by a vote of 11 ayes to 16 nays. Mr. McCall moved that the bill be laid on the table.

This was decided negatively by the same number of ayes and nays.

The bill thereupon being again before the Chamber on second reading, Mr. Cattell moved as a substitute for the bill under consideration the following: "An Ordinance to authorize the sale of the lot of ground in the Twenty-seventh Ward."

"SECTION 1.—The Select and Common Councils of the City of Philadelphia do ordain, That the Mayor of the city be and is hereby authorized to sell to the Trustees of the University of Pennsylvania, their successors and assigns, all that certain lot or piece of ground, being part of what is commonly known as the

Almshouse Farm, situate in the Twenty-seventh Ward of the City of Philadelphia, and bounded and described as follows, viz. : ' Beginning at a point where the northeastern boundary line of the said Almshouse Farm intersects the middle of the Darby road, thence along said boundary line southeastwardly to a point where the same intersects the middle of Thirty-fourth Street, as continued, thence along the middle of said Thirty-fourth Street southward, crossing Locust Street, to a point where the said line intersects the middle line of Spruce Street, thence as along the middle line of Spruce Street, continued, westward to a point where said line intersects the middle line of Thirty-sixth Street, as continued, thence northward along the middle line of said Thirty-sixth Street to a point where the said line intersects the middle line of said Darby road, thence along the middle line of said Darby road by its several courses northeastwardly to a point where said middle line intersects the said northeastern boundary line of the Almshouse Farm, being the place of beginning, for the price of eight thousand dollars an acre, the area of said piece of ground to be ascertained by a survey thereof, to be made by the proper survey officers of the City of Philadelphia : *Provided*, That before the deeds shall be executed the streets (excepting Irving Street) as proposed unanimously by the Committee on Poor, shall first be opened and dedicated to the public use, so far as the above property is concerned : *And provided, however*, That the proceeds of said sale shall be paid to the City Treasurer and form part of the Sinking Fund of the City of Philadelphia : *And provided also*, That the said Trustees shall, when requested by Ordinance or the Survey Department, duly dedicate to the City of Philadelphia, for public use as streets or highways, all the ground covered by the streets or parts of streets, which shall or may pass over said tract of land : *And provided also*, That they the said Trustees shall, at the time of the execution of the .deeds, enter into an agreement with the City as to require them, without expense to the City, to open, grade, pave and curb said streets and parts of streets and intersections thereof at such times and manner as may be deemed necessary by the authorities of said City : *And provided also*, That said Trustees shall, at the same time, enter into an agreement with the City, that said property or improvements to be made thereon shall not be exempt from taxation, except that portion thereof as is actually in use for University purposes, and that even such exemption shall not be claimed until such time as all the other real estate owned by said University becomes liable to taxation : *And provided also*, That the terms of sale mentioned in this Ordinance shall be accepted and fully complied with by said purchasers within six months from the date of approval by the Mayor of this ordinance, and said purchasers shall pay all expenses for stamps and conveyancing.'

" SECTION 2.—That the Mayor of the City be and he is hereby authorized to affix the Corporate seal of the City to each deed or deeds as may be necessary to convey the said tract of land to the said purchasers, in accordance with this Ordinance."

Mr. McCall moved that the bill and the proposed substitute be referred to a Special Committee of three members of this chamber. The motion was not agreed to.

The question being on the motion to substitute the bill offered by Mr. Cattell, it was agreed to by a vote of 21 to 5.

It will be seen that the Select Council bill reduced the area of ground very materially. The Common Council bill covered ground to the eastward of Thirty-fourth Street, running from Darby road (now Woodland Avenue) to Pine Street, and from Thirty-fourth Street, to the line which was at about where Thirty-first Street would be located.

The Select Council substitute included the ground extending from Thirty-fourth to Thirty-sixth Streets, and from Darby road to Spruce Street.

Upon the second reading of the bill Mr. McIlvain moved to amend by adding the words : " *And provided also*, That the said University shall pay the cost of curbing and paving said Woodland Street or Darby Avenue, along the front of said property now being curbed and paved," which was agreed to.

The question being on the section as amended, Mr. Duffy moved to further amend by striking out the words " eight thousand dollars " and inserting in their place the words " fifteen thousand dollars."

Mr. McIlvain moved to amend the motion by striking out the words " fifteen thousand dollars " and inserting into their place the words " thirty thousand dollars."

On Mr. McIlvain's motion the vote was: Yeas, Messrs. Duffy, Fox, Harkness, Hodgdon, Hookey, Hopkins, McCall, McCutcheon, McIlvain, Shallcross and Shermer—11.   Nays, Messrs. Armstrong, Bumm, Cattell, Cramer, Franciscus, Jones, Kamerly, Kersey, King, Marcus, Morison, Plumly, Ritchie, Smith and Stokley, President—15. So it was not agreed to.

On the motion to amend by inserting fifteen thousand in place of eight thousand the vote was: Yeas, Messrs. Duffy, Fox, Harkness, Hodgdon, Hookey, Hopkins, Kamerly, McCall, McCutcheon, McIlvain, Plumly, Shallcross, Shermer and Stokley, President—14. Nays, Messrs. Armstrong, Bumm, Cattell, Cramer, Franciscus, Kersey, King, Marcus, Morison, Ritchie and Smith—11. So the amendment was agreed to.

The question being on the section as amended, Mr. McCall moved to further amend by adding : " *And provided also*, That if any portion of said ground should be offered for sale by the said University, then and in that case, the portion so offered for sale shall revert to the City of Philadelphia at the original price paid to the City by the said University." This was agreed to.

On motion of Mr. Cattell further consideration of the bill was postponed until the next meeting.

On November 25th the bill was again considered, when Mr. McIlvain moved to amend by striking out the words " fifteen thousand dollars," and inserting the words " twenty thousand dollars " in their place. The call of the roll was:

Yeas: Messrs. Barlow, Fox, Hodgdon, Hookey, Hopkins, Kamerly, McCall, McIlvain, Shallcross and Shermer—10.

Nays: Messrs. Armstrong, Bumm, Cattell, Cramer, Franciscus, Jones, King, McCutcheon, Marcus, Plumly, Ritchie, Smith and Stokley, Pres't—13.

So the motion was not agreed to.

The question being on the section as amended, the vote was :

Yeas: Messrs. Armstrong, Barlow, Bumm, Cattell, Cramer,

INTERIOR OF A SURGICAL WARD.

Franciscus, Harkness, Hookey, Jones, Kamerly, King, McCutcheon, Marcus, Plumly, Ritchie, Smith and Stokley, Pres't—17.

Nays: Messrs. Fox, Hodgdon, Hopkins, McCall, McIlvain, Shallcross and Shermer—7.

The section as amended was adopted.

The second section and the title were agreed to, and the bill was read a third time and passed finally.

It will be noticed that all of the members voted for the bill as amended, making the price fifteen thousand dollars per acre, except seven of those who had voted to make it twenty thousand dollars.

The bill went back to Common Council for concurrence in the amendments. When it was called up for consideration, Mr. Shoemaker moved to amend by striking out the words " fifteen thousand dollars " and inserting in their place the words "eight thousand dollars," and to also strike out the two provisos.

On motion of Mr. Hetzell, the further consideration of the bill was postponed and made the special order for the next meeting at five o'clock, P. M.

When it was called up at the next meeting it was again postponed.

On December 9th it was considered. The question being upon the motion to amend by striking out " fifteen thousand dollars " and inserting " eight thousand dollars," and to strike out the two provisos.

The motion was agreed to by a vote of 26 to 19.

The bill was passed as amended and again went back to Select Council.

On December 16th, Select Council proceeded to consider the amendments of Common Council. They were read, and Mr. Franciscus moved to concur. Upon the vote to concur, the yeas were Messrs. Armstrong, Bumm, Cochran, Cramer, Franciscus, Hookey, Jones, Kersey, King, McCutcheon, Marcus, Morison, Plumly, Ritchie and Smith—15.

The nays were Messrs. Duffy, Harkness, Hodgdon, Hopkins, McIlvain, Shallcross, Shermer and Barlow, Pres't *pro tem.*—8.

19

So the motion to concur was agreed to, and Mayor Fox approved the bill on December 18th, 1869.

An ordinance was passed and approved December 18th, 1869, directing and authorizing the City Solicitor to prepare deeds of dedication for the following streets, so far as they lie within the Blockley Almshouse grounds, viz: Locust Street, sixty (60) feet wide; Spruce Street, eighty (80) feet wide; Pine Street, seventy (70) feet wide; Thirty-fourth Street, seventy (70) feet wide; also Thirty-second, Thirty-third, Thirty-sixth and Thirty-seventh Streets, each with a width of sixty (60) feet.

On July 7th, 1870, Councils appropriated $70,000 for the enlargement of the buildings of the Insane Department. Wings were added, running at right angles with the main building, in the rear of both the male and female ends. They were three stories in height, with cell-rooms on each side, and furnished accommodations for about 180 patients.

Another change in the method of selecting the members of the Board of Guardians was made in 1871, when the Legislature passed an Act which took the power of appointment from the Judges of the Courts and authorized Councils to elect four members each year thereafter, one of whom should be selected from the minority party.

Dr. William Pepper resigned from the position of Curator November 27th, 1871, and Dr. James Tyson was elected to fill the vacancy.

An Ordinance was passed and approved May 18th, 1872, which read as follows, viz:

"An Ordinance authorizing the sale and conveyance of a tract of land in the Twenty-seventh Ward to the Trustees of the University of Pennsylvania for hospital purposes.

" WHEREAS, An application has been made to the Councils of the City of Philadelphia by members of the Medical Faculty and Board of Trustees of the University of Pennsylvania, with other citizens, for the grant and conveyance to the said Trustees of the University of Pennsylvania, of a tract of land now the property of the City, for the purpose of erecting thereon a hospital and buildings pertaining to the instruction to be there given; and in consideration thereof, the said Trustees have agreed that the said tract of land, when so conveyed, shall never be alienated from the said University of Pennsylvania, and to erect and maintain forever on said ground a general hospital containing at least fifty free beds, for the care and relief of the poor in times of sickness or accident; and

"WHEREAS, We, the Councils of said City, believe that the proposed object is one of the purest benevolence, and a wise disposition of the property of the citizens entrusted to our keeping; therefore:

"SECTION I. The Select and Common Councils of Philadelphia do ordain, That for and in consideration of the sum of five hundred dollars ($500) in cash, to be paid to the Commissioners of the Sinking Fund of the City, and the covenants and conditions hereinafter set forth, to be kept and performed by the Trustees of the University of Pennsylvania, that the Mayor be and he is hereby authorized to sign, seal, acknowledge and deliver on behalf of the City of Philadelphia, the necessary and proper deed of conveyance, whereby all that certain tract or piece of land, situate in the Twenty-seventh Ward, bounded on the north by the middle line of Spruce street, on the east by that of Thirty-fourth street, on the south by that of Pine street, and on the west by that of Thirty-sixth street, containing five and a half acres, more or less, shall be sold, granted and conveyed unto the said Trustees of the University of Pennsylvania and their successors, in fee simple, in trust, for and subject however to the following uses, covenants and conditions, to wit:

" *First*—That the said tract or piece of land shall be forever held by the said Trustees of the University of Pennsylvania, for the purpose of erecting thereon and maintaining a building or buildings, to be devoted to general hospital purposes as aforesaid.

" *Second*—That the said Trustees shall erect and complete the said building within five years from the first day of July, A. D. 1872.

" *Third*—That the said Trustees shall set apart and forever maintain in said hospital, at no time less than fifty free beds, for the use of the poor of the City requiring hospital treatment.

"*Fourth*—That the said Trustees shall report to Councils in the month of January succeeding the erection and completion of said hospital, and annually thereafter, the number of free beds maintained, together with such information as may be desired by Councils.

"*Fifth*—That in the event of the failure of said Trustees of the University of Pennsylvania to erect and complete said hospital building within five years from the first day of July, A. D. 1872, or upon said completion they shall refuse or neglect to set apart and forever maintain at all times, not less than fifty free beds for the poor of the City, when requiring hospital treatment ; or shall sell or alienate the said tract or piece of land hereby authorized to be conveyed to them, or any part thereof, then such sale and alienation by said Trustees shall be null and void, and the tract or piece of land hereby authorized to be conveyed to them, with the building or buildings thereon erected, shall revert to, and again become the property and estate of the City of Philadelphia.

" SECTION 2. That the covenants and conditions set forth in the first section of this ordinance, shall be fully recited in and made a part of the deed and conveyance, to be executed by and between the Mayor on behalf of the City, and the Trustees of the University of Pennsylvania.

" SECTION 3. That all ordinances or parts thereof, so far as the same may be inconsistent with the provisions of this ordinance, be and the same are hereby repealed."

The terms of the ordinance must have been satisfactory to the Trustees of the University, as they sent a vote of thanks to Councils on the 4th of June, 1872, " for their very liberal grant of land, and accepted the ground on the conditions named in the ordinance."

Councils appropriated another piece of the Almshouse for a station house for the Twenty-first Police District. This property was on the angle formed by Spruce Street and Woodland Avenue at Thirty-seventh Street. It contained in front on Woodland Avenue

180 feet and 9¾ inches, and on Spruce Street, 175 feet and 5⅜ inches.

In September, 1872, Councils, by resolution, appointed a joint committee to consider the advisability of establishing a City Foundling Asylum, but nothing appears to have been done afterwards.

The Directors of the Pennsylvania Institution for the Deaf and Dumb made application for the grant of six acres of the Almshouse ground to erect buildings thereon, but no action was taken upon the request, except to table it.

Council Committee on Retrenchment and Reform presented the following report in June, 1873 :

" The Committee respectfully report that they have considered a resolution of instruction to this Committee, to consider the propriety of the transfer of the Almshouse to the House of Correction farm, cost of new buildings to accommodate the Almshouse purposes, and what can be realized from the sale of the property and buildings now occupied for Almshouse purposes, respectfully report that they have carefully considered the subject, having visited the grounds of the House of Correction in conjunction with the Managers of the House of Correction and Guardians of the Poor.

" It is evident that the time has come when some site more removed from the built up portions of the City should be selected for an Almshouse, and other institutions of a like nature, and your Committee is not aware of any other location so desirable as the House of Correction grounds, in the Twenty-third Ward.

" Placing these institutions in one place will be both economical and convenient, and likewise efficient, bringing them under a more direct and immediate supervision ; and if such institutions deteriorate the value of property in their vicinity, as has been alleged, that deterioration has already taken place by the erection of a House of Correction.

" If it should become necessary to procure more ground for the Almshouse purposes, it could be procured cheaper in the vicinity of the House of Correction than anywhere else, and by placing these institutions there, it will protect the citizens with their grounds, from deterioration in other localities. The Committee, therefore, submit the annexed Ordinance to provide for the removal of the Almshouse, and recommend its passage."

The Ordinance provided for the removal of the Almshouse to the House of Correction grounds, " as soon as suitable buildings can be erected to accommodate its inmates, and the Chief Engineer and Surveyor is hereby instructed to advertise for plans and specifications for the building of a new Almshouse on said grounds, said plans and specifications to be approved by Councils, and the following premiums shall be paid : For the best plan, fifteen hundred dollars ; second best plan, one thousand dollars, and third best plan, five hundred dollars. And he is also hereby directed to lay out in building lots of suitable size, all the present Almshouse grounds, in the Twenty-seventh Ward, lying north and west of the present Almshouse buildings, and submit plans to Councils."

The ordinance was passed by Common Council, but in the Select Chamber it was referred to the Finance Committee and that was the last of it.

The grounds and buildings would doubtless have brought enough to have paid for the erection of new buildings, and thus saved a large sum to the City, but for some reason that was not to be accomplished.

CHAPTER XXVII.

MR. MARSHALL HENZEY tendered his resignation as Steward on the 24th of February, 1873, after having served in that capacity for, a period of fifteen years. Major Ellis P. Phipps, who in the morning resigned his position as Chief Clerk in the U. S. Appraisers' Office, and in the afternoon, as a member of the Board of Guardians of the Poor, was unanimously elected to fill the vacancy.

An Ordinance was passed to appropriate a portion of the Almshouse grounds, bounded by Pine Street, Woodland Avenue and Thirty-sixth Street, to the Highway Department, to be used as a yard for storing material for the use of that department. It was inclosed and a tool house erected.

A bill was passed by the Legislature to provide for the removal of the Almshouse. Councils passed a resolution requesting the Governor to withhold his signature from it, as "Councils were moving in the matter to be accomplished.

The House of Correction, established principally to relieve the Almshouse of the vagrants, was opened for admissions on the 15th day of January, 1874. At that time there were 4,597 inmates in the Almshouse, according to the reports, 1,150 of whom were classed as vagrants. At the end of the year the number dropped to 3,972 with 421 vagrants.

It is interesting to note the great increase of expenditures at about this time. In 1873, before the House of Correction was started, the average population of the Almshouse was 4,069, and the cost of maintenance was $444,929.04 ; in 1874, with an average population of 3,764, a decrease of 305, it required $529,513.26, an increase of $84,584.22.

After one year's experience with the House of Correction, the appropriations for 1875 were—for the Guardians of the Poor, $529,408.62 and for the House of Correction, $378,298—making a total of $1,007,706.62, although the population of the Almshouse had been reduced to 3,658. Included in the appropriation to the Almshouse was an item of $50,000 to build five wooden pavilions for the use of the Hospital and Insane Departments. They did not remain long; when they were removed brick buildings were erected in their stead, much better, and at a cost of considerable less than $10,000 each. The appropriations made at that time were *very liberal*.

A piece of the marsh land of the Almshouse property, embraced within the following lines : " Beginning at a point on the eastern boundary of the said Almshouse property where the same is intersected by the southwardly boundary line of the right of way of the Junction Railroad (said point being 44 feet eastward of and at right angles to the easterly line of Marsden Street, from a point in the said easterly line six feet southward of the southerly line of Thirty-first Street); thence southwardly along the several courses of the said easterly boundary of the Almshouse property as aforesaid 507$^{4}{}{}^{0}$ feet, more or less to a point 40 feet southward of the centre line of Thirtieth Street; thence by and along the southerly boundary line of the right of way of the branch railroad belonging to the Pennsylvania Railroad Company, and between its main line at Haverford Street and its Delaware extension to its intersection with the easterly line of the right of way of the aforesaid Delaware extension of the said Pennsylvania Railroad Company, a distance of 2,480$^{9}{}/{}_{10}$ feet; thence northeasterly along said easterly line of the right of way of the Delaware extension of the Pennsylvania Railroad, 847 feet, more or less, to the southerly boundary line of the right of way of the Junction Railroad, 1,524$^{29}{}/{}_{100}$ feet, more or less, to the place of beginning; containing in area 9$^{194}{}/{}_{1000}$ acres," was sold at public sale by M. Thomas & Sons, Auctioneers, and William Hasell Wilson bid $14,600 for it. The sale was confirmed.

Dissatisfaction with the management of the Almshouse was manifested in the different bodies of citizens interested in charitable work. Rumors of all kinds seemed to be in the air. At last a number of petitions were sent to Councils, in which the signers declared their belief that " great injury had resulted to the interests of the City and to its poor from the appointment of persons to be Guardians of the Poor who do not possess the proper qualifications for that office.

" We submit that the dictates of humanity and the important financial interests involved in the care of the city's poor require that certain important qualifications should be kept in view in making these appointments.

" The Guardians should be men of sufficient leisure to give ample and studious attention to the duties of the administration of their department, and able and willing to respond promptly to the duties assumed by them.

" They should be persons of high character, and free from interested motives; of known benevolence and experience in charitable work; men of large intelligence and capacity to study practically the problems relating to the best treatment of the poor, their employment, their physical and moral welfare, and their elevation from pauperism.

" We earnestly urge that such considerations shall primarily govern the action of Councils in the appointment of the Guardians of the Poor."

On December 1st, 1881, Mr. J. L. Grim offered a resolution in Common Council to appoint a Committee of five members of that chamber " to investigate as to the truth or falsity of the charges of Maladministration and corrupt practices," and to enable the Committee to get at the facts, they were instructed to investigate the entire management of the Almshouse and the Board of Guardians of the Poor.

The resolution was adopted and Messrs. Grim, E. B. Morris, S. S. Hollingsworth, A. A. Catanach and William Conway were appointed as the Committee.

Another Ordinance was passed and approved on the 24th day of January, 1882, to sell and convey to the Trustees of the University of Pennsylvania and their successors the following described lots of land, being part of the Almshouse property, viz.:

" *No. 1.*—All that certain lot or piece of ground situate in the Twenty-seventh Ward of the City of Philadelphia, beginning at the northwest corner of Pine Street and Thirty-sixth Street, thence extending westward along the north side of Pine Street, one thousand and seventy--three (1,073) feet nine (9) inches to the southeast side of Woodland Avenue, thence northeastward along the same six hundred and twenty-six (626) feet nine and three-quarter (9¾) inches to the south side of Spruce Street, thence eastward along the same five hundred and thirty-four (534) feet nine and three-quarter (9¾) inches to the west side of Thirty-sixth Street, and thence southward along the same three hundred and twenty (320) feet to the north side of Pine street and place of beginning.

"*No. 2.*—All that certain triangular lot or piece of ground situate in the Twenty-seventh Ward of the City of Philadelphia, beginning at the corner formed by the south side of Pine Street and the northeast side of Cleveland Avenue, thence extending eastward along the south side of Pine Street nine hundred and ninety-two (992) feet five and three-eighths (5⅜) inches to the northwest side of Guardian Avenue, thence southwestward along the same seven hundred and eighty-six (786) feet five and three-eighths (5⅜) inches to the northeast side of Cleveland Avenue, and thence northwestward along the same six hundred and thirty-two (632) feet two (2) inches to the south side of Pine Street and place of beginning,

"*No. 3.*—All that certain lot or piece of ground situate in the Twenty-seventh Ward of the City of Philadelphia, beginning at the corner formed by the south side of Pine Street and the southwest side of Cleveland Avenue, thence extending southeastward along the southwest side of Cleveland Avenue six hundred and eighty (680) feet five and one-eighth (5⅛) inches to a a point, thence southwestward along other ground of the City of Philadelphia one hundred (100) feet and five-eighths (⅝) of an inch to ground of the Woodland Cemetery, thence northwestward along the same seven hundred and forty-one (741) feet eight and seven-eighths (8⅞) inches to the southeast side of Woodland Avenue, thence along the same twenty-nine (29) feet seven and three-quarters (7¾) inches to the south side of Pine Street, and thence along the same eastward eighty-nine (89) feet one and one-quarter (1¼) inches to the southwest side of Cleveland Avenue and place of beginning, reserv.

ing thereout a ground rent to the City of Philadelphia of five hundred (500) dollars per annum, redeemable at any time by the payment to the City of the sum of ten thousand (10,000) dollars, lawful money of the United States, to have and to hold the said land to the said Trustees for the use of the said University of Pennsylvania for its authorized educational purposes, and subject to the following conditions, to wit:

" That the said Trustees of the said University of Pennsylvania shall establish and forever maintain at least fifty (50) free scholarships of an annual value of not less than seven thousand five hundred (7,500) dollars per annum, to be awarded under such conditions as may from time to time be deemed suitable to worthy and deserving students of the Public Schools of Philadelphia: *And further*, That they shall cause to be made and maintained, on the line of Thirty-seventh Street, between Spruce and Pine Streets on the first lot of said ground, a flagged footwalk, open at all times to the public: *And further*, That said land shall never be alienated by the said Trustees without the consent of the City: *And further*, That no buildings other than for educational purposes shall ever be erected thereon: *And further*, That if Cleveland Avenue should be widened to a width of one hundred feet, the said Trustees will dedicate the land taken to public use."

Councils confirmed the sale of six and two hundred and ninety seven thousandths acres, more or less, of meadow land sold at public sale by M. Thomas & Sons, auctioneers, February 14th, 1882, to Henry K. Fox for the sum of eight thousand six hundred (8,600) dollars cash, with a proviso "that the Pennsylvania Railroad Company enter into an agreement that whenever the City shall pass an Ordinance to that effect the said Company will build and maintain a proper and suitable bridge over Thirtieth Street, at the point where the said railroad now or may hereafter cross said Thirtieth Street."

A piece of land adjoining the grounds of William C. Allison, ninety (90) feet wide on the east side of Thirtieth Street and extending eastwardly two hundred and ninety-five feet to the Port Warden's line in the river Schuylkill, containing five hundred and seventy-five thousandths ($\frac{575}{1000}$) of an acre was sold at public sale by the same auctioneers and on the same day. It was purchased by William C. Allison for the sum of three thousand eight hundred (3,800) dollars. The sale was confirmed.

Councils passed a resolution requesting the Trustees of the University of Pennsylvania to inform them as to whether they had complied with the provisions of the law of 1872, by which they were to set aside fifty free beds and also requesting them to send report at the next meeting and also in January next, in accordance with the Act of May 18, 1872.

Dr. William Pepper, Provost of the University, sent reply under date of June 14th, 1882, in which he said: "In reply to the request to the Trustees of the University of Pennsylvania for information respecting the University Hospital, I have the honor to state :

"That the Trustees received from the State of Pennsylvania $200,000, to be expended in the erection of a Hospital, upon condition that they would raise $350,000 additional, and that they would maintain therein 200 beds, free, for all cases of recent accidents occurring in the State of Pennsylvania : and further, that the Trustees were allowed to purchase from the City of Philadelphia, for a nominal sum, the lot of ground in West Philadelphia on which the Hospital now stands, on condition that they would maintain therein 50 free beds for the use of the sick of this city.

"Whereupon, after careful study of the best plans of hospital construction, the University Hospital was erected at a cost of $285,000, and with a capacity of 120 beds.

"It had been hoped that the appropriation received from the State would enable a Hospital containing 240 beds to be immediately erected; but the very high prices of labor and material prevailing in 1872–73, when the contracts were made, the cost of the building consumed the State appropriation and $85,000 additional, which latter sum was contributed by private individuals.

"The plans of the University Hospital, however, provide for a capacity of 500 beds, and it is the intention of the Trustees to complete the structure as soon as possible. During the present season a new wing has been constructed, with a capacity of 80 or 90 beds, which will raise the total to above 200.

"In addition to $200,000 received from the State towards the erection of the Hospital, the Trustees have received from private individuals, for the establishment and maintenance of the Hospital, more than $500,000, much of which is held as a special trust-fund for the maintenance of free beds in said Hospital.

"The expense of maintaining the University Hospital has been, from July 27, 1874, to June 1, 1882, $203,180.93.

"The pledge given to the State has been liberally fulfilled, since, from the day the doors of the Hospital were first opened, every case of accident or surgical injury brought to the Hospital has been freely admitted. The number of free patients treated in the Hospital in eight years has been 3,895, of whom about three-fifths, or 2,300, have been residents of this City.

"At all times the 50 free beds pledged to the City are available, and that number is frequently exceeded.

"The Trustees are conscious that there have been delays in carrying forward the great undertaking of establishing a large and fully-endowed Hospital, even as far as it has now progressed. But they feel that all who are familiar with the difficulties will realize that to have secured over $500,000 from private sources in nine years ; to have erected and maintained a Hospital recognized as a model of such an institution at a cost of $285,000 for construction, and over $25,000 per annum for maintenance, and in which 5,870 patients have been treated in its wards, and over 40,000 patients in its Dispensary department, proves an energetic determination to comply with and to exceed all the pledges given to the State and to the City. The above facts make this the more evident when it is noted that the Acts of the Legislature and the Ordinance of Council referred to do not fix any limit of time for the fulfillment of these pledges.''

The Provost had evidently overlooked or had forgotten the fifth condition of the Ordinance which granted the ground. It provided "That in the event of the failure to erect and complete said hospital building within five years from the first day of July,

A. D. 1872, or upon said completion they shall refuse or neglect to set apart and forever maintain at all times not less than 50 free beds for the poor of the City . . . . . . shall be null and void, and the tract or piece of land hereby authorized to be conveyed to them, with the building or buildings thereon erected, shall revert to and again become the property and estate of the City of Philadelphia."

CHAPTER XXVIII.

REPORT OF INVESTIGATING COMMITTEE.

ON June 12th, 1882, the special committee appointed to investigate the management of the Almshouse made a lengthy report, in which it appeared that more than 30 meetings were held for the examination of witnesses, and that more than 90 had been heard. About 1,450 pages of type-written testimony, apart from the exhibits, were taken. Some of the Guardians, as well as the Superintendent, were represented by counsel, and were permitted to call such witnesses as they desired. The Committee reported:

"*First.*—We find that the system of keeping accounts at the Almshouse is one which affords no sufficient check upon peculation; that it is so defective that those in control of the institution or their chief subordinates can, if they so desire, rob the city to almost any extent. An expert was employed to make an examination and he testified that they kept no commercial account books there; so much of a bill of goods as belonged to a particular item is charged up against that item, without detailing the goods purchased or their quantity. They kept no accounts of the distribution of goods, and the only way in which they could tell, or claimed to be able to tell, whether any specific article was exhausted, was by finding it no longer in the storehouse. No one, he said, could tell by the books, a month after entries were made, whether they were correct or not.

"The Storekeeper testified that he never balanced his books, and they were never audited.

"The man in charge of the manufacturing department testified that no invoice of stock had been taken for three years, and that he could not do it without an invoice book; and that the invoice book had been taken from him by a Committee of the Guardians.

"Mr. Huggard, a Guardian, testified that the mode of book-keeping was defective, and that there was no way in which the delivery of 900 pounds in place of 1000 pounds could be detected.

303

" A number of witnesses were examined on the subjects of food and clothing. The inmates all complained that the food was insufficient and of bad quality, and poorly cooked. This evidence was hardly contradicted, except in a general way by the Superintendent who said, ' there was nothing to complain of.'

" The flour inspector refused to pass some of the flour that was intended for the Almshouse, as it was unfit for human beings to eat.

" It was shown that J. B. Myers (who was then a member of Councils) furnished butter and eggs to the Almshouse worth from one-half to two-thirds the price paid for them, and just that much below the quality called for by the contract. W. W. Thompson also furnished butter of the same quality.

" More than fifty persons, who had furnished supplies, had been subpœnaed but none of them would testify.

" A woman, who had been chief nurse of the venereal ward, testified that in 1881 her patients suffered with the cold; that all they had for breakfast was bread and coffee, without milk or sugar, and only sometimes with butter; that for supper the diet was the same, except that tea was substituted for coffee. For dinner they had soup and about as much meat as one would give to a twelve-year old child; that they were without butter for three or four months at a time; that the bread was sour and bad; that there was no regular service of vegetables, and they had for the ward, containing from 25 to 30 patients, an allowance of half-a-dozen eggs per day.

" The story of the inmates was in its essential features corroborated by Mr. Wells and Mr. Harrah, gentlemen well-known in the community, and of extensive experience and knowledge of the management of public institutions.

" Mr. Wells said the food and clothing were insufficient, and the quality of the food injurious. Mr. Harrah found the bread in the hospital sour, the babies bottles unwashed, and the institution the worst managed that he had ever seen.

" The man in charge of the milkhouse testified that the milk was skimmed before it was served, and the fresh milk was mixed with the old milk, and often the whole made sour; and that during the two years he was there he saw some of the inmates of the Old Men's Department without bedding, and without under clothes.

" Most of the Guardians had very little to say about the food, clothing and attendance. The President of the Board said he knew nothing about bread, milk or beef, and had heard no complaints about clothing. Mr. Orr said the butter was sometimes not up to the standard, and the bread was sometimes sour. Mr. McAleer had seen bad flour, which he had ordered sent back. Mr. Daly said the tea and coffee ought to be better, and that the flour is sometimes good and sometimes bad, and Mr. Huggard considered the tea and coffee abominable, and the bread was sometimes sour."

The committee called attention to two facts which were not disputed, both of which they considered was a disgrace to the institution and all who had control of it. " The cruelty permitted towards old paupers and the insane, and the death of *all* found-lings brought to the place is difficult to write of with calmness. It is in evidence and not disputed—indeed Matthew McNamara, a witness called by the Guardians, testified that he was whipping from eight to ten people a day, when he suddenly went to Ireland in April, 1880, there being a great many complaints against him. He said that his stick was his best friend, that it had a large nail in the end of it.

" Richard Penn, a policeman, who in 1880 was an attendant in the insane department, testified that he had seen a man named Michael Houten, who was in charge of the sixth ward, frequently knock down old insane people. He said he complained to Major Phipps, but no improvement was made, and he (Penn) was finally discharged for making complaints.

" The death of all the foundlings brought into the children's department was attempted to be accounted for by Dr. Montgomery and the matron in charge on the theory that they were either so drugged or diseased when they got them that they could not be kept alive. The answer to this is the fact that when, in 1881, the thirty survivors out of sixty-six were received by the Society for

20

Prevention of Cruelty to Children, of those taken care of by the Society not one died.

" The testimony of Mr. Crew, President of the Society, and Mr. Harrah, who investigated this matter, is that the deaths of these infants was due to *ignorance* and *neglect*.

" That such barbarous cruelty should be allowed in any civilized community is almost incredible, and yet the Superintendent of this institution and the President of the Board of Guardians find nothing in regard to which they desire a change, unless it is in the smallness of the appropriations.

" There can be no right feeling person in this community who does not feel that he himself will in some degree be responsible for the continuance of such outrages, and it is the earnest hope of this committee that, whatever action Councils may take on this report, they will at least take such measures as will render impossible, in any of the institutions of this City, the beating of the poor, the crippled and the afflicted, and the abandonment of helpless infants to die for want of ordinary care."

The committee urged the necessity of separating the hospital from the Almshouse, using the argument that very few people are willing to go there for treatment, feeling that it involves being classed as a pauper, and it was recommended that the pauper element be placed elsewhere, leaving the Almshouse buildings for hospital purposes.

" The Committee found as a fact from the evidence, that the appropriations made for the Guardians had been to some extent, how far could not be stated, diverted from the purposes for which they were made, and had not been strictly accounted for. Warrants, signed by the President and Secretary of the Board, appear to have been drawn for supplies which never reached the Almshouse, or at least were never distributed there; and also for goods at a price higher than the market rate for the goods delivered.

" The evidence showed that supplies were regularly taken from the Almshouse and not accounted for.

" One of the officials received from six to twelve pounds of

INTERIOR OF DRUG STORE.

butter twice a week, made from the cream skimmed from the Almshouse milk. He also took meat.

"The receipts from the sale of empty packages, such as barrels, boxes, etc., fell off from $1,182.67 in 1873 to $150 in 1879. This could not be explained. The supplies were no less, or, to speak more accurately, the supplies *which are paid for* are no less, and presumably the packages in which they are contained are no fewer. The market prices of the articles were not shown to be lower. The only explanation of the shortage in the receipts is that this property of the City is either given away or sold and the proceeds not turned in.

"A Mr. Moore bid to furnish certain brushes at $128.40; he did not get the contract. Shortly afterwards he sold similar goods to Mr. Coyle, who was not in the business, who supplied them to the Almshouse at an advance of $79.20 over Moore's bid.

"Jacob Schleigh was a produce dealer, he was a clerk for W. W. Thompson when Thompson had a contract to furnish butter to the Almshouse. The butter furnished was worth about two-thirds of the contract sample; it was delivered early in the year, and Schleigh continued to ask for the warrant, without getting it until the ensuing fall. Major Phipps was written to several times about it. Schleigh then went to the Controller's office, and found that the warrant had been *paid* within four weeks after the delivery of the butter. Schleigh then visited the office of the Guardians on Seventh street, and was told that no warrant had come for him. He related what he had learned at the Controller's office, and received the money from the Penn National Bank, where two gentlemen, one of them the Treasurer of the Board, had driven him for that purpose. He was requested to not return to the Controller's, and he did not.

"Controller Pattison testified that in February, 1882, Mr. McFetrich, of the firm of Rocklean & McFetrich, called upon him to see about getting the money for liquors supplied to the Almshouse. It was discovered that the warrant, which was for $186.00, had been paid in February, 1881. Mr. McFetrich then produced a due bill given by Major Phipps for this amount, dated January

1882. Subsequently McFetrich and Phipps called together, and the latter said that the warrant had been given to the wrong man by mistake, and he had assumed the debt.

" The foreman of the carpenter shop at the Almshouse testified that his wages for one month in 1879 and for four months in 1880 were not paid until January, 1881, when, after being importuned very often for payment, Major Phipps finally gave him an order for the amount due him, on Frederick Sheeler, a grocer on Market street, who supplied the institution with groceries. The order was paid.

" An inventory was made by several experts of the carpets and furniture in the institution, and when it was compared with the books in the Controller's office, which showed the amounts purchased, there was found to be a deficiency of about 3,000 yards of carpet, which had been entered as costing from 75 cents to $1.00 per yard.

" A schedule was prepared by an expert showing the amount purchased and paid for by the city, and the amount consumed as per the diet card allowance of tea, coffee, sugar and meat in the year 1881; it showed a balance unaccounted for of 25.961 pounds of tea, 258,452 pounds of coffee and rye mixed, 72,449 pounds of sugar and 424,667 pounds of meat. The committee also had a schedule showing the amount of flour purchased and paid for by the city in 1865, when the population of the Almshouse was about the same as during 1881, which showed that while 4,296 barrels were sufficient in 1865, it required 6,999 barrels in 1881. The amount of tea and coffee *paid for* shows that it required three times as much tea and eight times as much coffee in 1881 as it did in 1865.

" The Controller testified that an item under the head of House receipts, representing money received at the Almshouse from various sources, and which was payable into the City Treasury monthly, had been omitted from the returns for the years 1876, 1877 and 1878. He wrote to the Treasurer of the Board of Guardians and afterwards to the President, calling their attention to this fact and asking explanation, but received none.

"He called the attention of Councils to the fact and gave notice that the money must be paid. This money was finally recovered, amounting to $26,398.51, according to the account presented, and paid to the City Treasurer. The explanation given by Major Phipps and the President was that the appropriations fell short for those years, and that the Guardians had authorized the Superintendent to use the money for the ordinary needs of the house. Major Phipps presented to the Controller receipts purporting to show that he had paid the money monthly to Mr. Lane, the Treasurer of the Board.

"Mr. Lane testified that he never received any portion of the money until immediately prior to his settlement with the Controller in June, 1879. Mr. Lane stated that in 1876 the appropriation ran short, and that the Board of Guardians gave its sanction to an arrangement by which certain contractors were to supply the goods required, and take their chances of getting their bills paid by Councils. That Councils refused to make an appropriation for this purpose, and that Major Phipps, with the knowledge of the Guardians appropriated the House receipts for the payment of these claims, and that when the Controller insisted upon the money being paid into the City Treasury, Phipps induced the contractors Mathews and Toy to return the money; that it was then for the first time handed to Mr. Lane, who at once paid it into the City Treasury. No official action of the Board was shown in relation to the misappropriation of this large amount of money, but unfortunately for the explanation given the annual reports of the Board show that the appropriations for the years mentioned *did not* run short, as there was an unexpended balance on December 31st, 1876, of $1,773.19 and on December 31st, 1877, there remained to their credit $1,344.96.

"The evidence, in the opinion of the Committee, established these facts:

"1. Goods have been furnished the Almshouse of a quality from 33 to 50 per cent. less in value than the contract samples.

"2. Goods have been paid for as furnished which have never been delivered.

" 3. Goods which had been delivered had been taken away and not accounted for.

"4. Warrants have been collected by others than those to whom they belonged, and the money retained until a settlement could no longer be delayed.

" 5. It would seem, though the fact is only shown in a single case, that Major Phipp's obligations were held by contractors whose warrants were overdue, and had been collected *but not by themselves.*

" These facts not only justify the finding of the Committee but make any other finding impossible. There is no evidence to show that any of the Guardians in any way participated in the misappropriation of the funds which should have gone to support the Almshouse.

" The retention of the House receipts by the Superintendent for the years 1876-7-8 was sanctioned by Mr. Chambers and acquiesced in by Messrs. Gill and Orr. The explanation given, that it was necessary to meet the expenses of the house, appears to be untrue. In view of the failure of these gentlemen to give any further explanation, the Committee recommends that they be requested to resign. Mr. Stewart and Mr. Keyser having been at the institution but a short time, the Committee have no positive fault to find with them. The remaining Guardians, except Mr. Jarden who has just been elected, and Messrs. Huggard and Daly, do not seem to properly understand the responsibilities of their positions. They have seen that the inmates of the Almshouse were neither properly fed, clothed, nor cared for; or if they have not they ought to have done so, and yet they have taken no steps to rectify those abuses.

" The Committee would feel it their duty to include Mr. Daly also in this criticism had he not wakened up, even at the last moment, and been very zealous in assisting the Committee in their investigation. These gentlemen, with exceptions already mentioned, have in the opinion of the Committee, all been too indolent and careless in attending to the duties of their position to be retained there, and the Committee recommend that they are, with the exception of Messrs. Jarden, Daly, Stewart, Keyser and Huggard, requested to resign.

"Over Major Phipps, Councils have no control. He is not elected by them, and is not responsible directly to them. It is eminently proper, however, for them to make a recommendation in regard to him to the Board of Guardians.

"The Committee appreciate all that has been said by the medical staff of the Almshouse about Major Phipps' executive ability, but they are of opinion that the facts developed before them, in regard to his relations with the contractors, his outstanding notes held by them, the delays in paying people for whom warrants had been cashed without their knowledge, his failure to correct abuses of which he could not be ignorant, demand imperatively that he should no longer be retained in the position he now occupies, and they therefore recommend his dismissal."

"The Committee submit herewith a joint resolution, embodying their recommendations, together with the testimony."

(Signed) JOHN L. GRIM, *Chairman.*
S. S. HOLLINGSWORTH,
A. J. MALONEY,
EFFINGHAM B. MORRIS,
ADAM A. CATANACH.

Mr. Maloney had been substituted for Mr. Conway, that gentleman having retired from Councils.

Mr. McAleer, one of the Guardians, sent a communication to Councils requesting that the report, so far as it related to him, should be returned to the Committee, in order that he might have the opportunity of proving that he had performed his duty as a member of the Board. He said in part:

"It is true that I was unable to attend to my duties for a length of time by sickness, yet this was my misfortune, and not my fault. As no man charges me with any sin of commission or any sin of omission, I think it hardly fair that any reflection should be cast on my character."

Upon the adoption of the report and resolution of the Committee, the name of Mr. McAleer was added to those to be excepted from the request to resign.

At this meeting an election took place for four Guardians to fill vacancies caused by the expiration of the terms of four of the old Board. Messrs. Edward F. Hoffman, John Ruhl, Lucien Moss and William McAleer were chosen.

During the term of Major Phipps the title of his position was changed from that of Steward to Superintendent, and the powers were considerably enlarged.

Councils took the usual summer recess, commencing June 19th.

CHAPTER XXIX.

TRAINING SCHOOL FOR NURSES ESTABLISHED—TERRIBLE FIRE IN INSANE DEPARTMENT—SUPERINTENDENT PHIPPS ARRESTED.

A CONFERENCE was held by the new and some of the older members of the Board of Guardians, and, after considerable discussion, in order not to appear as being hasty or harsh, a committee of three was appointed to wait on the Superintendent to request and advise his resignation, the same to take effect on September 1st, 1882. After some consideration he sent a communication dated July 3d, in which he said:

" GENTLEMEN—In compliance with the desire of the members of the Board of Guardians of the Poor, expressed at the conference held on 1st inst., I hereby tender my resignation to take effect as requested."

During the interval the Committee of One Hundred, citizens organized to procure better municipal government, were busy in procuring sufficient evidence to enter a criminal suit against him.

Mr. Morris M. Mathews made affidavit that on or about January 1st, 1882, and within nine months last past, that " said Ellis P. Phipps had defrauded the city of a large sum of money, to wit, over $5,000; that he obtained the money, and also that he had conspired with others to defraud the city of large sums of money, and that he had obtained and assisted others to obtain fraudulently and keep the money of the city." He also swore that Phipps had drawn warrants in payment for goods which had never been delivered, and the money had been obtained on these warrants.

Mr. Mathews confessed that he had presented bills during the first three months of this year for goods to the amount of $7,200, all of which, with the exception of one for $549.94, were fictitious, yet upon which warrants were drawn by Major Phipps, who also drew the money.

Upon the strength of this affidavit a warrant was issued and Phipps was arrested on September 1st, on the charge of embezzlement.   He was placed under $5,000 bail for a hearing, W. Elwood Rowan, a member of Common Council, becoming his bondsman.

Before the time set for the hearing he absconded and his bail was declared forfeited.   A new warrant was issued, a description of him was sent to all of the police stations and orders for his arrest were transmitted.

A search was made of the house No. 3419 Walnut street, which he occupied, where large quantities of all kinds of provisions, dry goods and notions, taken from the Almshouse, were found secreted in the cellar and locked in closets in the rooms.   The value of the goods recovered was estimated at $5,000.   In addition it was discovered that he owed to subordinates, whose wages he had retained, amounts running up into hundreds of dollars.   He also retained the House receipts of July and August, amounting to $1,500, and for which a demand had been made upon him a few days before his departure.   A number of promissory notes, amounting to about $200,000 were found.   They were dated in 1880 and 1881.   Some of them had been cancelled, and were in the names of prominent politicians and contractors.

Major Phipps was apprehended on the 18th day of September, 1882, in Hamilton, Ontario.   Upon being fully identified he was remanded.   It was necessary to have extraditien papers from the President of the United States to the Canadian government before he could be brought back to this city, and to obtain this object charges of felony would have to be established.   District Attorney Graham took the matter in hand ; witnesses were sent before the Grand Jury, and when they had been examined, three bills of indictment were found, charging Phipps with fraudulently making an instrument of writing and uttering and publishing the same. This constitutes forgery.

There were several counts contained in each bill.   The first charged that he, Phipps, had forged the name of W. L. Murphy to a receipt for a warrant for $389 ; the others charged the forgery of receipts for warrants in the names of A. J. Bellows & Co. for $377.80, and Seeds & Ferguson for $595.   These warrants were all paid by the City Treasurer.

The President issued the necessary papers, Mr. Graham took them to Canada and after a long delay Phipps was surrendered, brought to this City, tried, convicted, sentenced, and served a long term of imprisonment.

Major Thomas B. Scarborough had been elected Superintendent and took charge of the Almshouse on the 1st of September. Several of the employees of the institution were arrested, tried and convicted on the charges of larceny and conspiracy to defraud the City.

At the first meeting of Councils after the recess, Messrs. Lane, Gill and Spering tendered their resignations as members of the Board. Messrs. Joseph Paxson, William R. Chapman and Mark Balderston were elected in their stead.

The Board then consisted of Messrs. Jarden, Daly, Huggard, Stewart, Ruhl, Keyser, Hoffman, Moss, McAleer, Paxson, Chapman and Balderston. It was organized by the election of Mr. John Huggard as President and Robert C. Floyd as Secretary.

Mr. Jarden resigned on November 16th, and General Louis Wagner was elected to fill the vacancy.

President Huggard, in his report at the end of the year, said in part : " For reasons that are obvious and need no explanation the report for the first half of the year is—with the exception of that portion relating to the Hospital for the Insane—somewhat incomplete, but the facts have been arrived at as nearly as possible. Upon the showing of the last half of the year I congratulate the Board."

The new Superintendent said : " On assuming the duties of the institution, I need hardly remind you of the disorder and confusion which characterized some of its departments. Although my predecessor turned over no papers or books pertaining to the duties of the office, I have nevertheless, with your assistance, been able to appreciate to a certain degree its wants."

An item was inserted in the appropriations for the year 1883, to pay $555 to the paupers to repay the amounts belonging to them which had been taken by the late Superintendent.

On January 4th, 1883, Mr. Balderston resigned from the

Board, and Dr. W. H. Zeigler was elected to fill the vacancy. Mr. Moss resigned on March 8th, and Mr. Richard C. McMurtrie was elected in his stead.

Messrs. Paxson, Chapman, Zeigler and Daly were re-elected in June. The Board was re-organized by the election of Mr. Hoffman as President and Mr. Floyd as Secretary. Mr. George H. Smith was elected Superintendent.

Two Acts which had an important bearing upon the management of the Almshouse were passed by the Legislature and approved June 13th, 1883.

One of them provided that children over two years of age should not be kept in the Almshouses of this State for a longer period than sixty days, unless they were under medical treatment. It also provided for their maintenance in homes, the expenses to be borne by the municipalities in which they belonged.

This was intended to be of great benefit; it removed the children from the Almshouse surroundings and saved them from the taint of pauperism. It gave them the advantages of home care and treatment, thus fitting them to become useful, self-supporting men or women.

Councils appropriated $8,000 for the first year to "pay for the maintenance of the children sent to the various homes," in accordance with the Act. The number of children under the care of the department has so increased, since that time, that it now requires $20,000 per annum for that purpose.

The other Act was to provide for the surrender of the bodies of those who died in the Almshouse, etc., to the Anatomical Board for dissection.

After describing the method of forming the Board and providing for its appointment and duties, the Act sets forth :

"All public officers, agents and servants, and all officers, agents and servants of any and every county, city, township, borough, district and other municipality, and of any and every Almshouse, prison, morgue, hospital, or other public institution having charge or control over dead human bodies, required to be buried at the public expense, are hereby required to notify the said

Board of distribution or such person or persons as may, from time to time, be designated by said Board or its duly authorized agent, whenever any such body or bodies come to his or their possession, charge or control, and shall, without fee or reward, deliver such body or bodies, and permit or suffer the said Board, or its agents, and the Physicians and Surgeons from time to time designated by them, who may comply with the provisions of this Act, to take and remove all such bodies, to be used within this State for the advancement of medical science ; but no such notice need be given, nor shall any such body be delivered, if any person claiming to be, and shall satisfy the authorities in charge of said body, that he or she is of kindred, or is related by marriage to the deceased, shall claim the said body for burial, but it shall be surrendered for interment ; nor shall notice be given or body delivered, if such deceased person was a traveller who died suddenly, in which case the body shall be buried."

The Act provided for the distribution of bodies among the schools, colleges, etc., and required that bonds should be entered as a guarantee that the bodies should be used for scientific purposes only. A penalty was provided for the punishment of any person convicted of buying or selling bodies.

This Act put a stop to " body-snatching," " resurrecting " and " traffic in bodies," subjects that had caused much discussion and scandal in previous years, and had caused the Guardians to be designated as the " Board of Buzzards." Since the passage of the bill the Almshouse authorities have not buried any of the paupers who have died. Those poor persons who died in homes in the city and had no friends who were willing or able to pay funeral expenses, have been buried in an humble manner by an undertaker employed for the purpose by the Guardians of the Poor.

An ordinance of Councils was approved on the 6th day of July, 1883, which ordained "That all the Almshouse property in West Philadelphia, bounded by South Street, Spruce Street, Thirty-fourth Street, Vintage Avenue, on to the southern boundary of the city property, and thereto to the Schuylkill River, and the Schuylkill River, be and is hereby set apart for the purpose of being improved for the health and public welfare of the citizens of Philadelphia."

It provided for the appointment of two laborers to level the ashes, etc., that might be placed on the marshy part of the grounds so that it might be filled up to a proper level to the Port Warden's line. Citizens were authorized to dump ashes, etc., on the grounds.

This ordinance embraced all of the property south of Spruce Street that was not inclosed for the Almshouse buildings. It took in the grounds upon which stood the Children's Asylum, the stables and carriage houses, the farmer's and weigher's houses and the graveyard, in which the remains of hundreds are deposited.

On January 31st, 1884, General Wagner resigned from the Board, and Dr. Thomas Biddle was elected to fill the vacancy.

At the annual election in June, 1884, Messrs. Huggard, Stewart and Biddle were re-elected, and Mr. J. W. Durham took the place of Mr. Keyser. Mr. George H. Smith was elected Superintendent.

The office of Chief Nurse in the Hospital was created, and $800 were appropriated to pay her salary. On July 28, 1884, President Hoffman stated that for some time past efforts had been made to find a suitable person for head nurse of the proposed training school. Mr. George W. Childs and Mr. Anthony J. Drexel, having interested themselves in the matter, had submitted the name of Miss Alice Fisher, and she was selected.

In 1885 the salary was increased to $1,000, and in 1886 an assistant was provided for at a salary of $600 per annum. This was the *official* commencement of what has since been termed the "Training School for Nurses of the Philadelphia Hospital." Prior to that time the nursing was done principally by the inmates, and this movement was intended to introduce a different character of persons to perform that duty.

Young women and girls, who desired to become proficient in that line and who possessed the necessary qualifications, were employed at a small salary and placed under the direction of competent, practical teachers for a term of two, but subsequently changed to three years, during which time they had experience in all of the wards of the institution.

Miss Alice Fisher, a lady of much ability and of long experience in hospital work in England, was the first chief nurse and the organizer of the system. She served in that position until the time of her death, June 3d, 1888, when Miss Marion E. Smith, a graduate of the school, succeeded to the position. Miss Edith Horner, who is now the wife of United States Senator Hawley, was the first assistant. The school was started with about one dozen pupils, and from that small number it has increased until now there are more than a hundred attending the course.

The portion of the main hospital building that had formerly been occupied by the children was remodeled and repaired for a home for the nurses. Reception and class rooms were provided for them, and ward rooms were divided into sleeping apartments.

The old school room was fitted up for the Apothecary Store.

A new maternity building was erected on the ground where one of the old nervous pavillions had stood. It was finished in the latter part of the year.

One of the saddest calamities that had ever visited the Almshouse was the fire that occurred on the night of February 12th, 1885.

The main building of the Insane Department was entirely burned out, and nineteen of the poor patients lost their lives. It caused great distress, as there was no part of the institution where the homeless ones could be cared for. The Pennsylvania Railroad Company generously offered the use of the vacant depot at Thirty-second and Market Streets as a temporary asylum. It was accepted until arrangements could be made to send some of the patients to the State Hospitals.

Councils instructed the committee to make a thorough investigation of the origin of the fire and the conduct of the officials previous to the fire and at the time. The Committee submitted the following interesting report :

" *To the Select and Common Councils
of the City of Philadelphia :*

"The Committee on Prisons, etc., which was directed to make a
full and thorough investigation of all matters relating to the
late fire at the Almshouse grounds, etc., by Resolution passed
by your Honorable Bodies, February 19, 1885 (Appendix of
Select Council, No. 84), respectfully report:

"That at a meeting held on February 22, 1885, and at various
adjourned meetings thereafter, it examined a number of the Guardians of the Poor, and officers and employees of the institution, in
reference to the matters contained in said resolutions. Directly
after your Committee were instructed, as aforesaid, and before its
first meeting, the Coroner made an investigation of the fire, and
his jury, after listening to the evidence produced before it, found a
verdict implicating one of the inmates and two of the employees,
who were thereupon bound over for trial and are now confined in
the county prison. A majority of the members of your committee, while not in any wise adopting or rejecting the above verdict
as the true solution of the mystery, deem it inexpedient to interfere with the course of justice which would, in an orderly manner,
develop through the Courts an explanation more valuable than any
this committee could secure by further examination of the alleged
perpetrators of this terrible crime, and consequently it was determined to proceed no further in that direction. The investigation
of the origin of the fire being unnecessary, the carrying out of the
remainder of your instructions was expected to be rather perfunc-
tory in its character, but the statements of the Guardians, concerning the management of affairs at Blockley, displayed such a want
of harmony among themselves, and such an entire absence of attention to important details, that your Committee would fail in its
duty if it did not comment thereon and draw your serious attention
thereto.

Your Committee were surprised to find that no arrangements of any kind had been made for the prevention or suppression
of fire in the Insane Asylum, which contained over six hundred
male and female patients. The building was three stories high,

some seven hundred feet long, and about seventy-five feet deep. It was in shape a parallelogram, with wings at each end. The fire took place on Thursday, February 12, 1885, about eight o'clock P. M. It was discovered a few minutes after eight, and may have been smouldering some time. A mulatto boy, or man, named Naudine, shouted the alarm, and two attendants, who were a short distance away, hearing him, ran to the drying room, on the first floor, where they found the flames had made some headway. Without any appliances to extinguish or control the fire, the only resource was to assist the inmates to escape. There was not even a fire-alarm box on the premises, so that the building was a roaring furnace by the time the firemen arrived, and the difficulties of rescuing the unfortunates can hardly be exaggerated. Under the circumstances, it is remarkable that only nineteen of the inmates were burned up. The courage and energy of the firemen, assisted by the officers and employees of the institution, alone prevented a greater destruction of life.

"The fire completely gutted the main building, leaving nothing but the walls and the fire-escapes; but the wings, at either end, were only partially damaged, and are already almost entirely restored. They will certainly be ready for occupancy in a few days.

"In June, 1883, Councils provided the sum of $20,000 for erecting these fire-escapes, which consist of outside fire-proof staircases, and are attached also to the other buildings at Blockley. In the wreck of the Insane Asylum these staircases remained wholly uninjured, demonstrating their value at such times, and assisting in the saving of life.

"After the erection of these escapes there remained a balance of $1,490.20; and it is to be regretted that, with the subject before them, the Guardians did not purchase with this money some of the many modern chemical apparatus for use at fires inside the building. A transfer for this purpose was readily obtainable. A short time before the sad event the Board of Guardians had directed three members of the medical staff to make an examination of the building occupied by the insane, and report thereon. This report, dated January 30, 1885, called the attention of the Board to a number of

21

needed reforms in this department, and most particularly to the want of the proper provisions in case of fire, warning the members that should it occur 'a large proportion of the inmates would be burned to death.' These gentlemen say, ' there is not a fire-plug, a foot of hose, or a fire-extinguisher in the whole building; and in the upper stories there is no certain supply of water. They respectfully suggested changes and improvements in these respects, that were being considered by the Hospital Committee, but had not yet been acted upon at the time of the disaster.

" Before the receipt of this report the idea of fire seems never to have occurred to any member of the Board. The hospital and the out-wards, where the paupers are kept, containing some 2,500 persons in addition to the insane, were equally defenceless against that element.

" This oversight arose, no doubt from the general belief that such precautions had been taken. No one imagined the danger; each member elected to the Board, if the subject occurred to him at all, assumed that the buildings were perfectly provided, and troubled himself no more about the matter. What was everybody's business was nobody's. So far as your Committee could learn, there never had been, at any time in the history of the Almshouse, any provisions for security from or for the extinguishment of fire. At present each floor of the building is provided with chemical extinguishers. A fire-alarm box is located on the premises, and attachments will soon be made to secure a better water supply. The buildings now are ordinarily safe from fire.

"Your Committee cannot leave this branch of the investigation without alluding to the effort which was made to place the respon-sibility for this fire upon your Honorable Bodies. The present investigation has shown this to be entirely unsupported by any evidence whatever. In the first horrors of the occasion, inuendoes and statements were made, from what source exactly your Commit-tee was unable to discover, suggesting that the disaster was the result of some economies of the public money upon your part. Among other more indefinite assertions to support this, it was stated that two watchmen for the asylum were refused by the

Finance Committee; the inference being intended that, had they been granted—and this is suggested in a communication, signed by the members of the Board, to Councils of February 19, 1885 (Common Council Appendix, No. 251)—the fire would have been prevented. In the first place, they would have been useless without any means of extinguishing the fire; and, secondly, they were never requested. The application which was thus distorted into two watchmen for the insane asylum was actually for two policemen to guard the grounds, and particularly to prevent the inmates from passing their clothes and other articles through or over the fence to outsiders; and the men, if allowed, could therefore have been of no service whatever in preventing or extinguishing the fire.

"It was also asserted that the property at Blockley could have been sold for sufficient to put up new buildings, with modern improvements, etc., and leave a handsome surplus in the treasury; and that, therefore, Councils were responsible for the burning of the present tinder-box. The entire tract at the Almshouse being only sixteen acres, worth probably eight or ten thousand dollars an acre, the absurdity of this is apparent, even if such remote responsibility was not otherwise ridiculous.

"It was next insinuated that a better water supply would have aided in reducing the flames. This is undoubtedly true; and had the Guardians made attachments to the six-inch mains that completely surround Blockley, it could have been obtained; but it seems they did not know these mains were laid.

"These are sufficient as specimens, and it is unnecessary to allude to any more of these attempts to put responsibility for this disaster on innocent shoulders. It suffices to say, that no request of the Guardians for the protection of the lives and property entrusted to their charge has been refused by City Councils, and that three hundred and twenty-five thousand dollars, divided, as suggested by the Guardians themselves, was allowed for the expenses of the current year.

"The insight obtained by your Committee into the manner of government of the institutions at Blockley was not gratifying.

The character of the gentlemen constituting the Board is such that it is unnecessary to say that nothing affecting their integrity is suggested by this statement; but it cannot be denied that the efficiency of the body is greatly, if not totally, impaired by constant bickerings and an utter want of united action in any direction. The President of the Board, Mr. Edward Hoffman, frankly stated to your Committee that this was so, and, in his opinion, was caused by the struggle among the members for the patronage appertaining to the position; that is to say, the appointment of the numerous attendants, nurses, etc., required in the immense establishments. He presented a list of appointees in the Insane Asylum, and it was evident that politics had more to do with the appointments than fitness for office. Where the patronage was not retained by the members, it appeared to have been traded off for the support of measures of administration desired by the assignor of the patronage. That the appointments were the great lever and the chief cause of dissension was apparent, without the statement to that effect of the President. The report of the medical officers, before alluded to, says, with reference to the ability of the appointees, what would naturally be expected from such a system, 'The character and general fitness of the nurses is very low as a rule.' The list presented to your Committee by the President shows that painters, gardeners, car conductors, stablemen, laborers, sailors, and such like, were appointed nurses and attendants upon the insane, without any method of determining their qualifications. Your Committee respectfully recommend that this system be abolished, and hereafter fitness and character be made the sole test.

" Another weakness in the management your Committee deem it proper to suggest should be corrected; and that is the want of absolute authority in the heads of the departments. The report of the physicians speaks very strongly, but not too much so, upon this subject. In reference to the Physician-in-Chief of the Insane Asylum it says, ' All attendant nurses are appointed by the Committee on the Insane Hospital, and no matter how grave may be their offences—if they be drunk, brutal, or absent without leave, they are not removable by the physicians without a hearing before the

INTERIOR OF STORE HOUSE.

Committee.   A system which puts an end to all possibility of exact
and reasonable discipline.   This system stands alone in this Commonwealth in this hospital, and would be laughable were it not too
serious for mirth.   The Physician-in-Chief of the insane and the
Superintendent of the Almshouse should have power to dismiss or
punish any subordinate promptly, without any appeal, reporting
the same at once to the Board.

"Dr. Bennett, of the Norristown Insane Hospital, very properly said, 'The most unworthy attendants are those who are apt to
try to appeal to the Trustees, and if the latter listened to their
stories we would be involved in endless complications, and my
authority and discipline would be greatly weakened.'

"The management of the pauper establishments is, however,
entirely vested by law in the Guardians of the Poor, who have
complete jurisdiction and control; Councils being confined to electing four of these gentlemen every year, one of whom shall belong
to the minority, and appropriating the money for the maintenance
thereof; but the present members have always manifested such
deference to the wishes of your Honorable Bodies, and the desire to
promote the interests of the institution, that any suggestions that
are appropriate and useful will be cheerfully accepted and carefully
considered.   The office of Guardian is no sinecure.   It requires
conscientious attention and thought.   Experience is almost a necessity to the proper performance of its duties.   The gentlemen
who are willing to make the necessary sacrifices to hold the place
should receive the support of Councils, and be retained as long as
possible.   This Committee has endeavored, during the Council-
manic year now ending, to sustain the Board in the reforms which
it undoubtedly has accomplished; and can say that while obliged,
as you have seen, to criticise parts of the management, it recog-
nizes that there has been an endeavor, on the part of the members,
to promote the general welfare of the inmates and administer its
affairs honestly and economically.   With a mutual disposition all
around to surrender personal prejudices and unite their differences,
the present Board would secure admirable results.

"The resolutions adopted by your Honorable Bodies further

direct your Committee to report 'the demands of and appropriations to the Guardians of the Poor for the past five years, and the
expenditures of the same.' A statement showing the above has
been obtained and is herewith annexed.

"All of which is respectfully submitted.

"JOHN J. RIDGWAY, JR., *Chairman.*"

	Appropriations.	Expenditures.
1880	$405,476 00	$405,402 63
1881	436,976 95	436,093 90
1882	422,118 00	406,317 57
1883	386,304 00	365,401 56
1884	344,613 00	336,346 20

CHAPTER XXX.

BULLITT BILL GOES INTO EFFECT—CHANGE IN MANAGEMENT.

SHORTLY after the fire the effort to remove the pauper element of the Almshouse to another location was renewed. Petitions were circulated by the medical fraternity to obtain signatures of those in favor of it.

In compliance with a resolution, the Clerk of Common Council advertised for proposals for a tract of land in the City of Philadelphia, suitable for the purpose, price not to exceed $500 per acre, and tract to contain not less than 25 acres.

In compliance therewith, the following offers were received, viz:

From.	No. of Acres.	Price per Acre.
T. P. Smart	25	$473 00
John Hennig	not stated	400 00
Joseph C. Moore	34	475 00
James Clark	25	400 00
Edwin Martin	$41^{89}/_{100}$	238 72
David M. Hess	32	500 00
Jon'n Rowland	75	225 00
George S. Clark	$32^{2}/_{10}$	250 00
John Arthur	73	350 00
Mrs. Glackin	67	300 00
Dilworth Wentz	50	500 00
E. C. Chesebrough	190	400 00
Harrison Farm	156	500 00
E. V. Lansdale	100	500 00

President Hoffman, under date of May 9th, 1885, sent the following communication to Councils :

"*Gentlemen*—I respectfully tender my resignation as a Guardian of the Poor, to take effect forthwith.

"It is in the best interests of the institution that my place as President and member of the Board should be at once filled by a gentleman who commands the support of your body."

The resignation was accepted, and Mr. Thomas S. Keyser was elected to fill the vacancy on the Board.

327

Mr. Joseph Paxson was subsequently chosen for President. Dr. Philip Leidy was selected for Physician-in-Chief of the insane department.

The Councils Committee on Prisons was "requested to consider and report on the propriety of re-building the burned portion of the insane department at Blockley."

The Committee made report on May 28th, 1885, in which it was stated:

"The Board of Guardians of the Poor are unanimously of the opinion that they should be rebuilt on the present site, and this view is indorsed by your committee for the following reasons:

"*First.* The old walls now standing are worth between $30,000 and $40,000, which will be lost to the city if these buildings are erected elsewhere.

"*Second.* There are now about 240 insane patients in the portion of the building not touched by the late fire, who overcrowd the same, and in the event of a similar casualty, the same appalling result might happen as upon the prior occasion.

"*Third.* It is asserted that the State insane asylums are now full, and therefore the patients now remaining at Blockley cannot be removed to said asylums. The Norristown Asylum in particular is very much crowded.

"*Fourth.* While your Committee believe that the State should erect an insane asylum in Philadelphia, of sufficient size to accommodate and properly care for her insane citizens, inasmuch as Philadelphia pays into the State Treasury two-fifths of its entire receipts; yet, should the State authorities coincide with this view, it would be impossible to accomplish the said object by securing the proper legislation, the awarding of contracts and the erection of such buildings in a less period than four or five years, and in the meantime the insane poor of our city would be deprived of that care and treatment which is expected from a Christian community.

"*Fifth.*—There was an insurance of $10,000 upon the burnt building, which sum is now available, and which, together with the sum of $25,000, will rebuild these buildings and make them thoroughly fire proof and capable of accommodating 600 patients.

" *Sixth.*—The hospital facilities of Philadelphia are inadequate for the City's needs in case of an epidemic, and these buildings proposed to be rebuilt would be of great value for such purposes, if at any time hereafter other accommodations for the insane should be secured.

" The Board of Guardians of the Poor have had plans prepared for the rebuilding of these buildings, which they have unanimously approved, and which your Committee have also approved, and recommend their adoption."

The subject was referred to the Joint Committee on Finance and Prison. Upon their report Councils approved the plans prepared by Wilson Brothers & Co., and the work was ordered to be done.

Before the fire these buildings were three stories in height, the same as the other three, but when they were rebuilt only the centre portion was made that high, the extensions on each side of the centre being only carried up two stories.

On the first floor in the centre are located the physicians' offices and the reception rooms of the patients and their friends ; the assistant physicians' sleeping rooms and the sewing rooms are on the second floor, while the third floor was fitted up for the chapel and Amusement Hall.

Both floors of the extension on one side of the centre are occupied by male patients, while on the other side the female patients have accommodations.

The giving of money, provisions, and groceries as out-door relief (the propriety of which had caused much discussion) having been stopped, the City was divided into districts and a few physicians were employed at a salary of $120 per annum to attend the sick poor at their homes. Medicines and diatetic food were furnished free of cost to the patients. The number of physicians has been increased until now there are 25 of the old school and 25 of the new, with a salary of $240 per annum.

The medicines and food furnished cost the City about $8,000, which, added to the $12,000 paid the physicians, brings the cost of the item up to $20,000 per annum.

The position of hospital warden was abolished and that of physician-in-chief to the hospital was created in its stead; Dr. Thomas N. McLaughlin, who was warden at the time, was elected to the new position.

Mr. George Roney was elected Superintendent and assumed the duties on the 1st of January, 1886. Mr. Roney was an ex-member of Select Council, ex-fire commissioner, and a veteran of the civil war. Many noticeable improvements were made during his administration. During the year a brick pavilion, for the Men's Nervous Wards, was erected in the yard to the northeast ward of, and running parallel with, the main hospital building.

Miss Mary Shields, who died October 8th, 1880, bequeathed to the City of Philadelphia, one-twelfth part of her estate "to relieve and make more comfortable the sick and insane poor in the Alms-house in Philadelphia."

The Board of Directors of the City Trusts conferred with the Guardians of the Poor and adopted a plan for the disposal of the funds. This provided for the appointment of a physician of at least five years standing to act as Superintendent of what was termed the "Mary Shields Almshouse Fund."

Dr. W. H. Wallace was appointed, and he still holds the position. He visits the institution frequently, keeps himself informed as to the needs of the patients, confers with the officials, and reports to the Board of Directors of City Trusts. The accumulated income was applied to the erection of new kitchens, one for the insane and another for the hospital departments, supplied with the best character of cooking apparatus. In addition to these the fund has been used for supplying, as far as possible, such things as were necessary to the comfort and welfare of the patients, but which the authorities could not procure in the usual way. Some of these articles have been an organ, a piano, banjos, accordeons and other musical instruments, lawn seats, settees, water coolers for the wards, framed pictures and a number of games, both for out-door and in-door use. Concerts are given during the cold weather, and a band is employed to play in the yards of the insane department during the summer seasons. Stage coaches are also employed to take selected patients out for a ride, several times during the pleasant weather. A number of magazines, illustrated weekly and monthly papers are subscribed for, and a well selected library was presented to that department. On the holidays the patients are furnished with an excellent dinner of turkey and pies, and fruit is provided for them at different times. The amusement hall was supplied with the furniture, including a pulpit for religious services, tables, chairs and seats for the patients.

The hospital has been furnished with a number of useful articles, such as water and air beds, cushions, rockers, rolling chairs, trusses, etc.

The name of Mary Shields should ever be held in grateful remembrance for the great good that has been accomplished by her bequest through her representatives.

Dr. Joseph Leidy resigned his position as Physician-in-Chief of the Insane Department, and Dr. W. H. Wallace was elected in his stead, but he only served a few months.

The Act known as the "Bullitt Bill" went into effect in April, 1887. It revolutionized the management of the Almshouse. The Boards of the Guardians of the Poor and Managers of the House of Correction were abolished, and the two departments were consolidated in the Department of Charities and Correction. This department is under the care and management of a board consisting of a president and four directors, appointed by the Mayor for a period of five years, and all the authority of the two old boards is vested in them. The board is subdivided into two bureaus, one known as the Bureau of Charities and the other as the Bureau of Correction, the President being *ex officio* a member of both.

The Bureau of Charities is to look after the affairs of the Almshouse, meeting there at least once in each week. Reports are made to the Board at its monthly meetings. All of the members of the Board are expected to visit each of the institutions not less than once in each month. The civil service rules adopted in accordance with the law provided for the retention of faithful officials and employees, so there were very few changes made. These rules were complied with during several administrations with very beneficial results.

During previous years much of the business of the institution was intrusted to committees of the Board of Guardians. The old rules show that there were standing committees of three members each on the out-wards, children's asylum, hospital, insane department, classification and diet, manufacturing department, farm and garden, supplies and accounts, and a committee of five members on support and bastardy cases. The work of these committees has since been performed by the Superintendent, under the direction of the Bureau of Charities.

The first board of directors of the department was composed of Dr. James W. White, President, and Robert Laughlin, Dr. Richard A. Cleeman, Richard C. McMurtrie and James Stewart. They were appointed by Hon. Edwin H. Fitler, the first Mayor under the new law.

The last official act of the old Board of Guardians was the passage of the following preamble and resolutions:

"At a stated meeting of the Board of Guardians of the Poor, held March 28th, 1887, on motion of Mr. William McAleer, the following preamble and resolutions were adopted, viz:

" WHEREAS, This Board of Guardians in their experience as officials have been called in close contact with the President of Common Councils, who has at all times by his advice and influence been of great service to this Board; and

" WHEREAS, It is fitting the Board should take action before its dissolution upon the valuable services rendered by Charles Lawrence, Esq., President of Common Council, particularly for his untiring exertions after the disastrous fire at Blockley in securing for this Department the appropriation to complete the rebuilding of the Insane Department; therefore

"*Resolved*, That this Board tender to Charles Lawrence, Esq., President of Common Council, their hearty thanks for his energy and influence in obtaining from Councils the necessary means for the completion of the buildings for the insane poor.

"*Resolved*, That we recognize in Charles Lawrence a gentleman eminently qualified for the important and honorable position of a legislator in City Councils, and one whose heart prompts him to sympathize with and alleviate the sufferings of the poor.

"*Resolved*, That the members of this Board will always remember with gratitude his disinterested services and tender to him their best wishes for his success in whatever post of honor or duty he may be called upon to occupy."

A copy of the resolutions, handsomely engrossed and framed, signed by Joseph Paxson, President, and attested by Robert C. Floyd, Secretary, was presented to Mr. Lawrence, and is highly appreciated and valued.

Upon the re-organization of the hospital by the new board, Dr. George M. Wells was made Chief Resident Physician, and the position was now made to include that of Physician-in-Chief of the insane department. The rules adopted prescribed the duties, chief of which are:

" He shall have the general supervision of the hospital in all its departments; he shall be physician-in-chief of the insane department; he shall have full control of the resident physicians, and shall see that they faithfully perform their duties and conduct themselves with decorum at all times when within the institution, and shall report to the bureau any dereliction on their part; he shall have control and general management of all the nurses and attendants connected with the hospital. The library shall be under the superintendence and direction of the chief resident physician; and it shall be the duty of the person engaged for that purpose to see that all the books are catalogued, labelled and numbered."

During the year another brick pavilion for the men's nervous wards was erected; the apartments for the nurses and those of the resident physicians were renovated; the general laundry was enlarged and some new machinery introduced; a drying room for the laundry connected with the insane department was built; the outer walls of the buildings were rough coated; the outside woodwork was re-painted; balconies to the fire escapes were completed, and larger water pipes laid.

CHAPTER XXXI.

ON March 21st, 1888, an Ordinance was approved which authorized the Mayor to transfer to the Trustees of the University of Pennsylvania a certain lot of ground bounded as follows:

Commencing at the intersection of Woodland Avenue and Thirty-sixth Street, thence along Woodland Avenue, west, 248 feet and 3 inches to the grounds occupied as a Police Station House; thence along said grounds, west, 415 feet and 6 inches to Spruce Street; thence south 182 feet and 10⅝ inches to Thirty-sixth; thence north 237 feet and 11 inches to place of beginning; in consideration of the sum of one dollar, subject to the following conditions: "That the ground shall never be alienated by the Trustees of the University, without the consent of the City, and further that the said Trustees will erect and maintain a fire proof library building, and provide means to maintain it as a free library of reference open to the entire community, and that work thereon shall be begun within four months from the date of conveyance."

An ordinance was approved on the 22d day of March, 1888, "To authorize the location and erection of a new Almshouse; to provide for the removal of the indigent poor from Blockley Almshouse, and to make an appropriation therefor."

It provided "that so much of the House of Correction property as lies between the State Road and the Pennsylvania Railroad as may be required, is hereby set apart for the erection of buildings to be occupied, and used by the indigent poor, of the City of Philadelphia."

The Mayor was authorized to engage an Architect to prepare plans, and, under the direction of the Mayor, to supervise the work as it progressed. He was to be paid not exceeding three per cent. of the cost of the buildings. The sum of $150,000 was appropriated to pay for the buildings, plans, etc.

334

The Board of Charities and Correction was authorized and directed to remove the indigent poor from the Blockley Almshouse, upon the completion of the buildings. Work has not been started upon them up to the present time.

During this year the last of the old wooden pavilions were removed and two additional brick buildings substituted for them. More fire escapes were erected; and the laying of Asphalt paving, in place of the old cobble-stones in the streets within the inclosure, was commenced. It was found that the filling in of the marsh-land necessitated the extension of the sewer of the insane department, to carry the drainage into the Schuylkill River. An addition 450 feet in length was built, and the sewer was cleansed for the first time. It was stated that 142 cart loads of material were taken from it.

An effort was made to sell a large tract of the Almshouse property to a manufacturing firm for $50,000. After considerable deliberation Councils concluded to have it sold at public sale. M. S. Thomas & Sons were selected to sell it, which they did and the sale was confirmed on March 12th, 1889. The land was divided and the purchasers were named as follows:

"*Lot No. 1.*—All that lot of ground situate on the south side of Locust Street on the east side of 34th Street, on the northeast side of South Street and on the northwest side of 33d Street, containing in front on Locust Street 441 feet, 1⅛ inches, on 33d Street 442 feet, 5½ inches, on South Street, 236 feet, 3½ inches, and on 34th Street, 238 feet, 9⅞ inches.

"*No. 2*—All that lot of ground at northeast corner of 33d and South Streets, along 33d Street 346 feet; thence southeast 174 feet, 8¼ inches; thence northeast 96 feet, 5½ inches to Marston Street; thence along Marston Street, southeast, 354 feet to Meadland Avenue; thence along Meadland Avenue 442 feet, 5½ inches to South Street; thence along South Street 528 feet, 8¼ inches to place of beginning.

"*No. 3.*—All that lot of ground beginning at northeast corner of Meadland Avenue and South Street; thence along Meadland Avenue, northeast, 442 feet, 5½ inches to Marston Street; thence along Marston Street, southeast, 166 feet, 5⅜ inches to the land of the West Chester and Philadelphia Railroad Company; thence by the same, southwest, 446 feet, 9¾ inches to South Street; thence along that street, northwest, 214 feet, 3⅛ inches to place of beginning," all unto William Pepper, Provost of the University of Pennsylvania, for the sum of $149,800.00.

"*No. 4.*—All that triangular lot of ground at the northeast corner of Meadland Avenue and Marston Street, thence along Meadland Avenue 11 feet, 1½ inches, thence northwest 136 feet, 1⅜ inches to the northeasterly side of Marston Street, thence along Marston Street, southeast, 135 feet 8 inches to place of beginning.

"*No. 5.*—All that lot of ground on the northeast corner of Meadland Avenue and Marston Street, thence northeast along Meadland Avenue 16 feet 1½ inches, thence southeast 138 feet 8⅞ inches to the line of the West Chester and Philadelphia Railroad Company, thence south 29 feet 3 inches to Marston Street, thence along Marston Street 149 feet, 1¾ inches to place of beginning," to J. M. Gummey & Sons for the sum of $2,200.

It will be noticed that the sale realized $152,000, instead of $50,000.

In May, 1889, Dr. J. W. White retired from the Board, and Mr. Robert Laughlin succeeded him as President. Mr. Galloway C. Morris was appointed a Director to fill the vacancy on the Board, but he only served until December when he resigned and Mr. John Roberts took his place.

Mayor Fitler, in his annual message, opposed the removal of the Almshouse as provided for by the ordinance of March 22, 1888, and gave his reasons for so doing. The principal of these were, that it would be necessary to build an additional hospital in connection with the new buildings to accommodate the cases of sickness constantly occurring in the institution; that the removal of the Almshouse would greatly add to the cost of conducting two establishments separated by nearly ten miles; that for reasons of convenience and economy the Almshouse should be near to the city; that nearly all of the inmates of the Almshouse are proper subjects for hospital care ; that the separation would cause not only a large expenditure of money for the erection of new buildings, but would make necessary large additional fixed expenditures for management, with inconvenience and injury to the patients required to be moved from one to the other.

During the year new water closets were erected in the Outwards, the obstetrical ward and in the men's medical wards. This was a much needed improvement. Councils appropriated $5,000 towards starting an electrical plant to light the grounds and to put a few lamps in the buildings. This was done under the direction of the Electrical Bureau of the city.

Dr. George M. Wells resigned his position of Chief Resident Physician on January 13th, 1890, to take effect in one month from that time. Dr. Daniel E. Hughes was elected in his stead and went on duty in March. He still remains and has served with marked ability and faithfulness. Many improvements in the care and treatment of the patients have been inaugurated under his directions.

A brick kitchen for the use of the Outwards was erected and paid for by the Trustees of the Mary Shields estate. It is 93 feet in length and 20 feet in width ; it stands in the centre of the courtyard, adjoining the bakehouse and is fitted with the necessary cooking apparatus.

On July 1st, 1890, an ordinance was approved which authorized the sale of $6^{297}/_{1000}$ acres of the meadow land adjoining the Junction Railroad to the Pennsylvania Railroad Company for the sum of $10,000.

On the same day another ordinance was approved which transferred the $150,000 appropriated on March 22, 1890 for erecting new Almshouse on the grounds of the House of Correction, " For the purpose of erecting additional buildings to be occupied for an insane hospital, the Philadelphia Hospital, or as Outwards, such buildings to be either independent buildings or wings of buildings now existing on said grounds.

On October 1st, 1890, an additional sum of $75,000 was appropriated for the same purpose, to be taken from the special fund from the sale of the Almshouse ground.

22

Mr. George Roney resigned his position as Superintendent on April 6th, 1891, to assume the duties of Director of Public Safety, to which he had been appointed by Mayor Edwin S. Stuart. The vacancy was filled, after a competitive examination, by the election of Charles Lawrence, formerly President of Common Council and a veteran of the United States Navy during the Civil War, on May 11th, 1891.

An additional appropriation of $26,074, from the special fund, was made on June 11th, 1891, to complete the buildings provided for.

In April, 1892, Mayor Stuart appointed a new Board of Directors, consisting of Mr. James A. Freeman, President, and Messrs. William H. Lambert, Alfred Moore, William D. Gardner and John Huggard, the term of office of the old Board having expired, Mr. Freeman tendered his resignation on account of sickness on September 29th, 1892, when Mr. Lambert was appointed President of the Department and Dr. James W. Walk was selected to fill the vacancy on the Board. A series of resolutions expressing the regret of the members at the retirement of Mr. Freeman, were adopted by the Board.

On March 19th, 1892, an Ordinance was passed to "authorize the Trustees of the University of Pennsylvania to sell and convey part of the lot of land that was conveyed to them under the authority of an Ordinance approved on the 21st of March, 1888, to a corporation to be organized for the purpose of establishing a museum to receive and preserve anatomical and other specimens, and to promote the study of biology, anatomy and kindred sciences." This led to the erection of the Wistar Institute on that ground.

On June 21st, 1892, the sum of $50,000 was appropriated from the special fund, $40,000 of which was for the erection of a building for the accommodation of the nurses of the Hospital, and the balance for a brick structure for the care and treatment of any contagious diseases that developed in the institution.

The old Clinic Hall was remodeled and put in first-class order. The improvements were so marked that the medical staff concluded that there should be a formal re-opening, and it should be an event in the history of the Hospital. It took place on the 8th of October, 1892. Hon. Edwin S. Stuart, Mayor of the city, presided and delivered an address. A large audience was present, including the Directors of the Department, the members of the medical staff, a number of other physicians and prominent persons. Addresses were made by Dr. Roland G. Curtin, President of the Medical Staff, President Lambert, Messrs. Gardner, Moore and Huggard, of the Board of Directors, Dr. James Tyson and Superintendent Lawrence. As Dr. Curtin's address contained much information, some extracts from it are inserted. He said:

" *Mr. President, Ladies and Gentlemen :* The members of the Medical Staff of the Philadelphia Hospital have chosen me to speak for them on this important occasion—important not alone to the medical staff, but to the City of Philadelphia and its suffering poor who come to these doors for relief.

" The medical staff wish me to thank one and all who have been instrumental in bringing about this much needed improvement, in the planning and completion of which our Superintendent, Mr. Lawrence, has taken a continuous interest. This is what may be called practical reform. Let us at this time contrast the old with the new, and see what has been accomplished by the improvements made. The old amphitheatre or operating room, which stood between the walls that now surround us, was not up to the requirements of modern science. It was unsafe for operations ; it was dark and poorly ventilated. It answered well enough for the period in which it was built, but was wholly inadequate for this enlightened age. It had lived its life ; it had run its race. Until 1856 the old clinic room was not, as now, connected with the hospital by a covered way. The patients before that time were carried out in the rain or snow, often to their disadvantage. I was chairman of the committee of the resident physicians who asked the Board of Guardians to have the covered way built.

" The post-mortem room and dead house, where all the germ-exhaling bodies were carried after death, and where autopsies were held, were only twenty feet away, and opened into a hall that communicated directly with the old operating room.

"The pathological room, where specimens were taken to be mounted for the museum, was entered from the old clinic room, and the museum, where all the alcoholic and dried specimens were placed on exhibition, surrounded the top of the amphitheatre. These conditions, associated with an old wooden floor, which absorbed the fluids for germ-food and held it for their propagation, would make it an unsafe place for operations. The picture I have given would shock the nerves of a sensitive modern aseptic and antiseptic surgeon.

"But now how different! We have a light, roomy building, beautiful to look at, connected with the hospital by a handsome, enclosed passage-way, by means of which the patients can be carried to the clinics without exposing them to the outside air. The ample waiting and etherizing rooms which surround the new clinic are another very great improvement. You will all please observe that the new room has a hardwood wainscot and cement floor, glass shelves for instruments, also hardwood benches, all of which can be thoroughly cleansed. The heating registers are placed in the upper portion of the steps, so that the dust and fluids cannot gravitate into them with poisonous germs, there to be hatched and propagated by the general steam heat, to the disadvantage of the old sores and the freshly-made wounds of the surgeon. The dead house, post mortem room, the pathological laboratory and museum, with their dangerous effluvia, have been removed to another part of the grounds.

"The room has plenty of light and good ventilation, and can be properly cleansed, all of which gives increased safety to the sufferers undergoing operations. We may expect better results than could have been obtained in the past. It is a clinic room constructed in accordance to the rules of modern sanitation; it is now ample in size and as good and comfortable as any in the country. It is a great credit to those who have presided over the institution that holds the welfare of the indigent poor of the city in their hands. . . . . .

"The two side walls of the old clinic room were part of an entrance from the street ; two cross walls were erected and the enclosed square roofed over and the seats placed therein. After thirty years, in 1891, the roof was taken off and a new one placed on the old walls. This year, 1892, thirty-one years after its dedication, the whole has been torn out and made over, and the modern clinic room, in which we meet together to-day, appears as you see it now. Nothing remains of the former hall but the old stone walls, which have been renewed in appearance by the stucco covering. . . . . .

"It may not be amiss to call attention to some of the benefits derived from clinical teaching carried on in Blockley. "Old Blockley" is honored all over the land, and in many foreign countries by the teaching that has been given here by such lights as Benjamin Rush, Gerhard, Pennock, Gross (father and son) Pancoast the elder, Ludlow, Agnew, and others who have gone to their reward ; and among those now living who have long since retired from the staff, by Stillé, Da Costa, Penrose, Pepper, Wood, Tyson, Osler, the younger Pancoast, and many others who might be mentioned if time permitted. They gave their valuable time without pecuniary compensation to the poor of Philadelphia. How much they owed to Blockley for their information and experience, none can tell. We all—patients and doctors—have been directly or indirectly benefited by their teachings.

"Few have a conception of the multiplied labors of the chief resident physician, Dr. Daniel E. Hughes, in an institution like this. He acts not only as physician-in-chief to the insane department, but has many other duties connected with the medical work of the hospital.

"I have made a calculation that in thirty-one years fifteen to twenty thousand students have attended clinics in the old clinic room. This teaching has had much to do with making Philadelphia the medical centre of the United States. In this showing we are all interested, whether laymen or doctors. We have now in Philadelphia over one thousand medical students. Let us suppose that they spend six hundred dollars each year apiece ; this makes an average of six hundred thousand dollars.   Leave out one-sixth for medical students of Philadelphia, and you have half a million of dollars spent here every year.   This money is distributed not alone in the colleges, but also in the boarding houses, tailor shops, instrument makers, shoe stores and book stores. Moreover, the medical students who graduate here come back for medical and other supplies.

" By Philadelphia being a great medical centre, thousands of patients come here annually to be treated, and they also leave much money behind for board, nursing, shopping, etc. These facts prove that the city at large is benefited financially by the medical teaching; the material furnished by this hospital assists largely in giving us the reputation necessary to attract students. We should all be interested in keeping up that reputation, and proud to assist in adding to her honor and general welfare.

" The material furnished by this hospital has instructed also our family physicians; we know the benefit of their experience. Again, the researches here have settled some of the most important questions in medicine.   It was here that Doctors Gerhard and Pennock gave to the medical profession post-mortem evidence of the essential difference between typhus and typhoid fevers. They showed that the condition of the intestines in the one forbids solid food, and this one observation alone saved thousands of lives all over the world.

" Blockley has given the world much valuable statistics and information which have been published in journals, text-books, addresses, reports, etc., and this seed sown broadcast has ripened into multiplied harvests throughout the world.   Some of the notable literature that has thus emanated from the valuable experience here gained may be instanced: Gerhard and Pennock on the differential diagnosis between typhus and typhoid fever; Stillé on cholera and on epidemic cerebro-spinal meningitus; also Dr. W. H. H. Githens on the same subject; Pepper and Parry on relapsing fever, and many other valuable essays well-known to all the medical profession.   .   .   .   .   .   .

" The resident staff consisted of ten in 1866. The nurses were generally persons who had been patients and numbered about twenty. The visiting medical staff of physicians was composed of twelve members. The visiting staff has been increased to forty ; the resident staff now numbers twenty-three; and in the nurses school we have about one hundred nurses.

" The attendance on the Philadelphia Hospital clinics is from all the colleges in the city. The students are from all countries. I have seen on the benches Turks, Roumanians, Africans, Canadians, Burmudans, Brazilians, Chilians and Japanese—male and female—old style, new style and eclectic. All students are welcome, and are admitted on an equal footing without fee or reward, and receive the best practical instruction we can give. The facilities for clinical instruction in this hospital are excelled by only about four hospitals in the world, and by none on this side of the Atlantic. This hospital embraces what in New York is called Bellevue Hospital or City Hospital, and Charity Hospital, which is associated with the Almshouse, criminal institutions, and others that are under city control. The two together are larger than Blockley, but one is in the city and the other on Blackwell's Island. We have in the winter over twenty-two hundred sick and nervous patients to glean from. To this add the valuable teaching in pathology, to make which more effective we have sometimes opportunities to show the classes not only the case, but also the pathological specimens from the bodies of the patients previously lectured upon, verifying or disproving the opinions expressed to the students in the clinics. The teaching here is plain, practical instruction.   .   .   .   .   .   .

" You may ask what benefit the clinics are to the patients. I reply that the clinic cases are studied more carefully than the others. They are examined with great minuteness, often a long time before being shown to the class ; they are looked on in all their aspects. A doctor is very chary of the diagnosis he makes before a class ; he is always very careful how he presents the cases, and his treatment is thorough and scientific, for the students are great critics, and sometimes they have the chance of seeing the ' crucial tests ' commonly known as post-mortems.

" You may ask, do patients object to going before students ?

Such objections are exceedingly rare and are always respected. The members of the staff will all bear me out that it is not infrequent for the patients to ask to be lectured on.

"In concluding my remarks, ladies and gentlemen, I cannot do better than to make two brief quotations from Dr. Agnew's history of the institution:

"'On the 10th of September, 1860,' he says, 'the medical board addressed the Guardians on the propriety of throwing open the wards of the hospital for free clinical instruction. This proposition was considered from a liberal and intelligent stand-point, in its broader and more general bearings, and on the 24th of September, 1860, received their cordial sanction; and its doors have been opened to this time; and it is to be hoped through all time to come its doors may never be closed against or a fee craved from those who enter its halls in search of knowledge, which can alone render them qualified to discharge the functions of a divine art.'

"Again he says, 'It is difficult to over-estimate the importance of this institution to either the profession or the community. To say nothing of the multiform types of destitution and want which it meets and relieves, look at the field which it offers to the disciples of medicine, and no man will lightly esteem this who contemplates the prosecution of his profession with a conscience void of offence towards God and man. Here is a hospital in which over eight thousand cases of disease are annually treated; a children's asylum, offering illustration of all the complaints incident to this period of life; and there is an obstetrical department, in which as many as seven cases of labor have occurred in twenty-four hours, and where in the last thirteen years over two thousand six hundred children have been born. One year industriously spent in this institution will yield in medical experience the fruits of ten years gathered from ordinary practice. But to place the statement in another form; a graduate of medicine faithfully improving for a single year his opportunity for study of disease in the wards of the Philadelphia Hospital, will be better fitted to assume the responsibility of his profession than one who labors ten years in an ordinary city or country practice.'"

MAIN LAUNDRY BUILDING.

CHAPTER XXXII.

DESCRIPTION OF NURSES' HOUSE AND ISOLATING BUILDING—FIRE
IN LAUNDRY AND STOREHOUSE.

A N Ordinance entitled an "Ordinance to vacate a certain piece of ground at Thirty-third and South Streets for the purpose of straightening streets, and to convey the same to the University of Pennsylvania," was passed on the 5th of January, 1893. It provided :

"That all that tract of land beginning on the east side of Thirty-fourth Street at a point 225 feet 7½ inches south of the south side of Locust Street ; thence southwardly along the east line of Thirty-fourth Street 150 feet, more or less, to Spruce Street ; thence eastwardly along the north side of Spruce Street 190 feet, more or less, to Thirty-third Street ; thence along Thirty-third Street 15 feet, more or less ; thence 260 feet 3½ inches to place of beginning shall be vacated, and that so much of the Ordinance approved June 21st, 1892, providing for the paving of the said piece of ground hereby vacated be, and the same is hereby repealed."

It authorized the Mayor to sign a deed conveying the property vacated to the Trustees of the University of Pennsylvania for the use of the University for its authorized educational purposes, and subject to the conditions that said land should never be alienated, and further that no buildings other than for educational purposes should ever be erected thereon.

The erection of the building for the accommodation of the nurses in the hospital effected a great change in their mode of living. The structure is 134 feet 8 inches long and 78 feet 10 inches wide, with corridors ten feet wide the entire length of each story, terminating in bays, with transverse corridors seven feet wide, also terminating in bays, and with broad stairways at the intersection of corridors at each end of the building. The first story is twelve feet high in the clear, the second and third stories each nine feet high, plastered on hollow brick walls with hard polished finish coat cement, washboards or bases and rounded corners throughout, the amount of wood finish being reduced to a minimum.

There are accommodations on the three floors for 120 nurses, exclusive of the fourth floor, which has a central dormitory about 62 by 34 feet, and two (north and south) attics, 60 by 25 feet each. The exterior is of simple hard brick, with marble and terra cotta trimmings; the roofing is of green slate with copper flushings and gutters, and the porches on the east and west fronts are supported by brick arches and terra cotta with marble coping, the asphalt roofs of the porches serving for an open balcony, heavy glass floor lights having been introduced to prevent darkening of lower rooms.

Mr. John Huggard, of the Board of Directors, died on the 24th of January, 1894, after a lingering illness. Resolutions were passed by the Directors, expressing the appreciation of the members of the Board of the valuable services rendered by Mr. Huggard, and their sorrow for his death. Mr. John Shallcross was appointed by Mayor Stuart to fill the vacancy.

An ordinance was passed on March 30th, 1894, that ordained : ' That so much of the Almshouse grounds which was set apart for public park purposes under and by virtue of the ordinance approved July 6th, 1883, as is described as follows : ' All that certain lot or piece of ground in the Twenty-seventh Ward of the City of Philadelphia, beginning at the southeast corner of Thirty-fourth and Spruce Streets; along said Spruce Street to intersection with southwest side of South Street; thence to the northwest boundary of the right of way of the West Chester and Philadelphia Railroad Company; thence along the same to the northeast side of Almshouse or Blockley Lane ; thence along the same to the northwest boundary of the present Water Department storage yard; thence along this line to the northeastward 400 feet; thence northwest along a line parallel to and 30 feet to the northeast of the northeast wall of the present Almshouse stone barn for a distance of 350 feet; thence southwest along a line parallel to and about 30 feet to the northwest of the northwest wall of said barn to its intersection with the east side of Thirty-fourth Street; thence along the same to Spruce Street and place of beginning, containing eight acres, more or less, shall be forthwith opened to use as a public park forever.'

" For the purpose of securing the suitable improvement of the same, said lot of ground above described shall be conveyed to the Trustees of the University of Pennsylvania in trust to lay out and maintain the same forever as for a Museum and a Botanical Park and Garden, without expense to the City of Philadelphia, to be opened to the free access of the public at all times forever, under suitable regulations, to be from time to time agreed upon by said Trustees and the Mayor of said City, and also to erect thereon a Museum of Science and Art, without expense to the said City: Provided, that the said grounds shall be placed in the proper condition for the purposes of this ordinance within five years from the date of the execution of the deed creating and accepting said trust herein created, said deed of trust to be prepared by the City Solicitor, with all suitable covenants and provisions necessary to carry out the intents of this ordinance and secure the privileges of all parties named, to be executed by the Mayor of said City and said Trustees, with the proper legal authority accepting the same; and provided further, 'That in the event of the failure on the part of the said Trustees of the University of Pennsylvania to place said grounds in the proper condition for the purposes of this ordinance within five years, or of maintaining the same as a Museum and a Botanical Garden and Park and keeping the same open to the public as aforesaid, at all times hereafter forever, or shall divert the same grounds to any other purposes than those specified in this ordinance, then the trust created by this ordinance shall cease and determine, and this ordinance and all privileges granted hereunder shall become null and void, and the said property shall revert to the City of Philadelphia free and discharged of any and all trusts hereby created, or expense or obligation created by reason of this ordinance."

The passage of this ordinance necessitated the removal of the goods from the yard used by the Water Department for the storage of pipes, the large free public bath house on Spruce Street and several buildings belonging to the Almshouse.

The Isolating Building was designed by the Superintendent and erected from plans made by him. It was built of brick, one story high, and deserves more than passing mention. It is 88 feet in length and 26 feet wide, with an enclosed porch of wood and glass around one end and the two sides. A brick partition wall, extending to the roof, is built lengthwise through the centre, dividing it into two halves, one for males and the other for females. These parts are divided into rooms by brick partitions running to the roof, so that each room has a brick wall around the whole four sides. Doors open from each room to the porch, and there is no communication from one room to another. The floors are cement, and the walls and ceilings are covered with adamant cement painted. A register in each room furnishes the necessary heat, and the ventilation is secured by a ventilator through the ceiling and roof of each room, together with the windows and movable transoms over the doors. There are two rooms for the nurses at one end, and two for bath-rooms, lavatories, etc., at the other, with seven on each side for the patients, all supplied with gas. The floors are four feet above the ground, and as the walls are built on arches, a free circulation of air is secured under them.

The maternity wards were much improved by building an addition, which connected the two buildings and added a much larger room than any they had before.

A very important ordinance was approved on the 27th of June, 1895. It was entitled "An Ordinance to authorize the immediate opening of a portion of the Almshouse grounds, set apart for park purposes by the ordinance approved July 6, 1883, for public use as a park and for a museum, and conveying the same to the Board of Trustees of the Philadelphia Museum in trust for the purposes herein set forth." The full text of the bill follows:

" Section 1. The Select and Common Councils of the City of Philadelphia do ordain, That so much of the Almshouse grounds which was set apart for public park purposes under and by virtue of the ordinance approved July 6, 1883, as is described as follows: Beginning at a point in the northeast side of Cleveland Avenue, 100 feet wide, as the same is proposed to be laid out on the revised plan of the City, at the distance of 40 feet and ¼ inch northeast from the northwest line of the property of the Philadelphia and West Chester Railroad, and extending thence along the northeast side of the said Cleveland Avenue, north 4° 23' 19.4" west, 92 feet, 2⅝ inches to a point; thence along a line parallel with Vintage Avenue and 279 feet, 3⅞ inches southeast from the northwest side thereof, north 61° 28' 36" east 1,551 feet, 1⅜ inches to a point on the southwest of a certain 46-feet lane, known as Blockley Lane; thence along the southwest side of the said Blockley Lane, south 48° 59' 30" east, 248 feet, 2¾ inches to a point on the northwest side of a proposed 40 feet wide drive to be laid out along the line of the Philadelphia and West Chester Railroad; thence along the northwest side of the said proposed drive the following courses and distances thereof, viz: south 42° 38' 55.5" west 2 feet, 1⅝ inches to a point; thence south 58° 26' 25" west 34 feet, 5⅜ inches to a point; thence south 61° 15' 24.7" west 1022 feet, 5¼ inches to a point; thence south 68° 37' 50" west 57 feet, 10¾ inches to a point; thence south 70° 08' 50" west 79 feet, 11⅝ inches to a point; thence south 70° 38' 19" west 111 feet, 2⅛ inches to a point; thence south 76° 55' 59" west, 97 feet, ¾ inch to a point; thence south 77° 26' 21" west 101 feet, 2⅜ inches to a point; thence south 78° 41' 11" west 96 feet, ⅜ inch to a point; thence south 83° 36' 30" west 94 feet, 11¼ inches to a point in the northeast of the aforesaid Cleveland Avenue and place of beginning—containing eight acres of ground, more or less, shall be forthwith opened to use as a public park forever.

"Section 2.—Whereas the City of Philadelphia has come into possession of certain collections of great extent and value which have been presented to the City by various foreign governments upon the pledge that said collections shall be suitably cared for by the City of Philadelphia; and whereas by ordinance approved on the 15th day of June, 1894, there was created a Board of Trustees for establishing public museums to whose custody the aforementioned collections were consigned with instructions to secure funds and a suitable site for museum buildings to accommodate said collections, the present ordinance provides that the portion of the Almshouse grounds described above in Section 1, shall be entrusted to said Board of Trustees as a site for the museum buildings to accommodate said collections :

"*Provided*, That the said grounds and said museum buildings thereon to be erected shall be forever open to the free access of the public at all times forever under suitable regulations to be from time to time agreed upon by the said Board of Trustees and approved by City Councils ;

"*Provided*, That the said grounds shall be subject to the use and occupation by the Department of Charities and Correction for the purposes of its present use until the Board of Trustees of the Philadelphia Museums shall be ready to proceed with the erection of the museum building, it being further provided that no building or buildings of any kind, character or description shall be erected on said ground by the Department of Charities and Correction ; and

"*Provided*, That said Board of Trustees may go forward at once with the proper planting of trees and plants in accordance with the plans adopted for laying out said grounds as a public park."

This ground was part of the field in front of the institution, and was used as a garden for raising vegetables for the inmates, a number of whom were employed for that purpose and saved considerable expense.

On the night of August 14th, 1895, at a few minutes after eleven o'clock, fire was discovered in the ironing-room of the insane department. The stone wall that divided the outwards from the insane department, served to separate the laundry on the one side from the general storehouse on the other on the ground floors. On the second-story over the drying room, and extending over the rear end of the storehouse was located the ironing room. No person had been in either of these buildings after 5.30 o'clock ; one of the night watchmen passed them, while on his rounds through the institution, not more than five minutes before the fire was seen, and he reported that he did not see any signs of fire at that time, so it is impossible to say how the fire originated. The flames spread with wonderful rapidity, and the Superintendent immediately ordered the fire alarm to be rung at the Electrical Bureau. Men were sent to the gates to open them when the firemen arrived and to close them after they had entered. The hose was run out from the insane wards, and the hose cart and steam fire engine were taken over, and attachments made to the plugs. The water supply was so scant that the streams could not do much good and the storehouse was soon ablaze.

The safety of the inmates was looked after, and the insane patients were quickly and quietly removed from the building that faced the fire to wards in the rear. The inmates in the outwards were in condition to be taken out at any time if it became necessary. Everything was done to prevent a panic or undue excitement, and so well was the discipline maintained that not an accident occurred and no one was injured in the slightest manner.

Very little was left of the burnt buildings but the walls, and nearly all of the contents were destroyed or damaged. Temporary store-rooms were fitted up and food supplies for immediate use were ordered; the meals were served on the following day as usual.

President Lambert in his annual report said: "Great credit is due Superintendent Lawrence for excellent management under exciting circumstances, and for his prompt disposition to meet the emergency."

The Superintendent in his report said: "If the mains from which we draw our supply have not the proper pressure we could not get sufficient water even with a larger pipe. I would again suggest that a pumping engine could be placed on our wharf, to draw water from the Schuylkill River to supply the pipes for fire and other purposes that do not require subsidized or filtered water. Millions of dollars worth of property, belonging to the City and the University of Pennsylvania, are in adjoining blocks, and could be protected in this manner at a comparatively small cost. We have pipes run up through all our buildings and have hose attached at all times on each floor to be used in case of fire. If we do not have water in the pipes the hose is useless, and we have no protection. If there had been water and pressure enough, I have no doubt that the fire would have been extinguished in a short time, and with much less damage and loss."

The storehouse was rebuilt and very much improved by putting on a hip-roof with girders and trusses in place of the low, flat one that was on it previous to the fire. Two large skylights were erected, and now it is a well-lighted store with a cement floor 125 by 40 feet, entirely free of posts, with excellent ventilation and all of the modern appliances to do the work.

The laundry for the insane department was rebuilt of brick and made two-stories in height. There is no connection with the storehouse, and no danger of fire spreading from one to the other building. On the ground floor is the wash-room, then the drying room with about forty horses in the steam closets, and connected with the ironing room. On the second floor are three workshops, about 50 by 20 feet each, with windows on all sides.

In the Chief Resident Physician's Report, of that year, he says:

"The completion during the year of the Nurse's House has added nine elegant wards to the hospital service, and given much relief to the Men's Surgical, Men's Medical, and Women's Medical Sections. It may be safely stated that the surgical wards are not excelled by those of any hospital in the City, and with the addition of the proposed water, instrument, and dressing sterilizers, they will not be equalled."

President Lambert in his report of that year said: "The Directors of the Department are confident that neither of the institutions in their charge has ever been in better condition than now, and in this fact with its resultant benefits to the thousands of the sick, homeless and unfortunates who have care and shelter within these institutions, the Directors find compensation for the time and thought devoted to the City's interest.

"For the excellent condition of the institutions and for their efficient administration with their manifold and perplexing duties and details, the Department is indebted to the respective Superintendents, Charles Lawrence and Edwin A. Merrick, and I take pleasure in acknowledging my high appreciation of their faithful, intelligent and able discharge of duty, and in thanking them and their associates for their conduct of the important interests entrusted to their charge."

Another important bill was approved on the 10th day of October, 1896. It reads as follows :

" SECTION 1. The Select and Common Councils of the City of Philadelphia do ordain, That whereas the City of Philadelphia has received and agreed to care for extensive and valuable collections of Commercial, Educational and Scientific material, and has created a Board of Trustees of the Philadelphia Museums charged with this especial duty, and has made appropriations to said Board for the erection of suitable buildings and for the maintenance of said museums, and has by ordinance, approved June 27th, 1895, transferred to said Board in trust for the purposes of said Museum a certain portion of the Almshouse ground set apart for park purposes by the ordinance approved July 6, 1883, which certain portion of said ground is described in said ordinance, approved June 27th 1895, such additional portion of said Almshouse grounds was set apart for public Park purposes as is described as follows :

" ' All that certain lot or piece of ground in the Twenty-seventh Ward, of the City of Philadelphia, beginning at the southeast corner of Vintage Avenue and Blockley Lane, thence extending eastward along the south side of Blockley Lane to the line of the land described in ordinance approved June 27th, 1895, as transferred to the Board of Trustees of the Philadelphia Museums ; thence along the west boundary of said land to the north side of Cleveland Avenue, thence along the north side of Cleveland Avenue to the east side of Vintage Avenue thence along the east side of Vintage Avenue to the south side of Blockley Lane and place of beginning, containing seven acres, more or less ; and also that strip of land, forty feet wide, bounded on the east by the line of the Philadelphia and West Chester Railroad, and on the west by the line of the land described in ordinance approved June 27th, 1895, as transferred to the Board of Trustees of the Philadelphia Museums, and extending from the south side of Blockley Lane to the north side of Cleveland Avenue shall be forthwith

23

opened to use as a public Park for ever, and shall be, and is hereby assigned in trust to the Board of Trustees of the Philadelphia Museums for the purposes of said institution:

" ' *Provided*, That the said ground and the said museum buildings thereon to be erected shall be forever open to the free access of the public at all times forever under suitable regulations to be from time to time agreed upon by the said Board of Trustees and approved by City Councils: *Provided*, That the said property shall be subject to the use and occupation by the Department of Charities and Correction for the purposes of its present use until the Board of Trustees of the Philadelphia Museums shall be ready to proceed with the erection of the museum buildings, it being further provided that no building or buildings of any kind, character or description shall be erected on said ground by the Department of Charities and Correction: *And*, *Provided*, That said Board of Trustees may go forward at once with the proper planting of trees and plants in accordance with the plans adopted for laying out said ground as a Public Park.' "

This took the other part of the ground in front of the institution and left it surrounded by land that had been taken from the Department and transferred to other corporations, thus leaving it without any ground upon which to erect buildings to relieve the crowded condition of the institution.

The removal of the Almshouse has again been agitated, but the purchase of the ground for that purpose has not been accomplished; in fact the location has not been decided upon, and the Almshouse will remain where it is for some years longer.

CHAPTER XXXIII.

HOW to improve the condition of the insane patients caused much thought to the officials. Everything that could be done to accomplish that object was carried out. Fresh air and exercise was a policy of the management, no opportunity being omitted (weather permitting) during the entire year, to give walking exercises twice a day to all patients who were able. During the warm weather the patients were kept in the yards during the entire day and were encouraged to engage in games. Weekly concerts were given by a band employed by the representatives of the " Mary Shields Almshouse Fund." They also furnished stage coaches to take a selected number of the patients, with the necessary attendants, for a ride through the Park and to other places. Trolley car rides were arranged for by some ladies, and the patients were taken to the " McMurtrie " home at Chestnut Hill, where they were furnished with refreshments and given a delightful day's outing. During the fall and winter months the amusement hall was used frequently for concerts and other entertainments. The use of instrumental and vocal music was encouraged; an orchestra was formed under the direction of an employee in the Department, and as several of the patients were musicians, it soon became a valuable aid; a choir, consisting of forty voices, both male and female, was selected and trained by Mrs. D. E. Hughes, wife of the Chief Resident Physician, and after much patience, perseverance and labor, for which she is entitled to great credit, she succeeded in having it able to render the most difficult sacred selections for the religious services, which are held on every Sunday, as well as a great variety of songs and choruses for the secular entertainments.

These have been of great benefit to the poor unfortunates in that department. Music is beneficial to them in many respects; it breaks the monotony of their lives and takes their minds off of their imaginary troubles. If the truth were known there is no

355

doubt that many recoveries could be traced to the soothing influence of music and the songs furnished at the entertainments.

Employment is another great help, and every opportunity was embraced to introduce and extend it. At the request of the Superintendent, a workshop was fitted up in the kitchen that had been erected by the Mary Shields' estate, and which was replaced by the larger one erected in 1891, and the expense of alterations, tools, etc., was defrayed by the same estate. A brush-making shop was started with gratifying success, and furnished employment for thirty-three patients. After a sufficient number of brushes to furnish the institution was made, it was turned into a mattress factory. All of the ticking, fibre for filling, twine, etc., required has been paid for by the Mary Shields' estate, and while it has been the means of furnishing employment it has also given hundreds of first-class mattresses to the insane and hospital departments to take the place of the straw beds that had previously been used. The average number employed in various ways during the year was, males, 295; females, 313. Dr. Hughes in one of his annual reports said : "It is unquestionable that the prompt use of intelligent employment has done wonders in establishing rapid convalescence and complete restoration in a very large number of cases."

The astounding increase of insane cases that came to the institution that began in 1892, continued. The Superintendent in his report for the year 1896, said, "The crowded condition of the insane department was somewhat relieved by the transfer of 41 chronic cases to the asylum at Wernersville. We have good accommodations for 1050 patients, and all above that number is at the expense of the comfort of the others. It is necessary that steps should be taken at once to relieve the crowded condition of this department, and I would again suggest that the quickest and, I think, the best would be to have the Acts exempting the other poor districts in the County from the operation of the law placing Almshouses and Hospitals under the control and management of this Department, amended or repealed. If we had possession of the Oxford and Lower Dublin Almshouse, buildings sufficient for present purposes at least could soon be erected, and our surplus removed there."

President Lambert, in his annual report to the Mayor, said: "The most serious and urgent need of the Department is increased accommodation for the insane. The increase in number of these unfortunates demanding our care has exceeded our ability to properly house them—the number in the institution at this date is 1228, an increase of 337, since December 31st, 1891. The capacity of the insane wards is 1050, the excess of that number are cared for at the expense of all.

"The cession to other institutions of the greater and better portion of the grounds formerly controlled by the Department, outside of the walls surrounding its main buildings have rendered impossible the erection of additional and suitable buildings for the accommodation of our increased population. The number of buildings already within the enclosure precludes any material addition.

"Even if new buildings were allowed by the State Board of Public Charities, they would necessarily be small and give but scanty and temporary relief. The crowded condition of the State Hospitals for the Insane which has prevented them from relieving us to any appreciable extent forbids hope for help from them.

"Provision has been made in the recent loan bill for purchase of a site for a new Almshouse—but the relief which would be furnished by erection of the building is too far remote to assist in meeting present needs.

"In this emergency the only prospect of relief which presents itself is that which would follow such amendment to existing laws as would place within the control of this Department all of the poor-houses of the County—several of which are and have been since the Act of Consolidation in charge of separate boards of directors. Whatever local influences in earlier years sufficed to secure to these separate existence should have little force now—when the numbers sheltered in the suburban poorhouses are few in number, and utterly disproportionate to the space they occupy—whilst the main City institution is crowded to excess. The addition to our resources of the grounds of the Oxford and Lower Dublin Almshouse would enable us within a few weeks or months at most to give relief to our insane—provide for the City's needs in this respect for years to come, and permit the question of removal of the Almshouse and Hospital to be treated with proper deliberation and regard to the great interests involved. Humanity demands speedy relief for our insane patients, and we ask for our suggestion your earnest attention, and, if as we hope it shall meet with your approval, that by all means in your power, you strive to put it into practical effect."

That was an earnest plea, from a kind-hearted official, for relief for the poor unfortunate wards of the City, but it did not succeed in accomplishing the object sought.

The term of office of the President and Directors of the Department who had been appointed by Mayor Stuart expired on the first Monday of April, 1897, and Mayor Warwick appointed a new Board, composed of William H. Lambert, President, Messrs. Alfred Moore, William D. Gardner, Joseph H. Mann and Henry B. Gross.

Messrs. Lambert, Moore and Gardner had served on the old Board and were re-appointed; Messrs. Mann and Gross took the places of Dr. Walk and Mr. Shallcross.

President Lambert in his annual report for 1897, said: " The continuous increase in the number of insane committed to our care and our inability to provide adequate accommodations for them still constitutes the most serious condition which confronts the Department.

" We had hoped that favorable action would be taken by the Legislature of the State upon the proposition to place under control of this Department, the several poor districts of the County which are in charge of independent local boards of directors; but being disappointed in this we were forced to resort to other methods for the relief of our crowded wards. The practical impossibility of erecting new buildings within our enclosure compelled us to ask assent of the State Board of Charities to place an additional or third-story upon each of the four two-story buildings of the Insane Department; an assent which that Board was reluctant to give, because of its pronounced policy of limiting hospital buildings to

the height of two stories, but which they granted, because convinced that under existing circumstances there was no early prospect of relief in any other manner.

"So authorized, we received your consent to apply to Councils
for an appropriation of the balance, $40,663.83, remaining in the
Sinking Fund to the credit of this Department. The appropriation was made, plans were prepared which had the approval of the
State Board of Charities, and proposals were received from several
builders, including some of the highest standing; but, unfortunately, even under the lowest bid, the amount at our disposal was
only sufficient to allow the erection of the additional stories on two
of the four buildings, and to make no provision for the change in
heating. The pressure for room was, however, so great that we
could not postpone action until sufficient funds for the entire work
could be obtained, and accordingly contract was made for such of
the work as could be done.

"The additional stories, one in the male and another in the
female wings, have been erected, and though not yet completed, we
hope to have them available in the coming year, and thus have
space for about two hundred more patients; but as the number to
be provided for is still in excess of our accommodations, even with
the new wards, it is imperative that provision be made this year to
properly house at least two hundred more, and to this end we shall
ask your consent to apply to City Councils for an additional appropriation of $60,000, to enable us to complete the work.

"Humanity and sense of duty would demand that we urge
this appropriation in any event; but we are impelled as well by the
necessity of making adequate provision for the insane to enable us
to secure the benefit of recent legislation.

"At the last session of the Legislature an act was passed,
which was approved by the Governor, providing that "any county,
municipality, borough or township of this Commonwealth, which
has now or may hereafter supply, erect and equip a suitable institution for the maintenance, care and treatment of its indigent
insane upon plans and specifications approved in writing by the
Board of Public Charities, shall receive from the State Treasury

the sum of one dollar and fifty cents per week for every indigent insane person . . . . . so maintained . . . . . provided that the Board of Public Charities shall be satisfied that .the quality and equipment of such institution, and the manner and care and treatment therein furnished, is proper and suitable to the class or classes of the indigent insane so maintained, and shall so certify to the Auditor-General before any such payment shall be made.

" Under the provisions of this Act, which went into effect June 1, 1897, we have presented bills to the Auditor-General for the two quarters ending August 31st and November 30th respectively, amounting to $50,371.07.

" To comply with the terms of the Act, it will be absolutely necessary for us to increase our accommodations for the insane, because to crowd our wards still further will violate the conditions requisite to secure the compensation offered by the State.

" We have no choice between caring for the insane of our county in our own institutions and sending them to State hospitals, because they are filled to the limit of their capacity, and no provision has been made for increase of their size or for addition to their number.

" In fact the Act above referred to was passed because the State recognized the inadequacy of its provisions for the indigent insane, and in preference to increasing the number or the size of its hospitals, offered inducements to the counties to care for their insane in institutions of their own. The State Board of Charities, having recommended this action, is urging the several counties to accept the State's offer, so that it is probable the new policy will be permanent unless experience shall demonstrate its inadvisability ; but meanwhile this department must be empowered to care properly for its insane, and we shall confidently appeal to you, and through you to Councils, for the requisite means and authority."

The final transfer of Almshouse ground was made to the Trustees of the Philadelphia Museums on November 22d, 1897. This took in the marsh land between the line of the railroad and the Schuylkill river, which had been made a public dump and had been filled in with ashes, old tin cans and rubbish of all kinds. It is instructive as well as amusing to read the preamble and provisos attached to the ordinance. It was stated that the collections under the care of the said Trustees contained many seeds and plants particularly adapted to the development of a botanic and economic garden; and such a garden would be a great ornament and of much advantage to the City of Philadelphia; and those portions of the Almshouse grounds which were set apart for park purposes were specially adapted for the purposes of a botanic and economic garden.

The ordinance provided that the property should be forthwith opened for use as a public park forever, and should be assigned in trust, to the Board of Trustees of the Philadelphia Museums, for the purpose of developing and maintaining a botanic and economic garden and a public park. It provided that said garden and park should be forever open to free access of the public at all times, etc. It also provided that no building or buildings of any kind, character or description should be erected on the grounds transferred by the several ordinances save such as were necessary and suitable for the development and maintenance of the aforesaid park and botanic and economic garden.

How much of these agreements have been complied with can be seen by a visit to the grounds.

President Lambert made a final appeal for relief for the insane patients in his annual report for 1898. He said in part: " The following table exhibits the population of the insane department on the first day of January in each year for the past ten years and the number of admissions during that period :

Date.		Population.	Admissions.
January 1st,	1889	760	306
"	" 1890	824	283
"	" 1891	880	278
"	" 1892	891	497
"	" 1893	1010	466
"	" 1894	1050	479
"	" 1895	1114	521
"	" 1896	1149	591
"	" 1897	1228	592
"	" 1898	1327	598
"	" 1899	1378	. . .

"The steady and alarming increase in the number of insane patients demands increased provision for their proper care.

"The taking of the Pennsylvania Railroad, the transfer by ordinance of Councils, through sale, or gift, or in trust to the University of Pennsylvania and to the Commercial Museums have deprived the Department of the greater part of the land which had been dedicated to Almshouse purposes. The only ground now under our control is that portion within the walls occupied by the hospitals and out-wards, and the small exterior part occupied by the childrens' house, the barn and stable and appertaining buildings. There is, therefore, no land available for the additional buildings so greatly needed. In the judgment of the Directors there can be no enlargement of present buildings beyond the addition of stories to two wings of the insane wards, for which appropriation has been asked. For reasons stated in my last report, there is no probability that the State will relieve the City of the care of any considerable number of insane ; the hope that legislation could be secured, transferring to the Department the care and control of the three independent Almshouses in the county, appears to have been ill-founded, and there is little prospect that relief can be obtained in that direction ; and it is, therefore, imperative that measures be taken at once to obtain means for the purchase of ground elsewhere and the erection thereon of an Insane Hospital of modern construction and equipment large enough to accommodate the patients now in our charge, and to provide for the inevitable increase in their number.

"With such provision made for the insane and the relief which would thus be given to the institution, it is probable that the present buildings, with such alterations as could then be made, would suffice for the City's needs for years to come. . . . . .

"An insane hospital commensurate with the requirements of this municipality should provide at once for a much larger number than our present population, and be capable of expansion to meet the needs of the future, and in view of the probability that ultimately the other portions of the Almshouse will be removed from its present location, sufficient land should be secured also to

STABLE.

allow erection thereon of buildings for hospital and out-ward purposes."

This was President Lambert's last report, as he severed his connection with the Department shortly after it was written.

On January 8th, 1899, Mr. Joseph H. Mann died after a protracted illness. Mr. Mann had given active attention to his duties as a member of the Board during the time that his health permitted; the work was congenial by reason of his sympathetic nature.

Dr. Joseph S. Neff was appointed to fill the vacancy, February 2d.

On March 24th Mr. Henry B. Gross resigned, owing to pressure of business.

On April 3d Major William H. Lambert, who had been a member since April, 1892, and President of the Board since October, 1892, tendered his resignation and the City lost one of its best officials. Conscientious, proficient, impartial, attentive and kind in the discharge of his manifold duties he was eminently fitted for the office, and his loss was severely felt by all with whom he had been associated.

Mr. Wm. D. Gardner was appointed President pro tempore.

On April 20th, Mr. Albert H. Dingee, and on May 18th, Dr. C. S. Middleton, were appointed members of the Board.

CHAPTER XXXIV.

SUPERINTENDENT LAWRENCE tendered his resignation which took effect on May 15th, 1900. At the last meeting of the Bureau of Charities, previous to that date, he made the following statement, and as it gives a brief history of what was accomplished during his administration it is quoted :

" *To the President and Directors of the Department of Charities and Correction :*

" GENTLEMEN :—I respectfully submit the following statement : When I came to this Institution, in May, 1891, the grounds were surrounded by high wooden fences, some of which were shored up to prevent falling, unsightly in appearance, and frequently blown down. The interior walls and ceilings of most of the buildings had been white-washed year after year and were covered with scales. Floors and joists were rotten, and an unpleasant smell pervaded. Old, unsightly rookeries, which had long outlived their usefulness, could be seen on all sides. These conditions have all been changed.

" There was so much to do that it was a question as to which should be done first, as it was impossible to do all at once.

* " The erection of additional buildings for the insane was commenced. They consisted of two ward buildings, shaped like a T, on the ground plan, measuring 50 feet 9 inches by 80 feet 4 inches on the stem, and 50 feet 9 inches by 129 feet on the head. The associate dining room, 294 feet long and 104 feet wide, was built between these buildings, and separates the male and female grounds. In that year we commenced the erection of a stone wall around the grounds, to take the place of the old fences. We continued that from year to year until it was completed, it being about a mile in length, 2 feet thick, with foundations 4 feet below the

* See illustrations.

364

surface and 10 feet above ground, except that in front of the main building, which is 4 feet above ground, with a capping and an open iron fence 3 feet 6 inches high on top.

"It was estimated that it would cost $15,000 to fill in and grade the grounds between the insane buildings. It was decided to build the wall, on the west side of the grounds, on the line of Guardian Avenue, which was about 150 feet beyond the line of the old fence. It was necessary to establish a grade before the wall could be erected. W. H. Jones, Esq., the Surveyor of this District, kindly had the stakes driven for us. The grade fixed upon necessitated the removal of earth to the depth of 6 feet 9 inches at one point, running off to lower ground at the ends. As the ground to be graded was about 1000 feet long and 150 feet wide, a number of horses and carts were employed to remove the dirt, and it was used for filling in and grading the grounds of the Insane Department. As the cost for carts was only about $3,000, and the digging and grading was done by men from the House of Correction, it can be seen that a considerable part of the $15,000 was saved, and we graded two grounds instead of one. The stone used for the walls was sent from the House of Correction.

" I found the nurses in the hospital were sleeping in little cubbies erected in the wards. They were very much crowded and did not have the necessary accessories to make them comfortable. I recommended the erection of a building for their use for several reasons : First, to provide better accommodations for the nurses ; second, to obtain more room for patients in the hospital by vacating the wards occupied by the nurses ; third, to enable us to remove the old receiving wards to the rooms used as offices and reception room for nurses ; fourth, to enlarge the drug store by adding to it the room used as a class room for nurses, and also to tear down the old rookeries then used as the receiving wards.

" A brick building containing seventy-five rooms was erected for the nurses, and all of the other improvements were made.

" Back of the woman's outwards a lot of old buildings, built at different times of any and all kinds of material—part brick, an addition of stone and then another of wood, of all heights and shapes, with no regard to appearance, were used as a laundry. They were an eye sore and not fit for the purpose. A new building, equipped with modern appliances, including sterilizing, and having capacity for washing 35,000 pieces weekly, was erected on the reclaimed ground and the old buildings were demolished. All of the grounds back of that part of the institution have been beautified; grass plots and terraces have taken the place of dirt and mud, and cement walks have been laid where old boards had been used before.

" President Lambert remarked: ' One can hardly realize the great improvement made, as the entire character of the place is changed.'

" An old shanty known as the ' dirty wash-house ' was leaning against the wall in the hospital yard, opposite to the Maternity building. A tumble-down sort of fence running from wall to wall separated it from the men's nervous grounds; clothes lines were strung across, and all kinds of filthy rags, bandages and soiled bed clothes could be seen fluttering in the winds. Those conditions would have disgraced the slums of any part of the country. That blot was wiped out, the shanty torn down, the clothes washed in the laundry and the grounds cleared.

" The Clinic Hall was an old stone building with a flat roof, and no ventilation or light excepting what was furnished by two small windows. The interior was about like an old barn. During the clinical recess of one year we repaired and plastered the exterior and put on a pitched roof, with iron girders, and large skylight. In the next summer the interior was torn out and remodeled, new ash seats with walnut caps on the backs were put in, the operating floor was laid in cement, and the partitions faced with glazed tiles. The steam pipes were put under the seats, and iron steps with open rizers allow the heat to enter the building freely. The medical staff was so much pleased with the improvements made that it was thought proper to have the re-opening made an event in the history of the institution. President Lambert, in his report, said: ' Great satisfaction has been expressed concerning this improvement, and it has been declared to be the finest hall of its kind in this country.'

"An old wooden building known as Clover Hall, which was nothing but a disreputable loafing place, where some of the patients were in the habit of playing cards, and a small brick structure, together with a lot of rabbit boxes, coops, etc., at one time used for experimental purposes, were demolished, and on the place occupied we built a brick annex to the Clinic Hall, containing two rooms for sterilizing and dressings.

"Down by the stables a dilapidated, leaky white-washed shed had stood for years, and under it the wagons and ambulances were stored. A narrow stable and carriage house combined, in which a few of the driving horses were kept, stood opposite; the other horses were in an old cow stable, a few small holes having been knocked through the walls for ventilation. The old shed was torn down, and from designs which I made a neat brick structure was erected, in which there is room for all the carriages, wagons and ambulances belonging to the institution. It has two stories in the center, and two rooms, 18 by 18 feet, furnish sleeping accommodations for the drivers and stable help.

"I recommended the erection of an isolating building for the treatment of any contagious or infectious disease that might develop in the institution. It was built. President Lambert, in referring to it, said: 'The Isolating Building is of novel construction, was designed by the Superintendent, and erected from plans made by him. It is built of brick, one story high. It contains fourteen rooms for patients, two rooms for nurses, bath rooms and lavatories, and ample provision is made for heat and ventilation. The walls, floors and ceilings are covered with cement:'

"In the following year he said: 'The value of the isolation wards has been proved by the large number of cases treated there with success and without detriment to the other patients of the institution.' *

"I found that broken coal was being used for making steam. I recommended the changing of the grates under the boilers to allow us to use small coal, at a greatly reduced cost. Thousands of dollars have been saved by that change.

* See illustration.

" The Maternity buildings were supplied with heat and hot water from a boiler in a small building adjoining it. This was a very expensive plan, for aside from the cost of coal, two men were required, one during the day and the other at night, to attend the fire. I suggested that pipes be laid to the hospital cellar and connections made to the main steam pipes ; we laid the pipes, and now they are supplied from the main boilers and considerable expense saved.

" On the night of August 14, 1895, a fire of unknown origin occurred in the laundry of the Insane Department, and spread to the storehouse adjoining, destroying the two buildings and contents. The fire was confined to those buildings, and although it was in proximity to the Insane Department, there was no panic, the patients being promptly removed to the wards in the rear, and no one was injured. President Lambert, in his report, said: ' Great credit is due Superintendent Lawrence for excellent management under exciting circumstances, and for his prompt disposition to meet the emergency.' Supplies had to be procured immediately and temporary store rooms fitted up. The food was procured and the meals furnished as usual.

" We collected the insurance money and rebuilt the buildings ; we improved the storehouse very much by putting a hip roof with girders and trusses in place of the low flat one that was on it previous to the fire. Two large skylights were erected, and now we have a well-lighted store, with a cement floor, 125 by 40 feet, entirely free of posts, with excellent ventilation and the modern appliances. The laundry was built of brick, two stories high, with rooms for washing, drying and ironing on the lower floor and three work rooms, about 50 by 20 feet, on the upper.

" We planted a 70 foot mast, with 40 foot topmast, on the ground in front of the main building. It is fitted with cross trees and shrouds, and is one of the handsomest flagstaffs to be found anywhere. The American flag, 100 feet above the ground, can be seen flying from the staff whenever the weather permits.

" The ground upon which the barn stood was transferred to the University of Pennsylvania, and Councils made an appropriation of $6,000 for the erection of a new building to take the place of the old one, and we built a stable 100 by 40 feet, of brick, two stories in height. The lower floor is for the horses and has twenty-two stalls, two of which are large box stalls ; the floor is cemented and covered with plank, in the stalls, for the horses to stand on. It is supplied with water, gas and underground drainage ; harness and feed rooms are at one end and two stairways lead to the upper floor, A large room for hay and straw is secured in the second story, and as all of the straw beds required for the institution are filled there, it requires considerable space for that purpose. We laid a cement drive around the building, graded and sodded the grounds, and enclosed the whole with a neat picket fence. We could not have had as good a building erected by contract for $10,000. President Lambert's report said: ' The building erected on plans prepared by the Superintendent is commodious and well adapted for the purposes of the institution.'

"I recommended the introduction of a plant to manufacture the ice needed ; an old two-story stone building that had at one time been used to put old vermin-covered clothing into pickle, was remodeled, thoroughly repaired, new roof with skylight put on, cleaned and painted, and the machinery put in. We have not bought any ice since, the cost of the plant was saved in the first year, and we save thousands of dollars annually. Undertakers had been obliged to pay $1.00 for ice for each body removed from the Mortuary Building for burial. That imposition was stopped and no charge was allowed to be made. The money collected in that way was not paid into the City Treasury.

"I recommended the extension of the electric lighting system. We purchased the extra dynamos and engine, enlarged the dynamo house, laid the wires underground and made all connections with our own labor. All of the wards of the institution are lighted by electricity during the early evening, and the halls, stairways and lavatories have the light all night. This is a decided improvement, with less danger from fire, and if we had to use and pay for the gas that is dispensed with, it would cost thousands of dollars annually.

"Through the courtesy of Hon. A. M. Beitler, Director of
24

Public Safety, we procured a condemned steam fire engine. We put it in thorough repair and built a house to put it in. I recommended the purchase of a chemical engine. It was procured; and now, with these and the hose carts, hose on brackets attached to water pipes throughout the institution, fire extinguishers, etc., we are prepared for emergencies.

" Our water supply was furnished by a four-inch pipe, which had been in use for years and was not sufficient. I recommended and we laid a six-inch main, and connected the old one and the fire lines to it. We also succeeded in getting the Water Department to lay an eight-inch main around the outside of the buildings, and it is attached to those on the inside, so a largely increased supply is secured.

"As we did not have the proper facilities for making the large amount of bread required, we enlarged the bake house by adding an annex 16 by 32 feet. Another oven was built and a steam dough mixer erected. This machine will mix five barrels of flour at one time, and in about twelve minutes will produce better dough than men could make by hand. As we bake twenty-two barrels of flour per day during portions of the year, this is of great assistance.

" The meat house was remodeled and improved. The old floor and joists were taken out, new joists put in and a plank floor put down. A concrete surface was laid on the planks. An additional brick building was erected alongside of it, and in one end a refrigerator was built, lined with hard wood. This makes excellent cold storage for meat, milk and butter. The other end of the building is used as a fire engine house, in which our steam and chemical engines and hose cart are kept.

" We erected an additional story on the out-wards kitchen building, and made two large dining-rooms on the second floor for the use of the petty officers. In addition to furnishing them with better accommodations, it enabled us to largely increase the men's out-wards dining room by adding the portion formerly occupied by the petty officers to it.

" We procured a switch table from the Electrical Bureau, through the courtesy of Director Riter, and put telephones throughout the institution. The saving of time in sending messages in a place of this size and character is frequently of great importance.

"Of the many needs of an institution like this, none are greater than proper facilities for bathing. Cleanliness is absolutely necessary. We erected a bath house 50 feet by 20 feet in a corner of one of the male insane exercising yards, and put in eighteen booths with the rain or spray baths. Dressing closets are opposite the booths, and while some of the patients are being bathed, others can be prepared.

" The Chief Resident Physician, in his report, says : 'Another valuable addition to the department during the year was the men's bath house, fitted with the " rain bath," and capable of satisfactorily and thoroughly bathing eighteen patients at one and the same time. Two small bath rooms have also been completed in the women's wards, capable of bathing six women at one and the same time. It is impossible to speak of the value of this useful addition to the department, save in the most enthusiastic terms. The wonder is, how could the department have bathed its large and growing population without this form of bath ? '

" We have since fitted up bath rooms of the same character in all parts of the institution, so that every inmate can have the benefit of this great improvement over the old iron bath tubs.

" For the protection of the patients we erected open pavilions, 80 feet by 30 feet, with six rows of seats running lengthwise. One was built in the male insane yard, two in the women's insane yards and one in the hospital yard. It is a great comfort to the poor souls to sit under the shade of these roofs during the hot summer days.

" The walls along Vintage Avenue in front of main buildings were built four feet high, with open iron fence on top. As the spaces enclosed by these walls were each about 250 feet long and 60 feet wide, we embraced the opportunity of making a great improvement in the appearance of the entire front by placing a number of flower-beds there, instead of the dirt piles, chicken coops and dog kennels that had formerly occupied the grounds. A variety of beautiful plants were set out, making a handsome display. A garden was also arranged in the men's out-wards courtyard, in the place where the coal had been piled. With a fountain in the center, surrounded by beautiful flower-beds, it is very attractive. We erected a hot-house to enable us to propagate our plants: this allowed us to set out beds around the grounds, and we now have them wherever it adds to the cheerfulness of the place and beautifies the surroundings. *

"In improving the grounds we took up old worn out brick sidewalks and laid cement in their stead. All of the streets inside of the walls were covered with asphaltum, new inlets and drain pipes laid and curved curbing placed on all of the corners of the streets. Thousands of yards of cement floors and sidewalks were laid by our inmate labor and the expense was simply for the material used.

"Extensive repairs and improvements were made in all of the wards of the institution. In the Hospital Department the drug-store was enlarged, remodeled and put in first-class condition. New operating rooms were constructed and furnished with the latest style of instruments, sterilizing apparatus, operating tables, stretchers, etc. Walls between rooms were torn out and arches built, improving the light and ventilation. Old floors, joists and stairways were torn out and replaced by new. Walls and ceilings stripped, replastered and painted. Offices and library fitted up for doctors and nurses; in fact, from end to end and from top to bottom it has been improved and made new.

"In the outwards on both sides, the same kind of work was done. The remnants of the 'cubbies' or cell-like compartments into which the outwards had originally been divided were removed; all of the old plaster on walls and ceilings taken off and replastered with adamantine cement and painted; walls torn out and arches built, making one large ward of several small ones; wooden surbases removed and cement substituted; decayed floors, joists and other wood work condemned and replaced with new and everything connected with the buildings put in thorough repair. Every thing new except the outside walls.

* See Illustration.

"The old wards of the Insane Department were also entirely remodeled. We made one ward of five small ones in Ward 2, male side, and the improvement was so marked that Hon. M. H. Dickinson, President of the State Board of Charities, remarked, when visiting it, 'I do not believe there is an institution in the world that has a ward equal to this.' The old outgrown kitchen was turned into a well-equipped workshop.

"In the buildings in which are located Wards 6, 7 and 8, on both the male and female sides, there were brick walls extending from the cellars to the roofs, making bath rooms and water closets on each floor and occupying a space of 37 feet 6 inches by 11 feet 6 inches in the center of each room, leaving but a narrow passageway on either side. We tore the walls down, put in joists, floors and ceilings on each floor and built suitable structures on the outside of the buildings, with connections from each of the three floors. There we erected all of the necessary bath rooms, lavatories, etc., and have all the conveniences without any odors in the wards. In addition to the improved sanitary arrangements we gain space enough to accommodate about thirty more patients in each of the six wards. All of the wards and ceilings, as well as the corridors and stairways were plastered and painted. Cadwalader Biddle, Esq., Secretary and Agent of the State Board of Charities, upon the occasion of a visit remarked 'Nothing short of an inspiration suggested such a great improvement.'

" As a means of relieving the crowded condition of the Insane Department I suggest that, in my opinion, the best and quickest would be to repeal the acts which exempted the other poor districts in the county from the operation of the law placing the almshouses and hospitals under the control and management of this department. If we had possession of the Oxford and Lower Dublin Almshouses buildings sufficient for present purposes at least could soon be erected and our surplus sent there.

" As the Act to accomplish this failed to be passed I recommended the addition of another story on each of the two-story buildings in which are located Wards 1 and 2, and Wards 9 and 10 on both the male and female sides of the Insane department. By your request Councils appropriated the balance of $40,663.83 remaining in the Sinking Fund to the credit of this department for the purpose of commencing the work. Plans were prepared and approved by the Board of Public Charities, but the amount available was only sufficient to enlarge two of the buildings. Councils were applied to several times to appropriate the money to complete the work, but the request was not complied with. The work that was done increased the accommodations sufficient for about 175 patients.

"We built stone and brick tunnels from the main boiler house to the insane wards and from the manufacturing department to the Hospital buildings, completing underground connection with all the main buildings; in these tunnels can be placed all of the steam pipes and electric light and telephone wires, which are thus accessible for repair without excavation.

"We utilized the labor of men sent down from the House of Correction, in a great measure; the digging of trenches required for walls and tunnels, as well as the grading and filling in around new buildings was done by these men. The tearing down and removal of old buildings, hacking and scraping of walls and ceilings, preparing them for plastering; removing the dirt caused; tearing up the old floors and in other ways using the labor, saved the employment of other men and inasmuch as the City would have to maintain them, it seemed wise to get the benefit of their services in this manner.

"President Lambert, in one of his reports, said, ' So great have been the improvements made in the grounds and buildings, so well have they been kept in repair, that although the main buildings have been in constant use for more than sixty years without costly exterior structural changes, they compare favorably with buildings in similar institutions elsewhere of recent erection and elaborate and expensive equipment . . . . We believe that their condition and management will compare favorably with any of like character in the United States.'

"When persons are received in the Institution all money and valuables are taken from them and sent to the superintendent's office for safe keeping.   There was only $2,400 accounted for, in a loose sort of way, when I took charge, although the Institution had been in existence one hundred and fifty-nine years.   I had proper books prepared and accounts (now numbering 9,590) opened with every patient.   Receipts are given for everything received. Each person is credited for whatever is brought in; receipts are printed at the bottom of each account.   When the patients go out their effects are returned to them and they sign the receipts.

"If any of them should die and have enough to defray funeral expenses, they are decently buried, the undertaker is paid and his receipt taken.   Whatever is left is transferred to the 'deceased inmates' account,' and each year a list of the names of those who have been dead a year or longer is made, stating the name, date of death and the amounts standing to their credit.

"These sums are paid to the Treasurer and his receipt taken therefor.   As the credits vary from one cent upwards, it requires a considerable number of accounts to amount to much money. Nevertheless, I have paid $4,092.03 from that account to the Treasurer and have $4,903.62 deposited in bank belonging to the patients now here.

"To add what I paid to the City to the amount I have in bank would make $8,995.65, an increase of $6,595.65 over what was accounted for nine years ago.   Not one cent had ever been paid to the City from that account until I paid it.

"Prior to 1883 the several counties of this Commonwealth were compelled to pay the entire cost of maintaining their indigent insane, whether they were in a State Hospital for the Insane or in the county institutions, as the Commonwealth did not contribute anything for that purpose.

"The Act of June, 1883, provided that 'The expense of the care and treatment of the indigent insane in the State Hospital for the Insane shall be divided between the State and County: Provided, That the maximum charge to the county shall not exceed, including all charges, the sum of two dollars per week for each person.'

"The Act of May 21, 1889, fixed a rate of $1.75 per week for the county to pay, the excess over that amount to be paid by the State.

"No provision was made for the Commonwealth to pay anything towards defraying the expense of the care and treatment of the insane in the County institutions.

"I called the attention of the Bureau of Charities to the fact that nearly all of the counties had all of their insane in State hospitals, and it was only costing them $1.75 per week for their maintenance, the balance being paid by the State, while we had more than 1,000 in our institution that the State hospital would not receive; we received nothing from the Commonwealth for them, the entire expense being borne by the city. I suggested three remedies to correct the injustice.

"Alfred Moore, Esq., and Dr. J. W. Walk were appointed a committee to consider this important subject. A bill was prepared which provided 'That when the proper authorities of any county in this Commonwealth provide within the county accommodations for the support of indigent insane persons, which said accommodations are approved by the Committee on Lunacy of the Board of Commissioners of Public Charities, the said county shall be entitled to have maintained in the State Hospital for the Insane, for the proper district, free of cost to the county, as many indigent insane persons as are furnished accommodations within the said county.'

"The action of the Bureau of Charities was referred to Hon. Edwin S. Stuart, Mayor of the City. He approved it and sent the reports to Councils with a special message. (See Common Council Appendix, Vol. 2, October 1892, to March 1893, pages 826 to 833.) Both branches of Councils recommended the passage of the bill, and it was passed by the Senate and House of Representatives, but was vetoed by Governor Pattison.

"That bill would have saved the city nearly, if not quite, $100,000 per annum, as $91.00 was paid yearly to the State Hospital for each person from this city being maintained there.

"The Legislature of 1895 took the subject up again, and an Act was passed and approved by Governor Hastings on June 22d of that year, which provided 'That the same allowance shall be made to the counties as was given to the State Hospitals.'

"In other words, the State would pay the counties the amount of cost in excess of $1.75 per week for each indigent insane person cared for at the county institution. Under that act we collected and paid to the City Treasurer the sum of $67,996.39 for the care and treatment of the insane in this institution. That was the first money ever collected from the State for that purpose.

"The Legislature of 1897 considered the matter, as the State Hospitals were overcrowded, and the spending of millions of dollars to erect and support additional structures did not meet with favor. An Act was passed and approved by Governor Hastings May 25, 1897, and provides 'That any County, Municipality, Borough or Township in this Commonwealth which now has, or may hereafter supply, erect and equip a suitable institution for the maintenance, care and treatment of its indigent insane, upon plans and specifications approved in writing by the Board of Public Charities, shall receive from the State Treasury the sum of $1.50 per week for every indigent insane person of such County, municipality, borough or township so maintained, who has been legally adjudged to be insane and committed to such institution, or who may be transferred from a State Hospital for the Insane to such local institution, Provided, 'That the Board of Public Charities shall be satisfied that the quality and equipment of such institution, and the manner of care and treatment therein furnished is proper and suitable to the class or classes of the indigent insane so maintained, and shall so certify to the Auditor-General before any such payment shall be paid.'

"Our institution had been so improved and the character of the attendants and other help (upon whom the physicians must in a manner depend) had been so much elevated that we took rank with any hospital in the State, and were able to comply with all the provisions of the Act.

"The Committee on Lunacy made a special report regarding this hospital to the State Board of Charities, and I quote some of the statements:

" ' On November 4, 1895, there were present in the Department for the Insane 1,132 patients, or 570 men and 562 women. These being wholly drawn from the poorer classes of a large city are more difficult to manage than the average State Hospital population and present physically and mentally, very poor material for cure or relief. Notwithstanding this fact the percentage of recoveries on the whole number treated for the year just closed was $8\frac{1}{4}$ per cent.; on the number admitted during the year 28 per cent.

" ' In the State Hospitals of Pennsylvania in 1894, the percentage of recoveries on the whole number treated was 4 per cent.; on the number admitted during the year $21\frac{1}{2}$ per cent. These results require no comment.

" ' During the year past only eight patients had worn any form of mechanical restraint, and but one patient had been in seclusion. In the wards for refractory patients the single rooms have no doors, but open freely into the wide corridors. Restraint and seclusion of insane have been minimized here to a degree scarcely found elsewhere. Classification is made a leading feature, as it should be in all such institutions. There are separate wards for the acute cases ; for the epileptics ; for those ill in bed and feeble ; for disturbed and for untidy cases. The system of night watching and of special night nursing, is complete and admirably regulated.

" ' There is an exact day and night report submitted to the Chief Resident Physician, from each Ward, of the condition of each patient, and of every occurrence which takes place during the twenty-four hours. The records of the Hospital are full, accurate and reliable, as are also the returns made to the Committee on Lunacy.

" ' The proportion of attendants to the average number of patients is about 1 to 12, and the number of attendants is soon to be increased. Some of these are trained nurses, others are graduates of training schools for attendants to the insane, but all attendants receive special instruction in their duties by courses of lectures delivered by the Medical Staff. During the past year there occurred neither a serious accident nor a suicide, although there were present on the last day of the year 41 homicidal and 23 suicidal patients. . . . All the water closets and bath rooms are placed in towers or projections built outside the wards. These are well ventilated, perfectly clean and free from odor, and are supplied with excellent fittings and an automatic flush of water.

" ' All the patients sleep on wire-woven mattresses on neat iron bedsteads, supplied with good warm bedding. The beds are clean and free from vermin. The quieter patients sleep in large dormitories, which are entirely vacated during the day, the patients, when not in the open air, occupying large day rooms. The ceilings in most of the wards, corridors and dormitories are from 13 to 16 feet in height.

" ' The newer wards have always been excellent, but during the last few years all of the older wards have been torn out to the very walls and refitted in modern form, so that now these compare very favorably with the newer portions of the buildings.

" ' The patients take their meals in one of the finest and best equipped refectories in this country, connected with serving rooms and a main kitchen of great size and fitted with the most approved appliances for institution cooking. This group of buildings is of recent construction and is supplied above with sleeping quarters for attendants and employees. Of the 1,132 patients about 900 regularly use this dining hall. On the day of our last visit there 897 were at dinner. Each sex occupies half of the hall, which is divided in its length by a fixed screen about seven feet in height. The dinner was well cooked, well served and evidently much enjoyed, and the quiet and good order was rather better than is seen in the average hospital dining room. The buildings are now lighted with gas, but arrangements have been made to abolish gas and light entirely by electricity. The ventilation of the wards is very good and the general cleanliness admirable; there are no bad smells, no dirty corners, nor closets; no collection of rubbish. All spare clothing is neatly put by in clothes rooms.

" ' The patients are bathed regularly, under supervision of physician, are kept clean, and their clothing is warm, tidy and comfortable. . . . . The supplies of special diet, drugs, medicines and appliances are unrestricted and are subject to the requisition of the Chief Resident Physician. Politics are absolutely disregarded in the selection of physicians and in the employment of attendants and employees. Character and fitness for duty are the sole requirements to obtain and retain an appointment or position. Much to the contrary has been unfairly alleged. If it might have been true at some former time, it is no longer so. . . . . . This report, which is based upon repeated personal inspections by the Committee on Lunacy, was called forth by the injudicious, unjust and untrue publication which recently appeared in a justly popular periodical. There are many citizens and many of the medical profession who appear to content themselves with the remembrance of what "Blockley" used to be, rather than take the trouble to visit it now and to see what it has become under the leadership of the present Bureau of Charities, and under the admirable control of the present Superintendent, Mr. Charles Lawrence, and Dr. Daniel E. Hughes, the present excellent Chief Resident Physician, and of the Medical Staff at large. The present improved state of the Department for the Insane could never have been attained without the thorough co-operation and determination of those in control and of those in immediate charge. The results have only to be seen to be duly appreciated and highly commended. The improvements have steadily advanced, and will, doubtless, from year to year.

"'This report has shown that, with the single exception of outside exercising and working space (and this matter has been unduly exaggerated), the insane poor of this city are as well cared for at Blockley, in the present improved state, as are the patients in any other public hospital in Pennsylvania.'

"Signed by

"GEORGE I. McLEOD, M. D., *Chairman*.

"HENRY M. WETHERILL, M. D., *Secretary*.

"No such report as that could have been made previously. The conditions did not exist, and spare clothing was unknown, there being hardly enough to cover them. Many had no socks or stockings, and blankets were scarce articles. It is different now, and all are comfortably clothed.

"Dr. D. E. Hughes, Chief Resident Physician, said : 'In bringing to a close this report, I cannot allow the opportunity to pass of expressing my deep feelings of gratitude to Superintendent Lawrence.   Not only has he heartily co-operated in every effort to improve the work of the Hospital and Insane Departments, but he has raised and broadened the character of the institution by his wise suggestions, his enlightened views and his wide experience. The duties of a trying position have been made less arduous by his able and intelligent administration of the affairs of the institution.'

"Under the Act of May 25, 1897, we have collected from the Commonwealth $259,368.77, which, together with the $67,996.39 collected under the Act of June 22, 1895, makes a total of $327,-365.16 received for the maintenance of our insane patients.   In addition, we have another bill for the quarter ending February 28, 1900, amounting to $26,771.57.

"Not one dollar could have been collected unless the proviso had been complied with and the ' Board of Public Charities satisfied that the quality and equipment, and care and treatment furnished was proper and suitable.'

"A comparison of population shows :

1890, average population 2,919 } Increase 685—23.47 per cent.
1899,   "   "   3,604 }

" INSANE DEPARTMENT.

1890, average population   881 } Increase 501—56.87 per cent.
1899,   "   "   1,382 }

" The *net* cost per capita per day for maintenance and repairs for 1890 was :

Children's Asylum	Insane Dept's	Men's Outwards	Women's Outwards	Hospital Dep't	Institution Collectively
36.90	31.02	20.56	19.36	39.13	29.81

" The house. receipts were credited from the gross amount expended before the calculations were made.   To get the *gross* per capita cost, the $5,255.66, amount of house receipts, would be divided and added.   This would add to the institution collectively

.49 of a cent per day, making the per capita cost 30.30, instead of 29.81, which is the *net* cost.

" The *gross* cost per capita per day for maintenance and repairs for 1899 was :

Children's Asylum 31.76	Insane Dept's 31.54	Men's Outwards 19.15	Women's Outwards 21.08	Hospital Dep't 39.92	Institution Collectively 29.87

" It will be seen that the *gross* per capita for 1899 was .43 of a cent *less* than it was in 1890. When we credit the collections made and paid to the City Treasurer, the *net* cost per capita for 1899 was :

Children's Asylum 31.21	Insane Dept's 4.88	Men's Outwards 18.60	Women's Outwards 20.53	Hospital Dep't 39.37	Institution Collectively 19.31

" This shows that the cost to the City was 10.50 cents less per day for each person maintained than it was in 1890.

" The net cost for maintenance and repairs in 1890 was $317,638.94 ; in 1899, notwithstanding the largely increased population and superior accommodations and treatment, it was only $253,997.15, or $63,641.79 less. While the gross expenditures of the year 1899 were $392,973.72, we collected and returned to the City Treasurer during the year $138,976.57, or more than 35 per cent. of the entire amount. In a yearly report of the State Board of Charities occurs the following :

" ' Our visit of inspection was, as usual, made without any notification of the officials. Hence it was found in its general condition, and it reflected throughout great credit on Mr. Charles Lawrence, the Superintendent, and his subordinate officials and employees. Indeed, Mr. Lawrence has shown himself, in our opinion, pre-eminently qualified for the office he fills, and we believe him to be " the right man in the right place." '

Signed.   MAHLON H. DICKINSON, *President.*
                           CADWALLADER BIDDLE, *Sec. and Agent.*

"President William H. Lambert, after seven years' close connection with this department, and with a thorough knowledge of its conditions and management, in his last annual report, after referring to the improvements made, said : 'This work has been done under the direct supervision, and in most part because of the recommendation of Superintendent Lawrence, whose thorough acquaintance with the details and needs of the institution, and whose practical knowledge and executive ability especially qualify him for the management of the business of the great community in our charge; to him we are indebted for many valuable suggestions and improvements in buildings, grounds and administration.'

"William D. Gardner, Esq., after eight years' service on the Board, one of which was as President, said in his report, dated December 31st, 1899: 'I desire to thank the Secretaries of the Bureaus, the Superintendents and other officials of the various departments for their valuable aid and assistance, and for the deep interest evinced in the management of their affairs.'

"All of the gentlemen quoted have had years of experience and know whereof they speak. Their opinions are worth considering.

"Here is an institution which contains more than 4,000 poor people unable to care for themselves, suffering from all kinds of disease and infirmities, who are looked after by the officials of this Bureau after their friends have failed them. There were 8,043 patients under medical care and treatment during the year 1899. Four hundred and forty-two men and 358 women suffering from acute and chronic ailments were admitted to the Detention Wards during the year, and 329 men and 280 women were transferred from there to the Insane Department.

"Seven hundred and forty-six men and 86 women were treated in the 'Drunk Wards.' These cases were mostly brought in police patrol wagons from station houses.

"When these facts are considered, it can be seen that the safety, not alone of these patients, but of the public at large, is largely insured by the reception of these degenerates, many of whom are public nuisances and should not be allowed at large.

" Here is a city containing all kinds and all ages 'from the cradle to the grave.'

" The cleanliness of all parts of these immense buildings is remarked by all who visit them. The inmates are better cared for, have better food and clothing, at less cost to the tax payers of Philadelphia, than ever before.

" The Institution in all its parts will compare favorably with any of similar character in this or any other country, and what was once a ' stench in the nostrils of the people ' is now an honor and credit to the city. Thus I leave it to you."

Respectfully submitted,

CHARLES LAWRENCE,

MAY 11, 1900.   *Superintendent.*

Mr. Lawrence requested the City Controller to have all accounts audited. This was done and he paid to the Treasurer of the Board the sum of $5,280.54 which settled everything in full, according to the books.

When he found that the amount of money in his hands belonging to the inmates was increasing he deemed it prudent to arrange for a special deposit of a part of it upon which interest should be paid. The Centennial National Bank, one of the City's depositories, agreed to allow two per cent. interest, the same as was paid on the City's money. When his bank account was settled there was a credit for interest amounting to $285.69. The money from which this interest accrued did not belong to the City, and as it would be impracticable to attempt to distribute it amongst the inmates to whom it *did* belong, he asked the City Solicitor to advise him as to whom he would be justified in paying it, as he knew of no precedent to follow—as *principal is not always paid and interest is frequently overlooked*—and desired to be officially informed as to the proper course to pursue.

Some persons would not have taken the same trouble; they would simply end the matter by keeping the money, and saying nothing about it.

City Solicitor Kinsey, after considering the matter for about two weeks, replied by saying : " I think you should pay the interest into the City Treasury."

This was accordingly done, a receipt taken therefor, and the Superintendent retired from as clean an Administration as that, or any other institution, ever had.

No scandals of any kind, no reflections of mismanagement or dishonesty were even hinted during his term. He was instrumental in collecting, and turning over to the City Treasury, more money for the City than all of his predecessors combined. Not one dollar was expended extravagantly ; the City received full value in return ; every penny received was properly accounted for, and he had the proud satisfaction of feeling that no man had ever left a position of so much responsibility with a better or more honest reputation than he had earned. The following letter was sent to him by the Chairman of the Medical Staff, Dr. R. G. Curtin :

" *My dear Captain Lawrence :*

" I was sorry to hear of your departure from the Philadelphia Hospital and Almshouse.

" It is not often that a man remains in office nine years at ' Blockley' with the record that you left behind you—not even a whisper detrimental to your character—I never heard any one inti. mate that you had in any way deviated from the path of rectitude while Superintendent.

" Such a record you and your family may well be proud of. In your future days it will be a comfort to you to know that you not only served your country faithfully but also your city.

" I am with highest esteem,

Yours sincerely,

(Signed)   ROLAND G. CURTIN."

25

APPENDIX.

LIST OF THE FORMER RESIDENT PHYSICIANS OF THE PHILADELPHIA HOSPITAL.

By EDWARD R. STONE, M.D., W. A. N. DORLAND, M.D. AND C. K. MILLS, M.D.

The number in the second column refers to the year of appointment to the hospital ; the third column, to the college.

U. of P., University of Pennsylvania; Jeff., Jefferson Medical College; W. M. C., Woman's Medical College of Pennsylvania; Medico-Chi., Medico-Chirurgical College ' Univ. City N. Y., University of City of New York; Penna. M. C., Pennsylvania Medical College (extinct).

ABBOTT, HARVEY N.	79	U. of P.	BEVEA, HARRY D.	91	U. of P.
ABBOTT, W. L.	84	U. of P.	BIRKEY, THOMAS W., dec'd	51	U. of P.
ABEL, FRED. T., dec'd	76	U. of P.	BITTING, MIRIAM	89	W. M. C.
ALBERTSON, WILLIAM C.	86	U. of P.	BLACK, JOHN J.	65	U. of P.
ALLEMAN, FRANK	96	Jeff.	BLACKFORD, BENJAMIN	55	Jeff.
ALEXANDER, CLARA J.	89	W. M. C.	BLISS, A. A.	83	U. of P.
ALLEN, HARRISON, dec'd	61	U. of P.	BLOOMFIELD, J. C.	88	Jeff.
ALLIS, OSCAR H.	66	Jeff.	BOARDMAN, CHARLES H.	62	U. of P.
ALLISON, E. W.	80	U. of P.	BOENNING, H. C.	79	Jeff
ALLYN, HERMAN B.	85	U. of P.	BOSTON. L. NAPOLEON	96	Medico-Chi.
AMES, ROBERT P.	81	Jeff.	BOTSFORD, WILLIAM, dec'd	68	Jeff.
ANDERSON, GEORGE B., dec'd	77	Jeff.	BOWER, J. L.	88	Jeff.
ANGENY, GRANVILLE L.	95	U. of P.	BOWMAN, F. S.	97	Medico-Chi.
ANGNEY, WILLIAM M.	79	Jeff.	BOYD, JOHN S.	70	U. of P.
ARMSTRONG, ALEX.	96	U. of P.	BOYER, Z. P.	81	U. of P.
ASHTON, THOMAS G.	88	Jeff.	BRADFIELD, G. M.	91	Jeff.
ATLEE, WILLIAM A., JR.	87	U. of P.	BRADLEY, ALFRED E.	87	Jeff.
AUGE, TRUMAN	92	U. of P.	BRADLEY, MICHAEL	58	
			BRADY, ELLIOT T.	86	Jeff.
BAKER, P. B. L	49	U. of P.	BRAGG, J. C.	58	U. of P.
BALDWIN, HELEN	95	W. M. C.	BRAXTON, TOMLIN	54	U. of P.
BALDY. J. M.	84	U. of P.	BRECHEMIN, L.	76	U. of P.
BALL EDWARD S., dec'd	78		BRICK. JOSEPH COLES	95	Jeff.
BARDSLEY, GEO. ASHTON	97	U. of P.	BRICKER, CHARLES E.	81	Jeff.
BARKSDALE, R.	52	U. of P.	BRISTER, JOHN M.	98	Medico-Chi.
BARNES, CHARLES S.	98	Jeff.	BROOKE, BENJAMIN	89	U. of P.
BARTLES, WILLIAM H.	65	Jeff.	BROOKE, HARRIET W., dec'd	86	W. M. C.
BARRISTER.	43		BROWN, C. H.	78	U. of P.
BEECHER, A. C. W., dec'd.	67	Jeff.	BROWN, G. S.	85	Jeff.
BEHREND, MOSES	99	U. of P.	BRUEN, E. T., dec'd	74	U. of P.
BELLOWS, HORACE M.	61	U. of P.	BRUNER, W. E.	91	U. of P.
BENTON. CHARLES H., dec'd	59		BUCK, SAMUEL T.	90	
BENTON, JOHN H., dec'd	48	U. of P.	BUCK. W. P.	69	U. of P.
BERENS, BERNARD.	80	U. of P.	BUDD, A. V.	54	U. of P.
BERENS, JOSEPH, dec'd.	75	U. of P.	BUMSTEAD, CHARLES	98	U. of P.
BERENS, T PASSMORE	87	U. of P.	BUNCE, T. S., dec'd	82	U. of P.
BERTOLETTE, D. N.	72	Jeff.	BURTENSHAW, J. H.	91	U. of P.

387

GRIFFITH, S. H.	71	U. of P.
GROSS, S. W., dec'd	56	Jeff.
GUITERAS, DANIEL	74	U. of P.
GUITERAS, JOHN	74	U. of P.
GUITERAS, G. M.	85	U. of P.
GUTHRIE, G. W.	73	U. of P.
HACKLEY, C. E.	60	U. of P.
HAEHNLEN, W. F.	82	U. of P.
HAGY, J. A.	64	U. of P.
HAINES, JOSIAH	44	Jeff.
HALBERSTADT, GEORGE H.	78	U. of P.
HALE, GEORGE	70	U. of P.
HALL, JOHN C., dec'd . . .	69	U. of P.
HALL, J. H.	73	U. of P.
HALL, WILLIAM R.	71	U. of P.
HALLOWELL, WILLIAM H. .	80	U. of P.
HAMILL, R. H. . . .	79	U. of P.
HAMILL SAMUEL M.	88	U. of P.
HAMMOND, CLARA M. . . .	87	W. M. C.
HANCOCK, E. C.	81	U. of P.
HARDY, BENJAMIN F., dec'd	39	U. of P.
HARRIS, CHARLES M., dec'd	70	U. of P.
HARRIS, T. J.	89	U. of P.
HARRISON, J. M.	79	U. of P.
HAWLEY, B F.	82	Jeff.
HAZLETT. E. E.	80	U. of P.
HEARNE, JAMES C.	72	Jeff.
HEATH, WILLIAM H.	78	Jeff.
HELLER JACOB B. .	78	U of P.
HELM, WILLIAM H., dec'd .	64	U. of P.
HENDERSON	77	
HENLEY. LEO	47	U. of P.
HENRY, C. P.	82	U. of P.
HERCHELROTH, J. GRANT .	94	Medico-Chi.
HETRICK, CAROLINE	95	W. M. C.
HEWITT. GEORGE A.	77	Jeff.
HICKMAN, H.	84	U. of P.
HIGGINBOTHAM, EDWARD G.	45	U. of P.
HINKLE. WILLIAM H. . . .	92	U. of P.
HITSCHLER, WILLIAM . . .	94	U. of P.
HITZ, HENRY B.	91	U. of P.
HOFFMAN, JOSEPH E. . . .	83	U. of P.
HOFFMAN W. A, dec'd . .	68	U. of P.
HOLLAND, DANIEL J., dec'd	76	Jeff.
HOLLAND, J. W.	71	
HOLLOWAY, THOMAS B. . .	97	U. of P.
HOLMES, E. W.	80	U. of P.
HOONAMAN, G. H.	90	
HORWITZ, L. N., dec'd .	82	Jeff.
HORWITZ, THEO., dec'd . .	76	Jeff.
HOUGH, J. STOCKTON, dec'd	68	U. of P.
HOUSTON, JAS. P. S., dec'd .	69	U. of P.
HOUSEKEEPER, F. P.	74	U. of P.
HOWE, HENRY D.	95	U. of P.
HUG EDWARD V. . . .	93	Jeff.
HUGHES, D. E.	78	Jeff.
HUGHES, F. W.	80	U. of P.
HULL. GEORGE S.	77	U. of P.
HUME. J. E.	00	U. of P.
HUMPHREY, G. E.	90	U. of P.
HUNT, ELIZABETH G.	89	W. M. C.
HURLOCK, F. J.	82	Jeff.
HUTCHINSON, G. H., dec'd.	80	U of P.
HUTCHINSON, RANDALL . .	87	U. of P.
HUTCHINSON, R. C. . . .	80	U. of P.
INGRAM, SAMUEL D.	99	Medico-Chi.
IRISH, W. B.	94	Jeff.
JAMAR, JOHN H.	61	U. of P.
JAMESON, E. W., dec'd . . .	70	U. of P.
JAMESON, WILLIAM B. . . .	86	U. of P.
JAMISON, J. ROSS	94	
JANNEY, FRANCES S.	90	W. M. C.
JENKINS. S. R.	84	U. of P.
JENKS, WILLIAM F., dec'd .	66	U. of P.
JESSOF, S. A. S.	80	Jeff.
JEWITT, MARY B.	96	W. M. C.
JIMINEZ, J. M.	69	Jeff.
JIMINEZ, S. M.	79	Jeff.
JOHNSON, N. L.	91	U. of P.
JOHNSTON, A. R.	82	Jeff.
JOHNSTON, JOHN	99	U. of P.
KAHN, JOSEPH	89	U. of P.
KARCHER, WILLIAM L. . . .	00	Medico-Chi.
KEATING, JOHN M., dec'd .	74	U. of P.
KEATING, WM. V., dec'd . .	44	U. of P.
KEEFER, F. R.	89	U. of P.
KELLER, HARRY M.	87	U. of P.
KELLY, E. P. B.	58	Jeff.
KERLIN, E. J.	86	U. of P.
KERR, J. W., dec'd	77	Jeff.
KERR, JAMES W.	39	U. of P.
KETCHAM, S. R.	89	U of P.
KING	82	
KING, WILLIAM H.	94	Jeff.
KIRK, L. H.	78	U. of P.
KISTLER, CLINTON J	96	U. of P.
KLEINSTUBER, WILLIAM S. .	93	Jeff.
KLUTTZ, W. C.	99	U. of P.
KOCH JAMES L.	96	U. of P.
KOERPER, JOSEPH	62	Phila. Col.
KNOX, JOHN	77	U. of P.
KOLLOCK, CHARLES W. . .	81	U. of P.
KUGLER, G. W.	85	Jeff.
LAKE, DAVID H.	85	Jeff.
LANDIS, H. G., dec'd. . . .	70	Jeff.
LANDIS, H. R. M.	97	Jeff.
LAPIN, F. S.	81	
LARGE, OCTAVIUS P.	98	Medico-Chi.
LAZARUS, S. D., dec'd. . . .	83	Jeff.
LEE, CHAS. CARROLL, dec'd	60	U. of P.
LEETE, JAMES M.	61	U. of P.
LEIDY, PHILIP, dec'd	59	U. of P.
LEVY, HENRY H.	71	U. of P.
LEYS, J. L.	91	U of P.
LICHTY. JOHN A. . .	93	
LIGHT, SAMUEL D. W. . . .	99	U. of P.
LINCOLN, CLARENCE W. . .	93	U of P.
LINEAWEAVER, J. K.	61	Jeff.
LINN, G. WILDS	73	U. of P.
LIPPINCOTT. FRANKLIN . . .	40	U. of P.
LITTIG, LAWRENCE W. . . .	84	U. of P.

LITTLE, W. T.	94	U. of P.
LODER, PERCIVAL E.	76	Jeff.
LODGE, JOHN	59	
LODGE, WILLIAM J.	59	
LONG, WILLIAM S.	79	U. of P.
LUCAS, EMMA J.	93	W. M. C.
LUDLOW, JOHN L., dec'd	41	U. of P.
LUDLOW, R. G.	64	U. of P.
LYMAN, GEORGE H., dec'd	43	U. of P.
LYON, CHARLES H.	99	U. of P.
MACCOY, A. W	70	U. of P.
MACCRACKEN, G. Y.	77	U. of P.
MAGOFFIN, M. M.	62	U. of P.
MALONEY, S. O.	99	U. of P.
MANN, CHARLES W., dec'd	66	
MARCUS, HERMAN D.	92	Medico-Chi.
MARTIN, CHARLES S.	90	U. of P.
MARTIN, JOSEPH	78	U. of P.
MATLACK, ELWOOD	86	U. of P.
MATSON, E. G.	83	U. of P.
MATTHEWS, E. L. B.	91	W. M. C.
MATTHEWS, WILLIAM E.	87	Jeff.
MAURY, F. F.	62	Jeff.
MAY, JAMES V.	97	U. of P.
MCAULEY, JAMES A.	74	U of P.
MCBRIDE, G. W., dec'd	79	U. of P.
MCCAMY, R. H	79	U. of P.
MCCARTHY, DANIEL J.	95	U. of P.
MCCARTY, R. H., dec'd	79	U. of P.
MCCLEES, WILLIAM D.	85	U of P.
MCCLINTOCK, JAMES, dec'd	58	Jeff.
MCCOY, A.	88	Jeff.
MCCOY, HENRY W.	64	Jeff.
MCCONKEY, THOMAS G.	90	U. of P.
MCCLURE, W. W.	64	Jeff.
MCDONALD, A. A.	74	U. of P.
MCFARLAND JOSEPH	89	U. of P.
MCGILL GEORGE M., dec'd	61	U. of P.
MCGLINN, JOHN A.	99	Medico-Chi.
MCGOWN, D. J.	79	U. of P.
MCGUIGAN, J. J.	87	Jeff.
MCKEE. JAMES H.	92	U. of P.
MCKENYON	74	
MCLAUGHLIN, THOMAS N.	82	G'rg't'n Un.
MCMILLAN, JAMES H., dec'd	88	U. of P.
MCPHEETERS, WILLIAM M.	40	U. of P.
MEANS, J. S.	59	
MEARS, J. EWING	66	Jeff.
MENAH, W. MCC.	90	U. of P.
MERCUR, JOHN D.	78	Jeff.
MERILLAT, WILLIAM C.	64	U. of P.
MERRITT, VICTOR S.	98	Medico-Chi
MILLIKEN, C. W.	81	U. of P.
MILLIKEN, F. H.	79	U. of P.
MILLER, MILO G.	88	U. of P.
MILLER, ROBERT	64	Jeff.
MILLIGAN, JAMES E., dec'd	72	U. of P.
MITCHELL. JAMES	83	U. of P.
MOFFITT, WILLIAM J.	76	Jeff.
MONTEGUT, SIDNEY	92	
MONTGOMERY, E. E.	74	Jeff.
MOORE, DUNLOP, JR.	93	U. of F.
MOORE, EDWARD M.	39	U. of P.
MOORE, HENRY B.	80	Jeff.
MOORE, ISAAC H.	78	U. of P.
MORGAN, A. C.	97	Medico-Chi.
MORRIS, S. E.	90	
MOSELY, E. B.	68	U. of P.
MOSS, WILLIAM	54	Jeff.
MOWRY, WILLIAM B.	76	U. of P.
MOYER, SHERMAN T.	86	U. of P.
MUHLENBERG F., dec'd	68	U. of P.
MURPHY, JOSEPH A.	98	Medico-Chi.
MURRAY, G. D.	90	
MURRAY, JAMES M.	76	U. of P.
MURRAY, R. D.	70	Jeff.
MUSSER, MILTON B., dec'd	68	Jeff
MUSSER, JOHN H.	77	U. of P.
MUTTART, GEORGE W.	91	Un. C'y N.Y.
MYERS, SYLVAN	96	U. of P.
NAGLE, FRANK O.	79	U. of P.
NEAD, D W	82	U. of P.
NEALE, H. M.	80	U. of P.
NEARE, C. R.	99	Jeff.
NEWGARDEN, G. J.	89	Jeff.
NEWTON, R. D.	96	Medico-Chi.
NICHOL, WILLIAM L.	49	U. of P.
NICHOLS, HENRY D.	98	U. of P.
NICHOLS, W. V.	85	U. of P.
NICHOLSON, J. L.	91	
NICKERSON, L. H. A.	75	U. of P.
NORRIS, RICHARD F.	87	U. of P.
NOVAES, F. DEP	84	U. of P.
OHNESORG, KARL	95	U. of P.
OLIPHANT, N. B.	80	U. of P.
OLIVER, CHARLES A.	77	U. of P.
O'NEILL. J. WILKS	77	U. of P.
O'REILLY, THOMAS B.	94	
OWEN, J. J.	80	Jeff.
OWENS, JOHN E.	62	Jeff.
ORVIS, CHARLES, dec'd	67	Jeff.
PARISH, WILLIAM H.	71	Jeff.
PARKE, WILLIAM E.	86	U. of P.
PARKHILL, CLAYTON	83	Jeff.
PARRISH, ROBERT C.	98	Medico-Chi.
PARRY, JOHN S., dec'd	65	U. of P.
PATTERSON, JOHN P.	71	Jeff.
PECK, ELIZABETH L.	85	W. M. C.
PELHAM, J W.	88	Jeff.
PEPPER, WILLIAM	97	U. of P.
PERKINS, F. M.	76	U. of P.
PERRY, HEXT M., dec'd	73	Jeff.
PERRY, JOHN C,	40	U. of P.
PFAHLER, GEORGE E.	98	Medico-Chi.
PHILLIPS, WM. L., dec'd	76	U. of P.
PHILLIPS, R. J.	83	Jeff.
PHILLRICK. INEZ C.	91	W. M. C.
PICKETT, WILLIAM C.	96	Jeff.
PICOTT, MITCHELL H., dec'd	61	Jeff.
PLUMER, A. J.	85	U. of P.
POLK, W. ROBESON	81	U. of P.
POLLOCK, FLORA	91	W. M. C.

Name		
POLTER, THOMAS C.	71	U. of P.
PONTIUS, N. D.	97	Jeff.
PORTER, WILLIAM G.	69	U. of P.
PORTER, P. B.	69	U. of P.
POTSDAMER, J. B.	80	Jeff.
POTTS, CHARLES S.	85	U. of P.
PREFONTAINE, L. A.	92	U. of P.
PRESTON, SAMUEL P.	87	Jeff.
PRICE, HELENA J.	86	W. M. C.
PURVES, G. M.	96	U. of P.
RABINOVITCH, LOUISA G.	90	W. M.C.
RADEBAUGH, J. M.	74	U. of P.
RANDALL, EDWARD, JR.	83	U. of P.
RANSLEY, ALEXANDER W.	75	U. of P.
RATHBUN, F. D.	79	Jeff.
RECTENWALD, JOHN J.	96	U. of P.
REED, C. H.	82	U. of P.
REEDY, WALTER M., dec'd	93	
REESER, RICHARD	96	Jeff.
REEVE, JOSIAH	64	U. of P.
REYNOLDS, CHARLES R.	99	U. of P.
RIESMAN, DAVID	92	U. of P.
REX, OLIVER	67	Jeff.
REYNOLDS, F. P.	90	U. of P.
RHEIN, JOHN H.	90	U. of P.
RICHARDSON, D. D.	58	U. of P.
RICHARDSON, ELLIOTT, dec.	68	U. of P.
RICHARDSON, GEORGE H.	91	U. of P.
RICHARDSON, JOHN D.	39	U. of P.
RICIO, SEMFRIO, dec'd	61	
RITZ, CHARLES M.	67	U. of P.
ROBERTS, A. S., dec'd	77	U. of P.
ROBERTS, ISAAC E.	67	U. of P.
ROBERTS, THOMAS S.	85	U. of P.
ROBESON, W. F.	85	U. of P.
ROBINSON, EDWIN T.	00	U. of P.
ROBINSON, ERNEST F.	96	U. of P.
ROBINSON, GEORGE S.	81	U. of P.
ROBINSON, JOHN M.	91	U. of P.
ROHRER, GEORGE R.	81	U. of P.
RONALDSON, WM. R., dec'd	74	Jeff.
ROOKER, HERMAN S., dec'd	85	Jeff.
ROOT, M. P.	83	W. M. C.
ROSA, W. V. V.	39	U. of P.
ROSENAU, M. J.	89	U. of P.
ROTHROCK, J. L.	88	U. of P.
ROUSSEL, A. E.	82	Jeff.
RUSH, WM. H.	75	U. of P.
RYNIER, VAN NEST	80	U. of P.
SAGERSON, JOHN L.	98	Medico-Chi.
SAILER, J.	92	U. of P.
SCHIVELY, GEORGE S.	51	Jeff.
SCHNEIDEMAN, T. B.	83	Jeff.
SCHROEDER, HENRY F.	99	Medico-Chi.
SEARS, W. H.	98	Medico-Chi.
SEDGWICK, W. N.	94	Jeff.
SELTZER, C. JAY	91	U. of P.
SEYMOUR, A. J.	86	U. of P.
SHARPLESS, CASPER W.	88	U. of P.
SHARPLESS, WILLIAM T.	88	U. of P.

Name		
SHEPPARD, J.	62	U. of P.
SHERARD, C. C., dec'd	60	U. of P.
SHERK, HENRY H.	87	Jeff.
SHERMAN, M. H.	91	W. M. C.
SHERRER, FRED. A.	98	Medico-Chi.
SHEW, A. M.	65	Jeff.
SHIELDS, WILLIAM G., JR.	00	U. of P.
SHIFFERT, HERBERT O.	99	Medico-Chi.
SHIMER, WILLIAM S.	86	U. of P.
SHIMMELL, JAMES S.	81	Jeff.
SHUMWAY, E. A.	94	U. of P.
SMALL, J. F.	89	U. of P.
SMITH, A. S.	76	Jeff.
SMITH, ALLAN J.	86	U. of P.
SMITH, CHARLES E., JR.	65	U. of P.
SMITH, D. K.	96	U. of P.
SMITH, FISHER, dec'd	47	U. of P.
SMITH, H. A.	75	U. of P.
SMITH, ROBERT K, dec'd	58	
SOMMER, GEORGE N. J.	94	U. of P.
SOMMERKAMP, R. F.	99	U. of P.
SOUTHERN, F. L.	90	Jeff.
SPARKS, GEORGE W.	65	Jeff.
SPEAR, RAYMOND	95	Jeff.
SPENCE, J. E.	70	Jeff.
SPENCER, THOMAS R.	40	U. of P.
STACKHOUSE, C. P.	98	Medico-Chi.
STAHL, B. F.	87	U. of P.
STAMM, E. P., dec'd	81	U. of P.
STEELE, J. DUTTON	93	U. of P.
STEHMAN, H. B.	78	Jeff.
STENGEL, ALFRED	89	U. of P.
STELWAGON, H. W.	75	U. of P.
STETSON, J. B.	97	U. of P.
STEVENS, A. A.	87	U. of P.
STEWART, W. H.	92	Jeff.
STEWART, A. H., dec'd	82	U. of P.
STEWART, WALTER M., dec.	65	U. of P.
STILLE, ALFRED, dec'd	36	U. of P.
STIVERS, CHARLES G.	92	U. of P.
STONE, EDWARD R.	72	Jeff.
STRYKER, S. S.	66	U. of P.
SUTTON, R. S.	65	U. of P.
TABB, JOHN B.	43	Jeff.
TAGGART, THOMAS D.	96	Medico-Chi.
TAGGART, WM. H., dec'd	52	U. of P.
TALLY, FRANK W.	87	U. of P.
TALLY, JAMES E.	92	U. of P.
TAYLOR, G. B.	85	U. of P.
TAYLOR, J. L.	58	U. of P.
TAYLOR, ROBERT A.	86	Jeff.
TAYLOR, SARAH M.	90	W. M. C.
THOMAS, ADA R.	93	W. M. C.
THOMPSON, dec'd	78	
TOPPING, G. G.	73	Jeff.
TRUBY, WILLARD F.	98	U. of P.
TUCKER, HENRY	94	Jeff.
TUTEUR, EDWIN B.	90	Jeff.
TUTTLE, JAMES P.	81	U. of P.
UPSHUR, GEORGE L.	43	U. of P.

CHRONOLOGICAL LIST OF MEMBERS

OF THE

Medical Boards of the Philadelphia Hospital

From 1768 to 1900.

By CHARLES K. MILLS, M.D.

[This list probably contains many omissions and not a few mistakes, as many difficulties have attended its preparation, in which have been consulted Dr. Agnew's "Medical History of the Philadelphia Almshouse," Thatcher's "Medical Biography," Ruschenberger's "History of the College of Physicians," the Catalogues of the Alumni of the Medical Department of the University of Pennsylvania and of the Jefferson Medical College, the Annual Statements of the Boards of Guardians of the Poor and of the Board of Charities and Correction, and the written minutes of the Governing Boards since 1859. Members of the Medical Board have also been personally consulted in efforts at verification. I shall be glad to receive any corrections or additions from any one who may examine the table.—C. K. M.]

MEDICAL STAFF.

Name.	Service began.	Service ended.	Name.	Service began.	Service ended.
CADWALADER EVANS	1768		PHILIP S. PHYSICK	1801	1805
THOMAS BOND	1768	1779	CHARLES CALDWELL	1801	1804
ADAM KUHN	1774	1776	ELIJAH GRIFFITHS	1801	1810
BENJAMIN RUSH	1774	1777	BENJAMIN L. BARTON	1804	1805
SAMUEL DUFFIELD	1774	1801	SAMUEL STEWART	1804	1810
GIRARDUS CLARKSON	1774	1777	JOHN RUSH	1804	
GIRARDUS CLARKSON	1788	1790	JAMES REYNOLDS	1804	1807
THOMAS PARKE	1774	1779	JAMES HUTCHINSON	1805	1805
GEORGE GLENTWORTH	1779	1781	ISAAC CATHRALL	1805	1811
D. JACKSON	1779	1781	PETER MULLER	1805	1811
JAMES HUTCHISON	1780	1781	JOHN SYNG DORSEY	1805	1811
—— WILSON	1780	1781	JOHN SYNG DORSEY	1814	1815
CASPAR WISTAR	1788	1790	NATHANIEL CHAPMAN	1807	1815
J. R. RODGERS	1788	1789	NATHANIEL CHAPMAN	1822	1832
MICHAEL LEIB	1788	1790	JOSEPH PARRISH	1807	1811
JOHN MORRIS	1788	1789	SAMUEL STEWART	1810	1822
SAMUEL P. GRIFFITHS	1788	1789	JOSEPH KLAPP	1810	
N. B. WATRES	1789	1790	JOSEPH KLAPP	1815	1822
WILLIAM SHIPPEN	1789	1790	THOMAS HEWSON	1811	1822
—— CUMMING	1795		JOSEPH HARTSHORNE	1818	1820
—— PLEASANTS		1797	SAMUEL CALHOUN	1821	1822
SAMUEL CLEMENTS, JR.	1796	1797	WILLIAM P. C. BARTON	1821	1822
WILLIAM BOYCE	1796	1801	WILLIAM E. HORNER	1822	1833
SAMUEL COOPER	1796	1796	SAMUEL JACKSON	1822	1845
JOHN CHURCH	1797	1805	JOHN K. MITCHELL	1822	1827
THOMAS C. JAMES	1797	1811	RICHARD HARLAN	1822	1822
JOHN PROUDFIT	1801	1804	HUGH L. HODGE	1822	1835

393

MEDICAL STAFF—*Continued.*

Name.	Service began.	Service ended.	Name.	Service began.	Service ended.
SAMUEL GEORGE MORTON	1827	1835	WILLIAM ASHMEAD	1841	1845
JACOB RANDOLPH	1832	1837	N. STUARDSON	1837	1838
WILLIAM H. GERHARD	1835	1845	ROBLEY DUNGLISON	1838	1845
JOSEPH PANCOAST	1835	1837	EDWARD PEACE	1838	1841
WILLIAM ASHMEAD	1835	1838	MEREDITH CLYMER	1843	1845

SURGICAL STAFF.

Name.	Service began.	Service ended.	Name.	Service began.	Service ended.
J. CATHRALL	1811	1822	J. V. O. LAWRENCE	1822	1822
PETER MILLER	1811	1822	RICHARD HARLAN	1822	1838
JOSEPH PARRISH	1811	1821	WILLIAM E. HORNER	1832	1835
JOHN RHEA BARTON	1820	1822	JOSEPH PANCOAST	1837	1845
WILLIAM GIBSON	1821	1822	CHARLES BELL GIBSON	1838	1840

OBSTETRICAL STAFF.

Name.	Service began.	Service ended.	Name.	Service began.	Service ended.
THOMAS C. JAMES	1811	1821	CHARLES WISTAR PENNOCK	1835	1845
JOHN MOORE	1818	1821	WILLIAM D. BRINKLE	1837	1839
HENRY NEILL	1821	1835	CHARLES BELL GIBSON	1838	1840
NATHAN SHOEMAKER	1821	1827	ROBERT M. HUSTON	1839	1845
CHARLES LUKENS	1827	1827	JAMES McCLINTOCK	1840	1841
B. ELLIS	1827	1831	WILLIAM H. GILLINGHAM	1841	1845
F. S. BEATTIE	1831	1837			

Administration under Chief Resident Officer.

PHYSICIAN–IN–CHIEF.

Name.	Service began.	Service ended.
H. S. PATTERSON	1845	1845

CONSULTANTS.

Name.	Service began.	Service ended.	Name.	Service began.	Service ended.
WILLIAM BYRD PAGE	1845	—	N. D. BENEDICT	1845	1845
MEREDITH CLYMER	1845	—			

PHYSICIANS–IN–CHIEF.

Name.	Service began.	Service ended.	Name.	Service began.	Service ended.
N. D. BENEDICT	1845	1850	R. T. COLEMAN	1854	1854
—— HAINES	1850	1853	ARCHIBALD B. CAMPBELL	1854	1854
J. D. STEWART	1853	1854			

Administration by Residents-in-Chief and Board of Clinical Lecturers.

RESIDENTS-IN-CHIEF.

Name.	Service began.	Service ended.	Name.	Service began.	Service ended.
ARCHIBALD B. CAMPBELL	1854	1855	JAMES MCCLINTOCK	1857	1858
ROBERT K. SMITH	1855	1856	ROBERT K. SMITH	1858	1859
ARCHIBALD B. CAMPBELL	1856	1857			

LECTURERS ON CLINICAL MEDICINE.

Name.	Service began.	Service ended.	Name.	Service began.	Service ended.
J. L. LUDLOW	1854	1857	J. B. BIDDLE	1855	1857
ROBERT COLEMAN	1854	1854	J. B. BIDDLE	1858	1859
CASPAR MORRIS	1854	1855	J. AITKEN MEIGS	1858	1859
JOSEPH CARSON	1855	1857	SAMUEL DICKSON	1858	1858
JOSEPH CARSON	1858	1859	J. M. DA COSTA	1858	1859

LECTURERS ON CLINICAL SURGERY.

Name.	Service began.	Service ended.	Name.	Service began.	Service euded.
HENRY H. SMITH	1854	1857	R. P. THOMAS	1855	1857
D. H. AGNEW	1854	1857	W. S. HALSEY	1858	1859
D. H. AGNEW	1858	1859	RICHARD J. LEVIS	1858	1859
JOHN NEILL	1855	1857			

LECTURERS ON OBSTETRICS AND DISEASES OF WOMEN AND CHILDREN.

Name.	Service began.	Service ended.	Name.	Service began.	Service ended.
R. A. F. PENROSE	1854	1857	CASPAR MORRIS	1855	1857
R. A. F. PENROSE	1858	1859	E. MCCLELLAN	1858	1859
WILSON JEWELL	1855	1857			

MEDICAL STAFF.[1]

Name.	Service began.	Service ended.	Name.	Service began.	Service ended.
J. L. LUDLOW	1859	1885	J. T. ESKRIDGE	1882	
WILLIAM F. MAYBURY	1859	1861	W. G. MCCONNELL	1882	
CHARLES P. TUTT	1859	1866	JOSEPH F. NEFF	1884	1887
ROBERT SUCKET	1859	1859	JOHN H. MUSSER	1885	
J. M. DA COSTA	1859	1865	WILLIAM OSLER	1885	1889
O. A. JUDSON	1861	1863	F. P. HENRY	1888	
GEORGE J. ZEIGLER	1863	1867	J. M. ANDERS	1889	1896
ALFRED STILLE	1865	1872	WILLIAM E. HUGHES	1889	
J. S. DE BENNEVILLE	1866	1866	S. SOLIS-COHEN	1889	
EDWARD RHOADS	1866	1870	EUGENE L. VANSANT	1889	1896
WILLIAM PEPPER	1867	1884	F. A. PACKARD	1892	1900
H. C. WOOD	1870	1883	JUDSON DALAND	1892	1895
JAMES TYSON	1872	1889	SAMUEL WOLFE	1892	1900
JAMES TYSON	1893		JULIUS SALINGER	1892	
JOHN M. KEATING	1875	1877	H. A. HARE	1894	
JOHN M. KEATING	1878	1880	THOMAS G. ASHTON	1894	
EDWARD T. BRUEN	1875	1889	A. A. ESHNER	1896	
JAMES C. WILSON	1875	1889	ALFRED STENGEL	1896	
JOHN GUITERAS	1875	1880	HERMAN B. ALLYN	1900	
ROLAND G. CURTIN	1880		DAVID REISMAN	1900	
S. J. MCFERRAN	1880	1884			

[1] At this time the administration by a visiting Medical Board was resumed.

SURGICAL STAFF.

Name.	Service began.	Service ended.	Name.	Service began.	Service ended.
SAMUEL D. GROSS	1859	1865	W. S. JANNEY	1877	1890
D. HAYES AGNEW	1859	1865	GEORGE MCCLELLEN . . .	1880	1890
R. J. LEVIS	1859	1870	A. S. ROBERTS	1881	1887
R. J. LEVIS	1882		W. JOSEPH HEARN	1882	
EDWARD L. DUER	1862	1863	C. H. THOMAS	1882	1884
R. S. KENDERDINE	1859	1865	A. W. RANSLEY	1885	1892
J. W. LODGE	1864	1868	LEWIS W. STEINBACK . . .	1885	
W. H. PANCOAST	1865	1885	JOHN BLAIR DEAVER	1887	1899
F. F. MAURY	1865	1878	EDWARD MARTIN . . .	1888	1889
JOHN H. BRINTON	1866	1882	EDWARD MARTIN	1892	
HARRISON ALLEN	1870	1878	ORVILLE HORWITZ	1889	
SAMUEL W. GROSS . .	1874	1882	ERNEST LAPLACE	1889	
N. L. HATFIELD	1875	1884	JAMES M. BARTON	1890	1899
J. WILLIAM WHITE	1875	1889	J. CHALMERS DA COSTA . .	1895	
J. WILLIAM WHITE . .	1892	1898	ALFRED C. WOOD	1895	
WILLIAM G. PORTER	1875	1895	CHARLES H. FRAZIER . . .	1898	
A. A. MCDONALD	1878	1881	R. A. F. PENROSE	1859	1867

OBSTETRICAL STAFF.

Name.	Service began.	Service ended.	Name.	Service began.	Service ended.
JOHN WILTBANK	1859	1859	W. H. PARISH	1876	1889
WILLIAM D. STROUD	1859	1863	JOHN M. KEATING	1880	1890
LEWIS HARLOW	1859	1862	CLARA MARSHALL	1882	1895
GEORGE J. ZIEGLER	1859	1863	E. P. BERNARDY	1882	1884
A. H. SMITH	1862	1864	HANNAH P. CROASDALE . .	1882	
E. SCHOFIELD	1863	1870	THEOPHILUS PARVIN	1884	1892
F. F. MAURY	1864	1865	DONNELL HUGHES	1884	1884
EDWARD L. DUER	1863	1883	ELIOTT RICHARDSON	1886	1886
R. M. GIRVIN	1865	1876	BARTON C. HIRST	1887	
J. S. PARRY	1867	1876	EDWARD P. DAVIS	1889	
GEORGE PEPPER	1870	1872	WM EASTERLY ASHTON . .	1889	1894
J. V. INGHAM	1872	1874	ROBERT H. HAMILL	1890	1896
W. A. WARDER	1874	1881	GEORGE I. MCKELWAY . . .	1890	
J. R. BURDEN, JR.	1874	1876	J. W. WEST	1892	1894
E. E. MONTGOMERY . . .	1877	1884	R. C. NORRIS	1894	
E. E. MONTGOMERY	1886	1894	J. M. FISHER	1894	
JAMES B. WALKER	1876	1880	W. FRANK HAEHNLEN . . .	1895	
S. S. STRYKER	1876	1889	ELIZABETH L. PECK . .	1895	
G. W. LINN	1876	1882	JOHN B. SHOBER	1896	
M. B. MUSSER	1877	1887			

NEUROLOGICAL STAFF.

Name.	Service began.	Service ended.	Name.	Service began.	Service ended.
CHARLES K. MILLS	1877		JAMES HENDRIE LLOYD . .	1888	1889
H. C. WOOD	1883	1887	JAMES HENDRIE LLOYD . .	1890	1900
H. C. WOOD	1887	1888	WHARTON SINKLER	1888	1896
ROBERT BARTHOLOW	1887	1888	C. H. BRADFUTE	1889	1890
FRANCIS X. DERCUM	1887		CHARLES W. BURR	1896	

OPHTHALMOLOGISTS.

Name.	Service began.	Service ended.	Name.	Service began.	Service ended.
E. O. SHAKESPEARE	1877	1889	GEORGE M. GOULD	1889	1894
G. E. DE SCHWEINITZ . . .	1887		CHARLES A. OLIVER	1894	
CHARLES H. THOMAS . . .	1888	1888	HOWARD F. HANSELL . . .	1900	

DERMATOLOGISTS.

Name.	Service began.	Service ended.	Name.	Service began.	Service ended.
F. F. MAURY	1870	1870	J. A. CANTRELL	1889	1900
LOUIS DUHRING	1870	1877	MILTON B. HARTZELL	1900	
LOUIS DUHRING	1877	1889	E. S. GANS	1900	
HENRY W. STELWAGON	1887				

LARYNGOLOGISTS.

Name.	Service began.	Service ended.	Name.	Service began.	Service ended.
C. JAY SELTZER	1890	1900	GEORGE M. MARSHALL	1890	

PATHOLOGISTS.

Name.	Service began.	Service ended.	Name.	Service began.	Service ended
JAMES TYSON	1871	1875	W. M. L. COPLIN	1892	1895
R. M. BERTOLET	1872		H. W. CATTELL	1898	1900
JOSEPH BERENS	1876	1879	E. B. SANGREE	1895	1895
E. O. SHAKESPEARE	1882	1889	W. M. L. COPLIN	1896	
HENRY F. FORMAD	1887	1892	JOSEPH MCFARLAND	1900	
JOHN GUITERAS	1892	1899	SIMON FLEXNER	1900	

BACTERIOLOGISTS.

Name.	Service began.	Service ended.	Name.	Service began.	Service ended.
E. O. SHAKESPEARE	1889	1894	L. N. BOSTON	1898	
A. GHRISKEY	1894	1896			

ASSISTANT PATHOLOGISTS.

Name.	Service began.	Service ended.	Name.	Service began.	Service ended.
L. L. HATCH	1889	1891	ERNEST B. SANGREE	1892	1895
H. W. CATTELL	1889	1895	DAVID BEVAN	1892	1895
WILLIAM B. JAMESON	1892	1900			

CURATORS.

Name.	Service began.	Service ended.	Name.	Service began.	Service ended.
D. HAYES AGNEW	1860	1867	JAMES TYSON	1872	1875
WILLIAM PEPPER	1867	1871	JOSEPH BERENS	1876	1879
R. M. BERTOLET	1871	1872	E. O. SHAKESPEARE	1880	1882
R. M. BERTOLET	1875	1876			

MICROSCOPISTS.

Name.	Service began.	Service ended.	Name.	Service began.	Service ended.
JAMES TYSON	1866	1872	THOMAS B. REED	1875	1876
R. M. BERTOLET	1872	1875	H. F. FORMAD	1880	1892

PHYSICIANS TO THE INSANE DEPARTMENT.

Name.	Service began.	Service ended.	Name.	Service began.	Service ended.
L. HENLEY	1849	1852	A. A. MCDONALD	1880	1881
J. H. BENTON	1852	1852	PHILIP LEIDY	1885	1887
L. HENLEY	1852	1854	WILLIAM H. WALLACE	1887	1887
SAMUEL W. BUTLER	1859	1866	GEORGE M. WELLS	1887	1890
D. D. RICHARDSON	1866	1880	DANIEL E. HUGHES	1890	
D. D. RICHARDSON	1881	1885			

CONSULTING PHYSICIANS TO THE INSANE DEPARTMENT.

Name.	Service began.	Service ended.	Name.	Service began.	Service ended.
S. WEIR MITCHELL	1884	1886	PHILIP LEIDY	1886	1887
HORATIO C. WOOD	1884	1885	F. X. DERCUM	1890	
CHARLES K. MILLS	1884	1887	WHARTON SINKLER	1890	1896
CHARLES K. MILLS	1890		JAMES HENDRIE LLOYD	1890	1900
ANDREW NEBINGER	1885	1886	CHARLES W. BURR	1896	
JAMES A. SIMPSON	1886	1887			

Registrars.

MEDICAL.

Name.	Service began.	Service ended.	Name.	Service began.	Service ended
W. A. EDWARDS	1885	1886	H. TOULMIN	1895	1897
C. J. SELTZER	1886	1890	H. B. ALLYN	1895	1900
F. A. PACKARD	1890	1892	B. F. STAHL	1900	
ALFRED STENGEL	1892	1895	JOSEPH SAILER	1900	

SURGICAL.

Name.	Service began.	Service ended.	Name.	Service began.	Service ended.
EDWARD MARTIN	1885	1888	JOHN H. GIBBON	1895	1900
C. B. PENROSE	1888	1892	R. B. NEWTON	1900	
J. C. DA COSTA	1892	1895			

OBSTETRICAL.

Name.	Service began.	Service ended.	Name.	Service began.	Service ended.
H. A. PARDEE	1885	1887	R. C. NORRIS	1890	1894
EDWARD P. DAVIS	1887	1888	W. A. N. DORLAND	1898	
R. H. HAMILL	1888	1890			

NERVOUS.

Name.	Service began.	Service ended.	Name.	Service began.	Service ended.
GUY HINSDALE	1885	1892	B. F. STAHL	1896	1900
AUGUSTUS A. ESHNER	1891	1896	W. C. PICKETT	1900	

ANÆSTHETIZER.

Name.	Service began.	Service ended.
CHARLES LESTER LEONARD	1898	

SOCIAL PROBLEMS
AND
SOCIAL POLICY:
The American Experience

An Arno Press Collection

Bachman, George W. and Lewis Meriam. **The Issue of Compulsory Health Insurance.** 1948

Bishop, Ernest S. **The Narcotic Drug Problem.** 1920

Bosworth, Louise Marion. **The Living Wage of Women Workers.** 1911

[Brace, Emma, editor]. **The Life of Charles Loring Brace.** 1894

Brown, Esther Lucile. **Social Work as a Profession.** 4th Edition. 1942

Brown, Roy M. **Public Poor Relief in North Carolina.** 1928

Browning, Grace. **Rural Public Welfare.** 1941

Bruce, Isabel Campbell and Edith Eickhoff. **The Michigan Poor Law.** 1936

Burns, Eveline M. **Social Security and Public Policy.** 1956

Cahn, Frances and Valeska Bary. **Welfare Activities of Federal, State, and Local Governments in California, 1850-1934.** 1936

Campbell, Persia. **The Consumer Interest.** 1949

Davies, Stanley Powell. **Social Control of the Mentally Deficient.** 1930

Devine, Edward T. **The Spirit of Social Work.** 1911

Douglas, Paul H. and Aaron Director. **The Problem of Unemployment.** 1931

Eaton, Allen in Collaboration with Shelby M. Harrison. **A Bibliography of Social Surveys.** 1930

Epstein, Abraham. **The Challenge of the Aged.** 1928

Falk, I[sidore] S., Margaret C. Klem, and Nathan Sinai. **The Incidence of Illness and the Receipt and Costs of Medical Care Among Representative Families.** 1933

Fisher, Irving. **National Vitality, its Wastes and Conservation.** 1909

Freund, Ernst. **The Police Power:** Public Policy and Constitutional Rights. 1904

Gladden, Washington. **Applied Christianity:** Moral Aspects of Social Questions. 1886

Hartley, Isaac Smithson, editor. **Memorial of Robert Milham Hartley.** 1882

Hollander, Jacob H. **The Abolition of Poverty.** 1914

Kane, H[arry] H[ubbell]. **Opium-Smoking in America and China.** 1882

Klebaner, Benjamin Joseph. **Public Poor Relief in America, 1790-1860.** 1951

Knapp, Samuel L. **The Life of Thomas Eddy.** 1834

Lawrence, Charles. **History of the Philadelphia Almshouses and Hospitals from the Beginning of the Eighteenth to the Ending of the Nineteenth Centuries.** 1905

[Massachusetts Commission on the Cost of Living]. **Report of the Commission on the Cost of Living.** 1910

[Massachusetts Commission on Old Age Pensions, Annuities and Insurance]. **Report of the Commission on Old Age Pensions, Annuities and Insurance.** 1910

[New York State Commission to Investigate Provision for the Mentally Deficient]. **Report of the State Commission to Investigate Provision for the Mentally Deficient.** 1915

[Parker, Florence E., Estelle M. Stewart, and Mary Conymgton, compilers]. **Care of Aged Persons in the United States.** 1929

Pollock, Horatio M., editor. **Family Care of Mental Patients.** 1936

Pollock, Horatio M. **Mental Disease and Social Welfare.** 1941

Powell, Aaron M., editor. **The National Purity Congress;** Its Papers, Addresses, Portraits. 1896

The President's Commission on the Health Needs of the Nation. **Building America's Health.** [1952]. Five vols. in two

Prostitution in America: Three Investigations, 1902-1914. 1975

Rubinow, I[saac] M. **The Quest for Security.** 1934

Shaffer, Alice, Mary Wysor Keefer, and Sophonisba P. Breckinridge. **The Indiana Poor Law.** 1936

Shattuck, Lemuel. **Report to the Committee of the City Council Appointed to Obtain the Census of Boston for the Year 1845.** 1846

The State and Public Welfare in Nineteenth-Century America: Five Investigations, 1833-1877. 1975

Stewart, Estelle M. **The Cost of American Almshouses.** 1925

Taylor, Graham. **Pioneering on Social Frontiers.** 1930

[United States Senate Committee on Education and Labor]. **Report of the Committee of the Senate Upon the Relations Between Labor and Capital.** 1885. Four vols.

Walton, Robert P. **Marihuana, America's New Drug Problem.** 1938

Williams, Edward Huntington. **Opiate Addiction.** 1922

Williams, Pierce assisted by Isabel C. Chamberlain. **The Purchase of Medical Care Through Fixed Periodic Payment.** 1932

Willoughby, W[estal] W[oodbury]. **Opium as an International Problem.** 1925

Wisner, Elizabeth. **Public Welfare Administration in Louisiana.** 1930